Radio Propaganda and the Broadcasting of Hatred

Radio Propaganda and the Broadcasting of Hatred

Historical Development and Definitions

Keith Somerville
University of Kent, Kent, UK

First published 2012 by
PALGRAVE MACMILLAN

Palgrave Macmillan in the UK is an imprint of Macmillan Publishers Limited, registered in England, company number 785998, of Houndmills, Basingstoke, Hampshire RG21 6XS.

Palgrave Macmillan in the US is a division of St Martin's Press LLC, 175 Fifth Avenue, New York, NY 10010.

Palgrave Macmillan is the global academic imprint of the above companies and has companies and representatives throughout the world.

Palgrave® and Macmillan® are registered trademarks in the United States, the United Kingdom, Europe and other countries.

ISBN 978–0–230–27829–5

This book is printed on paper suitable for recycling and made from fully managed and sustained forest sources. Logging, pulping and manufacturing processes are expected to conform to the environmental regulations of the country of origin.

A catalogue record for this book is available from the British Library.

A catalog record for this book is available from the Library of Congress.

10   9   8   7   6   5   4   3   2   1
21 20 19 18 17 16 15 14 13 12

Printed and bound in Great Britain by
CPI Antony Rowe, Chippenham and Eastbourne

Contents

Preface

It was late evening on Wednesday, 6 April 1994 in studio S36 in Bush House, the home of the British Broadcasting Corporation (BBC) World Service. My *Newshour* team was coming to the end of a long shift and there were about 15 minutes of programme time to go. And then came the moment when a newsflash both set my pulse racing and also set off alarm bells in my head.

The breaking news came in on the BBC newsgathering system, from Agence France Presse. It said that the plane carrying presidents Juvenal Habyarimana of Rwanda and Cyprien Ntaryamira of Burundi had crashed near Kigali – all on board were presumed dead. It's not every day that you get two presidents killed in the same crash, so that alone meant that it would develop into a big story for the World Service audience. But these two men were from Rwanda and Burundi, two of the most volatile states in Africa. They were returning from Arusha, from a summit at which pressure was put on Habyarimana to proceed with implementing the Arusha Peace Accords designed to end four years of war in Rwanda. His death would at the very least put the accords in doubt but could lead to full-scale civil war or worse.

As I sought more information from BBC newsgathering and the African service at Bush, and checked incoming news wires, I was simultaneously assessing what we actually knew and could therefore report to the audience and whether we could cover the story accurately before the programme came off air. I checked with my trusted studio producer, Fred Dove, if we had room for the Rwanda story and, professional as ever, he said he could make room. So I had to decide.

While not an expert on the minutiae of Rwandan politics, I had been there, reported stories from there, followed the four-year civil war and had good background knowledge of the decades of conflict, massacres and repression of the Tutsi minority by the Hutu majority. I knew very well how unstable the ceasefire was between the government and the opposing Rwandan Patriotic Front (RPF), and how an event like this and any sugges-tion that the Tutsi-led RPF was responsible for Habyarimana's death could lead to not just renewed fighting but the mass killing of Tutsis. I did not want to risk having any role in starting rumours or broadcasting suggestions that could have catastrophic results – and I knew our programme was lis-tened to by English-speakers in East and Central Africa. All journalists want to report the news and report it now, but it is better to be a bit late on the news and get it right than to jump in fast, perhaps speculate and then have to take responsibility for the consequences.

I opted for safety and caution. When we had confirmation of the crash and the deaths of all those aboard, we still had time within the programme to broadcast a short newsflash. I decided not to try to get hold of the African service stringers in Rwanda, not all of whom broadcast in English anyway, or to go to our regional office in Nairobi, as the correspondents there would know little more than I did. The priority was to broadcast only what I could confirm and avoid potentially inflammatory speculation. When the programme came off air, we were none the wiser about the cause – a crash, shot down and, if so, by whom? But speculation was already being aired in some follow-up news agency reports, including accusations from Rwanda that the Tutsi-led RPF had been responsible.

I didn't get the chance to follow up the story on subsequent programmes. As it did for most of the continent of Africa and much of the world, my focus switched to South Africa. Within days, I was in Johannesburg leading the World Service news programme team reporting the elections that were to bring the African National Congress and Nelson Mandela to power and transform South Africa. But even in the hectic run up to the start of voting on 27 April, the horrifying news emerging from Rwanda was being discussed in South Africa – of the killing of the prime minister and several ministers in the coalition government, and reports of large-scale murders of Tutsis. Days before the official announcement of the election result by the election commission on 6 May, it was clear that the African National Congress (ANC) had won and that international leaders and diplomats were beginning to sound out ANC leaders about a South African role – political and military – in ending the Rwandan violence. The man soon to become South Africa's deputy defence minister and a key figure in the ANC military and intelligence set up, Ronnie Kasrils, told me that he was already having to fend off suggestions of a South African-led African force to keep the peace in Rwanda.

By the time I was back in London and running programmes again, Rwanda was one of the lead stories for the World Service, despite being ignored by much of the rest of the British and international media. They seemed only to be able to cope with one African story at a time and they already had South Africa. For many news editors across the world, the main questions were, 'Where the hell is Rwanda?' and 'Why should we care enough to report it?' Our programmes were different. We had correspondents there and I despatched one of our best radio documentary makers, Hilary Andersson, to Rwanda and Tanzania to get us more depth on the story – which was still patchy and unclear. Thousands, perhaps tens of thousands, were being killed but by whom and to what end?

Over the next couple of months the extent, intent and sheer horror of the attempted genocide became clear. What also became obvious was the role of the media in Rwanda in inciting hatred of and violence against Tutsis, and against Hutus seen as opposed to Hutu chauvinism. The phrase 'hate radio' became synonymous with Rwanda – 'radio that killed' and 'radio machete' were just a couple of the phrases used regularly to describe Radio Television Libre des Mille Collines (RTLM), the Hutu station that encouraged and aided the killings.

That radio should play such a role was anathema to someone like me who had worked for years in the World Service and was wedded to the motto on the BBC coat of arms that 'nation shall speak peace unto nation' – even though I knew well that, in its way, BBC World Service output was, like most other news, a form of propaganda even if it was a soft, benign and well-intentioned one. I was also aware that there was a wide spectrum of broadcasting, from the World Service near one end to stations like RTLM at the other.

Before working as a radio producer, reporter and editor, I had spent eight years at the BBC Monitoring Service directly monitoring Soviet, Czech, Israeli, Afghan, apartheid South African and, during the Falklands/Malvinas War, Argentinian news and propaganda broadcasts. I'd selected and edited for publication news and propaganda output from across Africa, the Middle East and Latin America – and for a brief period North Korea and China, too – for the BBC's *Summary of World Broadcasts*. I had few illusions about the purity of the broadcast media. But the first half of the 1990s brought home with violent force the ways that broadcasting, primarily radio, could be used to encourage, justify, incite and support violence, particularly in regional or civil conflicts. Even before the ghastly example of RTLM, Serb and Croat radio and TV, especially local stations like the Serb one in Knin, had shown how radio and other media could be used for other ends than informing people of news and information that could enable them to make sense of, and make rational decisions in, the world in which they lived. That radio could be used to incite hatred, to sanction, justify or encourage communal violence, was becoming clearer. Politicians, non-governmental organizations, journalists and academics were aware of this and were starting to call for ways of jamming or combating the hate broadcasts. But there had been little attempt to describe or define where and how this sort of hate broadcasting began, and where what one could call 'mobilizing propaganda' ended and incitement to hatred and violence began.

Other priorities as a BBC journalist meant that at the time I went no further into the dark side of broadcasting. I moved into academia in 2008 and started research on radio; this coincided with the investigations into the post-election violence in Kenya in 2007–2008 and the suggestions that once again radio had played a role in inciting violence and hatred. This rekindled my interest and, on further investigation, I found that there had been little progress in defining hate radio or providing any sort of realistic guide as to how or whether one could identify where propaganda morphed into something even more sinister. A research trip to Kenya in 2010, and subsequent dealings with the International Criminal Court in The Hague over the indictment of a Kenyan radio journalist whom I had interviewed, confirmed that an examination of Kenya's experience could throw a new light on the uses of broadcasting in times of conflict.

Research into the role of radio in the events in Kenya inevitably threw up comparisons with Rwanda. I also related it to what I knew of the break-up of Yugoslavia – which I had been involved in covering exhaustively as a programme editor at the World Service in the early 1990s. My research led me back to Cold War propaganda, the role of radio in the Middle East, and to the Second World War and Nazi Germany, and then further back to the early uses of radio for the purpose of propagandizing and the career of the 'hate priest', Father Coughlan, as an early exponent of bigoted and racist radio commentary. I found more and more material but struggled to put it into context, to find definitions, to delineate the different forms and motivations of propaganda, and to decide where, how and why propaganda developed into an open engendering of hatred and incitement to violence.

That is the basic purpose of this book – to tease out the strands of propaganda and present a more coherent analysis of how and in what circumstances propaganda becomes incitement and then to find definitions of hate media and, in particular, hate radio. The subjects under particular study are those perpetrators of hate propaganda who propagate their ideas openly – what has been called 'white propaganda', which comes from an identifiable source that tries to build credibility with the audience, whether or not it does so through distortion, outright lies or a manipulation of facts or interpretations (Jowett and O'Donnell, 2006, pp. 16–17). 'Black' or 'covert' propaganda is not the subject of this book, nor is the attempt by radio stations or other media to influence the beliefs or ideology of foreign audiences – as both the USA and the Soviet Union tried to do though their broadcasting during the Cold War. The focus is on those broadcasters and media that sought to influence their own populations – to incite them to hatred and violence against domestic or external enemies. I have omitted, after much research and deliberation, analysis of the American Shock Jocks, such as Rush Limbaugh, Bill O'Reilly, Glenn Beck and Don Imus. Bigoted and biased they might be but there is no evidence of a specific agenda of hate or incitement; rather just a stream of right-wing prejudice and abuse of perceived liberals and socialists, or mindless abuse of groups within American society. Under the First Amendment of the US Constitution, this is all legal.

The structure of the book reflects the origins of hate broadcasting in propaganda and how in certain circumstances nationalist, political party, racist or other forms of propaganda move into the area of incitement. Chapter 1 charts the development of propaganda as a weapon in conflict over history and the use of hate as the most deadly propaganda weapon of all. Chapter 2 follows the development of propaganda in the 20th century and charts how radio as a means of mass and targeted communication became such an effective propaganda tool and its utilization an extremely effective medium for inciting hatred. The first two chapters are also used to set out the methodology (qualitative and contextual rather than quantitative) for examining the broadcasts, their context as part of a political and social discourse, and their place in the historical and contemporary developments of the conflicts and political situations in which the use of broadcasting to incite hatred occurred. Chapters 4, 5 and 6 are case studies of radio propaganda in Nazi Germany, the role of radio in genocide in Rwanda and radio incitement during the political/violent conflicts in Kenya. The book ends (Chapter 7) with an examination of the conclusions that can be drawn from the earlier chapters on propaganda, hate, radio development and the case studies, and an attempt to define hate radio as a phenomenon that goes beyond what we normally understand as propaganda.

Acknowledgements

In many ways the work for this study started the moment I walked through the doors of the Monitoring Service, so there are many to whom I owe a debt. But I will keep this as brief and as to the point as possible and not make it into a tear-stained equivalent of an Oscar ceremony acceptance speech. My editor on the Middle East and Africa *Summary of World Broadcasts*, John Chadwick, was probably the best boss I worked for in 28 years in the BBC. Clear, focused and with a great knowledge of broadcasting, he was a model for ensuring accuracy and providing context in dealing with broadcast material. At the World Service, the late Kari Blackburn was a mentor and friend of huge importance in getting to grips with radio. Teresa Guerreiro is a close and valued friend and colleague (at the BBC and now in academic life) who has always been willing to ask questions that make me think very carefully about what I'm doing, how and why I'm doing it, and whether my conclusions stand up to scrutiny; she has been an immense support and has cast an experienced and critical eye over parts of the work – though any faults are all mine.

The support of colleagues and the Research Funding Department at Brunel University have been crucial in getting the time, the opportunity and the funds to carry out the research in Kenya – I'm particularly grateful for the support and friendship of Professor Julian Petley. Professor Jack Spence of King's College London has been a great source of support, advice and inspiration over my years of studying conflict and violence in Africa.

I'd also like to thank all those who spoke candidly to me in Kenya, especially those who did this at some risk and whose anonymity I have respected. In addition, Dennis ole Itumbi, Martin Githau, Ida Jooste, Brice Rambaud, Matthias Muindi and Moses Rono gave me a huge amount of help and advice. At BBC Monitoring, Mladen Bilic was invaluable in guiding me through the Balkan Broadcasting labyrinth and Chris Greenaway filled in a lot of gaps for me about what was monitored and when, notably in Rwanda and Kenya. Tim Butcher, despite once having tried to throttle me in a maul on the rugby field, gave me good advice and detail from his on-the-spot reporting in the Balkans and Africa. Marcus Tanner and Mark Thompson were hugely helpful on the media and the break-up of Yugoslavia. Samantha Blake and the staff at the BBC Written Archives have been consistently supportive in finding, sorting and supplying German wartime radio transcriptions for me. Paul Meller of the Economic and Social Research Council kindly cast a critical and expert eye over the chapters on propaganda before the radio era. Frank Chalk of the Montreal Institute for Genocide and

Human Rights Studies (MIGS) gave valuable advice and permission to use my MIGS occasional paper as the foundation for the Kenyan chapter.

Finally, and most importantly, I'd like to thank my wife, Liz, and son, Tom, for support, humour and constructive advice on grammar and tone as well as keeping me reasonably sane.

1

Propaganda: Origins, Development and Utilization

> Propaganda is not a modern invention. Ever since men have lived in communities, the propagandist has attempted to convince his audience of the righteousness of his cause and of the weakness, falsity and wickedness of the opponent's position. A limited audience could be secured by word of mouth. Pictures and then writing extended that audience. But the printed word was necessary before propaganda could assume its modern importance. Martin Luther's pamphlets are early examples of the new weapon's power. Now the circle has been completed. The radio has restored the predominant influence of the spoken word, while it has immeasurably increased the size of its audience.
>
> (Beller, 1940, p. 3)

The use of the electronic media, radio in particular, to promote causes, propagate ideologies, define or develop discourses of identity and also of 'otherness', ridicule, demonize, dehumanize and incite hatred and even violent action was a product of the technological advances of the 20th century. But the development of human discourses of identity and difference, the propagation of ideologies of enmity, hatred and violence go back to the start of human communication. So, inevitably, any study of the propagation of hatred as the extreme end of the propaganda spectrum must chart the development of propaganda, study its content, understand the ways in which it is utilized and try to identify where, how and, if possible, why it can develop into the incitement of extreme forms of hatred and violence.

This chapter attempts to set out to define the key aspects of propaganda through a review and synthesis of the substantial literature on the subject; describe the historical development of the phenomenon and seek to show where it has moved along a spectrum from the development of identity and the propagation of ideologies or discourses into incitement of hatred and to seeking violent responses to that hatred. Later in the book I go on to define and delineate hate propaganda as a point on the propaganda spectrum or as a subset of the wider field of propaganda, and establish a set of criteria for defining hate propaganda. It is important to emphasize here that the propaganda with which this study is concerned is that aimed by governments, movements and parties at their own populations to develop and maintain support for a regime or a set of policies, elicit active support or at the very least acquiescence in the face of a set of policies or actions by that regime and, in the extreme cases at the centre of this study, promote hatred and incite violence towards the objects of that hatred. This study is not concerned with propaganda aimed at foreign countries to undermine their systems or to promote a cause abroad – unless it is to recruit more adherents to the cause of hatred or the prosecution of violence against the target group. So, for example, German domestic radio propaganda will be examined extensively, but not its external broadcasts aimed at foreign audiences.

Defining propaganda

Propaganda is a widely used and frequently misunderstood word. Its image throughout the 20th century and into the 21st century has been a negative one. As Walton points out, 'the term "propaganda" has such highly negative connotations that people tend to see only the arguments of their opponents describable with this label, as if their own arguments could never be'. One of the key reasons for this is that during both world wars in the 20th century, Britain, the USA and their allies 'characterized only enemy opinion-forming activities as propaganda, and treated these so-designated enemy activities as composed mostly of lies' (Walton, 1997, pp. 383–4). The term 'propaganda' has become a stick with which to beat opponents – essentially the argument is that 'we tell the truth, you deal in propaganda'.

Following the widespread use of propaganda by all sides in the First World War, Harold Lasswell portrayed this popular view of propaganda when he identified the distaste with which many in the USA and Western Europe viewed the wartime use of information and disinformation to mobilize support for the war and develop and maintain a willingness to fight the enemy:

> they are puzzled, uneasy, or vexed at the unknown cunning which seems to have duped and degraded them [...] These people probe the mysteries of propaganda with that compound of admiration and chagrin with which the victims of a new gambling trick demand to have the thing explained. That credulous utopianism, which fed upon the mighty words which exploited the hopes of the mass in war, has in many minds given way to cynicism and disenchantment.
>
> (Lasswell, 1971, pp. 2–3)

Writing more recently, Phil Taylor referred to propaganda as a 'much misunderstood word' normally perceived as 'a dirty word involving dirty tricks, a process designed to seduce people into believing something that they would not otherwise have believed' (Taylor, 1997, p. 16).

The widely held, popular view of propaganda is a simplistic and very narrow image, with propaganda presented as something that only repressive, autocratic or essentially 'bad' regimes practise in order to lie to and control their subjects or to lie to the world to present a falsely positive view of an essentially negative regime. It ignores the wider meanings and uses of propaganda and its pervasiveness in social, economic, cultural and political life, clouding judgement about what propaganda involves and how it is used.

Propaganda has been in use ever since man could first communicate, even if the content, methods and effects were not the subject of study until the development of effective means of mass communication made the use and abuse of propaganda a very identifiable part of public discourse. Its name and basic definition come to us from the 17th-century Catholic Church. In 1622, Pope Gregory XV established the Sacred Congregation for the Propagation of the Faith (Sacra Congregatio de Propaganda Fide) charged with taking Catholicism to the New World, but it was also to be an instrument for maintaining the power of Catholic Church in the continuing spiritual and increasingly violent conflict with Protestantism. Gregory wanted the Congregation to prevent heresy, so that men would 'be placed in the pasture of the true faith, that they may be gathered together in saving doctrine and be led to the springs of the waters of life' (cited by Bernays, 2005, p. 10). The Pope's plan 'laid the foundations for modern propaganda techniques in that it stressed the control of opinions and through them, the actions of the people in the mass' (Jowett and O'Donnell, 2006, p. 73). It also introduced the word into the vocabulary of discourse – propaganda coming to mean the techniques employed by those propagating the Catholic doctrine rather than the doctrine itself. Jowett and O'Donnell suggest that one reason that propaganda has long been viewed with suspicion by many is that Protestants associated the term with Catholicism and Catholic reaction to the Reformation and so viewed it as suspect, devious and negative (ibid.).

To turn to basic definitions, propaganda is part of social and political life, however much people may want to wish it away as a tool of the evil. It is an inherent part of many forms of human communications and discourse; an ever-present part of life, whether political propaganda by parties, politicians and politically aligned media, the transmission of cultural values by the media in all its forms, the reinforcement of social norms or advertising to sell services or products. The phenomenon has been extensively analysed and a range of views has been propounded on what it is, how you identify it, what role it plays, how it is used and with what intended effect.

One of the first to analyse propaganda in depth – chiefly as a result of the use of it in the First World War – was the American political scientist and communications theorist Harold D. Lasswell. His work on analysing wartime propaganda really set the academic ball rolling. His key point is that 'propaganda is concerned with the management of opinions and attitudes by the direct manipulation of social suggestion rather than by altering other conditions in the environment or organism'; for him, propaganda 'refers solely to the control of opinion by significant symbols, or, to speak more concretely and less accurately by stories, rumours, reports, pictures and other forms of social communications' (Lasswell, 1971, p. 9). 'Propaganda in the broadest sense is the technique of influencing human action by the manipulation of representations' (Lasswell, 1934, p. 13). The core components are the management of opinion, control, manipulation and the variety of means or content used to achieve this. Control and manipulation seem at first sight, like the popular image of propaganda, to be devious tools relying on lies or distortions and so are automatically pejorative terms. But when we seek to persuade someone to accept or act on our own views, however laudable the purpose, we are trying to control or manipulate their opinions and then, if desired, their actions. Propaganda is deliberate, it is not accidental (Gulseth, 2004, pp. 26–8).

As Taylor argues, propaganda is very pervasive and democracies delude themselves into thinking they don't engage in propaganda. The very lauding of the values of democracy is propaganda on behalf of that form of government and of specific governments adhering or claiming to adhere to those ideals. So we should take propaganda as a value-neutral concept; as a process rather than as a negative label. And following Taylor's argument, we should have a different focus, intent. 'The intentions of those undertaking the process ought to be the object of scrutiny and judgement, not the process itself [...] if the intent is to persuade people to think and behave in a way desired by the source, then it is propaganda' (Taylor, 1997, pp. 16–17). This dovetails with the approach adopted by Jowett and O'Donnell that, 'propaganda is a form of communication that attempts to achieve a response that furthers the desired intent of the propagandist. Persuasion is interactive and attempts to satisfy the needs of both persuader and persuaded' (Jowett and O'Donnell, 2006, p. 1). This response could be as harmless as support for a local team in a major sports competition; or, more seriously, support and mobilization for war; implementation of or acquiescence in the face of a particular set of policies desired by a government; or the development of feelings of hatred and the initiation of violence against the object or objects of hatred.

In trying to achieve acquiescence, acceptance, support or action, the propagandist is carrying out a 'deliberate, systematic attempt to shape perceptions, manipulate cognitions, and direct behaviour to achieve a response that furthers the desired intent of the propagandist' (Jowett and O'Donnell, 2006, p. 7). Propaganda is 'an essential part of the political process' (Welch, 1983, p. 1), but becomes malign according to the content of the message it conveys and the intent of the propagandist. And for this study, intent and content are going to be key factors – when it comes to the case studies, emphasis will be placed on establishing intent and comparing that with the content and meaning of messages.

The targets of propaganda are individuals, groups and the mass of a population. Ellul argues that:

> modern propaganda will, first of all, address itself at one and the same time to the individual and to the masses. It cannot separate the two elements [...] the individual is never considered as an individual, but always in terms of what he has in common with others, such as his motivations, his feelings, or his myths.
>
> (Ellul, 1973, pp. 6–7)

Propaganda treating the individual in this way seeks to weaken his or her defences and so more easily provoke a reaction. Even when propaganda is read or heard by individuals alone, they absorb it in the context of being part of a group. So, the listener to a radio broadcast though actually alone, is nevertheless part of a large group, and 'he is aware of [...] Thus all modern propaganda profits from the structure of the mass but exploits the individual need for self-affirmation; and the two activities must be conducted jointly, simultaneously' (ibid., p. 8).

If the aim is to persuade the individual and the mass, what does it want to achieve through persuasion – mere adoption of idea in principle or something more? Ellul believes that 'It furnishes him with a complete system for explaining the world and provides immediate incentives for action.' For him, it is not just about opinions, 'the aim of modern propaganda is no longer to modify ideas but to provoke action' (ibid. pp. 11 and 25) – he says that this was at the centre of Goebbels's approach to propaganda. Morale and beliefs were important, but eliciting and maintaining the right behaviour was core. For propagandists, and he identifies Goebbels and also Mao as exemplars, Ellul argues that what is desired is achieving 'a minimum of participation from everybody [...] [this] can be active or passive, but in any case it is not simply a matter of public opinion' (ibid., p. 26). Jowett and O'Donnell agree with much of this, though don't place quite so much emphasis on eliciting action. They see the propagandist as providing the target audience with a comprehensive conceptual framework for dealing with social and political reality – 'the purpose of propaganda may be to influence people to adopt beliefs and attitudes that correspond to those of the propagandist or to engage in certain patterns of behaviour' (Jowett and O'Donnell, 2006, p. 271). The crux, though, is to form a critical mass of support for a particular programme or set of ideas – ideally, for the propagandist, this will involve fervent commitment but at the least must elicit passive acquiescence. But in many cases, what the propagandist wants is action, whether voting in a particular way in an election or taking up arms to fight or even exterminate a demonized enemy.

Ultimately, as Kallis deduced from his study of propaganda in Nazi Germany, 'by promoting a common cognitive environment for information acquisition and interpretation, as well as constant cultivation of perception of the world, propaganda aims to integrate the person both as an individual and as a member of a social group into a shared context of symbols, meanings and desired objectives' (Kallis, 2008, p. 2). He sees the function of propaganda as being, first, motivation and, second, mobilization or 'propelling people into modes of individual or collective action as desired by the propagandist' (ibid.). This study of hate propaganda will by its nature examine both phases, given that, as will be explored in the case studies, the intent of the propagandists is always to motivate and mobilize the target; in extreme cases through incitement to hatred and then the turning of that hatred into desired behaviour towards a target group.

The eliciting of behaviour desired by the propagandist further reinforces the basic motivational message – because that action by the propagandized binds the individual or group closer to the propagandist and his or her beliefs and objectives. A person persuaded to an act of violence or hatred by propaganda is bound by that action and less able or willing to then renounce the content of the propaganda or ideology it contains. Fear of retribution for an action by victims of that action provides a further incentive to adhere to the course of action ordained – to go back is to invite punishment, 'action demands more action ... and he gets more deeply involved by repeating the act in order to prove that it was just' (Ellul, 1973, p. 29).

Two other key points need to be emphasized. Firstly, propaganda is aimed at the masses and, as the arch-propagandist Josef Goebbels repeated again and again in his diaries and at daily briefings in his Propaganda Ministry (see Boelcke, 1967; Goebbels, 1982, 1984; and Heiber, 1962), it must be simple, have emotional impact and repeat the same basic messages over and over again. It must also, as Ellul states, be continuous and lasting (Ellul, 1973, p. 17). Secondly, however simple and repetitive the message, it does not seek to change ingrained or established beliefs or opinions. Propaganda may seek to gradually alter opinion or guide opinion in new directions, but not to dismantle or destroy strongly or long-held beliefs. Rather, the propagandist seeks to reinforce audience predispositions or to create new attitudes in evolving circumstances (Jowett and O'Donnell, 2006, p. 279; see, also, Ellul, 1973, p. 35). Propaganda does not create something from nothing, there must be fuel for the propaganda fire. If propaganda does, on occasion, seek to change beliefs, it must do so by utilizing:

the vocabulary, terminology and fundamentals of the existing value system [...] in this way the audience can be brought to believe that the way the propagandist addresses a particular pressing issue of the day either accords with convictions and attitudes that have been long held within society, or at least does not violate them

(Kallis, 2008, p. 4)

If a belief can be undermined in this way, the way is open to consistently reinforce the process of change and so over time alter opinions and ultimately behaviour. Kallis demonstrates this well in the study of Nazi propaganda – where the German National Socialists worked to replace traditional views with their own, they did it slowly with constant repetition and reinforcement of their new message (Kallis, 2008, p. 4).

Propaganda works primarily on the emotions and feelings – the propagandist is concerned much more with how people feel than about deep thinking. It is essentially emotional manipulation through the transmission of ideas and ideology (O'Shaughnessy, 2004, p. 41). Propagandists make use of the whole gamut of emotions – love, anger, fear, hope, guilt and hate, to name but a few (Gulseth, 2004, p. 38).

A final point before moving on to the historical development of propaganda – this study will not attempt to assess the effect of propaganda on target audiences or try to quantify it. Rather, it will examine the content, identifiable intent and historical, social, economic and political context of propaganda and attempt to define the nature, deployment and motivation of hate media. There is no consensus among those who have studied propaganda in detail and over time about how media or propaganda effect beliefs, emotions and behaviour – this will be demonstrated particularly in the case of Rwanda, where interviews with and study of the behaviour of those who carried out the genocide brought researchers no nearer to understanding, let alone measuring, the effect of hate propaganda (see Rwanda case study). As Taylor points out, a fierce and inconclusive debate still rages over the impact of media messages. He gives the example of 40 years of study of the effects of TV and film violence on the behaviour of children and concludes that there is 'no conclusive evidence either way that satisfies researchers' (Taylor, 1997, p. 6). This is supported by Kris and Leites, who note that 'we do not know of the existence of data comprehensive and reliable enough to demonstrate in quantitative terms broad hypotheses about changes in response to propaganda' (Kris and Leites, 1953, p. 267). Nicholas O'Shaughnessy supports this view when he posits that 'The salience of propaganda texts and events in history is not in doubt, although the measure of its impact is impossible to gauge and therefore permanently subject to dispute' (O'Shaughnessy, 2004, p. 37). So, this study will start with the basic assumption that propaganda has an effect, is a form of social manipulation and control, and that its content relates directly to the intent of the propagandist. This doesn't mean that the effects of propaganda will not be addressed, but where they are addressed there will be no assumption that they can be accurately measured or treated as a discreet factor that can be separated from other instruments of social control or manipulation.

The history and development of propaganda and the incitement of hatred

Social communication predates man. You only need to watch a herd of deer during the rut to see the way that competing stags advertise their worth to hinds or their strength and prowess to competing stags to know that some basic form of propaganda is in operation; the birds of paradise of Papua New Guinea have even more extravagant propaganda displays to gain and control territory and seek mates. Stags, and other animals competing to mate, for territory or food will use display to deter or intimidate opponents or attract mates. The side-on, antler-up strut of a stag is communication in the form of propaganda. Scent marking, fraying tree bark and roaring or calling by animals are all forms of propaganda.

Early man will have been no different. But being an even more social creature with a greater range of means of communication, man took propaganda to new levels. Who knows the intent of early cave or rock paintings depicting hunts or warfare – the oddly, in fact totally incorrectly, named White Lady of Brandberg in Namibia shows early man hunting. This could have been a celebration of the hunt, a form of communication to others in the same population group or perhaps a sign to other groups that this was occupied territory – it could equally have been a depiction of the strength or abilities of a particular group.

Of more obvious communicative significance were early uses of art, monuments and decoration to convey political messages. Taylor points to the monuments and symbols of Assyrian rulers of the first millennium BC as forms of communication intended to create desired behaviour among subjects and to demonstrate divine support for the ruler (Taylor, 2003, pp. 22–3). Architecture, murals and stelae illustrated the support of the gods for the rulers and emphasized the ability of the rulers to vanquish enemies. The Assyrians portrayed the kings' campaigns on glazed bricks set in walls of palaces to demonstrate his invincibility – an early example of military propaganda aimed at internal rivals but also potential external enemies. More explicitly and with the clear intent to inspire awe and fear to deter rebellions, at the royal palace of King Assurnasirpal II at Nineveh an inscription describes how the king dealt with a rebellious Assyrian city:

> I built a pillar over against the city gate, and I flayed all the chief men who had revolted, and I covered the pillar with their skins [...] some I impaled upon the pillar on stakes [...] many within the border of my own land I flayed, and I spread their skins upon the walls: and I cut off the limbs of the officers, of the royal officers who had rebelled. Ahiababa [the rebel

leader] I took to Nineveh, I flayed him, I spread his skin upon the wall of Nineveh.

(Taylor, 2003, p. 24)

A clear message for the king's subjects – I am powerful, I cannot be overthrown and I will wreak brutal vengeance on those who challenge me. The combination of violent repression of enemies and public propaganda is one that is repeated down the ages. The propaganda of repressive rulers or those seeking to mobilize a population in anger and hatred against others will be seen to go hand in hand with violence and the threat of terror. Taylor, in his comprehensive work on the history of propaganda, identifies the way in which propaganda is used as a societal tool and a military one, citing Plato, Aristotle and Xenophon and describing how Alexander used his image as the invincible conqueror to increase his power and prestige (Taylor, 2003, pp. 33–5). Herodotus used his *Histories* not only to inform literate Greeks of the conduct of wars against the Phoenicians and Persians but also to attribute blame and to extol the virtues of cooperation between the different states of Ancient Greece, arguing for cooperation between them and against inter-state warfare (Herodotus, 1998). Carolyn Dewald, in her introduction to the *Histories*, points to the theme of glorifying unity: 'finishing his work on the *Histories* in the early years of the Peloponnesian War, Herodotus intends to save the memory of a moment in the recent past when Greeks for once worked together to repel the invader' (Herodotus, 1998, pp. xxxv–xxxvi).

Rome replicated the use of architecture, art and also the role of the gods in its republican and imperial propaganda. With the spread of Roman power, coinage bearing the heads of emperors became not only a means of exchange but also a very effective form of propaganda. Roman works of history and literature glorified Rome. Julius Caesar no doubt intended his histories of the Gallic and Civil Wars to extol Roman power and virtue and glorify his own military prowess as he sought to increase the power of his faction in Rome, as Napoleon later emulated. Caesar also used his works to demonize enemy peoples as barbarians. In his accounts of the civil wars in Rome and the Gallic and African wars, he refers repeatedly to the 'Roman people', but to the 'tribes' of Gaul and Germany (Caesar, 2006, p. 27) to the 'barbarian tribe' of the Albici, and to 'the Lusitanians and other barbarian tribes' (Caesar, 1976, pp. 53–8). Later emperors had their predecessors or themselves declared gods to further exalt their worth and emphasize their right to govern. Triumphal processions through Rome for victorious emperors or generals and the staging of historical battle in circuses were living propaganda (Taylor, 2003, p. 45). The glory that was Rome was built and maintained through violence or the threat of it and the deliberate use of forms of propaganda that sought to bind Roman citizens together and create a sense that anyone not a Roman citizen was inferior and 'other'.

With the advent of Christianity as both a state religion and as a supra-state locus of power and belief, religious propaganda became an instrument for achieving social cohesion but also one of exclusion and control – 'of maintaining the prevailing social, political and religious order' (Taylor, 2003, p. 52). The most emphatic demonstration of religious propaganda came with the church's exhortations against the Muslim Turkish expansion in the east, the capture of Jerusalem and the threat to the Christian Byzantine state. Despite the schisms between the Catholic, Orthodox and eastern churches, in Western Europe the Catholic Church and the Pope had a virtual monopoly over cultural/religious power and through churches, pulpits, monasteries (as seats of learning and orthodoxy) and preachers had the means to propagandize and exert control over belief and behaviour. The power of religion as a social force was spread and maintained through preaching, religious rites and visual images in the form of church architecture, statues and paintings – for a largely illiterate world, the spoken word and visual communication were vital.

In 1095, the power of church preaching was made flesh. It was a time of warfare within Europe as kings tried to extend their power, often against the resistance of powerful regional leaders and the nobility. Pressure for land and resources increased as populations grew but food production was static, leading to social and economic discontent. At the same time, Christian power in the east was diminishing. By 1073, forces of the Seljuk Turk leader Alp Arslan had weakened and come to dominate the Fatimid dynasty, which had led the Muslim world and held the position of Caliph. The Caliphs had controlled Jerusalem since 636, when Caliph Umar ended the brief Byzantine period of control. Arslan's forces had defeated the Byzantine forces at the battle of Manzikert in 1071 and taken much of Anatolia. In 1073, they captured Jerusalem. This meant that Muslim rule over Jerusalem continued, but under the Caliphs there had been tolerance of Christianity, cooperation over maintenance of Christian holy sites and regular pilgrimages by European Christians. The Seljuks took a less tolerant view, especially after an uprising by the inhabitants of Jerusalem (Christians and Fatimid supporters), which led to the violent re-assertion of Seljuk control and the massacre of many Christians. Pilgrimages became more perilous.

In 1074, Pope Gregory VII had called on all Christians to aid the Byzantine empire against the Turks but had not developed this into a campaign, unlike his successors who followed preaching with campaigns to fight the Turks, and little happened. But in 1095, his successor but one, Urban II, made a crusade against the Turks the centrepiece of his papacy. In answer to further Byzantine appeals for aid against the ever more powerful Seljuk Turks, Urban convened a council in the city of Clermont in the Auvergne of 13 archbishops, 82 bishops, numerous abbots and other church leaders and, crucially, temporal leaders from the diocese of the clerics attending. Aware of the political, social and economic threats to peace and unity in Western

Europe, Urban used his speech at the end of the Council of Clermont to call for a Christian crusade to fight the Turks and protect Christians and to recapture Jerusalem. His speech contained appeals to fear, anger, hatred of the unbeliever, greed and the desire for freedom from the burden of sin:

> Although, O sons of God, you have promised more firmly than ever to keep the peace among yourselves and to preserve the rights of the church, there remains still an important work for you to do [...] you must apply the strength of your righteousness to another matter which concerns you as well as God. For your brethren who live in the east are in urgent need of your help, and you must hasten to give them the aid which has often been promised them. For, as the most of you have heard, the Turks and Arabs have attacked them and have conquered the territory of Romania [the Greek empire] [...] They have occupied more and more of the lands of those Christians, and have overcome them in seven battles. They have killed and captured many, and have destroyed the churches and devastated the empire. If you permit them to continue thus for awhile with impurity, the faithful of God will be much more widely attacked by them [...] Let those who have been accustomed unjustly to wage private warfare against the faithful now go against the infidels and end with victory this war which should have been begun long ago. Let those who for a long time, have been robbers, now become knights. Let those who have been fighting against their brothers and relatives now fight in a proper way against the barbarians [...] Behold! On this side will be the sorrowful and poor, on that, the rich; on this side, the enemies of the Lord, on that, his friends.
>
> (Medieval Sourcebook, 1966)

Urban promised absolution and the remission of all sins of those who went on the crusade. His progress around France preaching the crusade lasted until September 1096, when he returned to Rome. He exhorted Christian kings and nobles to join the crusade, offering not just spiritual cleansing but holding out the lure of lands and wealth in the east. By joining the crusade to the east and helping establish a Christian kingdom based on Jerusalem 'they would be joyful and prosperous and true friends of God' (Runciman, 1951, pp. 107–8). His call was met with cries of *Deus lo volt* (God wills it) from his audience of clerics and nobles. Urban is also quoted as saying in support of the crusade and as a fierce attack against and a demonization of the Turks that,

> it is the imminent peril threatening you and all the faithful which has brought us hither. From the confines of Jerusalem and from the city of Constantinople a horrible tale has gone forth ... an accursed race, a race

utterly alienated from God has invaded the lands of those Christians and has depopulated them by the sword, pillage and fire.

(Jowett and O'Donnell, 2006, p. 63)

In terms of the framing of its language and the representation of the threat and the enemy, Urban's call to arms contains the emotional appeal to fear of invasion, the description of atrocities against co-believers, the responsibility of a race apart from God for this threat and these atrocities and a call to spiritually and materially benefit from bringing them to an end. It could have been designed as the model for propaganda. Urban repeated much of this on his progress around France, as did clerics charged by him with mobilizing men and finances for the crusade. As Taylor points out, the preachers of the crusade struggled to find real, current atrocities to blame on the infidel and Urban just made up stories claiming that 'the barbarians in their frenzy have invaded and ravaged the churches of God in the eastern regions', while his acolyte, Robert the Monk, said that the Saracens had forcibly circumcised Christians, putting the blood on their altars and disembowelled other Christians before killing them – he was graphic in his detail:

And they cut open the navels of those whom they choose to torment with a loathsome death, tear out most of their vital organs and tie them to a stake, drag them around and flog them before killing them as they lie prone on the ground with all their entrails out.

(Taylor, 2003, pp. 73–4)

Such oft-repeated atrocity propaganda was designed to build a fierce and militant hatred among those who took the cross and joined the crusade – the incitement effect of such atrocities stories cannot be ignored.

This was not just a holy war to regain Jerusalem and protect Christian Byzantium, it was a war of violent hatred against Turks and Muslims. They were systematically dehumanized and turned by preachers into inhuman, ravenous monsters dedicated to the torture, mutilation and murder of Christians. Peter the Hermit preached the crusade so successfully that thousands of peasants joined his disastrous expedition, few surviving. He combined apocalyptic teaching about the Second Coming with economic inducements. The doyen of crusades historians, Steven Runciman, writes that 'many of Peter's hearers believed that he was promising to lead them out of their present miseries to the land flowing with milk and honey' described in the Bible (Runciman, 1951, p. 115).

The sermons and preaching in the open air to mass audiences predated Hitler's and Goebbels's Nuremburg and Berlin rallies by 850 years but they used the methods that they were to use to such good effect – simple, repetitive messages combining fear, threat, atrocities, demonization and lures of a better future – to both mobilize support for a campaign but also build up real fear and hatred of an enemy who stood for everything that was alien to the target audience. Fact was mixed with myth and outright lies to build a picture of atrocities and their perpetrators. This was not just propaganda to mobilize, it was to develop hatred. As with much incitement to hatred, the crimes laid at the doors of the enemy were the very ones that the propagandists would encourage through their messages of fear and atrocity.

The crusading propaganda and the hardships of the crusade before it reached Jerusalem perhaps explain the frenzy of killing when the crusaders finally took Jerusalem after a final assault on 15 July 1099. Victory was not celebrated with religious worship or thanks to god but with a massacre of all encountered – Muslim and Jewish inhabitants of Jerusalem alike. Crusader Raymond of Aguilers described knights in front of the al-Aqsa mosque wading through blood up to their horses' knees, while other Christian sources of the time spoke of Jews and Muslims being tortured to death or burned alive (cited by Tyerman, 2007, pp. 157–8). In campaigns to launch the later crusades, Bernard of Clairvaux effectively declared war on all Muslims (throwing in the Slavs for good measure), while Pope Innocent III, in raising the fifth crusade, spoke of 'the perfidious Saracens' who were enslaving Christians (Taylor, 2003, pp. 76–9).

Printing and the Reformation transform propaganda

By the Reformation and the religious wars of the 16th and 17th centuries, there had been a revolution in communications through the invention of printing. While only a small proportion of people could read, the effect on propaganda was huge. Messages could be more effectively spread, with greater uniformity of content. Images as well as words could be printed and the small but growing educated middle class could now read for themselves what had once been the preserve of clerics and the educated few among the nobility. A technological revolution led to more efficient and widespread use of propaganda and incitement – with the printed word and image adding to the word spoken from the pulpit or open air preaching sessions. As metal printing plates replaced woodcuts, printing became more sophisticated and could be carried out on a larger scale. The growth of education beyond the church – the setting up of universities and schools outside the monastic system – diversified the sources of knowledge, opinion and debate. The Reformation and Counter-Reformation swept across Europe with the preached and printed word a key factor in the spread of Protestantism and in the Catholic Church's response.

The printing of bibles in vernacular languages rather than just Latin was part of the religious thrust of the reformers and it encouraged literacy and added to the efficacy of Protestant propaganda. Despite the poor literacy rates, Luther's writings sold over 300,000 copies. Luther's preaching was a departure from the style of Catholic theologians. Just as the reformers printed bibles in local languages, Luther in his preaching appealed directly to ordinary people in language they could understand – he used 'plain German laced with the common idiomatic expressions of Northern Germany and Austria and based his sermons on metaphor and folk wisdoms' (Jowett and O'Donnell, 2006, p. 68). This down-to-earth approach to the language of propaganda, using local vernacular, but also simple, earthy expressions and colloquialisms was to be used time and again in propaganda, but was particularly a characteristic of propaganda seeking to incite hatred and violence – targeting the poor, unemployed and less educated sectors of society – as will be demonstrated in the case studies – not that Luther was inciting hate, but propagandizing for church reform. Luther's nailing of his 95 Theses to the church door in Wittenburg was in itself an act of propaganda that ensured a far greater public reaction than just submitting them to the church hierarchy.

It was as part of the Counter-Reformation that the word 'propaganda' came into our vocabulary when Pope Gregory XV established the Sacred Congregation for the Propagation of the Faith in 1622. He also formed the Collegium Urbanum, whose role was to train Catholic propagandists. Through these efforts, in the words of Jowett and O'Donnell, his plan 'laid the foundations for modern propaganda techniques in that it stressed the control of opinions and through them the actions of the people in the mass' (Jowett and O'Donnell, 2006, p. 73). The propagandists of the crusades had effectively used all the techniques but now there was a very conscious attempt to create and spread propagandistic messages. The Thirty Years' War was a vicious war that swirled across northern and central Europe in the first half of the 17th century without clear boundaries and with betrayal a common feature. Bound up with the religious schism of the Reformation, it saw theologians and religious propagandists become 'specialists in the permanent intellectual warfare which this division made inevitable' (Asch, 1997, p. 16). The war was about religion but also the power of princes vis-à-vis both the church and the Holy Roman Empire, the desire of princes and other rulers to increase power and wealth and the growing economic power, and influence of cities and the growing bourgeois and more educated guild and artisan classes therein.

It was a period when theological debate became a hot issue, with the burnings of books that were deemed heretical and burnings of their authors and readers, too. The debate was bound up closely with the earthly ambitions both of clerics and rulers. The burnings of books and 'heretical' authors or preachers did not stop the flood of propaganda, 'both sides in the Thirty Years' War turned out massive quantities of leaflets, pamphlets, and line drawings – including vicious caricatures' (Davison, 1971, p. 2; for more complete coverage of propaganda during this war, see Beller, 1940). The spread of printing was key in developing propaganda and, to quote Taylor, 'the printing press certainly provided the artillery that enabled lines to be drawn in an unprecedented religious war of ideas' (Taylor, 2003, p. 97). Religious works became part of the arsenal of the conflicts of the 16th and 17th centuries – one example was the printing of more than 30 editions of the Catholic work on witchcraft and heresy, *Malleus Maleficarum*. It was effectively a working guide as well as a theoretical work and instructed Catholic clergy and their secular supporters how to recognize and persecute heretics. Burnings of heretics reached epidemic proportions in Germany during the early years of the Thirty Years' War as the guide was put into effect and the Catholic Church sought to burn out heresy and support for the Reformation. The speed of production and of local distribution of pamphlets was important in eliciting responses from supporters and the winning over of communities. As Beller points out, referring to the fate of Catholic regents in Bohemia in 1618 when they fell foul of the Bohemian Protestant hierarchy and were thrown from the windows of the Hradshin Castle, 'the victims of the "defenestration" had scarcely crawled out of the castle moat when the presses poured forth a stream of pamphlets and broadsides' (Beller, 1940, p. 3).

Massacres were commonplace during the conflict – it was a war of extermination of religious opponents as well as one of territory and seizure of power. On 20 May 1631, Catholic forces took the Protestant-held town of Magdeburg – the garrison was wiped out and the inhabitants put to the sword or burned alive when the Catholic forces torched the town, 20,000 civilians being killed in the massacre or fire. This was the sort of atrocity that acted as a rallying call for Protestants – preachers throughout Germany called for violent revenge against the Catholics and pamphlets and songs were used to attack the Catholics and the Holy Roman Emperor, Ferdinand II (Asch, 1997, pp. 105–6). Pamphlets decried such atrocities but also, at times, threatened vicious retribution against enemies. Beller reproduces some of the prints of the period, including one Protestant print threatening the castration of Catholic priests. The artistically produced print shows a priest being castrated and the accompanying verse accuses priests of sleeping with the wife of an artisan. The verse threatens that:

> They (there is no begging off), Must all be castrated. Prelates, abbots, priors, bursars, Jesuits, it cannot be helped. The good fathers must now give up their *Fraterculos*. Then without a shudder, their baggage is cut out completely. They may die or recover from it, No great attention is paid to their great fuss.
>
> (Beller, 1940, pp. 21–3)

A Catholic print shows the army of the Swedish king, Gustavus Adolphus, as being made up of barbarians, while another Protestant print depicts Catholics as the seven-headed beast of the Apocalypse and as a another beast vomiting Jesuits on to Protestant cities.

These prints, reproduced by Beller with their verses and translations, show the variety of methods of propaganda. Some are clearly there to glorify one side or the other, others are more violent or inciting, and demonize the opponents and threaten death or mutilation. Pamphlets were the most common form of propaganda, along with single page 'broadsides' with large illustrations. Verse forms were used to make them easier for propagandists to recite them from memory to the masses who couldn't read. For those who could read, or the masses who could see the illustrations and have verses of proclamations recited to them, the printed materials were such that 'the simplest and most evident fears and prejudices could be emphasized' (Beller, 1940, p. 7).

Myths and biblical metaphors were common – the Swedish king depicted as a brave lion chasing a Catholic beast or as Achilles; angels supporting the Catholics thrown from the Prague Castle windows; Catholics as apocalyptic figures or representatives of the anti-Christ. All were designed to win over waverers, instil fear of the opponent and, frequently, to incite hatred and encourage attacks on the enemy or to encourage men to join one army or another in defence of their town, region or religion – propaganda was aimed at developing specific attitudes but also at direct recruitment of supporters and fighting men. Beller points out that each side's propagandists were well aware, as later and more technically sophisticated exponents would be, that 'the identification of the enemy with unfavourable existing attitudes is at least as efficacious as a positive statement of the righteousness of a cause' (ibid.).

The propaganda war was concerned primarily with religion, but atrocity stories abounded as a means of blackening the image of your religious or secular opponents. Sir Thomas More, philosopher and Catholic ideologist, wrote of the occupation and sack of Rome, alleging the 'torture and mutilation of its inhabitants' by the invading opponents of the papacy (Taylor, 2003, p. 94) – his words drawing clear parallels between the physical mutilation of the people of Rome and the spiritual torture being inflicted by those he viewed as heretics. Atrocity, and through it the demonization of the enemy, was a key aspect of the propaganda throughout this period. Atrocities by one's opponents became a theme of sermons on both sides and of the growing use of pamphlets that could be printed cheaply and distributed widely.

The printing revolution also saw the advent of the newspaper. One of the first, strongly bound up with the dynastic and religious wars of the time, was the *Strasbourg Relation*, which appeared in 1609, followed soon after by the weekly *Frankfurter Zeitung* in 1615. The first English newspaper, printed in 1620, was produced by English Protestants in Amsterdam reporting on the horrors of the Thirty Years' War – it was contained news but also propaganda against Catholicism. The pamphlets produced at the time were often luridly illustrated with caricatures of opponents or glorifying the home side – such as the print of a great lion devouring Catholic priests, believed to be a glorification of King Gustavus Adolphus of Sweden, who fought for the Protestant cause during the war. During the war, the French government, directed by Cardinal Richelieu, established the first government newspaper, *La Gazette de France.*

In 16th-century England, Henry VIII and his minister Thomas Cromwell used the printing presses to justify and spread the ideology of the English Reformation. Later, early newspapers, pamphlets and leaflets became key means of spreading the puritan and radical messages of King Charles I's opponents before and during the English Civil War. The abolition of the Court of Star Chamber by the Long Parliament in 1641, gave particular impetus to printers and pamphleteers. The chamber had operated as a supreme court but also as the main scourge of dissent, sedition and those accused of fomenting public disorder. Puritan and radical pamphleteers took full advantage of the effective lightening of censorship and used the printed word and, as in the Thirty Years' War examples, printed images to vilify their opponents and the religious, monarchical/aristocratic establishment. One of the innovations in news and propaganda was the appearance of what were called newsbooks – weekly collections of news reports and comment anything up to 15 or 16 pages long. The first, snappily entitled *The Heads of Severall Proceedings in this Parliament, from the 22 of November to the 29, 1641,* reported on the work of parliament and clearly placed it within a timespan and, by having clear dates, suggests that it will be part of a series. It was the first move to report domestic news following the abolition of the Star Chamber and the effective lifting of a ban on reporting what happened in England.

Charles I had resisted reporting of English affairs believing that 'liberty of discourse' would undermine his position and authority (Cull et al., 2003, p. 85). The government tried to suppress the outpouring of works critical of the monarchy by imprisoning authors and printers, but failed to stem the tide. The abolition of the chamber and the decline in the powers of the Stationers' Office, the government body that had a monopoly over printing and copyright and was used to try to suppress independent printing, reduced the royalist government's ability to control printing and the production of political pamphlets or broadsheets. The works were of key importance in shaping opinion, despite continuing high levels of illiteracy. They might not have determined the course of the Civil War but as Cull et al. assert,

> the authorities could not control the press and its propagandistic writings, which, whether actively or passively, shaped the public sphere of debate by providing information to the masses and the provinces about the working of government. The distribution of news and opinion forced people to take sides on issues and drove a wedge between the king and Parliament.
>
> (ibid.)

During the Civil War, the two sides each produced their own newspaper to report the war and political developments from their side – the royalists printed *Mercurius Aulicus* and the parliamentarians *Mercurius Britannicus*, the latter famed for its denunciations of royalists as 'anti-patriotic social parasites, who did not know honest labour' (Hill, 1991, p. 64). They reported the news in a highly partial way and were aimed at maintaining support for each side and winning over waverers. They were works of propaganda, though rarely of the violent incitement or extreme religious hatred seen during the Thirty Years' War. They were really a forerunner of the highly 'patriotic' and partial press output to be seen in later wars, particularly during the Napoleonic period and the First World War. The pamphleteers were even more propagandistic – supporting or attacking each side during the war but also in the debates within the parliamentary and radical camp. During the Putney Debates of 1647 between Cromwell and his radical Leveller critics, pamphlets were a key means of each side propagating their arguments and gaining support (Robertson, 2007, pp. xvi–xvii).

Jumping ahead to the late 18th century and the Napoleonic era, access to the written word had spread to the emerging bourgeoisie and to some of the more prosperous urban skilled workers and artisans, and newspapers were increasingly important alongside and illustrated sheets. The 17th and 18th centuries had seen improvements in education for some classes, more efficient and cheaper production of paper and faster means of distribution, all increasing the spread and potential power of the written word (Jowett and O'Donnell, 2006, pp. 74–5). Papers like William Bradford's *Pennsylvania Journal* had been important in developing anti-British sentiment and bolstering the cause of independence during the American Revolution (Jowett and O'Donnell, 2006, p. 77). The wide distribution of the works of Thomas Paine and the effective propagandizing of Thomas Jefferson and Benjamin Franklin all played their role in building up opposition to rule by the British monarchy and in favour of independence. Franklin engaged in black propaganda, putting out on one occasion a fake version of the pro-British newspaper that appeared to boast about scalp-hunting by pro-British forces – a practice reviled by the colonists and so designed to discredit the British and make them appear as brutal oppressors (Jowett and O'Donnell, 2006, p. 83).

In the final years of the ancient regime in France, 66 newspapers were published regularly but none of them was permitted to carry domestic or political news – this was strongly enforced by law. Literacy was gradually improving – especially in urban areas – and Hanley estimates that by the late 1780s, just prior to the revolution, 37 per cent of the population could read (50 per cent among men) and in northern France rates were as high as 66 per cent of men (Hanley, 2005). There was a growing audience for the written word and greater potential for written propaganda to be transmitted by word of mouth at public meetings. Taylor writes that when the Estates-General was convened in Paris in May 1789 because of the growing political and economic threat to the monarchy – the first meeting since 1614 – it did so amid debates about the economic crisis which 'exploded into a torrent of political propaganda. In that month over a hundred pamphlets appeared [...] and the figures rose to 300 in June' (Taylor, 2003, p. 147).

During the period from the revolution in 1789 to the appointment of Napoleon as First Consul in 1799, over 515 newspapers appeared, though most were short-lived – 172 lasted only a month or less – but the rise along with greater literacy meant as many as six million French people could read the news and the opinion and propaganda contained in the papers. During the first ten years of the revolution, newspapers and pamphlets were used by the competing factions to advance their own positions but also to denigrate royalists and republican opponents. After the fall of the monarchy, constraints on newspaper publishing and on free expression fell away. But 'it was a freedom that often degenerated into licence, as the press was used to slander individuals, to vent personal grievances or to further the interests of a faction' (Gilchrist and Murray, 1971, p. 1).

The post-revolutionary press in France was highly politicized and highly propagandistic. At times, it directly advocated or incited violence, generating support for the execution of opponents. During the terror in 1790, the politician and revolutionary journalist, Jean-Paul Marat, used his newspaper *L'Ami du people* to call for revolutionary violence and insurrection against opponents. On 18 December 1790, the paper issued this strident call:

> it is not on the frontiers, but in the capital that we must rain down our blows. Stop wasting time thinking up means of defence; there is only one means of defence for you. That is what I have recommended so many times: *a general insurrection and popular executions*. Begin then by making sire of the king, the dauphin and the royal family: put them under strong guard and let their heads answer for events.
>
> (Gilchrist and Murray, 1971, p. 268)

Marat goes on to call for the beheading of generals, counter-revolutionary ministers, mayors and councillors. He advocated putting all counter-revolutionaries 'to the sword'. The language is simple and direct and was, according to the increasingly established pattern of propaganda and incitement, repeated constantly and consistently.

Antoine Gorsas, another radical revolutionary, used his papers to incite violence and insurrection – and is believed to have played a major role in inciting the popular insurrections of June and August 1792. In 1793, in his *Le Courier des departements*, he wrote:

> the terrible moment has arrived. Hordes of cannibals, greedy for blood and pillage, have violated the asylum of liberty [...] They want the death of the patriots [...] It is therefore today a fight to the death![...] Let them

perish [...] We are in open conflict with the enemies of our liberty; either we must perish at their hands or they must perish by ours.

(Gilchrist and Murray, 1971, p. 270)

Again, there is no doubt about the use of language, the open incitement and the extreme portrayals of opponents. In the violent and unstable environment of revolutionary France, Gorsas is no doubt right that it was a case of kill or be killed – but the ascribing of murderous intent to opponents to justify or incite one's own violence is a tool that crops up again and again in the cases where political or military propaganda goes beyond just vilifying the enemy and mobilizing support for a cause, and becomes incitement to extreme hatred and individual or mass violence.

As Napoleon used his military successes to develop his political profile and to seek power, he demonstrated an acute awareness of the role of the press and propaganda (Holtman, 1950, p. 245). He combined military with political campaigning, used military despatches, newspaper articles, proclamations and, later, paintings, medals and medallions to promote himself and get his face known throughout France. Hanley captures the step up in sophistication and understanding well: 'although the other historical figures had manipulated various media for political gain, Napoleon Bonaparte was the first non-monarch in the modern era to realise the limitless possibilities of propaganda'. Early in his military career in 1796, he used despatches from campaigns in Italy to foster his own image as a general and potential leader and rapidly learned how to manipulate the French press. He founded his own newspaper and used the expansion of the popular press and growth in literacy to boost his profile. He also encouraged his armies to produce their own newspapers, which of course gave pride of place to their general's military achievements and leadership qualities.

The prestige gained from military successes and his carefully cultivated public image helped to get him appointed as First Consul in 1799, following his Egyptian campaign. He had an engaging style in his speeches, proclamations and despatches – his military despatches (widely published in the pro-revolutionary press and notably in the semi-official newspaper, the *Moniteur*) were written in a new and personal style – in the first person and with praise for soldiers and officers but always depicting him as controller of events (Hanley, 2005). Hanley details how, between 19 April and 28 November 1798, 54 stories about Napoleon's Egyptian campaign were published in the revolutionary *Journal des Hommes Libres* (Henley, 2005). His campaigns in the press as well as on the battlefield were successful as he progressed from First Consul to Consul for life in 1802 and Emperor in 1804 (Jowett and O'Donnel, 2006, p. 87). Propaganda was a device to maintain or increase his popular support and mobilize resources for his foreign wars. There was not the same incitement to terror that had been present in the immediate post-revolution period, although on occasions attempts were made to whip the populace into a frenzy. Following his appointment as Consul in 1799, French envoys to Austria were assassinated. The government under Napoleon declared a national day of mourning and a proclamation was sent to local leaders that left little to the imagination about how to mark the period of mourning:

> Miss no opportunity to give the ceremonies a solemn, inspirational character. On urns, mausoleums, pyramids and funerary columns let artists place broken olive trees stained with blood, Nature veiled, Humanity in tears... Show Despotism gathering their blood in a goblet. Depict all evils which come in its train: famine, fire, war and death; depict republicans rushing to arms to withstand the monster... Let funeral music of desolating sadness be followed by a period of silence and then – suddenly – let it be broken by the cry: Vengeance!
>
> (cited by Taylor, 2003, p. 154)

Once entrenched in power, Napoleon used newspapers in France and abroad to bolster his power and policies and also employed censorship to prevent domestic criticism. Papers were closed if they dared to criticize. By 1810, there were only four newspapers left in Paris and he limited each department of France to a single paper (Cull et al., 2003, p. 260; Taylor, 2003, p. 155).

The whole revolutionary and Napoleonic period saw a qualitative change in attempts to influence masses of people. Political crises, wars and revolutions were all meat and drink to propagandists and the 19th century saw enough of these to ensure that the role of propaganda was undiminished after the Napoleonic wars. Newspapers gained in readership and so in importance throughout the century, and rulers – whether democratic or autocratic – had to take more note of the importance of public opinion.

The use of the press to inform and to propagandize was key during the Crimean War. The French and Russians closely controlled their press through censorship but the British press was less constrained and over the period of the conflict both supported war and engendered public backing for the expenditure of men and money, and criticized the conduct of the war and the appalling state of medical facilities. The famous early war correspondent, William Russell, emerged during the war and with his despatches published in the *Times* set the scene for war reporting – with its opportunities for influence and propaganda (see Meller (2010), for a full account of propaganda during the Crimean War and also Cull et al. (2003, pp. 99–100)). His and other journalists' despatches from the front and from military hospitals portrayed the appalling conditions and unnecessary suffering – sent by steamship and telegraph, they helped lead not only to the fall of the Aberdeen government but also to the development of a new, punchier and faster style of reporting. It was, to cite Knightley, 'an immense leap in the history of journalism', as it 'marked the beginning of an organized effort to report a war to the civilian population at home using the services of a civilian reporter' rather than through the words of military despatches, letters from serving officers and soldiers or straight lifts from foreign papers (Knightley, 1982, p. 4).

The effect of reporting, especially that of the influential *Times*, was such that Lord Newcastle said to Russell after the war, 'It was you who turned out the government, Mr. Russell' (Meller, 2010, p. 84). Lord Palmerston succeeded Aberdeen, even though he was viewed with great suspicion in parliament and both main parties, yet 'public opinion and the press forced the government and monarch to allow it' (ibid.). It is important to point out that the reporting from the front, especially by Russell, highlighted the incompetence of those directing and supplying the army but also directly supported the prosecution of the war. Russell was no opponent of the war and his despatches can be seen as effective propaganda for the pro-war camp rather than criticism of the war per se, as was found in the writings of those like as the radical politician and pamphleteer Richard Cobden.

One of the central characteristics of propaganda before and during the Crimean War, was the way in which Lord Palmerston – as foreign secretary, home secretary and then prime minister – engendered anti-Russian opinion to support war against Russia and then try to maintain that support as the war become less and less popular and the poor conditions of the troops and the wounded became ever more widely known. Palmerston was a Russophobe and had developed a keen understanding of both the power of public opinion (at a time of coalition or minority governments and shifting political fortunes) and the ability of politicians to manipulate it. He was more than willing to use all methods he could to get backing for his view that Russia had to be opposed and to develop a nascent suspicion of Russia into something more substantial. As Meller contends, 'his role in kindling this xenophobia and turning it to his own ends is important both as a demonstration of his own early experiences of coordinating a propaganda campaign and of the forces that lay behind the success of patriotic propaganda during the Crimean War' (Meller, 2010, pp. 68–9). At one stage, in an early reference to the importance of the chattering classes in affecting public policy, Palmerston spoke of the need to develop strong anti-Russian feeling, saying 'I am all for making a chatter against her [Russia]' (Meller, 2010, p. 69).

It is notable that despite the scandals over equipment, the conditions in field and military hospitals and disasters like the charge of the Light Brigade, there was not a strong wave of public opposition to the war, per se, and Palmerston was able to take a hard line against Russia at the peace talks. The propaganda effort maintained support for the war until its end. It was anti-Russian in tone, presenting Russia as expansionist and aggressive. While it did not develop into such full-scale vilification of the Russians that it presented each and every Russian as cruel, barbarous and inhuman, it did use events like the Russian attack on the Turkish fleet at Sinope in 1853 to portray the threat posed by Russia as a major power and the alleged cruelty of Imperial Russia's conduct of the conflict with Turkey (Meller, 2010, p. 70). The war showed that public opinion mattered and could be manipulated. Meller summed it up succinctly: 'Whereas the efforts of the *Times* during the Crimean War demonstrated the power of the media in orchestrating propaganda campaigns and organizing public opinion, Palmerston demonstrated that officials could utilize that media to their own, and the government's, ends whether in war or in peacetime' (Meller, 2010, p. 98).

At times during the course of the war, vilification of the Russians was used to bolster pro-war feeling by portraying the Russians as barbaric:

> Popular culture was also fed a diet of atrocity propaganda [...] An abundance of stories circulated in Britain concerning the Russian treatment of prisoners and wounded British soldiers [...] There were numerous reports of the Russians illegally using flags of truce or neutrality to fool the British, consolidating the idea of Russia as an uncivilized and dishonourable nation.
>
> (Meller, 2010, p. 72)

But while this was regular fare in the newspapers, it was not used to incite lasting hatred of Russians individually or en masse but rather to maintain a spirit of determination to continue the war against what was depicted as an aggressive state prepared to use barbaric methods to pursue its geopolitical and military objectives.

The American Civil War saw another step change in the reporting of war and its uses in governing public opinion. The development of the telegraph enabled the faster transmission of news and huge numbers of correspondents covered the campaigns – 500 alone on the Union side and around 100 on the Confederate side (Taylor, 2003, p. 166). The papers brought the war to ordinary Americans. As in the conflicts already described, the war reporting was used not only to inform but also to form opinion. Horace Greeley's *New York Tribune* was an exemplar of the way in which journalism was used to bolster morale rather than give a true account of events. As Taylor has noted, Greely's newspaper 'spearheaded the northern propaganda cause in words' (ibid.). Overall, though, the Northern press was freer and more critical than that in the Confederacy which 'lent itself to the government's propaganda line much more readily than did the Northern press' (Knightley, 1982, p. 25).

The last quarter of the 19th century saw the continued use of propaganda at times of international, regional or national tension – notably the expert use of the tool by pan-Slavists during the Russo-Turkish and Balkan conflicts and the widespread use during the Franco-Prussian War and the Paris Commune. Newspapers were still dominant and the relationship between the media and politicians continued to develop. The speed of dissemination was faster due to the extensive network of telegraph cables connecting Britain,

Europe and North America and the cables connecting the colonial powers with their major colonies. Britain, by 1902, owned 63 per cent of the cables laid, giving it speed of communication for administrative and military purposes but also for news transmission and propaganda. Control of the cables was to be key in the First World War.

The dissemination of news and, if necessary, the control of that flow and the ability of one side in a conflict (initially Britain had the advantage in this sphere) to get across its side of events was further enabled by the rise in the 1860s of news agencies – typified by the British-based and owned Reuters agency. It had a wide network of correspondents serving newspapers. There was simply more and more news and comment. And, as Meller identified, 'Ubiquity was highlighted as one of the prerequisites of the modern form of propaganda and the mass media of this period was undoubtedly pervasive in this way. With such a ready and fast supply of information, there was inevitably more scope for its manipulation for the purposes of propaganda' (Meller, 2010, p. 115). As theorists and practitioners of propaganda are well aware, the quantity, repetition and ubiquity of propaganda are keys to its success. Alongside the development of the speed and scope of the media would come government efforts both to censor and harness media output for their own opinion forming and direct propaganda ends. This coincided with societal evolution, particularly in the industrialized world, that saw the development of what one could call mass-consciousness and mass media. This created fertile conditions for mass propaganda, which could be used for a variety of purposes, including, as was the case during the Crusades, and Thirty Years' War, the use of myth, atrocity stories and other devices to provide propaganda with content and emotional power that could not only develop, manipulate and mobilize mass public opinion but also incite hatred and action. Politicians were well aware of the changes and they soon developed propaganda accordingly.

Propaganda in the 20th century

The new century started with a major war in progress – the South African or Boer War – and it was one in which imperialist propaganda and the manipulation of opinion played a major role and presaged the use of propaganda in the decades to come.

In the run up to the war, the British High Commissioner for South Africa, Sir Alfred Milner, assiduously used the press to gain public support for the annexation of the Transvaal and to denigrate the Boer leader, Paul Kruger. By the time of the ultimatum to the Transvaal government over the British demands for votes for the Uitlanders (non-Afrikaner, mainly British, residents of Transvaal who were denied the vote under the Transvaal Republic's Constitution), Milner had lined up major newspapers like the *Times, Daily Mail, Morning Post, the Westminster Gazette* and *Pall Mall Gazette* (Milner had worked for the latter as a journalist before becoming a civil servant and diplomat) behind them. They were banging the imperialist drum and demanding that Kruger and the Transvaal concede the vote to the Uitlanders on British terms or face the threat of war. This was to develop a wave of public support for action against the Boers and put pressure on the colonial secretary, Joseph Chamberlain, who was less than enthusiastic about a possible war in southern Africa.

Careful utilization of government despatches from Milner in Cape Town and the financial backing of the gold and diamond magnates Rhodes and Beit had enabled a mounting campaign of criticism of the Transvaalers and the building up of the Uitlanders as victims of an autocratic and repressive government. Liberal papers such as the *Daily News* and *The Chronicle* were less jingoistic and either called for compromise or opposed war but even they were critical of Kruger and the Boers. But the weight of press opinion was pro-imperialist and behind the move towards war, particularly the popular press (Taylor, 2003, p. 174).

When the British ultimatum was rejected and war started, it was again a war with correspondents tagging along with the armies – some cultivated for their pro-imperialist views and given access and briefings by the army staff, others tolerated or obstructed because of their perceived critical stance. The main papers, *Times, Mail, Telegraph* and *The Chronicle* sent out correspondents (Pakenham, 1979, p. 136). Their reports, telegraphed back, brought the news far more quickly than in the past to the breakfast tables and drawing rooms of Britain. The conservative and popular press kept up a stream of pro-war output, only moving to criticize when the British campaign faltered and ran into the ground with the sieges of Ladysmith and Mafeking, the defeats at Talana, Modder River and Colenso, and then the disaster at Spion Kop. The sieges enabled an 'our brave boys' style of reporting and comment to maintain pro-war opinion – the dastardly Boers were contrasted with the brave defenders of the besieged towns. As in the Crimean War, alleged abuses of the white flag by Boers were used to depict them as villainous and cruel. But, despite the vilification of Kruger and the caricaturing of the Boers in text and cartoons, the thrust of the propaganda was to mobilize and maintain support at home for the war, rather than incite lasting hatred of the Afrikaners or encouraging indiscriminate killing of Boers. There were examples of the British retaliation for Boer actions, such as the indiscriminate killing of fleeing Boers at Elandslaagte in October 1899 by the British cavalry, following the accusation that Boer abuse of a white flag that led to the deaths of a number of British officers and soldiers, but these were the exception rather than the rule (Pakenham, 1979, pp. 139–40; see, also, Meller, 2010, p. 11 on British press comments on reported abuses of the white flag).

The abuse of the white flag, periodic reports of the abuse of prisoners and other atrocity stories were highlighted in the imperialist press. This was both to maintain the image of the Boers as unfit to govern in Transvaal and the Orange Free State but also to combat the feelings of compassion and respect for the Boers among many British people (Meller, 2011). The propaganda aimed at creating a negative, brutal image of the Boer was intended to undermine compassion and respect – 'Depictions of Boer barbarism served to dispel the belief that they were simple, honest, courageous farmers defending their land. Atrocities reported from the front were eagerly taken up by the Unionist campaign, often with a flagrant disregard for verification' (Meller, 2010, p. 192). Yet, this never completely counteracted a certain residual sympathy for the 'plucky' Boer republics resisting the British imperialist steamroller – the traditional British habit of backing the underdog. Compassion for the Boers, especially non-combatants, was increased by Emily Hobhouse's reports of the appalling conditions, disease and high death rates in the concentration camps in which Boer civilians were incarcerated.

As the critic of the war, J.A. Hobson wrote, the British government's and the imperialist press's actions before and during the war involved the modern manufacture of public opinion (cited by Meller, 2010, p. 2). This was standard war and imperialist propaganda rather than the propagation of hatred for the Boers, white flag stories notwithstanding, and it was reaching, in Britain, a mass audience. The atrocity stories were there to maintain support for the war and justify British actions rather than lead to a war of extermination – what was at stake was public support for the imperialist venture rather than survival in the face of a brutal and implacable enemy. Education reforms in the last 40 years of the 19th century had massively expanded the literate population. The war saw the inexorable rise of the popular media – the forerunner of the tabloids of today – in the form of the *Daily Mail*, whose sales reached one million during the war. Its populist and avowedly imperialist content was a potent form of propaganda helping to form and develop public opinion. The *Daily Mail* published verses and opinion from the poet of imperialism, Rudyard Kipling, and the music halls were essentially conservative and pro-imperialist, staunch supporters of the soldiers and fierce caricaturists of the Boers and played a role in maintaining mass support for the war. Not that the British media had one indivisible aim – that of supporting the war and imperialism. The *Daily News*, *The Chronicle* and the *Manchester Guardian* remained critical of the war and the imperialist policies behind its prosecution.

The First World War brought about the next revolution in the scale and style of propaganda, building on the foundations already in place – notably the use of fear, atrocity stories and demonization or caricatures to attack the enemy. The war was a watershed, but as Meller has expertly demonstrated, it saw the development and evolution of modern propaganda, not its invention (Meller, 2010, p. 2). The role of propaganda during the conflict gave rise to the first serious studies of propaganda and brought it into the political lexicon of the 20th century – generally as a form of abuse of the actions of an enemy. In Britain, France and the USA during the war, the view taken by politicians and most people was that propaganda was what the Germans indulged in but not the noble allies! In his seminal work *Propaganda technique in World War I*, Harold Lasswell wrote that 'A word has appeared, which has come to have an ominous clang in many minds – Propaganda. We live among more people than ever, who are puzzled, uneasy, or vexed at the unknown cunning which seems to have duped and degraded them...' (Lasswell, 1971, pp. 2–3).

In the run up to the war, newspapers (often fed stories by increasingly aware governments) played their role in influencing public opinion in Britain, France and Germany in the growing competition between the imperialist powers. Right-wing, populist newspapers like the *Daily Mail* in Britain, had played a major role in building suspicion of Germany – particularly over the naval arms race and the building of dreadnought battleships. Newspapers in France and Germany played similar roles. While many papers across Europe represented views critical of the momentum towards war, the most popular ones were pro-war and helped build enthusiasm for war – with, as Taylor notes, celebratory 'dancing in the streets throughout Europe's capitals' on the outbreak of war (Taylor, 2003, p. 176). The propaganda during the war was aimed principally at convincing domestic audiences of the rightness of each country's cause and the injustices or evils represented by the enemy. More than ever before, government propaganda and the propaganda of the pro-war parties and papers worked to develop and maintain public support for the war, encourage recruitment and, as the war dragged on, to sensitize populations to accept massive casualty rates and economic privation in the cause of defeating the enemy. Atrocity propaganda and dehumanizing of the enemy played crucial roles.

The organization of propaganda differed from state to state. In Britain, despite the recent experience of the Boer War, there was no fully developed government 'organisation or plan for propaganda or the manipulation of public opinion' (Badsey, 2011). France similarly lacked a single organization, but by 1916 'had established the Maison de la Presse as the official agency for the conduct of French propaganda, under the control of the Ministry of Foreign Affairs' (Davison, 1971, p. 8). German propaganda was under the control of the military and, as Hitler and Goebbels were to proclaim fervently during and after the rise to power of the National Socialists (see German case study), was poor and failed to combat the much more sophisticated propaganda of the British, French and, later, Americans. The Germans were on the back foot – even with some of their own population – from the start having taken the offensive in the West and invaded Belgium and France. By invading a neutral country, Germany effectively 'forfeited the moral high ground the German government had hoped to secure by its pre-war propaganda' (Taylor, 2003, p. 176).

British domestic propaganda and its output aimed at influencing American government and public opinion was able to use 'Poor Little

Belgium' as a rallying point (ibid.). The scale, death toll and sheer horror of the war – on a far greater scale than anything seen before – required a more organized, consistent and targeted propaganda effort. It led to the formation and development of institutions and government strategies for propaganda and, where the privately owned newspapers were dominant, the development of closer and more complex relations between owners, editors, journalists and politicians. In Britain, politicians, particularly those like David Lloyd George who were more aware of the power of public opinion, both feared and feted the press barons – notably Lords Northcliffe (owner of the *Times, Daily Mail, Evening News, Sunday Dispatch* and *Sunday Times* and Beaverbrook (who owned the *Daily Express)* – and worked with them to build and maintain public support for the war. There were anti-war newspapers before and at the start of the war, notably the *Manchester Guardian*, the *Labour Leader* and the *Daily News*, but they did not have the mass circulation of the Northcliffe papers and did not seriously challenge public support for war.

The press weapon was a two-edged sword and Northcliffe's support for the war in the early years was combined with criticism of the government for poor recruitment (despite the initial fervour for war), the inefficiency and corruption of the munitions industry and military failures like Gallipoli. By 1914, Northcliffe controlled 40 per cent of Britain's morning papers and 45 per cent of evening papers (Lee Thompson, 1999, p. 2). Towards the end of the war, both Beaverbrook and Northcliffe were co-opted as part of the government's information and propaganda effort.

One of the key factors in the success of the British propaganda effort was the combination of government and 'independent' newspapers putting out strongly pro-war messages and stories, but with periodic bouts of press criticism. The ability and relative freedom to criticize and to report defeats (even though this was often incomplete reporting that was delayed) established a level of trust that meant propaganda messages were more readily accepted. In the early days of the war, the *Daily Mail* (edition of 3 August 1914) exhorted its readers that 'Our duty is to go forward into the valley of the shadow of death with courage and faith – with courage to suffer and faith in our country.' Although Northcliffe's papers supported the appointment of Lord Kitchener as minister of war, Kitchener was intensely suspicious of the press after his experiences in the Boer War and he set up the Press Bureau under F.E. Smith (later ennobled as Lord Birkenhead) to try to control press coverage of the war. Kitchener resisted the sending of correspondents to the front but was forced by political pressure on the government to allow correspondents to be attached to the British Army headquarters on the Western Front in 1915 – a pool system of reporting was developed that involved strong elements of army control over movements, heavy reliance on official briefings and 'multiple layers of censorship in France and Britain'; press photographs were banned but papers got round this by getting photos from serving soldiers (Badsey, 2011). Censorship and the barring of reporting of some aspects of the war was enabled right at the start of the conflict by the Defence of the Realm Act – this gave powers of censorship and the right to examine incoming and outgoing cables (Knightley, 1982, p. 64).

At the start of the war, Britain was a step ahead in international propaganda as it controlled the majority of the undersea telegraph cables between Europe and America and at the start of the war cut the cables between Germany and North America. As Taylor argues, this gave the allies a huge advantage in the propaganda battle for the sympathies of the US government and people (Taylor, 2003, p. 177). Combined with the advantage given allied propaganda by the lasting image of Germany as the aggressor, this interruption of Germany's communications eventually helped Britain and France to win the international propaganda battle, helping to smooth the way for American involvement, despite the strong strand of isolationism in American public opinion.

But for the purposes of this study, the key area of propaganda in the First World War was the home front and the use of propaganda to influence and manipulate opinion towards the war and, crucially, towards the enemy. As Lasswell put it in his classic study of propaganda during the war:

> by far the most potent role of propaganda is to mobilize the animosity of the community against the enemy [...] war propaganda rose to such amazing dimensions in the last war, because the communization of warfare necessitated the mobilization of the civilian mind. No government could win without a united nation behind it, and no government could have a united nation behind it unless if controlled the minds of its people.
> (Lasswell, 1971, p. 10)

This control and unity was achieved through the constant repetition of basic, easily understood ideas – a technique to be used to great and evil effect in Germany in the Second World War and then later in Serbia and Rwanda.

At the core of the successful allied propaganda during the war was the presentation of their cause as just and, crucially, a defence of civilized values against a brutal aggressor. Fear of the war and public opinion against war had to be overcome and the war presented as necessary for the survival of the public's way of life and values. Lasswell summed it up well: 'So great are the psychological resistances to war in modern nations that every war must appear to be a war of defence against a menacing, murderous aggressor' (Lasswell, 1971, p. 47). The German invasion of Belgium and France and its offensive into Russian territory served to give content to British and French propaganda and deprived German propaganda, even at home, of the argument that it was a war of defence. German propaganda could rail against British, French and Russian imperial ambitions and their ganging up on Germany, but it could not present itself as fighting a war of defence against an invading enemy.

Menacing and murderous were qualities that allied propaganda could use to great effect – not just defence of territory against German invasion, but also defence of the weak (Belgium) and of a particular idea of justice and civilization. The French and British publics were left in no doubt about who to hate – the Germans. The sole responsibility of the Germans for the war was the core of the message (Lasswell, 1971, p. 47). As the war gained pace, vivid reports of German atrocities became the most potent means of maintaining emotions at a high level and reinforcing the message that this brutal enemy must be resisted at all costs. Linked to this, among the pro-war papers, was the presentation of the allied armies in a positive light. Despite initial frustration over government attempts to have a new blackout on the Western Front in the early weeks of the war, by its edition of 31 August 1914, the *Daily Mail* was reporting the 'heroic' fight by the British Expeditionary Force (BEF) in Belgium, calling it an 'army of exhaustless valour'.

The 'our boys' approach was maintained throughout the war, as was the atrocity angle. As early as 21 August 1914, the *Mail's* reporter Hamilton Fyfe was writing of German 'sins against civilization' and 'barbarity', accusing the German army of cutting off the hands of captured Red Cross personnel and using women and children as shields against allied fire (cited by Lee Thompson, 1999, p. 36). On 26 August, the *Daily Mail* reported that the Germans were guilty of 'a catalogue of horrors that will indelibly brand the German name in the eyes of all mankind'. The language was simple, emotional and effective – the Germans during the war were seen through the frames of aggressor, torturer, rapist and murderer. But it went further and declared,

> the measured, detailed and we fear unanswerable indictment of Germany's conduct of the war issued yesterday by the Belgian minister is a catalogue of horrors [...] After making every deduction for national bias and possibility of error, there remains a record of sheer brutality that will neither be forgiven nor forgotten.

The German capture and destruction of much of the Belgian city of Louvain was an important point in establishing the brutality of the German army towards civilians and the threat they posed to civilized values. Reporting in a number of newspapers, but most vividly in the *Daily Mail* of 18 September 1914, described how after the capture of the town, the Germans accused civilians of firing on them and launched a murderous reprisal campaign involving the summary execution of hundreds of civilians, the depopulation of much of the town, the burning of a sixth of the entire town, including the library housing thousands of medieval books and historical manuscripts. The episode was named the Horror of Louvain. Estimates are that 248 civilians were killed and thousands made refugees. The *Mail's* coverage included a photograph described as a Belgian holding the burned remains of his daughter's foot.

The execution of Nurse Edith Cavell by the Germans, the Zeppelin raids against British towns and the bombardment from the sea of coastal towns and ports all added grist to the propaganda mill and enabled the British and French to continue to add to the list of German atrocities and the image of sheer brutality. This 'atrocity propaganda continued to fuel public hatred of Germany, producing a conviction that only total victory is acceptable' (Lee Thompson, 1999, p. 42). The newspapers, like the Northcliffe's *Times, Mail* and *Evening News* and Beaverbrook's *London Evening Standard* upheld this view and the stream of heroic allies and brutal Germans stories. The information system was refined during the war with the creation of the Ministry of Information (Beaverbrook was appointed minister), with Northcliffe becoming Director of Propaganda responsible for propaganda aimed at the USA. In the USA, the American Committee on Public Information was formed to direct the American war propaganda effort. The British, French, Americans and Germans also used film to report on the war and mobilize opinion – with newsreels becoming standard fare in the early cinemas.

Throughout the war, as Taylor describes, atrocity stories remained at the centre of war propaganda, so that:

> Images of the bloated 'Prussian Ogre', proudly sporting his pickelhaube, the 'Beastly Hun' with his sabre-belt barely surrounding his enormous girth, busily crucifying soldiers, violating women, mutilating babies, desecrating and looting churches, are deeply implanted [...] Evoked repeatedly by Allied propagandists during the Great War, the British stereotype of the Hun and the French image of the 'Boche' provided them with the essential focus they needed to launch their moral offensive against the enemy, at home and abroad.
>
> (Taylor, 2003, pp. 179–80)

Despite the heavy emphasis on German guilt and German atrocities, it did not become a campaign of incitement to violent hatred rather than an atrocity-laden war propaganda campaign. Newspapers like the *Daily Mail* were distributed free to troops at the front and the troops were exhorted to fight the hated Germany, but even in the face of the brutal stereotypes there wasn't serious incitement to hate each individual German – it was more the country and the image of its government and army as a whole. The propaganda did not prevent the famous Christmas fraternization of British and German troops in 1914 – there was no clear engendering of absolute and murderous hatred of the ordinary German.

Newspapers, film and even the music halls were part of the propaganda array during the war. Radio played no meaningful part as it still was not developed as a publicly available medium on any scale and broadcasting organizations did not exist. However, there were signs of changes in the technology of information and, therefore, of propaganda. The American Committee on Public Information deployed 75,000 'four-minute men' who were briefed to give short, inspiring speeches in cinemas and theatres across America – reaching an estimated 400 million people (Davison, 1971, p. 4; Taylor, 2003, p. 185). This was to show how speech would come to rival and even overtake the printed word as a source of news, information and propaganda. An inkling of how radio might develop to use the voice rather than the printed word was given when the US News Brunswick Marconi radio station in 1918 broadcast President Woodrow Wilson's 'Fourteen Points' speech to Europe. It was aimed at Germany and used the US radio call sign of NFF (Cull et al., 2003, p. 331). There is no record of how widely this was listened to in Germany or any effects, but it indicated the recognition of the potential of radio as a means of communication and of influencing both domestic and foreign audiences.

To return to the opening quotation of the chapter, 'The radio has restored the predominant influence of the spoken word, while it has immeasurably increased the size of its audience' (Beller, 1940, p. 3) – and radio and its role in the further development of propaganda and hate propagation is the subject of the next chapter.

2
The Advent of Radio: Creating a Mass Audience for Propaganda and Incitement 1911–1945

> Radio is the media genie, small enough to fit into a bottle, big enough to cover a continent [...] radio has developed into the most intimate of media, the principal one-to-one means of communication. At the same time, in remote agricultural communities the radio receiver may still be the focus of family life as it was during the Second World War in Europe, gathering people to listen to news that affects all their lives.
>
> (Kaye and Popperwell, 1992, p. 11)

Radio did not figure as a major form of communications or propaganda in the First World War. Radio telegraphy had speeded communications, enabled newspapers to get news more quickly and facilitated the faster spread of information. Telegraphic messages had to be typed out and distributed. There was no human voice – delivery was still at a remove and in print – so only available to those to whom it was distributed directly and to those who could read. Propaganda so distributed could be read out at public meetings or printed in newspapers or news sheets. But it wasn't direct communication.

Direct broadcasting to an audience was in its infancy. Radio sets were cumbersome, expensive and rare. Broadcasters were only really experimenting with the medium and had not developed plans for, or the means of, mass broadcasting. Yet, radio was there and being used – as the broadcasting of Wilson's Fourteen Points demonstrates. The Germans had started limited broadcasting – this was acknowledged when the victorious powers drew up the Treaty of Versailles, which included a three-month ban on a number of small German radio stations and a block on the construction by the German government of new stations (Robbins, 2001, p. 13; Taylor, 1983, p. 29). This was early recognition that radio would have a major role to play in mass communications and propaganda and inter-state relations.

The birth of radio

Experiments with radio had begun at the close of the 19th century, after James Clerk Maxwell had demonstrated theoretically that electromagnetic waves could propagate through the air and Heinrich Hertz had proved in laboratory experiments that radio waves could be transmitted. Work on the medium continued in Britain, the USA and Germany into the 20th century. The first audio radio broadcast was transmitted on Christmas Eve, 1906 at Brant Rock in Massachusetts – when Reginald Fessenden broadcast speech and and he played *O Holy Night* on the violin during the broadcast (Wood, 1994, p. 10). It was audible to ships off the North American coast. Two years later, Fessenden broadcast audio material from the top of the Eiffel Tower in Paris. Work continued on radio during the First World War, but Wilson's broadcast apart, it was not a key medium until after the war. In 1916, an American radio pioneer, Lee de Forest, had set up a small station in New York, but it had few listeners and they were generally professional wireless operators or gifted amateur enthusiasts; a small station was set up in Pittsburgh in 1918 by Frank Conrad, but it too had a tiny audience (Coe, 1996, p. 26).

The first overtly political use of radio to spread news and propaganda was in revolutionary Russia. Radio telegraphy and wireless radio signals were used to spread the news of the seizure of power by the Bolsheviks and the formation of the Soviet government by the All-Union Congress of Soviets in October 1917 (Jowett and O'Donnell, 2006, p. 124). Radio telegraphy was used to send the message of the establishment of the workers' government and the decrees calling for an end to the war and announcing the abolition of land ownership across the expanses of the tsarist Empire, and also to Germany – in the hopes of encouraging a workers' uprising there. The announcements were broadcast in the name of the Council of People's Commissars and couched in Leninist language – this wasn't just news, it was clearly propaganda aimed at informing and eliciting the support of workers across Russia for the new government formed in Petrograd and encouraging them to join the workers' movement (Hale, 1975, pp. 16–17).

As the Bolsheviks fought attempts to overthrow the new Soviet government, they brought the press and embryonic radio systems under the control of their party and its government. In the years preceding the 1917 revolutions, and especially in the run up to the October Revolution, Lenin had been clear about the need for the revolutionary movement to have its own newspapers and means of getting their message to workers. In 1901, he wrote that a party newspaper was essential, because 'without it we cannot conduct that systematic, all-round propaganda and agitation, consistent in principle, which is the chief and permanent task' (Lenin, 1971, p. 9). This key Leninist approach to the media was to become the dominant factor in the development of the Bolshevik, and then Soviet, use of the press and broadcast media.

The Soviet approach right from the revolution was to follow Lenin's linked two-stream model of propaganda and agitation – the former aimed at further educating party members politically, the latter intended to educate and win over those who had not adopted Marxism-Leninism as their political creed, in other words, the mass of the Soviet population.

The combined system, known as AgitProp, was to be at the centre of Soviet media and culture policy for 80 years – all output was there ultimately to serve Soviet construction and the development of Marxism-Leninism (Oates, 2007, p. 279). Close party and state control of all forms of mass media ensured a system in which, in Soviet terms, only 'organizations of the working class' had access to radio broadcasting, newspaper and periodical publication and printing; and tight control over the appointment of editors and senior journalists and the setting of news and current affairs agendas was in the hands of the propaganda and agitation department of the Communist Party of the Soviet Union (CPSU) Central Committee (Hough and Fainsod, 1979, pp. 284–5). The Soviet Union developed a network of radio stations across the Union of Soviet Socialist Republics (USSR) and, by 1922, had the world's most developed and largest radio network. In 1925 it set up its first shortwave station, which could reach throughout Soviet territory and had considerable reach abroad. In the same year, it started broadcasting in English as well as Russian – something that was to be a cause of huge of alarm to the British government during the General Strike of 1926, as Soviet broadcasts urged British workers to support the strike (Jowett and O'Donnell, 2006, pp. 124–5).

In stark contrast, radio broadcasting in the USA was entirely commercial to begin with. The first major station to be set up was Marconi's New Brunswick Marconi Station in New Jersey in 1914. It could transmit to ships and to receivers in Europe. There was a brief period of government control during the First Word War when, after the USA's entry into the war, the majority of private radio stations were ordered by President Wilson to be shut down or taken over by the government. Even before US entry into the war, Wilson tried to impose censorship on radio stations. Marconi resisted this, despite government accusations that it was not behaving in a neutral fashion (its parent company being British Marconi). Marconi's station in Massachusetts was closed for three months. It was allowed to reopen again in January 1915 only after agreeing, unwillingly, to abide by US Navy regulations about shore-to-ship broadcasting (White, 1980 p. 2). On 7 April 1917, the radio station run by Marconi at New Brunswick was taken over by the Navy to provide the government with wireless transatlantic communications – it was from there that Wilson's Fourteen Points were transmitted to Europe.

After the war, commercial dominance over radio was reasserted. There is no general agreement on which was the first station to broadcast publicly after the war. On 17 February 1919, a station calling itself 9XM at the

University of Wisconsin in Madison, Wisconsin, broadcast human speech to those who had radios to receive it. It wasn't until January 1921 that it began to regularly broadcast of voice and music (WHA, 2011). Perhaps the most significant development in US radio is attributed to KDKA in Pittsburgh, Pennsylvania. It received a radio licence in October 1920 and started transmitting as the first US-licensed commercial broadcasting station. KDKA was linked to the giant Westinghouse Electric Company and, while broadcasting from Pittsburgh, was able to generate a signal that could be heard across most of mainland USA (Coe, 1996, p. 26).

Many stations were owned by major electrical manufacturers, which started stations to encourage people to buy radios. Other stations were set up by companies or even newspapers to advertise their existing products or get a foot in the door of an expanding market. Soon after its launch, KDKA joined forces with the *Pittsburgh Post* to broadcast the results of the 1920 presidential elections as the results were announced. This was a major breakthrough in the use of radio to broadcast news, though the commercial stations that dominated in the USA concentrated more on music, speech and entertainment, only interspersed with occasional news broadcasts (Wood, 1994, p. 13). The stations owned by manufacturers and department stores were often established to sell radios. Major companies like Westinghouse, General Electric (GE) and American Telephone and Telegraph (AT&T) were heavily involved in developing radio stations as well as making radios. Network broadcasting began in the USA in 1926 and by 1928. National Broadcasting Company (NBC) (owned by General Electric), the dominant national radio network broadcaster with two national networks, estimated that there were 9.6 million radio sets in the USA (Cull et al., 2003, p. 331). The commercial dominance over radio, and the lack of a major state role or the formation of independent radio station or network under the aegis of the government or a non-profit public body, meant that a corporatist, capitalist approach dominated radio and effectively led to influence over the nature of news and political or social comment on the stations. The poorly funded and financially vulnerable National Public Radio was established in later decades to offer an alternative radio voice – it developed a network of local public radio stations with a national hub, providing news and current affairs output to supplement local output. This capitalist owned and influenced system and its effects have been described most effectively by Herman and Chomsky:

> It is our view that, among their other functions, the media serve and propagandize on behalf of the powerful societal interests that control and finance them. The representatives of these interests have important agendas and principles they want to advance and they are well positioned to shape and constrain media policy.
>
> (Herman and Chomsky, 2002, p. xi)

The implicit, and sometimes very explicit, pro-capitalist and conservative outlook of the dominant commercial broadcast media in the USA was demonstrated in the development of radio in the 1920s and 1930s. The range of opinions expressed on air represented, or at the very least supported, those of the companies or individuals owning the stations or the advertisers helping to fund them. The views aired and the thrust of the news agenda were conservative and veering more to the right of the political spectrum than the centre, and there was very little that one could describe as left or socialist. In this media environment, there was little that was critical of capitalism and much that was bordering on racism, prejudice and bigotry. The most celebrated example was Father Charles Coughlin. A Catholic priest and radio presenter, he came to have a major radio presence on national as well as local and religious networks. His highly opinionated and controversial content and style of broadcasting led to him being labelled 'The Father of Hate Radio' (Warren, 1996).

Father Coughlin and hate radio

Father Charles Coughlin was a Canadian-born Catholic priest who set up a religious broadcasting operation when he was the priest at the Shrine of the Little Flower in Royal Oak, Michigan. A charismatic speaker, he started broadcasting his sermons via local radio stations in 1926. A natural public speaker and instinctive propagandist with strong political, social and racial opinions, he began to move from purely religious themes to wider societal ones. Between 1926 and 1930, he evolved from being a sermonizer who included social topics in his weekly sermons to being an almost wholly political broadcaster (Jowett and O'Donnell, 2006, pp. 223–4). His first radio show was entitled *The Golden Hour of the Shrine of the Little Flower* and it gained a loyal and regular audience, which spread from the immediate environs of Royal Oak to state-wide and then national radio audiences as his output was re-broadcast. His critical biographer, Donald Warren, believes that he was 'one of America's most persuasive mass media orators' of the period between the two wars (Warren, 1996, p. 1). His audience – in a telling parallel to that of Hitler and the National Socialists in Germany – was small farmers, the lower middle-classes, small town traders and shopkeepers and pensioners. As he moved from religion to politics, just as the USA moved into the Depression, his broadcasts became replete with attacks on bankers, 'plutocrats', 'atheistic Marxists' and 'international financiers', the latter generally identified as Jewish and part of a conspiracy against the American way of life.

He had an engaging style of broadcasting that won over his audience as he started developing the themes of his talks. He used his position as a priest and the respect accorded religion in America to give respectability to his views and to appeal to ordinary Americans very directly through the power of his voice projected into their own homes – he set himself up as the defender of the 'little man' attacked on the one side by atheistic communists and on the other by rampant capitalism, and always with the little man's religion and way of life threatened by Jews. As one writer has described him:

> Most important was the warm, inviting sound of his voice, a sound that could make even the tritest statements sound richer and more meaning-ful than they actually were... the ability to make the sermons accessible, interesting, and provocative to his audience [...] Coughlin used a variety of rhetorical techniques: maudlin sentimentality, anger and invective, sober reasonableness, religious or patriotic fervor.
>
> (Brinkley, 1982, p. 97)

Starting with a small local audience, syndication by major broadcasters like NBC enabled him to reach millions. He sent out newsletters, appealed for donations and set up a whole organization funded by his supporters, enabling him to replace the small church of the Shrine of the Little Flower with a huge church with the offices for his growing enterprise attached. He built his own radio station and had a large staff answering listeners' letters fast and in detail – building on the very personal link created by his Sunday evening radio sermons. The timing of the broadcasts was key, in what was a very religious country – Sunday, the day of rest and worship. His sermons and political broadcasts had credibility with his audience by being seen essentially as extensions of religion and backed by the prestige of the Church. Right up until his open advocacy of Nazi-style anti-Semitism and his involvement with militia groups, he was supported by his local Catholic bishop and supported or at least tolerated by the Vatican, even though more liberal members of the Catholic hierarchy were critical of his anti-Semitism and extreme views.

As was to be the case in Germany with the Nazis, Coughlin's views on capitalism, communism and Jews were designed to appeal to the victims of the economic catastrophe of the Depression – people who needed someone to blame for the loss of the American Dream (Warren, 1996, p. 2). He castigated those with wealth and power and the 'red serpent' of socialism and communism (Barnouw, 1968, p. 45). Warren sums it up well:

> Millions of bewildered and angry men and women turned to this radio priest for solace and solutions. In his weekly newspaper, *Social Justice*, and in his radio broadcasts, the priest became the voice of the people against a political elite and against alien minorities whom they thought were intent on betraying the nation.
>
> (Warren, 1996, p. 2)

Coughlin started as a supporter of Franklin D. Roosevelt's populist approach to combating the effects of the Depression but rapidly fell out with him and started attacking Roosevelt and the New Deal for 'selling out to the bankers' (Warren, 1996, pp. 64–5).

In 1934, as he took up an increasingly critical stance towards the government, Coughlin and his supporters set up the National Union for Social Justice. He used his radio broadcasts to attract members and organized several nationwide speaking tours to promote the union and its objectives. By this time, he was a national figure. His sermons had been broadcast nationally since 1930, when Columbia Broadcasting System (CBS) started carrying them. They continued to be broadcast on national networks even as they became more extreme, more anti-Semitic and more pro-fascist. Coughlin developed the argument that communism and socialism were breaking down the basis of American family life and belief in God and that communism was a product of the Jews, claiming that 90 per cent of the Soviet government was Jewish (Warren, 1996, pp. 31–3).

In line with this outlook, he became a supporter of Italian fascism under Mussolini and a sympathizer with Hitler's National Socialism. His anti-Semitism was open and loudly proclaimed though he never, despite the accusations levelled at him at the time and more recently by right-wing commentator Glenn Beck (2009), openly advocated the mass killing of Jews. Beck claimed this in a broadcast on *Fox News* when he was accused of being a modern-day version of Coughlin. During the Spanish Civil War, Coughlin strongly supported Franco and advocated American support for the Nationalist cause in Spain, arguing that they were part of a crusade against communism. In 1936, Coughlin supported the presidential ambitions of the corrupt, violent and demagogic Governor of Louisiana, Huey Long. The two shared much in the way of ideology and had similar styles of demagogic populism. Long's assassination in 1935 led Coughlin to give his support to a former Republican, William Lemke. Lemke's overwhelming defeat dented Coughlin's image and self-esteem, but he soon bounced back and became 'more openly fascist in his methods and his pronouncements' (Institute for Propaganda Analysis, 1939, p. 11). According to a study by the American Institute for Propaganda Analysis (IPA), he began to speak in favour of the establishment of a corporatist-style state on the lines of fascist Italy with a single state religion and he started to devote 'hours of radio time to the cultivation of anti-Jewish prejudices' (IPA, 1939, pp. 11–13).

One of the techniques that the IPA identifies Coughlin as employing to great effect was 'card-stacking' – 'the selection and use of facts or falsehoods' to give undue prominence to the best or worst possible case for an idea, programme or person (IPA, 1939, p. 24). So, for example, in a broadcast of 4 December 1938, he stacked the cards against Jews, not only blaming them for the Depression and their role in international capitalism and banking but also saying that 'Jewish international bankers [were involved] in helping to plot [the Russian] revolution with its subsequent murder and practical atheism'; in an article in his publication *Social Justice* on 5 December 1938,

Coughlin used large parts of a speech recently given by German Propaganda Minister Josef Goebbels at a rally at the Nuremberg Stadium, presenting this as his own views (cited by IPA, 1939, pp. 84–5). In speeches and radio addresses in 1938, he began to quote extensively from the anti-Semitic fabrication *The Protocols of the Elders of Zion* to ratchet up the list of crimes of which he could accuse Jews (Warren, 1996, p. 150). He openly referred to Hitler's National Socialism as 'a defense mechanism against Communism' (cited by Warren, 1996, p. 156) and, on 18 December 1938, he accused Jews of being responsible for the death of Christ and said that Jews believed in 'the subjugation of all nations to the naturalistic philosophy of race supremacy' (Warren, 1996, p. 164).

By 1938, Coughlin's policies had begun to go beyond just words and he called, both through the radio and the pages of *Social Justice*, for the formation of anti-communist militias. He advocated the formation of a Christian Front – a title that, he said in an edition of *Social Justice* in October 1938, he had borrowed from Franco's fascists in Spain. The priest now told his audience that 'Our people have passed beyond the point of being satisfied with a mere study club. I am convinced we are ripe for action clubs' (Warren, 1996, p. 189). In a later edition of *Social Justice* (31 July 1939), he said that the front was 'organized along militant lines, as a defense mechanism against Red activities and as a protector of Christianity and Americanism'. When, in January 1940, 18 members of the Christian Front were arrested in Brooklyn and charged with stockpiling arms and making bombs, Coughlin continued to express support but distanced himself and denied that he was a leader of the organization (Warren, 1996, p. 192). By this time, according to Warren, there was growing criticism of Coughlin from the Catholic hierarchy in the USA (Warren, 1996, p. 215) and he was eventually denounced by Archbishop Mooney of Detroit as expressing views in opposition to those of Pope Pius XI.

Following the outbreak of the war in Europe, the American National Association of Broadcasters adopted a code placing greater restrictions than had previously existed on broadcasters who aired very strong views on controversial public issues. For the first time, the Association told its members (including the major national networks) that on controversial issues, notably the war and US policy towards it, manuscripts of talks had to be submitted in advance of broadcasts. Stations faced the possible loss of broadcasting rights if they failed to comply. The adoption of the code effectively pushed Coughlin off air. In the 23 September 1939 issue of *Social Justice*, Coughlin said he had been forced off air by those who controlled radio stations (Marcus, 1972, pp. 173–7).

In 1941, when the US Lend-Lease Bill to assist the British war effort was signed into law, Coughlin spoke against it but no longer had a radio presence and so was limited to articles in *Social Justice* and public speeches or sermons. His outlook on the war and US policy was openly praised at editorial meetings of the German Propaganda Ministry at the time, which lamented that he was no longer broadcasting as 'it is at times like this the nation needs a speaker like Father Coughlin' (cited by Linkugel and Carpenter, 1998, p. 123). There is no conclusive evidence of direct contacts or cooperation between Coughlin and the Nazi regime, but Warren cites Dr Otto Ernst Braun, who worked in the German Foreign Ministry under Ribbentrop, as testifying that the German Foreign Ministry covertly sent funds to Coughlin and that he was held in high regard in the ministry because of the pro-fascist and other content of his radio broadcasts and newspaper articles (Warren, 1996, pp. 234–5).

The USA's entry into the war after Pearl Harbour and Hitler's declaration of war on the USA hardened American public attitudes towards fascism and towards the views of public figures like Coughlin. His support base had dwindled by this time and he effectively disappeared as a public figure after May 1942, when Archbishop Mooney of Detroit, backed by the Catholic Church, banned him from any further role in *Social Justice*.

While it is not possible to identify the extent of Coughlin's influence on American public opinion, let alone whether his broadcasts increased anti-Semitism or incited hatred and violence towards American Jews, the content of broadcasts, sermons, speeches and newspaper articles was clearly anti-Semitic and had a clear intent to persuade Americans to adopt a strong anti-Semitic and anti-communist attitude. His representation of the Jews and communists or socialists was always negative and designed to encourage dislike or even hatred, while his framing of references to them was always in the context of threat or danger. Whether his support for and involvement in the Christian Front would, had the war not effectively cut away public support for him and his policies, led to direct action based on Coughlin's stated views can only be speculated upon, but it is hard to disagree with Warren's labelling of him as 'the father of Hate Radio' (Warren, 1996).

Wartime propaganda – the role of radio

Europe had an early taste of radio's potential in wartime during the Spanish Civil War. When the war started, on 17 July 1936, there was no national system of broadcasting – unlike in Britain, Germany or Canada. The country had a regionalized system with eight main transmitters broadcasting mainly to urban areas and their immediate locales and then 60 low-powered local transmitters. But the republican government had some experience of utilizing these stations during times of crisis – government information had been broadcast by the stations during an attempted military rising in 1932 and during the miners' revolt in the Asturias in 1934 (Davies, 1999, p. 473). When the Nationalist rising started, the potential of radio was recognized by both sides. The Republican government moved to control the regional stations, suspended the 60 smaller stations and banned amateur radio.

On the first day of the rising, Nationalist forces tried to occupy Seville but early on captured the radio station and used it to broadcast denials that the rising had been crushed and to encourage the people of Andalusia to join Franco's forces. The leader of the Nationalist forces there, General Queipo de Llano, made the first of a long series of harangues of the audience:

> In a voice seasoned by many years' consumption of Manzanilla, he declared that Spain was saved and that the rabble who resisted the rising would be shot like dogs [...] Queipo's rousing speech did much to rally Andalusia to the rising. The possibility of denying on the radio that the rising had been crushed played an essential part in the rebels' success.
>
> (Thomas, 2003, pp. 211–12)

The word 'rabble' for the Republican forces was to be the keyword in Llano's broadcasts during the war. As the war progressed and Germany and Italy gave military, financial and other help to Franco's forces, Hitler's government gave the Nationalists a huge Lorenz transmitter, with three times the broadcasting power of any existing transmitter in Spain. This enabled Nationalist broadcasters based in Salamanca and Burgos to reach both Nationalist and Republican Spain. Llano remained one of the key broadcasters, with his mix of black humour, harangues and threats to the 'rabble'. In one famous broadcast he boasted, 'tonight I shall take a sherry and tomorrow I shall take Malaga' (Thomas, 2003, p. 504). He broadcast most nights at 10 pm until mid-1938, when he stopped abruptly, having been left out of the new Nationalist cabinet. The content of his broadcasts was colourful and he was listened to even in Republican areas – where leaders of the government accused him of being drunk. In Nationalist areas he was listened to by people not only at home but also in cafes and restaurants, where his broadcasts would be played to the customers. This was an indication of the way in which radio could and would be used for decades to come – it could be listened to alone or in groups, while concentrating solely on the output or doing other things. Another aspect of Nationalist broadcasts was the airing of implicit threats that resistance would be crushed and those deemed socialists, communists or anarchists would be liquidated. Radio broadcasts ahead of offensives and sieges were aimed at creating panic and encouraging immediate surrender – the use of Moroccan troops by the Nationalists was emphasized in their own broadcasts and they often implied that the troops were brutal and that the Nationalists could not be held responsible for their actions. These broadcasts were designed to create fear among the civilian population in Republican areas.

On the Republican side, the government sought to control radio stations and brought together those stations it held to form the Radio Union network. This was used, at first, to deny rebel claims of success and to try to reduce fear of a rebel victory. As the war progressed and factions, parties and the trades unions on the Republican side jockeyed for power nationally and regionally, many stations became dominated by, or at times shared by, competing unions and parties, somewhat diluting the power and impact of the Republican message (Davies, 1999, p. 474). Their transmitters were less powerful than Llano's in Seville or the German one at Burgos and they lacked a charismatic broadcaster like Llano – although the Communist Party activist Dolores Ibarruri (La Pasionaria) was renowned for her fiery rhetoric and regularly went on air to exhort the workers to resist the rebels and to demonize the Nationalist leaders and their supporters (Davies, 1999, p. 487). The Nationalists had another big advantage – prior to the rising they had encouraged the development of short-range radio within loyal military units and the development of amateur radio by supporters. Following the rising, this was invaluable in developing pro-Nationalist local broadcasting to supplement stations seized in Seville, Burgos, Navarra and Salamanca – eventually creating a national network that became the Franco government's mouthpiece, Radio Nacional de Espana.

As with the woodcuts, pamphlets and sermons of the Thirty Years' War and the newspapers of the First World War, radio was also used during the Spanish Civil War to accuse opponents of atrocities. The rebels were particularly skilled at using alleged or invented atrocities to demonize the Republicans, endlessly reporting the rape of nuns, killing and torture of priests. The nationalist side assiduously fed these stories to sympathetic journalists and newspapers in Europe and America. The *Daily Mail* in Britain was a strong supporter of the Nationalists and printed the stories regularly. The Nationalists combined propaganda with control of the press and foreign journalists based in areas controlled by the rebels were banned, on pain of arrest or expulsion, to avoid using the term 'rebels' for the Nationalists or 'loyalists' for the Republicans (Riegel, 1937, p. 133).

If the Spanish Civil War saw the first major test for the uses of radio during wartime, the early 1930s had already seen the growth (notably in Italy, Germany and the USSR) of radio as a tool of ideological education and indoctrination. The Soviet Union had developed the most powerful shortwave transmitters to broadcast to its own population and to spread the Marxist-Leninist message through an expanding external broadcasting system. Soviet domestic broadcasting was used to develop 'political consciousness that supports the ideology of the party' through agitation, political education and propaganda (White, 1980, p. 323). Radio, domestic and external, was also used to critique the capitalist system, call for the liberation of colonized peoples and warn of the dangers of fascism in Europe. A constant refrain of Soviet radio between the wars and later, during the Cold War, was the desire for peace (Griffith, 1979, p. 245).

Germany's close ally in Spain and, in the Second World War, fascist Italy, were also quick to recognize the power and uses of radio at home and abroad. Mussolini and his movement were adept in using roman history, pageantry, music, parades, rallies, art and broadcasting to 'create a culture of Fascism' in Italy (Cull et al., 2003, p. 197) and to develop a personality cult around Il Duce. Domestically, the media was used to condemn and overwhelm opponents in the centre and on the socialist and communist left. Externally, radio was to play a strong role in furthering Italy's colonial policy in North Africa and the Horn of Africa. The first external Italian broadcasts were transmitted in 1930. The Italian fascist state developed a large external broadcasting capability aimed at supporting the war in Abyssinia and opposing the British presence in East Africa, the Horn of Africa and the Middle East.

The British government was so concerned that in 1937 it funded the British Broadcasting Corporation (BBC) Empire Service (established in 1932 after requests from colonial administrators for a radio service that would be the British voice around the world, partly to counteract the propaganda of Soviet and Italian stations) to start broadcasting in Arabic (Wood, 1994, p. 39). The first BBC Arabic broadcast was on 3 January 1938. While the Italian stations broadcast heavily slanted news and obvious propaganda, the BBC Empire Service and Arabic Service took the approach of broadcasting straight balanced news and comment, 'so that it was able to set a standard of service and gain a reputation for being a reliable source of information, objectively reported and independent of government control' (ibid.); the Foreign Office kept a close eye on the content of broadcasts, while not actually directing or censoring material.

In the late 1930s, there was a growing expectation of war in Europe as Germany sought to regain German territory and unite German speakers in an expanded state. Fear of war was prevalent both in Europe and the USA and was only slightly lessened by the Munich agreement of 29 September 1938, ceding the Sudetenland to Germany. It was soon after Munich that an incident happened in the USA that, while not of huge political or social import in itself, did demonstrate the power of radio to cause fear and elicit behaviour in response. On 30 October 1938, the CBS national radio network broadcast a dramatization of H.G. Wells' book *War of the Worlds*. It was the brainchild of the actor and director Orson Welles. Despite being introduced as a drama, the way that Welles had set the action in the USA and started off with a series of acted-out radio news broadcasts convinced many Americans listening at home that this was a real story and that the news bulletins were real. The news reports in the drama said that aliens had landed at Grover's Mill, Trenton, New Jersey, and had killed scores of people at the site of the landing. The dramatization is effective with a series of bulletins of news about Mars, followed by live reporting of the scene of the alien landing and the start of the invasion of Earth.

This is how the *New York Times* reported what happened in its edition the following day:

A wave of mass hysteria seized thousands of radio listeners throughout the nation between 8:15 and 9:30 last night when a broadcast of the dramatization of H.G. Wells's fantasy, *War of the Worlds* led thousands to believe that an interplanetary conflict had started with invading Martians spreading wide death and destruction in New Jersey and New York.

There was panic, with people rushing into the street, others packing belongings into cars and fleeing New Jersey and areas of New York state. Hundreds of listeners phoned their local police stations to seek reassurance. There are no reliable reports of just how many people reacted in some way to the broadcast and most accounts remain anecdotal and have an exaggerated feel, yet there was clearly a strong reaction and there were behavioural responses to the broadcast. As reports of the panic emerged, CBS broadcast reminders to the audience that this had been a drama and was not real. In the following month, over 12,500 articles appeared in American newspapers about the responses to the programme and even Hitler is reputed to have commented on the event as 'evidence of the decadence and corrupt condition of democracy' (Hand, 2006, p. 7), while no doubt noting and relishing this demonstration of the power of radio.

Listening to the original broadcast and surveying the reports of the public reaction one cannot but agree with Cantril when he concludes, 'The broadcast was masterful in its use of devices designed to construct an impression of authenticity. It capitalized on radio's public credibility with the scripted interruption of an on-going music program to bring "news"[...] A sense of real-time urgency was created as developments were subsequently "reported" from specific locations' (ibid.). As Cantril wrote less than two years after the events and soon after the start of the war in Europe, with its accompanying battles of the airwaves, 'by its very nature radio is the medium par excellence for informing all segments of a population of current happenings, for arousing in them a common sense of fear or joy and for enticing them to similar reactions directed toward a single objective' (Cantril, 1940, p. viii).

Radio during the Second World War

The rise of the Nazis in Germany, the fascists in Italy and the development of the Soviet system had all involved propaganda to an unprecedented degree. All three systems openly proclaimed its importance. In international politics, propaganda was becoming an acknowledged part of inter-state relations. The ability to broadcast across borders to promote ideologies, incite rebellion, national liberation or manipulate opinion had been vastly increased by radio. The German-Polish non-aggression pact of January 1934 and the German-Soviet one (often called the Molotov-Ribbentrop pact) of August 1939, specifically forbade the broadcasting or spreading by other forms of propaganda by one pact member against another. The day the German-Soviet Pact was signed, German anti-Bolshevik and anti-Soviet propaganda stopped – it was like turning off a tap. The tap was to be turned on again on 22 June 1941, when Germany invaded the Soviet Union.

Propaganda and the broadcasting of it had become a greater feature of domestic and international politics between the wars because of 'the general increase in the level of popular interest and involvement in political and foreign affairs as a direct consequence of World War I [...] [and] technological developments in the field of communications which provided the basis for a rapid growth in propaganda' – and these developments were tied to the rise of highly ideological movements (Taylor, 1983, pp. 19–20).

By 1938, a year before the outbreak of war, there were broadcasting networks operating in 30 European countries, as well as developed countries outside Europe, such as the USA, Canada, Australia and Japan. Of the European stations, 13 were state broadcasters, 9 were government monopolies operated by autonomous public bodies (e.g., the BBC in Britain), 4 were directly government-owned companies run by the governments concerned and 3 were privately owned. Italy, Germany and the Soviet Union were open about propaganda being part of their domestic political systems and their diplomacy. They made no secret of utilizing propaganda and Germany, for example, named the government department controlling radio the Ministry of Public Enlightenment and Propaganda. In Britain and the USA, they had departments or ministries of information (Short, 1983, pp. 1–2). As wartime US radio writer Erik Barnouw put it, 'much of what we radio writers did during those years, whether called fiction or non-fiction, I now feel can be described as *propaganda*, but we zealously avoided that word. Propaganda was what others did, especially the Germans' (cited by Short, 1983, pp. 1–2).

The main combatants in the war all conducted propaganda battles on a number of fronts. The key one for this study is the domestic front – so the main focus of this section is on how governments used broadcasting as a tool to influence their own populations during the war; how radio was used to promote the war effort and maintain hostility or even hatred of the enemy. The other fronts were external – maintaining the support of allies, winning over neutrals and seeking to undermine the morale and support for their governments of enemy populations. The latter is not ignored but emphasis is strongly on domestic broadcasting.

Britain was less geared up for a propaganda war than its opponents. Despite having set up the Empire Service in 1932 and having 17 years of domestic broadcasting experience, at the start of the war the British broadcasting system wasn't prepared for war and appeared totally unprepared to compete with the well-drilled propaganda machine in Germany or even the Italian one. The domestic BBC radio network was publicly funded but independent of government and while government directly funded the Empire Service it had considerable independence under the auspices of the BBC. This had its advantages and disadvantages for British propaganda during the early stages of the war. The government did not directly control broadcasting and machinery was not in place for control, prior censorship or influencing of output. But, and this proved to be a huge boost for the BBC domestically and abroad, its relative independence and growing reputation for impartiality gave it a level of trust that was never to be achieved by its wartime or later Cold War competitors.

Within Britain the BBC was seen as fair-minded, balanced but very much part of the liberal democratic establishment. And, as Nicholas points out, 'In a dangerous world listeners turned to the BBC, its most famous public corporation and newest national institution, as a source of stability and continuity' (Nicholas, 1999, p. 68).

Abroad the BBC's reputation was strong, despite the relatively short period it had been operating. Between the launch in 1937 and the start of the war, the BBC Arabic service had developed the image of being an impartial and balanced broadcaster 'so that it was able to set a standard of service and gain a reputation for being a reliable source of information, objectively reported and independent of government control or censorship' (Wood, 1994, p. 39). The BBC had started broadcasting in German and Italian in 1938, added Portuguese and Spanish before the start of the war and then French. By the start of the war, it had two 50,000-watt sort-wave transmitters, giving it the most powerful broadcasting capability in the world (Davison, 1971, p. 6).

The government machinery to cope with the demands of broadcasting, propaganda and censorship was disorganized, even though planning for a possible war had started as early as 1935 and been accelerated after the 1938 Munich agreement. The Ministry of Information was starting to get to grips with what was likely to be demanded of it but 'amidst chaos and confusion' and the early weeks of the war and the attempts to censor press reports of the British Expeditionary Force going to France were farcical (Taylor, 1981, p. 57). Few seemed to be confident, as Taylor points out, that the ministry could 'combat effectively the already tried and tested machinery of Dr Goebbels' (Taylor, 2003, p. 212).

The ministry and the government adopted the concept that it was most effective to 'tell the truth, nothing but the truth and, as near as possible, the whole truth' (Ministry of Information statement cited by Taylor, 1981, p. 58). The ministry saw its role as mediating information and of convincing the educated minority, as it put it in a 1939 memorandum, through 'subtle and indirect' propaganda and for the less educated masses having simple and direct messages focused on a definite object and appealing to instinct rather than reason (Ministry of Information memorandum on propaganda of 21 June 1939, reproduced in full in Taylor, 1981). The ministry took the basic approach that the role of domestic British propaganda was that it should be guided by the question 'will this measure increase people's desire to serve and keep on serving' (ibid.). The role of propaganda, through careful but subtle control of the news that was printed or broadcast, was to serve the war effort and not to incite hatred or promote killing beyond that necessary to achieve Britain's war aims of defeating Germany, Italy and Japan. The mainstream media reported Churchill's exhortations to defeat the Nazis but the message was one of victory in war over what was presented as an aggressor rather than annihilation, ethnic cleansing or killing the enemy because they were German, Italian or Japanese.

The BBC was the sole open broadcaster in Britain during the war. Covert 'black propaganda' stations were set up by the government (with assistance from the BBC and through the Political Warfare Executive) to broadcast disinformation and propaganda to Germany and occupied Europe, but the mainstream BBC domestic and external output remained committed to broadcasting the truth – even if censorship or careful filtering of news by the Ministry of Information meant it was not always the whole truth or the most up-to-date news. But the willingness to report British defeats and criticism of aspects of the war effort gave the BBC a lasting air of balance and honesty. News was censored at source (notably the agency material supplied to the BBC) but editorial opinions weren't, though most editors and broadcasters exercised a degree of self-censorship.

The combination of a fair degree of consensus and an unobtrusive but routine form of censorship and news flow control was very successful and many British people were not always aware of the censorship. 'This system operated so effectively on a day-to-day basis that many observers were unaware that a compulsory pre-censorship system was in fact operating and it helps to explain why Britain's wartime propaganda gained its reputation for telling the truth when, in reality, the truth was rarely being told whole' (Taylor, 2003, p. 213). Even if the truth told was incomplete or slow, the basis of truth and the reporting of defeats in comparison, for example, with Germany's failure to report the surrender at Stalingrad, was to serve the BBC well during the after the war and help establish its global reputation as a broadcaster (Tusa, 2009). The exhortatory aspect of British propaganda came via the speeches of Churchill and other leaders and the public information and poster campaigns. But it cannot be denied that Churchill used the BBC assiduously, despite his doubts about its reliability, to get his messages across to the nation and that the underlying message of the output of the corporation, 'as it believed its listeners expected this, was the absolute necessity of beating Hitler' (Nicholas, 1999, p. 72). The BBC as far as possible tried to tell the truth and was able, despite considerable self-censorship and interference but no direct control by the government, to say that it had been as independent as circumstances of war allowed (Seaton, 2003, pp. 139 and 145). Briggs in his history of the BBC refers to the impediments the BBC had to overcome in reporting news quickly when the Ministry of Information wanted to stop or at least delay the reporting of the news (Briggs, 1970, pp. 38–43).

The BBC's foreign broadcasts maintained their reputation for integrity but there is no denying the link between BBC broadcasts to Europe and aspects of resistance to German occupation and that the BBC 'did more than any comparable agency both to pull together different elements of resistance in each separate European country – by giving news... by providing ideas and inspiration and at certain stages by passing on operational orders – and to spread relevant information between countries' (Briggs, 1970, p. 11).

The government tried to interfere in all sorts of ways and often slowed the reporting of news or the reporting of a full version of events. It also interfered in the broadcasting of comment and opinion. One of the most popular opinion programmes in 1940 and early 1941 was the *Postscripts,* which followed the news on a Sunday evening. It was presented by the left-wing writer J.B. Priestley and he often used the talks to look ahead to a post-war world. He was accused by Churchill of left-wing bias and of being damagingly critical of the government (see Nicholas, 1995, for a full account of the dispute) and he was taken off air. Priestley claimed that he had been sacked from the programme because of his views, on the orders of the Ministry of Information (Seaton, 2003, pp. 137–8). There is no doubt, as Briggs says, that there was 'a real conflict of views in 1941 between Priestley and the government about domestic social policy and international war aims' and that this led to him being taken off air (Briggs, 1970, p. 294). This demonstrated the limits to the BBC's independence and also shows how the BBC would bow to pressure or self-censor to keep broadly in line with the wishes of the government, while trying to appear independent.

The radio and media in the USA was still privately owned and run at the start of the war. True, during the post-Depression era and the implementation of Roosevelt's New Deal, radio had been increasingly used to disseminate information in support of government policy and Roosevelt had started his regular 'fireside chat' broadcasts in cooperation with commercial broadcasters. But US broadcasting remained in private hands. Prior to the USA's entry into the war, the State Department and the Federal Communications Commission (FCC) secured the agreement of a number of small shortwave broadcasting companies to expand their overseas broadcasting to ensure that the USA's views began to be projected abroad (Washburn, 1992, p. 21). It was only in February 1942, two months after Pearl Harbour, that the government-run Voice of America (VoA) station started broadcasting (Robbins, 2001, p. 21). VoA, as it became known, was an external broadcaster, like the BBC Empire Service, and there was still no major domestic public service broadcaster. Americans remained dependent for news of the progress of the war on major commercial networks, though the military news and related issues were reported via the Office of War Information (OWI), established by the government. OWI's role was to 'achieve enthusiasm for America's war effort' (Short, 1983, p. 4). The corporations, like CBS, used the news routed through OWI and reports and commentary by leading commentators such as H.V. Kaltenborn, William Shirer from Berlin (prior to the German declaration of war on the USA), and (from London and then Western Europe after D-Day) by Ed Murrow.

Murrow's broadcasts from London during the German air raids were particularly powerful and had great influence over American sympathy and support for the British prior to the USA's entry into the war. Murrow showed clearly his sympathy and admiration for British resistance during the Blitz – he was particularly effective as he was experiencing the same peril as those he was reporting about (Horten, 2003, pp. 36–7). His broadcasts reported what was happening from the viewpoint of someone sharing the danger of those about whom he was reporting and evinced a clear empathy and admiration for British resistance in the face of German bombing raids. He was never overtly propagandistic but, as Seib records, 'if there was a clear message in Murrow's broadcasts it was to demonstrate to Americans "the evil of Hitler's Germany"' (Seib, 2006, p. 56).

While the networks did not become pure propaganda stations, there was considerable propagandizing to support the war effort and the role of big business in arming and supplying the troops. As Ehrich has identified, 'Wartime radio programs have been criticized as blatant propaganda not only for the U.S. military effort but also for big business' (Ehrlich, 2011, p. 25). He cites radio journalist and documentary-maker Norman Corwin as saying that during the war journalists had no qualms about 'indoctrination' of listeners as too much was at stake (ibid.). Broadcasting corporations, journalists, politicians and their audiences saw the war as one in defence of democracy and human values – a level of propaganda, especially anti-Japanese, was deemed acceptable. Following Pearl Harbour, the Japanese were vilified and as reports of their brutality multiplied, a strong measure of racism and hatred emerged in some broadcasts. The tenor of much of the broadcasting by the leading correspondents can be captured in Ed Murrow's famous broadcast from the Buchenwald concentration camp as US forces liberated it from the Germans:

Permit me to tell you what you would have seen, and heard [...] It will not be pleasant listening [...] for I propose to tell you of Buchenwald. It is on a small hill about four miles outside Weimar, and it was one of the largest concentration camps in Germany [...] the prisoners crowded up behind the wire. We entered [...] There surged around me an evil-smelling horde. Men and boys reached out to touch me; they were in rags and the remnants of uniform. Death had already marked many of them, but they were smiling with their eyes [...] We proceeded to a small courtyard. The wall was about eight feet high [...] There were two rows of bodies stacked up like cordwood. They were thin and very white. Some of the bodies were terribly bruised [...] Some had been shot through the head [...] all except two were naked [...] more than five hundred men and boys lay there in two neat piles [...] the country round about was pleasing to the eye, and the Germans were well fed and well dressed.

(Murrow, 1968, pp. 90–4)

The import of the words is clear but there is no outright condemnation of the Germans. This form of factual but empathetic reporting, which got across what the journalists saw as the crimes and inhumanity of the Germans and Japanese was common in US and British reporting of the war. There was a message but it was not an overt one and it was delivered through first-hand reporting and interpretation of what was being reported. The words used, in reporting events factually but with human empathy for suffering, spoke for themselves, without the need for overt propagandizing.

On the other side of the war, Japan had a well-developed and tightly controlled system of broadcasting – the national broadcasting network, NHK, had been operating across the country since 1928, three years after the launching of Japan's first domestic radio broadcasts. It gained early experience of wartime and propaganda broadcasting following its invasion of Manchuria in 1931 and the resulting war in China. From the start, the media and broadcasting were under close official control. There was a tradition of central direction of many aspects of life in Japan. As Daniels puts it, 'Confucianism was the ideology of government, and moralistic exhortation was an important aspect of administration' and this was rapidly applied to the infant broadcasting sector with regulations set out by the Ministry of Communications ahead of the first public broadcasts by radio stations (Daniels, 1982, p. 115).

Initially, the development of radio was in private hands but the government rapidly grasped its social and political significance and NHK was formed as a private but government sponsored broadcasting monopoly effectively under government control. In 1934, by which time NHK was a national broadcaster with seven stations, a Central Broadcasting Council was established run by representatives of the Ministries of Communications, Education and Home Affairs; in 1934, as the war in China continued, the Army, Navy and Ministry of Foreign Affairs were also represented and military influence became more and more important. The war led to an increase in broadcast hours and in the proportion of news to entertainment. Propagandistic commentaries on the war and strongly patriotic material became routine fare on radio with a very clear attempt to create a very supportive link between the home audience and soldiers fighting on the Chinese mainland. This pattern was to become ingrained and there was increasing military control and military-governed output on the radio leading up to and during the Second World War.

The themes of broadcast content were primarily patriotic, pro-war and absolutely subservient to the imperial system. During the war they gained, especially in the external services, a strong anti-Semitic edge under the influence of Japan's German allies; seizing on the alleged role of Jewish families and businesses in controlling commerce in Shanghai and other areas of East Asia, Jews became the arch-capitalists who were working against Japan's economic interests (Robbins, 2001, pp. 226 and 228). The careful censorship and direction of domestic broadcasts to ensure a patriotic, pro-war, pro-imperial discourse was supplemented by the banning of the ownership shortwave radios in Japan to prevent citizens hearing foreign broadcasts. Japanese shortwave broadcasting was aimed at Asia, Australia, New Zealand, the Pacific islands and at British, US and Australian forces – the most famous broadcasts at enemy troops were by Iva Toguri, an American citizen of Japanese descent stranded in Japan by the war. She became known as Tokyo Rose and broadcast to foreign forces, trying to play on their homesickness (see Keene, 2009).

During the war, there were regular broadcasts by the prime minister and foreign minister of Japan, explaining government policy. A Cabinet Information Bureau was set up in 1940, which took control of most aspects of radio. Its purpose, according to the government, was to aid 'the establishment of a military state through the unity and solidarity of the public,' and it aimed at 'raising morale by radio, particularly among farmers and young people' (Daniels, 1982, p. 117). Under its auspices, a Government Hour was broadcast every night nationally during which ministers, civil servants or military officers explained the 'meaning' of issues of the day and set out government policy. With the attack on Pearl Harbour and the declaration of war on the USA and Britain, the full Imperial Proclamation was read out on air and on the first day of hostilities 15 extra news bulletins were broadcast to report Japanese successes. A day later, Miyamato Yoshino of the Cabinet Information Bureau broadcast this clear exposition of policy and use of radio:

> Now is the time for all people to rise for the nation. The government and the people must be united. One hundred million Japanese must join hands and help each other go forward. The government will inform the people over the radio of where our nation will go and how they should behave. All the people of Japan please gather round the radio. We expect you to wholeheartedly trust the government's announcements over the radio because the government will take responsibility and will give you the complete truth. Please obey all instructions which the government issues over the radio.
>
> (cited by Daniels, 1982, p. 118)

To supplement news, commentary and government instructions, city, town and hamlet 'neighbourhood associations' were established to encourage people to listen to the radio and to carry out additional propaganda work. The meetings of the associations were frequently times to coincide with planned special broadcasts on important duties to be carried out or events/policies to be explained. They served to reinforce the propaganda by making it a communal or mass activity and not just an individual one, reinforcing the objective of all mass propaganda – of making the individual part of a greater whole and binding him or her to the mass. As Daniels had identified, the discourse of Japanese radio broadcasts was based on three key principles:

> Japan had been compelled to declare war on the Anglo-American powers to survive and maintain her prestige; the main cause of the war was the enemies' ambition to conquer the world; Japan's purpose was to establish a new world order to assist all nations to take their rightful place in a spirit of universal brotherhood.
>
> (Daniels, 1982, p. 118)

During the course of the war, army and navy personnel appeared more and more on the radio and became key voices in reporting successes. The radio was used to broadcast air raid warnings but less so to report damage or casualties after raids. As Japan's fortunes in the war suffered and defeat became a possibility, censorship of news increased as did delays in reporting setbacks; there was even a suspension of the broadcasting of casualty figures from the regular earthquakes that afflicted Japan. As Japanese territory was invaded by American forces, special broadcasts were made to the garrisons of those territories (notably Iwo Jima and Okinawa) with inspirational messages from government leaders and emotional appeals for resistance from the families of soldiers, sailors and airmen. Following the dropping of nuclear bombs on Hiroshima and Nagasaki, the official surrender proclamation was read on air by the emperor – to forestall military or nationalist efforts to thwart the decision to end the fight.

The content of Japanese broadcasts during the war was patriotic, stressing the need for sacrifice and national unity and highly critical of the enemy. But, apart from the forays into anti-Semitism, it was not laden with messages of hate, rather it appealed constantly to duty, obedience and a sense of the rightness of the Japanese cause. The news was often inaccurate, slanted to avoid admitting defeats and overblown in its reports of victories and their meaning, while commentary was chauvinistic and highly nationalistic.

Soviet radio broadcasting during the war started off on the back foot. Stalin's adherence to the pact with Germany and his disbelief when Hitler launched the invasion meant that Soviet citizens were not prepared mentally for the war. Since the signing of the pact with Germany in 1939, both sides had refrained from broadcast propaganda against each other. Germany had its propaganda offensive against the Soviet Union and Bolshevism primed to start from the firing of the first shots in Operation Barbarossa. The Soviet propaganda machine was as unprepared as Stalin for the German attack. Even after the initial reports of invasion and the defeat of Soviet forces on the border, he refused to accept that this was a full-scale invasion and so the broadcast news and comment reflected his perplexity. Once it became evident that this was a full-scale invasion and the USSR devoted all its energies to the war, the propaganda output, especially on radio, was geared towards defence and then the achievement of victory. Defence came to mean not just the defence of Soviet socialism but also of Mother Russia – all possible means were used to generate and maintain unity against the invader and a determination to liberate Soviet territory and defeat National Socialism. Symbols of Russian stoicism previously discarded by the Communist Party – such as Suvurov and Kutuzov, the hero of the defeat of Napoleon's invasion in 1812 – were revived and used in speeches, broadcasts, posters and medals. While communism was not totally forgotten, the struggle became the Great Patriotic War and patriotic resistance became the watchword rather than building communism or spreading revolution.

With a highly organized propaganda machine in place since the early years of communist rule, the propaganda effort was highly centralized with the Council of People's Commissars and the Politburo of the Communist Party in ultimate control. Radio news output was closely controlled and only officially sanctioned news was broadcast, while commentaries were exhortatory and part of a discourse across radio, newspapers, art, literature and cinema that glorified and sought to bolster patriotic resistance. As the war neared its end, the propaganda began, again, to stress the building of socialism and the rebuilding of the areas devastated by German invasion. Radio output was highly propagandistic, demanding justice and highlighting German atrocities but did not become violently anti-German in the sense of advocating mass killings or ethnic cleansing, even though Soviet troops took the opportunity of the defeat of Germany to exact retribution and tens of thousands of German prisoners of war died in Soviet camps. The officially broadcast policy was not one of retribution against individual Germans, it was one of extremely rigorous pursuit and punishment of the leaders of Nazi Germany.

3
The Cold War and After: Propaganda Wars and Radio in Regional Conflicts

Media loom large in accounts of the war that killed Yugoslavia, and they will figure no less in histories of the conflict. There are several reasons for this. Since the war began in summer 1991, it has been waged among people who had lived peacefully as compatriots in Yugoslavia all their lives (except those born before 1918 and except for the period 1941–1945, when Yugoslavia was carved up among Germany, Italy and their fascist allies). A campaign of intense propaganda was needed to mobilize the population, to make thinkable in Yugoslavia [...]

(Article XIX, 1994, p. 1)

The euphoria that greeted the end of the war was part and parcel of the belief that new societies and international cooperation would be built on the ruins of war. In the USA, for example, there was a widely held view that the role of radio was to play a constructive role in building a better society and world. There was a public mood that supported the development of socially useful radio. In the Soviet Union, the stress was on rebuilding after the huge destruction of the war – rebuilding, that is, according to Stalin's blueprints and autocratic style and involving a campaign against internal enemies when deemed necessary. Radio was again used to propagandize in this cause and in the cause of building Soviet-style socialism in Moscow's new sphere of influence and control in Eastern and central Europe.

Although the Korean War was to turn the war hot for a while, the period of the Cold War from 1946 through to the fall of the Soviet Union in 1991, was marked by ideological conflict, often conducted via the airwaves. There was the need to bolster the resolve of domestic populations in opposing the opposing bloc and creed and supporting the ruling ideology, but there was also the battle for the middle ground in the neutral states and populations not already part of the US-led or Soviet blocs. International radio broadcasting became a key weapon in the war of ideologies. European states not strongly aligned with the North Atlantic Treaty Organization (NATO) or the

Warsaw Treaty members were immediate targets for broadcasting followed by the Middle East, Asia, Africa and Latin America (Washburn, 1992, p. 25). As the wars of national liberation, post-colonial civil and inter-state wars and the conflict in the Middle East gained pace, radio became an integral part of these struggles with, as is demonstrated in this section and in the case studies, varying levels of propaganda and outright incitement over the airwaves.

Immediately following the end of the Second World War, the USA started scaling back its international broadcasting from 119 hours programming daily in 50 languages to 65 hours in 24 languages (ibid.) but this was soon reversed as wary post-war cooperation turned into outright competition and bitter hostility. By 1955, Voice of America (VoA) had expanded again to 850 hours a week, supplemented by the Central Intelligence Agency (CIA)-funded stations Radio Free Europe (RFE) and Radio Liberty, aimed at the Eastern European states and the Soviet Union, respectively (Taylor, 2003, p. 258). VoA, Radio Liberty, RFE and the British Broadcasting Corporation (BBC) Overseas Service, as it had been renamed in 1939 to avoid the stigma of 'empire', on the one hand, and Radio Moscow, East German and Czech radio on the other, were at the forefront of the broadcasting battle. The competing broadcasters demonstrated commitment to their respective ideologies (even if, in the case of the BBC, this was a subtle background adherence to broad values of liberal democracy and concepts of individual human rights rather than a clearly stated ideology) and sought through their broadcast content to persuade, educate and inform but also to give their version of news and major global events and their interpretations of those events (Hale, 1975, p. x).

The Soviet Union's well-developed radio propaganda system for domestic and international audiences was expanded in terms of power of transmitters, languages broadcast and daily hours of broadcasting. By 1962 and the height of the Cold War, Radio Moscow was broadcasting 1200 hours a week to foreign audiences with a reach that covered every continent and all major languages – 250 hours a week were directed at Western Europe. Soviet propaganda was aimed at the capitalist states, their ruling ideology and socio-economic system and media output was replete with critiques of that system and consistent criticism of capitalism and the domestic and international policies of the USA and its allies. But the central feature of post-war Soviet propaganda was the issue of peace (Griffith, 1979, p. 245). The other key plank of propaganda policy in the 1950s to the 1980s was anti-imperialism and support for national liberation movements fighting colonial or settler rule.

When, as a BBC Monitoring service journalist in the 1980s, I monitored and edited the transcripts of Soviet radio broadcasts to Africa and Asia, peace, anti-imperialism and criticism of the West and calls for states and peoples in the developing world to combat what was termed Western economic imperialism or neocolonialism were central to the output. These basic positions, alongside criticism of the path chosen by China under Mao and his successors, provided the prism through which events were explained for global audiences but also for the audience inside the Soviet Union. This first-hand experience of Soviet output accords with the analysis of Soviet broadcasting over the post-war period and up to the fall of the Soviet Union (see CIA, 1948; Griffith, 1979; Hale, 1975; Paulu, 1975; Wood, 1994).

In the early years of the Cold War, even the CIA concluded that the presentation of the Soviet Union as 'peace-loving' and the promotion of peace was at the heart of Soviet broadcasting. A report in 1948 stated that, 'American policies are universally attacked, but are never depicted as reaching a point where they could no longer be tolerated by the USSR' and broadcasts contained nothing to suggest that the Soviet Union was promoting 'the desirability of hating the West', nor were broadcasts within the Soviet Union or externally preparing people for war (CIA, 1948, p. 3). The USA and its allies were consistently presented as being in opposition to the 'true' democratic socialist values of the Soviet Union and its allies, who were always portrayed as championing world peace. In a similar vein, the American people and their allies 'are never singled out for attack, only the system or government policies' (CIA, 1948, p. 5).

Soviet and East European broadcasting was marked during this period by strong centralized control and elite-controlled content, in the same way that in the privately/commercially owned media in the capitalist world the content was governed by ownership and control (Oates, 2007, p. 1283). Centralized media control meant that political elites directed the messages being broadcast to their populations and to foreign audiences. There were shades of opinion and elements of criticism allowed within the Soviet media, but always within strict limits set by the party and government elite and termed in a way that they come across as efforts to strengthen socialism and improve the system's efficiency – outright criticism of the system itself was not permitted (Hough and Fainsod, 1979, p. 291; Nove, 1977, pp. 348–9). This control of domestic media was supplemented by attempts to jam foreign radio stations (notably the BBC, VoA and RFE/Liberty) to prevent alternative accounts of events and interpretations reaching audiences (Wood, 1994, p. 163).

On the other side of the Cold War divide, the BBC and VoA were the public/government-funded stations broadcasting to the world and in effective opposition to Soviet and East European radio stations. VoA was far more of a government broadcaster and received guidance of key aspects of editorial line and content on major issues from the State Department (Rawnsley, 1996, pp. 21–2). It broadcast news and comment and was less obviously propagandistic than Radio Moscow, its ideology being more in the background, though its opposition to communism and the Soviet bloc was there for its audience to hear and immediately understand. The BBC Overseas Service (which started as the Empire Service in 1932, became the Overseas Service in 1939 and was renamed the World Service in 1965) was more independent of government. Funded, until 2011, by a grant from the Foreign Office but run independently as part of the overall BBC, the World Service was free of government control and resisted attempts to bow to the government on content. In the author's experience as a producer and programme editor with the BBC World Service for 25 years, there were periodic bouts of pressure from governments to influence output. In the late 1980s, for example, the British government was supporting the Siyad Barre regime in Somalia as bulwark against the pro-Soviet government in Ethiopia and sought, unsuccessfully, to limit the broadcast by the World Service and its African and Somali services of news or commentary that highlighted or implicitly criticized the brutal nature of the Barre regime. While the BBC refused to accede to this, it did subject commentary on Somalia to close editorial scrutiny to ensure, not conformity to a government position, but accuracy and sourcing of what was broadcast (author's personal experience as a commentary and talks writer in the African Service in 1987 and the World Service news department from 1998).

Using the original definitions of propaganda set out in first chapter, despite the BBC's line that it does not broadcast propaganda, output was and remains a form of propaganda. The stated aim is to inform and educate and to provide balanced and accurate news and comment. But behind the day-to-day output, the BBC operates within the broad system of liberal democracy with a stress on freedom of speech – governed though it may be by defamation and contempt laws and restrictions relating to national security, as regulated through the D-notice system, the Official Secrets Act and other legislation. This broad intent clearly has an effect on content. The propaganda is subtle and relates to commonly held sets of values, rather than being overtly ideologically driven, as was the case with Soviet and, to a less overt degree, US broadcasts during the Cold War.

More obviously propagandistic and, at times, moving into incitement to rebellion or violence was the CIA-sponsored RFE. Set up along with Radio Liberty (whose target audience was the Soviet Union), RFE was presented as a privately funded, independent broadcaster targeting the communist states of Eastern Europe. In fact, they were funded by the US CIA and were clear propaganda tools aimed at undercutting the belief of people in Eastern Europe in communism and undermining the governments of the Warsaw Treaty states (Wood, 1994, p. 177). The CIA later set up similar stations in the Caribbean broadcasting anti-socialist propaganda aimed at Cuba and Nicaragua under the Sandinistas – notably Radio Swan and Radio Marti (Taylor, 2003, p. 265). The clear aim of the stations was a form of political warfare – the broadcasting of 'liberation-style psychological or political warfare,' as Granville describes it (Granville, 2005, p. 811).

RFE and Hungary – from propaganda to political warfare by radio

From 1950 to 1956, RFE broadcast a diet of news and anti-Soviet commentary. The key event, though, in its first decade of broadcasting and one that was to lead to a watering down of its very blunt propaganda was the Hungarian uprising of 1956. The political struggle within the Hungarian Communist Party between Imre Nagy, leading the reformists, and the conservative wing under Rakosi and Ernst Gero, engendered public demonstrations in support of reform, backed by those supporting reform of the communist system and by many seeking the overthrow of the system. The demonstrations initially supported the cause of reform, including loosening of control over the media and major economic reforms. Soviet-backed attempts by the conservatives to derail reform and oust Nagy initially failed amid growing popular support, particularly among students and young people but with support also from sections of the armed forces, which increased the momentum for change. Popular protests took place in Budapest in favour of the reformist camp – on 25 October 1956, Soviet troops opened fire on demonstrators killing 12. Rather than halting reform, this led to the sacking of Gero as Communist Party leader and the promotion of Janos Kadar to head the party (Nagy had been appointed as Government Head by the Hungarian Communist Party's Central Committee on 24 October).

Over the following days Nagy, supported by Kadar and other reformers, released a number of prominent dissidents and announced a programme of reforms. These were opposed by Hungarian party hardliners and viewed with extreme suspicion by the Soviet leadership. But it was Nagy's decision, announced on 1 November, to pull Hungary out of the Warsaw Treaty Organization that turned the tide. On 4 November, Soviet tanks and troops moved into Hungary to crush the Nagy government and the popular uprising in support of it. There was fighting, mainly in and around Budapest, in which 3000 Hungarians were killed and 12,000 were arrested. Nagy was overthrown and eventually arrested and executed, while his erstwhile supporter, Janos Kadar, changed sides and supported the Soviet suppression of the reform movement.

Prior to and during the uprising, RFE took its usual strongly anti-communist line. It not only supported reform but also urged a more complete break with the Soviet Union and communism, which was consistent with its broadcasts in the preceding years. While run and funded by the CIA, those broadcasting in Hungarian were largely anti-communist exiles violently opposed to the Communist Party. As the extent of the reforms and the growing evidence of mass popular support for reform or replacement of the communist system became apparent, RFE's broadcasts were aimed at stirring up the revolt and consisted of 'crude and insensitive propaganda' (Hale, 1975, p. 41). Even a former director of RFE, George Urban, who worked for the station for 31 years, admits that 'in retrospect, these broadcasts were clear acts of incitement, by the peaceable standards of Western liberal democracy' (Urban, 1997, p. 212). The content of many of the broadcasts was inflammatory, inciting violence, giving instructions about how to carry it out and calling for destroying railway lines and other infrastructure. This went far beyond the anti-communist propaganda which had been RFE's standard fare.

In his book on RFE, Urban quotes in detail many of the broadcasts. Content rapidly developed from general support for change and repeated calls for the overthrow of communism but then developed a sharper edge – saying that in Hungary there were no communists, only 'murderers' (Urban, 1997, pp. 216–7). A broadcast on 27 October by a Hungarian émigré, Julian Borsanyi, told Hungarian listeners (of which there were reputed to be millions) that there was enough ammunition and spare weapons in Hungarian People's Army depots across the country to enable Hungary to fight communists and the Soviet forces for three weeks. Borsanyi told Hungarians that 'all railway lines and others means of communication that support the Soviet troop movements must be destroyed'. Two days later, another émigré Imre Mikes, broadcast that if 'our victorious revolution surrenders its weapons before it has attained its goal [...] if it abandons its blood-soaked, sacred ramparts before it has turned the sacrifices if its martyrs in to the golden currency of freedom, then tyranny may have lost the war but won the peace'. Despite Nagy's ultimate fate, RFE broadcasters were not supporters of his version of reform and repeatedly talked of him using bullets, 'the hangman's noose' and Soviet troops against those fighting for freedom (all quoted from Urban, 1997, pp. 216–17, 221–2). He was called a murderer and a 'foul Muscovite [organizing] [...] a bloodbath in the country'.

Urban denies that broadcasters ever promised that the USA, or through it the UN, would support the uprising with weapons or direct military help. Wood, in his study of international broadcasting, opposes this view, stating that on 27 October a Colonel Bell broadcast on RFE promising military support for the uprising, and Wood says that RFE carried out a covert survey of listeners in Hungary suggesting that, as a result of RFE broadcasts, a large majority of Hungarian listeners were expecting intervention (Wood, 1994, pp. 177–8). Granville contends that, on 4 November, a broadcast by RFE promised US military help, to the huge embarrassment of the Eisenhower administration (Granville, 2005, p. 823). Her view is supported by Hale, who says that RFE was guilty in 1956 of 'peddling the view' that the USA would intervene or bring about some form of UN intervention on the side of the rebels (Hale, 1975, p. 41). CIA head Alan Dulles was forced to admit at an inquiry that followed the revolution that 'RFE broadcasts went somewhat beyond specific guidance in identifying with Hungarian patriot aims and in offering certain tactical advice to the patriots' (Granville, 2005, p. 823). RFE did not cause the Hungarian Revolution but certainly gave it encouragement, tried to instruct Hungarians in tactics of resistance and effectively promised support, thereby giving impetus to and prolonging the fighting without there being any realistic US intention to intervene. Granville puts the argument, with strong evidential support, that what RFE did beyond encouraging anti-communist Hungarians to lay down their lives was to push the Soviet Union into taking a harder line in suppressing the revolt because of its fear that RFE was both inciting rebellion and representing a view from Washington that at some stage intervention might happen (Granville, 2005, p. 836). Even the former director, Urban, says that during the Hungarian Revolution, right-wing Hungarians were able to use the station for their ends and were 'inciting the population to fight or not to give up fighting the communist system' and quotes a Hungarian general who joined the resistance, Bela Kuraly, as saying that RFE had told him to fight and that he believed this represented the policy of the US government (Urban, 1997, p. 232). The major result for RFE of this episode was a wholesale purge of personnel, especially in the Hungarian section, and a return to a diet of carefully targeted news and anti-communist propaganda.

The Middle East, national liberation and post-9/11 broadcasting

The ideological conflict between East and West was far from the only conflict in the decades following the Second World War to involve radio as a major instrument of policy and propaganda. Following the war in Palestine in 1948, which culminated in the formation of the state of Israel and the expulsion of a large part of the Palestinian population from land occupied by the Israelis, a focus of conflict developed in the region around the state of Israel, the fate of the Palestinian lands and refugees and the conflict both between Arab states and Israel, and between Arab nationalism and Western imperialism and political/economic hegemony in parts of the region. These developments and the progressive decline of French and British economic and military power, and so their ability to retain control or at least dominate what they had seen as vital spheres of influence after the Second World War, helped create the conditions for the rising tide of Arab nationalism across the Middle East, a tide whose waves are still buffeting states across the region today.

The 1950s saw the overthrow of the monarchy by radical military officers in Egypt, the overthrow of pro-Western governments in Iraq and Syria and the start of the Algerian war of independence. Radio was to become a key weapon in the Arab nationalist armoury. The Free Officers Movement, which overthrew the pro-British regime of King Farouk in Egypt in 1954, was not slow to grasp the potential of radio for spreading its message of radical Arab nationalism. It set up a national radio station broadcasting across the region – calling it Voice of the Arabs. Copying the successful strategy used by the Italians in the 1930s when attacking the British, the Nasser government in post-coup Egypt distributed tens of thousands of radios across the Arab-speaking world to aid the propagation of its message. This message was of the need for Arab unity under the flag of radical nationalism, anti-imperial struggle against the British and French, criticism of pro-Western governments in Iraq and Jordan and opposition to Israeli occupation of Arab lands. The anti-imperialist writer Franz Fanon credited the station and the distribution of radios by the Egyptians with helping galvanize Algerian nationalism and a willingness to fight the French (cited by Hale, 1975, p. 71). The first communique issued by the Algerian National Liberation Front, on 1 November 1954, was broadcast across the Middle East by the Voice of the Arabs.

Egyptian radio supported the nationalist cause and opposed the British attempts to form a pro-Western defence organization along the lines of NATO, which became known as the Baghdad pact, but was short-lived as nationalists overthrew the pro-Western government in Iraq and undercut Jordan's interest in being part of the pact. In the run up to the Suez War of October 1956, the Voice of the Arabs was vehement in its criticism of Britain and in support of Nasser's decision to nationalize the Suez Canal. By the 1960s, Cairo radio was broadcasting not just in Arabic but in 15 African languages – again encouraging the struggle against European colonialism (Hale, 1975, p. 67). In a region with widely spread, diverse populations, the prevalence of Western colonial rule or direct influence over governments/rulers in nominally independent states but a common language, Arabic, radio could become a powerful weapon. It not only overcame the problems of low rates of literacy, but also delivered nationalist messages and versions of events in Arabic, spoken by Arabs and broadcast from the region.

The Voice of the Arabs was seen as so influential that when the British invaded the Suez Canal zone of Egypt at the end of October 1956, the Voice of the Arabs transmitters were among the first targets. But before they went off air, the station broadcast appeals for support and anti-imperialist action across the Arab world, particularly in oil-producing states. *Time* magazine reported that:

> Before British bombers knocked Egypt's Voice of the Arabs off the air, the International Federation of Arab Workers broadcast an appeal to Arab field hands to blow up Western oil installations – 'even if it means blowing up all the pipelines in the Arab world!' Promptly, workers in tiny Bahrain set fire to a British oil company office. Three big explosions were reported along the Iraq Petroleum Company's 556-mile pipeline to the Mediterranean. Saboteurs may have acted on their own. At least, none of the oil-producing or oil-transmitting Arab nations officially ordered the sabotaging of oil installations.'
>
> (*Time*, 12 November 1956)

There is no proof, though, that the broadcasts directly led to the sabotage.

Radio broadcasting remains a powerful weapon in the conflicts continuing in the Middle East. During the Six Day War, in June 1967, the Voice of the Arabs was key in rallying support within Egypt and across the Arab world following Israel's pre-emptive military strikes against Egypt, Jordan and Syria. Radio Cairo's broadcasts convinced many in the Arab world that US and British forces had joined the Israelis in attacking Egypt. The radio reported that British Canberra bombers had carried out raids against Egypt, while US planes were operating against Egypt from Libya and British and American pilots were flying Israeli combat aircraft (Radio Cairo, 1967). Podeh, in his study of the Egyptian media during the war, concludes that the false reports of early victories by the Egyptians and the alleged collusion between the USA, Britain and Israel had a strong and lasting effect on Arab opinion (Podeh, 2004). While one can question the objectivity of some of his observations in what is clearly a pro-Israeli account of events, there is no denying the strong effect of such accusations on Arab attitudes towards the Western policies in the region – not the least because of the basically pro-Israeli character of Western policies and actions.

Following the coup in 1969 that removed King Idris and his pro-Western government from power and saw the assumption of power by Muammar Gaddafi, Libya's Voice of the Arab Homeland claimed to have superseded Voice of the Arabs as the voice of Arab nationalism (Kazan, 1993) – it broadcast throughout the region and to Africa in Arabic and number of African languages, propagating Gaddafi's concept of Green Revolution, attacking Western policies and those Arab and African states that were deemed pro-imperialist, the latter definition being Gaddafi's idiosyncratic one – so at one stage Nyerere's African socialist experiment in Tanzania was labelled pro-Western because of Nyerere's use of his army to overthrow Libya's ally in Uganda, Idi Amin. During the Arab spring revolt in Libya in 2011, Libyan radio and television remained a powerful weapon for Gaddafi in presenting his interpretation of events, rallying his supporters and threatening the rebels with bloody retribution, though with little ultimate success as his overthrow and killing demonstrated.

Radio remained a major propaganda weapon throughout the last four decades in the Middle East – during the 1973 war, the successive invasions of Lebanon, the Intifada and the Israeli re-invasion of Gaza. Arab and Palestinian radio stations were vociferous in their condemnations of Israel and its Western allies – except of course the stations in those states that either tolerated or supported aspects of Western policy. Israeli radio (and later television) was a powerful unifying force within Israel. Although less obviously the voice of the government than Arab stations, mainstream Israeli radio and television were government-owned and like all media in Israel were subject to strict military censorship when it comes to stories or comment related to military of security issues. And, as the Israeli academic Amit Schejter has pointed out, 'I argue that Israeli media law and policy have been designed to serve an interpretation of Israeli culture that supports the perpetuation of non-egalitarian structures built in to Israeli society'(Schejter, 2009, p. xviii). Mainstream radio, Kol Israel's (Voice of Israel) domestic and external services are publicly owned and the other major broadcaster is the Israeli defence force radio, Galey Tzahal, which curiously has a reputation for greater detachment than Kol Israel to the extent of being regularly criticized in Israel for interviewing Hamas and Palestinian spokesmen (BBC, 1999). These broadcasters work from the position of support for Israel's policies towards its neighbours and, while critical in the short-term, do not challenge long-term assumptions about Israeli aspirations.

Beyond the mainstream, since the early 1980s there has been a growth in religious and ultra-nationalist private stations – often broadcast outside the media laws, but without serious government attempts to act against them. In the 22 years between 1985 and 1997, the number of pirate stations broadcasting on behalf of Israeli settler groups in the occupied territories, ultra-nationalist or religious groups grew from 35 to 117. Laws were passed in 1997 legalizing some stations – this was carried out by Prime Minister Netanyahu to retain the support of the religious Shas Party, which ran six religious stations. The most influential and widely held pirate station is the pro-settler Arutz Sheva network. This radio station – now largely broadcast via the internet – is strongly pro-settler and violently anti-Palestinian and anti-Arab. In 2010, a US State Department human rights report said that the radio station and other settler-run stations depicted 'Arabs as sub-human and called for the expulsion of all Palestinians from the West Bank' (US Department of State, 2010). Israeli law prohibits hate speech and incitement to violence, but no action has been taken to stop the broadcasting of racial hatred and incitement to violence by settler stations. Schejter believes that the proliferation of unlicensed religious and settler stations has effectively undermined freedom of expression and democracy within Israeli (Schejter, 2009, pp. 29–30).

The settler radio stations are just one example of the use of radio for propaganda and the incitement of hatred in the Middle East. Radio, television and latterly the internet and SMS messaging have all been used, by settler groups and by Hamas or Hezbollah in southern Lebanon to promote their causes – the latter two groups being vehement in their propaganda against Israel, denying the state's right to exist and inciting popular uprising and armed attacks against Israeli targets.

Radio propaganda and the break-up of Yugoslavia

Just as the Second World War led to a restructuring of the political map of Europe and to the successful rise of the nationalist and national liberation movements across the world, so the denouement of the Cold War led to major changes in Eastern Europe, notably the crumbling of Soviet power, the demise of the USSR and the fall of pro-Soviet governments across Eastern Europe. Yugoslavia had not been part of the Warsaw Treaty Organization and had been distanced from the USSR following Tito's split with Stalin, which led to Yugoslavia's expulsion from the Cominform in 1948. Under Tito, Yugoslavia followed its own path towards state socialism. But some of the same political and economic pressures that were behind the fall of communism in the Soviet Union were at work in Yugoslavia after Tito's death in 1980.

Tito's Yugoslavia proclaimed itself a socialist state committed to building communism according to its own model rather than Moscow's. The Yugoslav model involved central planning and the subsuming of national differences through a federal structure that gave considerable power to the Yugoslav presidency and the League of Communists. Tito personally played a dominant role as the binding force that helped overcome or at least mask differences between Serbs, Croats, Slovenes, Bosnians, Montenegrins, Macedonians and Kosovan Albanians.

Socialist Yugoslavia had inherited the territory of the multinational Yugoslav state established following the break-up of the Ottoman and Austro-Hungarian empires after the First World War . The state was an unstable mix of territories and nationalities, which had to try to coexist in a new and rather artificially created state ruled by a Serbian monarchy but supposedly committed to equality. Bringing with it the historical, nationalist and mythical baggage of centuries of warfare, revolt, imperial competition and forced migrations, the Yugoslav state formed after Versailles and then reformed under Tito and the League of Communists of Yugoslavia (LCY) (the outgrowth of his communist-dominated partisan movement) contained an unstable mix of constituent parts.

The crisis that developed in the 1980s, and which became the explosive force which ripped Yugoslavia apart in the 1990s, was not caused by national differences alone. It was the agency of powerful political leaders, with their own agendas and ambitions, that utilized the republican rivalries and national suspicions, took and developed historical grievances and built mythical discourses of fear, threat, dispossession and persecution that characterized the 1990–95 conflict and the later Kosovan-Serbian conflict of 1998–99. These discourses were to be the basic content of the competing media – used most extensively by the Serbs but also the Croats and, to a lesser extent, the Bosnian Muslims – during the break-up of Yugoslavia, instruments to mobilize support for political agendas, to justify war and to encourage and justify ethnic cleansing, the use of concentration camps and mass killings. The media (print, radio and particularly television) became a key weapon in the fight for power as Yugoslavia fragmented. It can be strongly argued, as William Shawcross does, that 'Propaganda used especially to incite national hatreds and fears, has been one of the most important weapons of war in the annihilation of former Yugoslavia' (reface to Article XIX, 1994, p. vii).

Post-Versailles Yugoslavia was officially described as being made up of three religions and three peoples – Catholic, Orthodox and Islamic; Croat, Serb and Slovene (Pavkovic, 2000, pp. 4–5). No mention was made of the Bosnian Muslims, the Albanian Muslims of Kosovo, the Macedonians or Montenegrins. The Serbs and Croats were the largest and politically dominant forces – their national struggles had developed in the 19th century as the Ottoman and Austro-Hungarian empires, which between them had divided up the Balkans over centuries, began to weaken. The desire that grew among communities for liberation from Turkish or Austrian rule took on the form of nationalist ideologies, built up by nationalist intellectuals and political leaders. The nationalists took the earlier histories of linguistic communities to build 'historical myths' of the past glories and future destinies of the Serb and Croat peoples:

> patriotic historians and intellectuals of the emerging smaller nations of Eastern Europe started, in the 18th century, to search the history of their peoples for suitable independent and sovereign states which could be used to prove that they too have a history on a par with those of dominant nations. In the process, these intellectuals came to interpret the history of their emerging nations as a mission of recovery of the freedom and independence which these nations possessed in the past.
>
> (Pavkovic, 2000, p. 6)

The different communities of what were to become the Serbian and Croat regions of the future Yugoslavia were not divided by language or history as much as by religion and the different cultural traditions that had evolved through this. But the emerging nationalist theoreticians and leaders worked to create the concept of enduring national identities that included religion, language, literature and constructed versions of national histories. The invention of these new nations from the past in the 19th and early 20th centuries was to be revisited in the 1980s and 1990s, when Serb and Croat politicians and intellectuals would take these historical myths and use them to convince Serbs and Croats of their specific inalienable rights to distinct nationhood on what were claimed to be the historical territories of previous national incarnations.

Croat nationalists claim as part of their historical myth a continuity of the Croat Diet or assembly, which, in Croat accounts but with little basis in recorded history, continued:

> a protracted political struggle for the preservation of the old historic rights of the Croatian state against the encroachments of the Austrian Habsburgs and, later, the Hungarian [...] This protracted struggle,

according to this myth, continued in the Yugoslav state in which Serbs, like the Austrians and Hungarians before them, denied the Croats their distinct national identity as well as sovereignty and political independence.

(Pavkovic, 2000, pp. 7–8)

The ultimate aim of this invented and mythical nationalism was the formation of an independent Croatian state.

The Serbs had their own history and their own myths, which had been drawn from that history and used as a basis for Serb nationalism. One of the key historical events that came to underpin the whole concept of Serbian nationhood and later dominated the Serbian nationalist discourse under Milosevic was the defeat of the Serbian ruler, Lazar, by the Turks at the highly symbolic battle of Kosovopolje (the Field of the Blackbirds on 28 June 1389, St Vitus Day – 15 June on the old calendar). As MacDonald points out, 'In the Serbian legend of the Battle [...] the Serbs lost and were thereafter subjected to five centuries of Ottoman rule' (MacDonald, 2002, p. 69). The battle itself was not a conclusive one, but it had the effect of so weakening Serbia that the Turks were able over the next three years to achieve hegemony over the Serbian areas.

The Kosovo battle has become sanctified as one of the key events in Serbian national mythology – a symbol of sacrifice to protect Christian Europe from the Turk. The Serbian Orthodox Church and 20th-century Serb nationalists would portray the battle 'as a moral and spiritual victory for the Serbs; the victory of the divine over the secular, the eternal over the temporal [...] the martyrdom of Lazar and the Serbian nation raised the Serbian people and made them divine, holy, chosen, special' (MacDonald, 2002, p. 70). It also placed Kosovo at the heart of Serbian nationalism and had an element of promise for the future of regaining lands and reuniting all Serbs. The defeat and the symbolism surrounding it were used assiduously by Serb intellectuals and historians and nationalists in the 19th and 20th centuries to exhort their fellow Serbs to unity, sanctifying the fight for Serbia and demonizing those who stood against the tide of Serbian nationalism. It was on the 600th anniversary of the battle that Slobodan Milosevic was to make one of his most important speeches (at the site of the battle) rallying Serbs to the nationalist cause and sending tremors through the other Yugoslav republics (MacDonald, 2002, p. 71).

It was the gradual weakening of the Austro-Hungarian and Ottoman Empires and the changes in the balance of power in Europe in the late 19th century that helped give impetus to growing Balkan nationalism. The two Balkan wars of 1912 and 1913 were inextricably bound up with Serb ambitions.

These two wars saw accusations of genocidal acts by the Serbs against Albanians, Bosnians and Macedonians following the pre-war spate of killing of Croatian political leaders. In its report on the conduct of the war, the American Carnegie Endowment was very clear in its condemnation of the crushing by the Serb forces and their allies of resistance by Kosovo Albanians during the Balkan wars, reporting that, 'Houses and whole villages are reduced to ashes, unarmed and innocent populations massacred *en masse* [...] with a view to the entire transformation of the ethnic character of regions' (cited by Judah, 2000, p. 85). Such tactics and brutality were to be a hallmark of the Serbian wars in the 1990s against Croats, Muslims and Kosovan Albanians.

The First World War led to the break-up of the Ottoman and Austro-Hungarian empires and the redrawing of the political map of the Balkans. The post-war settlements saw the formation of a Yugoslav state, uniting Serbia, Croatia, Bosnia-Hercegovina, Slovenia and Kosovo – under a Serb monarchy, which headed the state put together by the National Council of Slovenes, Croats and Serbs in Zagreb in October 1918 before the end of the war. It became known as Yugoslavia in 1929 after the royalist coup by King Alexander Karadjordjevic. Most moderate Croats had been willing to join the state and accepted the status quo – though the nationalist Croat Peasant Party had resisted a centralist, unitary state under the Karadjordjevic dynasty. This was the strain of nationalism that was to rise again in 1941 and under Franjo Tudjman.

In 1941, the Yugoslav government joined Hitler's Tripartite Alliance, but a coup followed and the new pro-British government was intent on pulling out of the alliance. On 5 April, German forces supported by Italian, Hungarian and Bulgarian forces invaded and defeated the weak Yugoslav forces in just two days. The victorious Germans installed an Ustasha (Croat ultra-nationalist) government in Croatia under Pavelic. Most Croats welcomed the invasion and the birth of an independent Croat regime. The rest of Yugoslavia was carved up between Germany, Italy, Hungary, Bulgaria and Italian-controlled Albania. Bosnia-Hercegovina and Srem became part of Ustasha Croatia. The Germans controlled the remainder of Serbia (Pavkovic, 2000, p. 32). Initial resistance came from the monarchist Chetnik group of General Mihailovic, but communist partisans under Tito took up the fight after the German invasion of the Soviet Union in June 1941 and became the most effective military force.

In the newly established Independent State of Croatia, oppression of the Serbs through forced conversions to Catholicism, murders of Serb leaders and deportations of Serbs who would not convert, led to a Serb uprising in August 1941 and a retaliatory wave of repression by the Ustasha regime. Pavkovic and Judah both refer to the massacres of Serb civilians that led to the uprising and the brutal crackdown by Pavelic (Judah, 2000, pp. 125–6; Pavkovic, 2000, p. 36). The Croat intentions were summed up in the statement by Mile Budak, the Croat minister of education and faith on 22 June 1941, that one third of Croat Serbs should be killed, one third driven out and one third converted (Judah, 2000, p. 126).

The Ustasha under Pavelic developed their ideology and nationalist discourse in a way that paralleled that of Nazi Germany towards the Jews. Ustasha ideology was that Yugoslavia was an artificial creation imposed on Croat Serbs and that 'like the Jews to the Nazis, the Serbs were for the Ustasha not only exploiters but also representatives of degraded humanity. The hatred of Serbs came to be the core emotional element of Ustasha ideology' (Pavkovic, 2000, p. 37). Despite the downplaying of Ustasha crimes by subsequent Croat leaders and intellectuals, 'the scale of the atrocities was immense. Large numbers of Serbs, Jews, Gypsies, Communists and Croatians hostile to the regime were interned in concentration camps, while countless others were massacred in towns and villages' (MacDonald, 2002, p. 134).

Two other ideologies were important during the Second World War: the Chetnik one of Serb nationalism and monarchism and the communist/ partisan ideology of unity and socialism, which for over 40 years was to become the dominant discourse of Yugoslav politics, swamping and then banning nationalist ideologies. The partisans fought the Germans, the Ustasha and the Chetniks. Led by Tito and the communists, they developed an ideology both of pan-Yugoslav inclusiveness and equality but also of setting Yugoslavia on the road to socialism. Serbs, Croats, Slovenes, Montenegrins and Macedonians all had national status within the partisan movement, but not Bosnian Muslims. By the end of the war and the defeat of the Italians and Germans, the partisans had succeeded in crushing the Chetniks and Ustasha – Mihailovic was shot and Pavelic escaped to Franco's fascist Spain.

The partisans were reborn as the LCY just as Yugoslavia was reborn as a socialist federation of republics and autonomous regions. The new ruling ideology blotted out the old nationalisms and buried them along with what happened during the war. There was no post-war assessment or process of reconciliation or organized trials of those guilty of atrocities. Between 20,000 and 40,000 Ustasha, Croatian refugees, Chetniks and Slovenes fled Yugoslavia into British occupied areas of Austria after the war but were returned to Yugoslavia, most of them being executed with little formal investigation of what they had or had not done (Judah, 2000, p. 130). The lack of investigation of the nature and extent of crimes on all sides during the war was to be a major problem when nationalisms re-emerged. There was no agreement, for example, on the numbers of Serbs killed by the Croats, particularly in the concentration camps like Jasenovac – the Serbs claim over a million dead, Croat nationalists like Tudjman put the figure at the ridiculously low level of 30,000. MacDonald puts the figure of Serbs killed by the Ustasha at 300,000, in addition to 100,000 Serbs killed by the Germans in Serbia. The killings by the Ustasha 'left deep traces in the collective memory of the Serbs in Croatia and Bosnia-Hercegovina. In particular, it has produced a feeling of insecurity and fear of any government which, like the Ustasha one, insists on the Croat domination over the Serbs' (MacDonald, 2002, pp. 42–3).

Under the new socialist federation, there were a variety of forces at work – those that were committed to socialism and making the federation work as a step beyond nationalism; groups nationally and within the individual republics who accepted the new framework and sought power and influence within it but with no intrinsic attachment to socialism or to federation; and nationalists who subsumed their nationalism within the new framework and sought to use the republican structure to have some sort of autonomy for nationalities. There developed a dualistic view of the importance of the federation: 'non-Serbian republican elites generally expected Yugoslavia to be a genuine multi-national federation, the increasingly-influential nationalist-minded elites in Serbia saw the federation primarily as a compromise solution that allowed all Serbs to live in one state' (Mihelj et al., 2009, p. 41). Serb nationalism was damped down – as were all overt representations of old-style nationalism – in the new Yugoslavia, but Serbs gained a sense of security by all being within the federal state with a strong voice in federal institutions as well as republican ones. Pulling the levers of power in the new state was a leader with a non-nationalist ideology and Slovene/Croat parentage, Tito. If there was tension in the early decades, it was between the Serb desire for strong federal institutions to safeguard Serbs living in Croatia, Bosnia and Kosovo and non-Serb republican leaders who did not want to surrender too much power to Belgrade. Tito tried to balance out these tensions while imprinting the dogma that 'nationalism, given its head, will naturally and necessarily lead back to the horrors of inter-ethnic strife experienced in the Second World War' (Allcock, 1992, p. 277).

The late 1960s and early 1970s saw a rise in Croat nationalism, with a historian and general in the Yugoslav National Army (JNA), Franjo Tudjman, as one of its main voices. The movement was crushed. Many of the leaders, like Tudjman, were imprisoned, while others fled abroad to keep the flame of Croat nationalism alight outside Yugoslavia. At the same time, there was a gradual growth of Serb nationalism. This was represented in the views and writings of people such as Dobrica Cosic, a Serb intellectual. He believed that the Serbs had won the war for Yugoslavia and then, as always in their tragic history, had lost the peace. Cosic was expelled from the LCY but not arrested and drew around him Serb nationalist intellectuals. The Serb nationalist view was that in the formation of the new Yugoslavia, Serbia had lost Macedonia, Montenegro and had been forced to accept autonomy within the republic for Vojvodina and, worst of all, for sacred Kosovo (Judah, 2000, p. 138). After Tito's death on 4 March 1980, there was a leadership vacuum and nationalist rivalries re-emerged within and between republics.

Despite the maintenance of central power under Tito, republican powers were gradually expanding. Each republic developed its own secret police and aspiring politicians came up through republican ranks with loyalties to republican party structures rather than to the federal machinery. The tension between federal and republican authority and the ability of republican elites to consolidate areas of power and control was manifested in the media.

The media system that developed under the LCY was not a free press in the Western sense of the term but, as Mark Thompson has set out in his extensive study of its role in the break-up of Yugoslavia, the media in Yugoslavia 'were more abundant, varied and unconstrained than in any other Communist state' (Thompson, 1999, p. 7). Newspapers, periodicals, journals, radio and TV were all produced under the direct or indirect control of the LCY in the six republics and two autonomous provinces. By 1989, there were 9 television stations (one for each republic or province and an extra one for the Italian minority in Slovenia), 202 radio stations (from federal down to municipal level), the federal state news agency Tanjug, 27 daily newspapers, 17 news magazines and hundreds of local papers and special interest publications (ibid.).

As Yugoslavia gradually liberalized and powers were gained by the republics, so the republican rather than national press became more important and more 'ethnic', especially after the death of Tito in 1980, 'as the republican Communist elites became overtly competitive and critical of each other and of the federation, the media were allowed to become critical too. The media were manipulated to enhance the republican elites' authority, usually by appealing to national sentiments' (Thompson, 1999, p. 8).

Under federal and republican law, the freedom of the media was guaranteed but with the proviso that, according to the 1974 constitution Article 203, 'No one may use the freedoms, and rights [...] to disrupt the foundations of the socialist self-management, democratic order [...] violate the freedoms and rights of man [...] stir up national, racial or religious hatred or intolerance'. But, of course, the laws were applied by the elites, and republican elites seeking to enhance their power vis-à-vis federal institutions and to use nationalism to create a power base did not apply these restrictions as long as the press and broadcasters were saying what the elites wanted them to say.

Radio and television had been closely controlled by the federal government – each republic and autonomous province had its own radio and TV service but their programming and schedules were coordinated federally with most programmes being broadcast on all stations. Coordination was strongest in television and involved TV Belgrade (Serbia), TV Zagred (Croatia), TV Sarajevo (Bosnia), TV Titograd (Montenegro), TV Novi Sad (Vojvodina) and TV Pristina (Kosovo). The Slovene and Macedonian stations produced programmes in their own languages rather than Serb-Croat (Thompson, 1999, p. 16). This meant considerable sharing of output. It also meant that programmes from one republic, with that republic's viewpoint represented, would be broadcast by the other republics. In the 1980s, these different viewpoints became more pronounced and the major broadcasters started putting their own reporters in other republics rather than automatically taking that republic's news.

The most obvious example of this, according Goran Milic, a former head of Belgrade TV news, was when TV Belgrade put its own correspondent in Kosovo and stopped taking reports on the province from TV Pristina. This led to the feeding of Serbian reports on Kosovo into the federal TV system – coverage of Milosevic's famous speech in Kosovo in April 1987 was broadcast across Yugoslavia but giving the Serb rather than Kosovan viewpoint. Milic said that this was the key moment that led to the break-up of the federal broadcasting system into republican stations (cited by Thompson, 1999, p. 25). Soon the Croatian and Bosnian stations had pulled out of the sharing of news and current affairs. This foreshadowed the break-up of the whole federal system.

Radio stations had not been as closely coordinated as TV stations, but republican and local radio stations became more and more partisan and had particular influence regionally and locally. But TV was the dominant media for most Yugoslavs in political terms and was watched across the republics, especially in the evenings and at weekends. The republicanization of the media was 'a basic fact of Yugoslav public life and is one of a number of factors which push in the direction of disintegration of the country' (Ramet, 1992, p. 437). Thompson and De Luce go further and say that 'the media were highly influential on public opinion in the former Yugoslavia during the country's terminal crisis and violent disintegration. Regime-controlled media helped create the conditions for war by attacking civic principles, fomenting fear of imminent ethnic assault and engineering consent' (Thompson and De Luce, 2002, p. 201). None was more assiduous in using the media for his own ends than Slobodan Milsoevic in Serbia. Not a great speaker himself or particularly charismatic, he had, however, a grasp of how the media and television, in particular, could be used to build and bolster his power. As the journalist Maggie O'Kane, who reported from the fomer Yugsolavia during the conflict, has said:

> To understand the background to the wars in Croatia and in Bosnia there needs to be an acknowledgement of how absolutely and completely the media has been controlled by the political leaders in the former Yugoslavia.
>
> Milosevic and Franjo Tudjman, the Croatian president, both realized how important it was to instigate a propaganda campaign that would prepare the country of Tito's children – essentially an ethnically mixed country – for the division of the Yugoslav ideal.
>
> (O'Kane, 1996, p. 2)

Ethnic discourses in Yugoslavia and the descent into war

The first real demonstration of this use of the media came in 1987 with the crisis in Kosovo and Milosevic's use of it to build his Serbian power base through naked appeals to nationalism and the development of discourses based on the alleged threats facing the Serbs as a nation. The growing dominance in demographic terms of the Albanians in Kosovo, the lower birth-rate of Serbs in the province and the exodus over decades of Serb families – particularly during the two world wars – had left the Serbs as a minority population in the province seen as the heartland of Serb nationalism and national myths – their share of the population was down from 27.5 per cent in 1948 to 14.9 per cent in 1980. In the late 1970s, there was a rise in Albanian nationalism in the province, culminating in riots in 1981 over the declining state of the economy but also over continued Serb control over the province. More Serbs left after the riots, despite a Serbian-led crackdown on Albanian nationalists.

For many nationalist-minded Serbs, this development was a threat to Serb unity and to the desire to restore the old Serbia. It was reflected in the document that was to become the modern cornerstone of the Serb nationalist revival. This was the Memorandum of the Serbian Academy of Arts and Sciences. Extracts were published on 24 and 25 September 1986 by the Belgrade paper *Vecernje Novosti*, accompanied by very critical comments on the nationalist views expressed (Judah, 2000, p. 158; MacDonald, 2002, p. 65; Silber and Little, 1996, pp. 31–2). The Memorandum, drawn up by a group of Serb intellectuals within the prestigious Academy, fell like a bombshell on the Yugoslav political scene. In extreme and inflammatory language, it spoke of the genocide of Serbs in Kosovo. It argued that the Serbs had been treated so unjustly within Yugoslavia since the war 'that their very existence was threatened' (cited by Silber and Little, 1996, p. 31). The document claimed that Serbs alone were the victims (the familiar refrain) – and the culprits were Croats and Slovenes, who were discriminating against Serbs economically and politically. It went on to say that Serbs 'have never been as endangered as they are today' (Silber and Little, 1996, pp. 31–2). The most extreme part of the memorandum concerned the Serbs in Kosovo. It spoke of the danger of the genocide of Serbs in Kosovo and demanded that Serbs act collectively to prevent this (MacDonald, 2002, p. 65). As Judah says, the memorandum moved from strong language to 'shrill hysteria' over Kosovo and it claimed that in the previous 20 years, 200,000 Serbs had been 'forced to leave' (Judah, 2000, p. 158). The memorandum also lamented the threat to the Serbs of Croatia, which was said to be as bad as under Pavelic's NDH (Independent State of Croatia) in 1941. Once more the valiant, sacrificial Serbs were about to suffer genocide at the hands of their enemies – be they Kosovo Albanians or Croats.

The Serbs, of course, had their own republic but now Serb nationalists were once again bringing back in to the political equation the idea of a Greater Serbia in which all the Serbs of Yugoslavia would be united in a single entity instead of spread across republics or provinces. Slobodan Milosevic, then head of the Serbian Party's Central Committee, called the memorandum a representation of 'nothing else but the darkest nationalism. It means the liquidation of the current socialist system of our country, that is the disintegration after which there is no survival for any nation or nationality' (Judah, 2000, p. 160). His words were to change dramatically within a year and he was to implement nationalist policies of the darkest kind, which ensured the disintegration of Yugoslavia.

The change in Milosevic's rhetoric and political direction took place, not surprisingly, as a result of events in Kosovo. In April 1987, he was sent to Kosovo by the Serbian leader Stambolic to meet local party leaders and to calm angry Kosovan Serbs, who were demonstrating against the Kosovan province party and regional leadership. Meeting with those leaders at the House of Culture at Kosovo Polje on the outskirts of Pristina, Milosevic was confronted by angry crowds of Serbs threatening violence and to march on Belgrade to air their grievances about their lot in Kosovo. Whether this was planned by the Serbian party leader or was spontaneous, Milosevic was transformed. The Kosovan party leader asked him to speak to the crowd to calm them down. But far from calming them and trying to get them to accept the leadership of the Kosovan party, he shouted to them, 'No one should dare to beat you.' With this one sentence, he got the crowd on his side and they started chanting 'Slobo, Slobo, Slobo'. He had become their man – but his words did not stop the Serbs attacking and beating the Kosovan police. He then told the crowd:

> You should stay here. This is your land. These are your houses. Your meadows and gardens. Your memories. You shouldn't abandon your land just because it's difficult to live, because you are pressured by injustice and degradation. It was never part of the Serbian and Montenegrin character to give up in the face of obstacles, to demobilize when it's time to fight [. . .]
>
> (Silber and Little, 1996, p. 38)

After Milosevic had spoken, representatives of the Serbs addressed the crowd and called for the abolition of Kosovo's autonomy, for a state of emergency and some for the expulsion of the Albanians. Milosevic now built a political platform on which 'he embraced nationalism with opportunistic fervour'; the US Ambassador to Yugoslavia, Warren Zimmerman, said he made 'A Faustian pact with nationalism' (MacDonald, 2002, p. 65).

Milosevic built around him a coterie of nationalist intellectuals and set himself up as the nationalist messiah of the Serbs, while using all his skills as a lifelong apparatchik to take over the Serbian party and state machine. In this he also used his grasp of the growing importance of the media, especially television, along with the use of mass rallies and demonstrations. To ensure the necessary nationalist fervour at such rallies, he would have militant Kosovan Serbs bussed in to what were called 'Meetings of Truth' (Judah, 2000, p. 163). He also worked hard to get the Serbian media under his control and through *Politika Ekspres* and *Politika* was able to attack his critics. He used his skill as a bureaucrat to outmanoeuvre his enemies and gain control. Once in charge, Milosevic purged the Serbian party, the media and administration of his opponents, placing loyal supporters in key posts.

Nationalism now began to take centre stage. The federal state and party institutions weakened progressively and republican leaders began to build power bases utilizing appeals to nationalism. There was a range of nationalist strands that appeared, from those seeking greater autonomy within the federation to those favouring secession and complete independence. The latter strands became dominant in Slovenia and Croatia and later Bosnia. Early on, Milosevic raised the nationalist stakes throughout Yugoslavia by moving to end the autonomy of the autonomous Serbian provinces of Vojvodina and Kosovo. Milosevic's arguments with the Slovene party leader, Milan Kucan, over his increasingly liberal attitude towards the Slovene media and youth groups widened the republican divides. The arguments, in which Milosevic adopted a seemingly federalist point of view, enabled the Serb leader to cement an alliance with the JNA, the armed forces seeing themselves as guardians of federalism and centralism. Defence Minister Vejko Kadijevic called the increasingly free media in Slovenia counter-revolutionary and Milosevic supported him.

In Serbia, Milosevic used his ability to organize massive demonstrations to unseat the leadership in Vojvodina and take over the province (Silber and Little, 1996, pp. 58–60). The same happened in Montenegro and he then cemented his control fully in Serbia and in Kosovo in late 1988. He played the dual game of invoking 'the supremacy of the federal institutions over the republics; but when it was in his interests, he claimed that Serbia would not obey the dictates of the federation' (Silber and Little, 1996, p. 62). He was able to get army support and used the JNA and the survival of the federation as a stick with which to beat the Slovenes and Croats (Pavkovic, 2000, p. 89).

His control of Serb radio and TV and of major newspapers like *Politika* meant that Serbs were fed a media diet of nationalism and attacks on critics within Serbia and the other republics. Milosevic ally and Serb member of the Federal Presidency, Borisav Jovic, was quoted in evidence to the International Criminal Tribunal for the Former Yugoslavia (ICTY) as saying that,

> For years, he [Milosevic] paid the biggest attention to the media, especially television, He personally appointed editors-in-chief of the newspaper and news programs, especially directors-general of the radio and television. Perhaps in no other area was he in direct communication with all editors who 'fed' the public with the news, comments and generally with information. He was deeply convinced that citizens formed their

view of the political situation on the basis of what they were presented and not on the basis of their real material and political position.

(ICTY de la Brosse, 2003, p. 5)

The evidence to the ICTY made clear that journalists who tried to be independent were demoted, sacked or persecuted, while taxes and fines were imposed or the withdrawal of broadcasting licences was used against independent radio and TV stations or newspapers that did not fall into line (ICTY de la Brosse, 2003, pp. 5–6).

On 28 June 1989, Milosevic gave a speech at the site of the battle of Kosovopolje on the 600th anniversary of the battle, which set the tone for the coming conflict of nationalisms. Speaking to a crowd of around one million Serbs, many bussed in by the Serb party and government, Milosevic gave his version of Serb history and aims in simple direct language that seized the moment, latching on to historical strains of nationalism and the Orthodox religion (Pavkovic, 2000, pp. 89–90) . He said that the:

> Serbs in their history have never conquered or exploited others. Through two world wars, they liberated themselves and, when they could, they also helped others to liberate themselves. The Kosovo heroism does not allows us to forget that at one time we were brave and dignified [...] Six centuries later we are in battles and quarrels. They are not armed battles, though such things should not be excluded yet.

(cited by Silber and Little, 1996, p. 72)

The Slovenes and Croats, already moving towards national autonomy or secession, now pushed on harder fearing Serbian attempts to centralize power and dominate them. Slovenia tried to push through federal constitutional changes that would give Slovenia the power to stop the army being deployed there and the right to secede. The Kucan leadership was able to argue that the Serbs had changed their constitution and ended the autonomy of Vojvodina and Kosovo, so the Slovenes had the right to change their republican constitution and gain federal approval for changes. But the Serbs blocked this. As a result, on 27 September 1989, the Slovene parliament adopted all the constitutional amendments and Slovenia declared its right to become a sovereign state. In April 1990, elections were held in Slovenia that allowed a multiplicity of parties to stand. Kucan was elected at the head of a coalition of centrist and right-wing groups committed to maintaining the republic's sovereignty.

This bitter process of federal disintegration hastened the development of Croat nationalism. Nationalist intellectuals highlighted what they said was an unbroken line of statehood since the 10th century – a myth, but one widely accepted as affirming Croat sovereignty. Franjo Tudjman, jailed by Tito for his nationalist activities, emerged as the spokesman and dynamic force of Croat nationalism, eclipsing the Croat Communist Party leader Ivica

Racan, who had supported Slovenia against Serbia. As Tudjman began to expound his plans for the future of Croatia, he also revisited the still open wound of Ustasha atrocities against Serbs – he strongly denied the claims that hundreds of thousands of Serbs died at Croat hands, claiming that only 60,000 people were killed in Croatia during the NDH period and that most of these were Jews and gypsies rather than Serbs. He also argued against specific rights for the Serb minority in the Krajina and Slavonia. Just as Milosevic's stance encouraged nationalism in the other republics, so this approach sharpened the contradictions between Serbs and Croats within Croatia and between Serbia and Croatia within the federation.

When free elections were held in Croatia in May 1990 and Tudjman's Croatian Democratic Union (HDZ) was voted into power, one of the first moves was to delete from the republic's constitution the status of Serbs as a constituent nation. Tudjman then started to purge Serbs from positions of authority in the government, economic and media hierarchies. Just as Milosevic had done, he ensured that radio, TV and the major newspapers in Croatia were under his control and toed the HDZ line. Croatia was declared to be a national state of the Croatian people. 'The result of the Croatian elections fuelled the next round of Serbian nationalism, both within Croatia and within Serbia' and helped to ensure Milosevic's re-election in Serbia in December 1990, though now at the head of what had been renamed the Socialist Party of Serbia (Judah, 2000, p. 165). It was only in Bosnia where, despite a split between Muslim, Serb (the Serbian Democratic Party of Radovan Karadzic) and Croat (effectively the HDZ) parties, a significant number of people, 28 per cent, voted against the parties based on ethnicity.

In Croatia, one of the parties that came into being as the communist party fell apart was the Serbian Democratic Party (SDS). This was separate from the one in Bosnia but essentially developed the same aim of opposing the inclusion of Serbs in Croatia in the new republic; fighting instead for the maintenance of all Serbs in one state, whether a federal Yugoslavia or a Greater Serbia. Initially, it was moderate and sought to protect Serb rights. But it soon developed a more nationalistic programme and came under the influence of Milosevic and then of Croatian Serb nationalists committed to demands for territory to be recognized as Serb. Under Milan Babic, a Serb leader from the Krajina town of Knin, it became Serbia's ally in Croatia. With assistance from the Serbian secret police, Milosevic was able to utilize both the Bosnian and Croat SDS parties and the territorial defence units that existed throughout Yugoslavia to build up and arm Serb militias in the two republics (Judah, 2000, pp. 169–70). This increase in Serb military strength was complemented by the support of the JNA for Milosevic and for his centralist approach. In the Croatian Krajina area, the JNA commander in the town of Knin was Colonel Ratko Mladic. He was 100 per cent behind Milsoevic and Babic and their building of Serb militias. In Serb areas of Croatia and Bosnia, this process was also assisted by the dominance of Serbs within local police forces. In Knin, for example, the police chief Milan

Martic became the leader of the Krajina Serb militia. Weapons for the militias came from Serbian police arsenals and then from the territorial defence units and the JNA.

As the militancy of Serbian nationalism was growing alongside the development of militant Serb nationalist parties in Croatia and Bosnia, Serb radio and TV did all it could to build tensions and create ever greater fear among Serbs about Croat intentions – 'Serb television played its part by the constant screening of documentaries about the Ustashas and Jasenovac, implying all along that President Tudjman was the heir of Ante Pavelic'; a climate of fear, anxiety and hatred was built up by Serb TV and radio over what was said to be the impending persecution of Serbs in Croatia (Judah, 2000, p. 171; this view was echoed by BBC Monitoring's Mladen Bilic, and Claire Hardy, and the *Daily Telegraph's* Tim Butcher in interviews with the author). The media propaganda campaign went hand-in-hand with the political and military preparations to prevent Serbs coming under Croat rule and, if possible, to bring Yugoslavia's Serbs together in a single state – whether a remodelled Yugoslavia or a Greater Serbia. The media was used by Milosevic and his allies to convince Serbs across Yugoslavia that they were 'dispersed members of a "national entity". Least of all were they Croatian or Bosnian citizens of a given national or ethnic genealogy, faith or culture' (Thompson, 1999, pp. 51–2). Ensuring that this message went out clearly and consistently along with the message of fear of what was to come from the Croats was achieved by strict control over the media through rewarding loyalists and threatening waverers or opponents, using the methods noted earlier (see also, Thompson, 1999, p. 52).

The Serb propaganda campaign was undoubtedly assisted by the strongly nationalist discourse developed by Tudjman and other Croat nationalists both before and after the April 1990 elections that brought him and the HDZ to power. While Silber and Little see Tudjman's rhetoric as something that many Croats welcomed and as 'an antidote to the fervor coming from the east [Serbia]' (Silber and Little, 1996, p. 83), it is very clear that the two discourses, while on a collision course, were, in their way, mutually reinforcing – each seeming to justify the nationalism and the fear element in the discourse of the 'other'. They quote Croatia's Communist Party chief Ivan Racan (defeated by Tudjman in 1990) as saying that, 'Milsoevic's aggressive policy was the strongest propaganda for Tudjman. Milosevic was sending his gangs to Croatia, where they were dancing and singing: "This is Serbia" which provoked and liberated the national pride and the nationalist reaction of Croats which was effectively used by Tudjman' (Silber and Little, 1996, p. 84). There is no doubt that Tudjman was a convinced Croat nationalist and would have pursued similar policies in the circumstances of the break-up of Yugoslavia, but the growing Serb nationalist propaganda and actions among Serbs in Croatia, added a further edge and haste to his approach once elected.

From 1990 onwards, the path to war was trodden by nationalists on both sides of the Serb-Croat divide and then by the Bosnian Muslims. The short-lived military intervention in Slovenia by the JNA, backed by the Serbs, was unsuccessful, partly because Slovenia was not key to Milosevic's ambitions. Its independence and resistance to the attempt to keep it within Yugoslavia, added impetus to the nationalists in Croatia and to Bosnian Muslims, who were becoming ever more fearful of domination by either of, or both, the Serbs and Croats. This section does not detail the progress of the wars and international intervention – this has been done elsewhere to great effect (Glenny, 1996; Judah, 2000; Silber and Little, 1996; Thompson, 1999) – but looks at the content and language of the media output (primarily radio) of Serbia to identify the way that the conflicts and opponents were framed and represented as the federation fragmented and descended into conflict.

Serbian Radio and Television (RTS) was the key Serb broadcaster, supplemented by regional or local stations in Novi Sad, Pale, Knin, Pristina and other Serb areas, and was a key instrument for Milosevic. He used it to vilify domestic opponents (as during the March 1991 demonstrations against his policies and his hegemony over the media) and to mobilize Serb opinion in favour of his nationalist line and elicit support for the war. He controlled much of the printed press, too, especially the *Politika* group. There were independent media – such as B-92 radio, Studio B television and the publication *Vreme*, but these were harassed constantly and had to fight to survive and to maintain an alternative if small voice (see Collin, 2001).

The tenor of the news reporting, the unchallenged assertions of politicians interviewed or allowed to broadcast and the commentary by presenters and other journalists was such that Serbs were fed a diet on radio and TV of consistent vilification and condemnation of the Serb and Bosnian Muslims, their representation as Ustasha, Jihadists and as genocidal killers and the presentation of Serbs as brave but vulnerable victims of aggression and planned genocide by their neighbours (ICTY de la Brosse, 2003, p. 30). The existence of Serbia and the rights of Serbs was continually presented as at risk.

Serbian Radio Knin in the Serbian-populated areas of the Croat Krajina was, as Misha Glenny, BBC correspondent in Yugoslavia throughout the conflict, maintains:

> one of the most important actors on the Knin stage which transformed the consciousness of this dozy town [...] The people of Knin are extremely dependent on this radio station [...] much of the news broadcast about the political situation is tendentious nonsense put out by the army or Babic [...] And yet like all the other media in Yugoslavia, with a few dazzling exceptions, Srpski Radio Knin is a vital accomplice in the dissemination of falsehoods and the perpetuation of divisive myth which

has turned one hapless *narod* against another equally innocent one. The only truth in the Yugoslav war is the lie.

(Glenny, 1996, p. 21)

Unfortunately, there was little if any monitoring of Knin radio by the BBC or the American Foreign Broadcast Information Service but the centrally controlled Yugoslav Tanjug news agency and RTS frequently quoted it.

As the tension increased and conflict approached in August 1990 – with Babic as president of the Knin Municipal Assembly, founder of the nationalist and anti-Croat Serbian National Council and effective head of the SDS, working hand in glove with Milosevic and Mladic to create a Serb entity in Knin and the Krajina – Radio Knin provided a running commentary of his statements. On 17 August, according to Tanjug (Tanjug, BBC SWB – Summary of World Broadcasts), Radio Knin broadcast Babic's statement that Krajina was in a state of war because of the threat from Croatia. On the same day, RTS's Belgrade Radio (BBC SWB), said that they had been unable to contact 'our friends' at Radio Knin but that there were reports from Krajina of Serbs demanding and receiving arms to protect Serb areas from the Croat government. Tanjug also reported that day that Radio Knin was being used by the Serbs to pass military information and instructions to the Serb population in the face of this threat. The agency also reported (Tanjug, BBC SWB) that Croatian President Tudjman had denounced Radio Knin and called on Serbs 'not to be taken in by provocateurs and those who are inciting them'.

When Babic, with Milosevic's support, held a referendum in Knin on autonomy on 19 August, Radio Knin was used to encourage Serbs to vote in the referendum. After the referendum, which overwhelmingly supported Babic, the conflict between the Croatian government and the self-styled autonomous Serb areas worsened, with Serb militias formed with arms from the territorial defence organizations, the JNA and the Serbian police. The Knin JNA garrison headed by Mladic was important in assisting with weapons and training. On 29 September 1990, Tanjug quoted Radio Knin as broadcasting a statement by the Serb Council for National Resistance as saying, 'The Serbian nation has not risen against the Croatian nation, but will resist the Ustashas until the last drop of blood' (Tanjug, BBC SWB). This formulation of denying that they were anti-Croat but just anti-Ustasha was to become a regular theme in Serb propaganda discourses in the media. But Ustasha had become the label of choice for Croats. The massacres that took place during the war in Croatia – notably during and after the capture of Vukovar by the Serbs – showed that all Croats were deemed legitimate targets for Serb forces with no discrimination between Croat nationalists and innocent bystanders or between combatants and non-combatants.

The conflict over the self-proclaimed Serbian autonomous region of Krajina and the Serbian areas of Slavonia kicked off in February and March 1991. Serbs forces tried in February to seize the police station in Pakrac but were then surrounded by Croat forces. Belgrade radio put out reports of attacks on Serbs and of tens of thousands of Serb refugees flooding into Serbia – ignoring that the Serb militias had started the affair. There was a stand-off between Croatian special forces, who had taken control of the town, and JNA units supporting the Serbian rebels. This was followed by a Serbian attempt to stop the setting up of a Croatian police station in the Plitvice National Park. Clashes followed and Radio Knin called on Serbs to resist. The radio also broadcast an appeal on 31 March, reported by Belgrade radio the same day, to the Yugoslav and Serbian presidencies from the Serbian Council for National Defence 'to take urgent measures or we will all be liquidated' (BBC SWB).

Throughout the spring, Radio Knin kept up the tempo of inflammatory broadcasting, which seemed designed to ramp up fear and anxiety among Krajina Serbs and to feed into RTS's media campaigns against the Croatian government. On 9 May 1991, the local radio broadcast a statement in which the presenter praised Serbia and elements within the Yugoslav federal presidency for coming to the aid of the Krajina Serbs 'to prevent civil war' and to 'prevent further barbarity and terrorism by the Croatian leadership against the Serbs' (Tanjug, BBC SWB). Using the familiar mirror technique of propaganda, the Serbs through their media reflected their own plans and motivations onto their enemies so as to blame them for any conflict. The Serbs were planning to carve Serb areas from Croatia, as they were later to try to do in Bosnia, and to use violence as necessary. But their propaganda reversed this and accused the Croats of attacking and persecuting the Serbs – while it is true that Tudjman and his party intended to progressively remove Croat Serbs from positions of influence in public service and the police, they generally reacted to Serb arming and occupations rather than initiating actions.

The declarations of independence of Slovenia and Croatia on 25 June 1991 moved the level of conflict from brutal skirmishes and small-scale actions to full-scale warfare. While the JNA move into Slovenia was short-lived and involved few casualties, the Serb-Croat war involved the JNA and Serb militias on one side and the Croat armed forces and police on the other. The fighting was bitter and intense involving bloody sieges and large-scale loss of military and civilian lives. Gung-ho or atrocity-laden reports by Serb radio – lauding the heroic Serb fighters and accusing the Croats of all manner of atrocities against innocent Serbs – were accompanied by political commentaries on Serb radio and television attacking Croat leaders as fascists and direct heirs of the Ustasha. Zagreb radio, controlled closely by Tudjman, for its part constantly accused the Serbs (often with due cause) of atrocities and accused them of being heirs of the Serb monarchist Chetnik movement, which fought Tito's partisans during the Second World War.

The war escalated in Croatia as JNA units and Serb militias sought to end Croat control of areas they deemed to be Serb and tried to end Croat blockades of JNA garrisons. Belgrade Radio warned on 16 September that 'those who attack and oppose the JNA will be destroyed'. This coincided with the offensive by Mladic's Knin JNA brigade to end the blockade of the JNA base at Vukovar in Croatia. This became a brutal siege in which hundreds of troops on each side were killed and there was a high toll of civilians. The siege lasted three months. When it ended, with the JNA over-coming Croat resistance on 20 November, journalists who entered the town after the Yugoslav army found the streets littered with human and animal corpses and many buildings reduced to skeletons by Serb bombing (Silber and Little, 1996, p. 180). The *Observer* correspondent who was in Vukovar at the time, John Sweeney, told the author on 24 November 1991 that he had seen the bodies of large numbers of civilians in Croat areas and had been taken to what he termed a 'ghouls banquet' by JNA officers in a building outside which there were bodies littering the street (Sweeney, 1991).

On the night of the capture of the town, Belgrade television broadcast a report saying that 41 Serbian children aged between five and seven years old had been massacred in a school in Vukovar by the Croats before they surren-dered, along with countless adults. They were actually reporting something that was unconfirmed but they did not say that and interviewed a Serbian Reuters photographer, Goran Mikic, who spoke in graphic detail of seeing the bodies of Serbs murdered with knives and axes and of piles of children's bodies, some in plastic bags. Photos of dead adults were shown but not of the dead children. Reuters denied the story and said there was no truth in it but Belgrade TV and radio continued broadcasting reports of the massacre of children, saying they had all had their throats cut by 'bloodthirsty Croats' (ICTY de la Brosse, 2003, p. 8). As de la Brosse said in his report to ICTY on the media war, this and reports like it were used to reinforce the image 'nurtured by the Serbian media of a *"criminal and genocidal"* Croatian people to undermine opposition to the war and encourage recruitment to the army and militias' (ibid.).

Similar false atrocity stories were used by the Serbs when the conflict in Bosnia started. One of the most outrageous was the claim that the besieged Muslim defenders of Sarajevo were feeding Serbian children to Sarajevo zoo's starving animals. This was broadcast by Bosnian Serb TV in Pale, repeated by Tanjug and reported by RTS in Belgrade. There was no evidence for the report but Belgrade TV's correspondent in Sarajevo reported that 'the Musim extremists have come up with the world's most horrible way of torturing people. Last night, they threw Serb children to the lions in the local zoo' (ICTY de la Brosse, 2003, pp. 8–9).

Throughout the war Belgrade TV and radio, Pale TV and Radio Knin kept up the barrage of anti-Croat and anti-Muslim propaganda (as did Zagreb radio and TV with its anti-Serb and, at times, anti-Muslim broadcasts and Sarajevo TV and radio to a lesser extent with its open support for the Bosnian Mulsims led by Izetbegovic). Serb victories were praised as heroic; atrocity story followed atrocity story to try to prove to a Serb population divided between supporting and opposing Milosevic that he was their saviour in the face of genocidal threats. Serb atrocities such as those at Vukovar and the later massacre of thousands of Bosnian Muslim men after the capture of Srebrenica were denied. When the pressure from the European Union, the USA and NATO forced concessions and eventually the adherence to the Vance plan and the Dayton agreements, Serb radio and TV was then turned against Babic in Krajina and Karadzic in Bosnia when they stood against international agreements that Milosevic saw as his only way of preserving his power – they suddenly became traitors or dangers to the Serb nation and its survival.

The media in the former Yugoslavia was an important weapon in the political and military conflict. It was used to incite fear and hatred and to mobilize support for the competing nationalisms. What it didn't do directly, and this was confirmed to the author by Serbo-Croat monitors at BBC Monitoring (interviews with Hardy and Bilic, 2010), by former *Daily Telegraph* Defence correspondent Tim Butcher, who covered the Balkan wars of the 1990s (Butcher, 2010) and by Balkan media experts Marcus Tanner and Mark Thompson (email correspondence with the author), is incite direct attacks on Croats or Muslims or say where and when they should be attacked. Real or imagined threats of attacks in particular places were reported, the 'genocidal intent' of enemies was endlessly emphasized and the enemy attacked as Ustasha, fascists or Jihadis, but Serb and Croat media outlets did not take the line of Radio Televison Libre des Mille Collines (RTLM) in Rwanda (see Chapter 5 case study) or suggest the necessity of the complete extermination of enemy populations – even if this is what was clearly attempted at Srebrenica alongside the policy of ethnic cleansing in areas deemed Serb. The role of the Serb media in Milosevic's aggressive policy in the region was seen as so vital that when the Kosovo conflict restarted in 1998 and the Serbs moved to crush the Kosovo Liberation Army, the NATO intervention that eventually created the state of Kosovo started with the air attack on government targets in Belgrade, including RTS. The media war, as de la Brosse emphasized in his report to the ICTY, was characterized by the 'waging of an intense media battle of hateful propaganda and biased and untrue information' (ICTY de la Brosse, 2003, pp. 6–7).

The end of history and the war on terror

The post-Cold War world, far from seeing the 'end of history', witnessed continuing conflict in Asia, Africa and the Middle East, with growing conflict between radical Muslim groups and the USA and its allies becoming dominant globally in the first decade of the 21st century. In the wake of the 9/11 attacks, the US-led invasions of Afghanistan and Iraq led to long-term conflict not only in those countries but also in Pakistan. The ambiguous position of the Pakistani government and the military/intelligence establishment meant that the conflict involving Pakistan, radical Pakistani Islamic groups, the Afghan Taliban, groups claiming allegiance to Al-Qaeda and the USA was particularly complex – a complexity that is not the topic of this study. However, as part of the conflict in Pakistan, it is worth noting the role of radio in the conflict in the Swat Valley in North Western Pakistan. There, radical Islamic groups fighting both the government of Pakistan and, by proxy, the USA, used radio to both incite the local population and to threaten them – warning of the consequences of continued support for the government and failure to back the Islamic groups.

The respected Pakistan daily newspaper *Dawn* reported, on 7 July 2011, that a top commander of the Pakistani Taliban in the Swat Valley, Maulvi Faqir Mohammed, has resumed FM radio broadcasts in the region. He used radio to send out a mix of religious and political propaganda, warning that 'all those who have turned their backs on us, like we are gone for good, should seek forgiveness from Allah'. The newspaper noted that militant Islamic groups in Pakistan had long used mobile transmitters to broadcast localized messages of incitement against the government and it supporters (Dawn, 2011). Maulvi Faqir Mohammed's broadcasts repeated consistently that it was the duty of every Muslim to fight the infidels and warned them after his group carried out attacks that killed soldiers and government officials that they should not dare 'stand in the way of those who are following the path of God'. Another Taliban leader in the region, Maulana Fazlullah, became so prolific as a broadcaster that he was dubbed the FM Mullah. His broadcasts and those of other groups in contested areas of Pakistan mixed incitement to fight the government with the furthering of local rivalries and conflicts – so at one stage there was a radio war reportedly going on between Sunni groups and Sufi Muslim groups in the Swat Valley (*Asia Times*, 2009).

Case Studies

4
Nazi Radio Propaganda – Setting the Agenda for Hatred

> The *psyche* of the broad masses is accessible only to what is strong and uncompromising [...] the masses of the people prefer the ruler to the suppliant and are filled with a stronger sense of mental security by a teaching that brooks no rival than by a teaching that offers them a broad choice.
>
> (Adolf Hitler, *Mein Kampf*, p. 50)

> As a speaker he [Hitler] has developed a wonderful harmony of gesture, histrionics and spoken word. The born whipper-up! Together with him you can conquer the world.
>
> (Goebbels, *The Early Goebbels Diaries*, p. 91)

> The voice on the radio [Goebbels) begins softly. It seems friendly and familiar. It could belong to a favourite uncle. Slowly, it becomes louder and more excited. Then something snaps. The voice snarls. Words explode from the radio, spewing hatred.
>
> (Roberts, 2000, p. 5)

The voices of Hitler and Goebbels were to become two of the most effective tools of the National Socialist German Workers' Party (NSDAP – hereafter the Nazi Party). It was through Hitler's vision of a National Socialist Germany and his ability to inspire and manipulate audiences that he was able to seize control of the party and to form it into a vehicle for his political ambitions and programme.

Prior to the First World War, Hitler was politically aware and, in *Mein Kampf*, wrote of how when living in Vienna in 1910 he read the Austrian Social Democrat party newspaper, *Arbeitzeitung*. Already a fierce anti-communist, he was fascinated by the power of the paper and its ability to mould the opinions and beliefs of its readers and noted how the paper:

> inculcated this new doctrine of human redemption in the most brutal fashion. No means were too base, provided they could be exploited in the

campaign of slander. The journalists were real virtuosos in the art of twist-ing facts and presenting them in a deceptive form [...] The newspaper propaganda was intended for the masses.

(Hitler, 1988, p. 49)

Critical of the paper because of its Marxism, he was impressed by the power of the media to manipulate or inspire – a power he was to harness and develop by adding the effect of the human voice at rallies and on the radio.

His ability to do this and his recognition of the power of propaganda led to the development of a party machine in which propaganda was as important as organization and action. Hitler and the Nazis demonstrated the ways in which the voice, radio and newspapers – supplemented by education, film, art, culture and sport – could be turned into instruments of political mobi-lization and control. They were integrated into the overall Nazi philosophy and have become both a propaganda model and the image of propaganda at its most extreme. The image of Nazi propaganda led to the idea that while Hitler and Nazi Germany lost the 1939–1945 war, they won the propaganda battle. In his book *The War that Hitler Won*, Robert Herzstein sets out the case for the totalitarian approach to analysing Nazi Germany and its propa-ganda campaign. While he is right when he says that 'Nazi ideologists and propagandists employed the enormous party propaganda apparatus and the directly or indirectly state-controlled mass media for intensive campaigns, blanketing the whole country with a single message' (Herzstein, 1979, p. 15), he overplays the totalitarian and totally uniform character of the Nazi media and, when combined with the title of the book, the implication is that Nazi propaganda was ultimately successful and flawlessly organized. This approach, very common in the decades immediately after the war, has now been questioned more and more by the studies of Kershaw, Kallis, Welch and others (Kallis, 2008; Kershaw, 1983; Welch, 1983, 1993).

The propaganda campaigns that helped the Nazis to gain power, build and maintain that power, took an unwilling German population into war and kept them in that war to the bitter end were powerful weapons in the Nazi armoury, but they were never used in isolation. While Herzstein has a strong point when he says that 'the greatest success of the Goebbels propaganda apparatus was reflected in the continuation of the struggle by the German people into 1945 until practically every Gau was in Soviet or Western Allied Hands' (Herzstein, 1979, p. 22), the propaganda campaigns were part of an overall system of control of information, opinion and phys-ical actions. Propaganda worked hand in glove with the repressive power of the state – the security police (SD), the SS (Schutzstaffel) and the Gestapo. The campaigns worked alongside the ever-present threat of force – of the concentration camp, or worse, for those who questioned the propaganda or sought alternatives.

Care needs to be taken not to take the scale, short-term successes of the propaganda campaigns and the ability of propaganda to work on a cowed population as signs of the overall success of propaganda per se. Echoing the Clauswitzian view of war as the continuation of politics by other means, so propaganda was another means to an end – an end that was not ultimately achieved. Furthermore, Hitler's propaganda did not always persuade the German public. As Kallis points out, when Germany was threatening war over the Sudetenland, 'Hitler himself commented unfavourably on the depressed mood of the German public' (Kallis, 2008, p. 94). He had failed to win them over and they opposed war to recover territory claimed as German or unite all German speakers in one territory; however much they supported the aims in principle. Propaganda failed to generate enthusiasm for war, though it did help achieve acquiescence, but always backed up by force and a lack of choice. The scale, importance of and nature of propaganda, though, were defining characteristics of the rise and rule of the Nazi Party. Propaganda was central to its modus operandi.

Note on sources

There was little if any concerted monitoring of German domestic radio from Hitler's accession to power in 1933 up to the outbreak of war in 1939. Accounts of broadcasts in that six-year period rely heavily on reports of Hitler's and other leaders' speeches that were broadcast, and on secondary sources reporting radio activity. For the period of war, the daily reports by the British Broadcasting Corporation (BBC) Monitoring Service are the primary source of radio content (in sourcing the material I give the date of broadcast rather than the dates of the BBC summaries) along with Goebbels's diaries and Boelcke's invaluable edited reports of Goebbels's daily conferences for press and radio (that end in 1943). The historical context sets out the main events of the period under study and charts the rise of propaganda and incitement to hatred as instruments of policy and power in the context of historical developments and the evolving political discourse of the Nazis. In charting this history, the works of Alan Bullock, Ian Kershaw, William Shirer and Richard Evans have been invaluable and are extensively quoted, as are David Welch's incisive examinations of the propaganda of the Third Reich.

Propaganda and the rise of Hitler and the Nazi party

The following historical narrative of the development and use of propaganda by Hitler and the Nazi Party is not a new history of the development of Nazism and Hitler's rise to power but focuses on propaganda as an instrument in that rise to power, its use of incitement to hatred (chiefly its use of anti-Semitism as a major plank and foundation of policy) and its harnessing of the power of radio as a propaganda tool. Necessarily, this is put in the context of post-First World War Germany's social and political environment and of the development of a Nazi ideology that exploited Germany's decline and its bitterness at defeat. Propaganda cannot but be viewed in its historical, political, social and cultural context.

Ideologically, Hitler was drawn to the pan-German policies of right-wing nationalist parties and to the political tactics of the Austrian Christian Social Party in appealing to the petit-bourgeoisie – the small shopkeepers, artisans, skilled workers, petty officials and state employees. Hitler was to combine aspects of each of these approaches in his political programme. As Bullock writes, 'Hitler was to show a brilliant appreciation of the importance of these same classes in German politics' (Bullock, 1962, p. 45). Just as he was impressed by what he saw as the power of the Social Democrat press, so he was in awe of the political skills of the Christian Social Party. He wrote that, 'Their leaders recognized the value of propaganda on a large scale and they were veritable virtuosos in their working up the spiritual instincts of the broad masses of the electorate' (cited by Bullock, ibid.). The ability to appeal to instinct or latent prejudices and anxieties was to be a lasting facet of Hitler's appeal and propaganda tactics.

Hitler's adherence to pan-Germanism meant that at the outbreak of the First World War, though an Austrian, he wanted to join the German army and successfully petitioned to be allowed to enlist in a Bavarian regiment. He saw the war as something welcomed by the masses of Germans and Austrians. In *Mein Kampf,* he said that from the moment war was inevitable,

> the conviction grew among the masses of the people that now it was not a question of deciding the destinies of Austria or Serbia but that the very existence of the German nation itself was at stake [...] it was not a case of Austria fighting to get satisfaction from Serbia but rather a case of Germany fighting for her own existence – the German nation for its own to-be-or-not-to-be, for its freedom and for its future.
>
> (Hitler, 1988, pp. 155–6)

Hitler enrolled in the 16th Bavarian Reserve Infantry Regiment, which served in France, where Hitler first experienced war at the First Battle of Ypres in October 1914. For the majority of the four years of the war, he served as a runner between his company and regimental headquarters and was at or near the front – he was wounded in fighting on the Somme in October 1916 and sent to Germany for treatment before returning to France. He won the Iron Cross for bravery. A month before the end of the war, he was gassed and sent back to Germany. He was there when Germany surrendered. Hitler believed that defeat was the result of the campaigns in the social democrat press against the war, the failure of government propaganda, the machinations of the Jewish financiers – who he claimed controlled German industry – and betrayal by politicians. He wrote that he'd not taken much interest in politics during the war, but at the end, 'I intensely loathed the whole gang of miserable party politicians who had betrayed the people' in order to line their own pockets by sacrificing Germany and her soldiers (Hitler, 1988, p. 186). Hitler believed that the German army had been stabbed in the back by Marxists, Jews and politicians working hand-in-hand. He began to conceive of a new approach to politics,

> a new movement, something more than a parliamentary party, which would fight Social Democracy with its own weapons [...] power lay with the masses, and if the hold of the Jew-ridden Marxist parties on their allegiance was to be broken, a substitute had to be found. The key, Hitler became convinced lay in propaganda.
>
> (Bullock, 1962, p. 55)

Hitler's observations on Germany's defeat in the propaganda war provided the basis for his very active propaganda to promote the Nazi Party and then imprint it on the German people. He viewed it as an art that had massive practical value in politics. He was full of praise for British propaganda, which was 'exploited by the enemy in such an efficient manner that one could say it showed itself as a real work of genius' (Hitler, 1988, p. 167). In his view, 'propaganda is a means and must, therefore, be judged in relation to the end it is intended to serve. It must be organized in such a way as to be capable of attaining its objective' (ibid.). He condemned German propaganda as failing in the basic objective of strengthening fighting spirit and so helping to achieve victory.

Hitler very clearly understood the key mechanisms of propaganda:

> Propaganda must always address itself to the broad masses of the people. For the intellectual classes, or what are called the intellectual classes today, propaganda is not suited, but only scientific exposition. Propaganda has as little to do with science as an advertisement poster has to do with art [...] The purpose of propaganda is not the personal instruction of the individual, but rather to attract public attention to certain things [...] Here the art of propaganda consists in putting a matter so clearly and forcibly before the minds of the people as to create a general conviction regarding the reality of a certain fact, the necessity of certain things and the just character of something that is essential [...] it must appeal to the feelings of the public rather than their reasoning powers.
>
> (Hitler, 1988, p. 170)

And Hitler proved adept at gauging the feelings of important sections of the German public. As Welch argues, while pre-1933 Nazi propaganda reflected many 'of the aspirations of large sections of the population' and played to their post-war grievances over the Treaty of Versailles and the decline of the economy, the efficacy of the propaganda is sometimes over-emphasized and ignores 'the failure of the Weimar system to solve prevailing economic and social problems' (Welch, 1993, p. 8). Nazi propaganda did not have to create discontent but to harness and reinforce grievance. It could then promote solutions that fed on people's anger and anxiety, positing a formula for German rebirth and resurgence. It utilized existing trends and beliefs and sought to manipulate emotions and thereby control popular opinion. In doing this, Hitler displayed massive contempt for his audience, believing them to be 'malleable, corrupt and corruptible', not sophisticated or complex but 'simple and consistent' (Zeman, 1964, p. 5).

In the violent and turbulent years following the war, Hitler was instruction officer in the press bureau of the political department of the German Army's VII District Command in Munich. His role was to inculcate resistance to socialist or pacifist ideas among soldiers (Bullock, 1962, p. 65). He worked alongside right-wing nationalists in the army, who were supporters of the Freikorps movement, which was assisted by the army in fighting communist and socialist revolutions in Bavaria and other parts of Germany after the war. His work involved investigating the Munich-based German Workers' Party of Anton Drexler – not a socialist or Marxist movement but an aspiring populist, working-class nationalist party. Despite it having just six members, Hitler joined the party and put all his energy into it, developing from being a rather uninspiring public speaker into one who could grab the audience's attention and hold it. He spoke at small public meetings called by the party in beer halls – his main subjects being the iniquities of the Treaty of Versailles (which had taken Germany's colonies, reduced its territory, demilitarized the Rhineland, limited the size and nature of the armed forces and imposed war reparations), Germany's betrayal by politicians, the role of the Jews and the threat of Bolshevism.

In 1920, Hitler was put in charge of the German Workers' Party propaganda. In April, Hitler left the army and devoted all his time to party work. There were at the time other national socialist movements in Bavaria (one led by the fanatically anti-Semitic Julius Streicher, who in 1923 founded his own violently anti-Jewish Nazi newspaper *Der Stürmer*, which became the spearhead of the Nazi anti-Semitic press campaign) and national social-ist parties in Austria and the German-populated Czech Sudetenland. These were not part of Drexler and Hitler's party but there were frequent meetings between them and they shared basic pan-German, nationalist and anti-Jewish beliefs. Hitler developed links with Captain Ernst Rohm of the army's VII district command, for which Hitler had worked. Rohm had connections with the Freikorps and other paramilitary groups. As Hitler worked to build the party, Rohm's contacts proved invaluable in recruiting new members and establishing squads of former soldiers for party security and to break up communist meetings. Under Rohm, these were to become the Nazi Storm Troopers (Sturm Abteilung – the SA).

While Hitler worked on party propaganda and widened his network of contacts among right-wing businessmen, army officers and other Bavarian movements, the provision of funds from the army and from a nationalist and violently anti-Semitic journalist, Dietrich Eckart, enabled the party to buy a weekly newspaper, the *Volkischer Beobachter*. Eckart became editor but Hitler controlled the ideological content. Important though the paper was, it was Hitler's speeches at public meetings that helped the party expand and put him in position to outmanoeuvre Chairman Karl Harrer, and President Anton Drexler. Kershaw writes that 'It was largely owing to Hitler's public profile that the party membership increased sharply from 190 in January 1920 to [...] 3300 by August 1921. He was rapidly making himself indispensable to the movement' (Kershaw, 2001a, p. 149).

As he concentrated more and more on public speaking and propaganda, he came to develop further his contempt for the masses but alongside it his belief in concentrating propaganda efforts on them rather than educated people. He wrote in *Mein Kampf*:

It is not the purpose of propaganda to create a series of alterations in sentiment with a view to pleasing these blasé gentry. Its chief function is to convince the masses, whose slowness of understanding needs to be given time in order that they may absorb information; and only constant repetition will finally succeed in imprinting an idea on the memory of the crowd. Every change that is made in the subject of a propagandist message must always emphasize the same conclusion. The leading slogan must of course be illustrated in many ways and from several angles, but in the end one must always return to the same formula. In this way alone can propaganda be consistent and dynamic in its effects.

(Hitler, 1988, pp. 174–5)

Between 1920 and 1924, when Hitler was imprisoned for his part in leading the abortive Munich putsch against the Bavarian government, the various national socialist parties campaigned against the policies of the Weimar Republic government in Berlin and against the Bavarian state government in Munich. The national socialists were also active in opposing socialist and communist movements. Hitler told a meeting in a beer hall on 4 January 1921, that, 'The National Socialist Movement in Munich will in future ruthlessly prevent – if necessary by force – all meetings or lectures that are likely to distract the minds of our fellow countrymen' (cited by Bullock, 1962, p. 72). The combination of propaganda and violence was to become the *leitmotif* of Nazi activity – once the Nazis controlled the state and so the instruments of state power, opponents were hunted down ruthlessly, imprisoned, beaten or killed. Hitler always believed that not only was the party's propaganda paramount in the struggle for control of opinion but also that it must be accompanied by the suppression of all competing opinions. In the early 1920s, the SA (largely recruited and trained by Rohm and made up of ex-soldiers and ex-Freikorps members) was the weapon Hitler used to complement his propaganda.

By late July 1921, Hitler had become president of the Nazi party. He retained the basic programme of the party – based on pan-German nationalism, anti-Bolshevism, anti-Semitism and total opposition to the post-war treaties. While you could not doubt the depth of his anti-Semitism and nationalism, Hitler viewed ideology as a tool to gain power rather than as an end in itself, though anti-Semitism was to be part of the path to power and a major plank of Nazi policy once in power. As Bullock argues, for Hitler, 'all programmes were means to an end' and he wanted the support of the lower middle classes and working class, not because of sympathy for them but 'their grievances and discontents were the raw stuff of politics, a means, but never an end' (Bullock, 1962, p. 75).

Success in fundraising meant that by February 1923, *Volkischer Beobachter* was published daily – with Hitler contributing a stream of articles. By then, the German Republic was at the point of crisis – the French had occupied the Ruhr over non-payment of reparations, the Stresemann government in Berlin had given up its attempts at passive resistance to the French occupation and was proposing the resumption of reparation payments. As Shirer observed, the end of resistance and the reparations plans 'touched off an outburst of anger and hysteria among the German nationalists' (Shirer, 1960, p. 89). The government called a state of emergency, giving massive powers to the Ministry of Defence and the army. Bavaria called its own state of emergency and put power in the hands of State Commissioner Gustav von Kahr.

Encouraged by the national socialists, the Bavarian state government tried to resist the federal government's attempts to impose its directives. A complex struggle developed within Bavaria over the state's ability to resist Berlin and the role of the national socialists. They at times supported von Kahr and at others threatened to destabilize or even overthrow the government. The struggle has been described in detail by Bullock and Kershaw (Bullock, 1962, chapter 2; Kershaw, 2001a, chapters 5, 6 and 7). Hitler sought to influence the Bavarian government through cajoling and threats to follow policies supported by the Nazi Party. The state government, like the army in the early 1930s, thought it could use Hitler and his party and control them. At a rally in Nuremberg at the beginning of September 1923, he spoke alongside the hero of World War I and a leading nationalist, General Ludendorff – an important figure as he had strong support in the army and was intransigently opposed to the Berlin government. As a figurehead but with no party of his own, he was useful to Hitler as one who would bring prestige to the Nazis if he was seen to support the same policies as them.

For Hitler, the growing crisis of the German government and the strains between Berlin and Bavaria seemed to him to bring him a step closer to power. Kahr realized this and was increasingly concerned that he would attempt a coup to replace the Bavarian government (Kershaw, 2001a, p. 205). Hitler begged Kahr to march on Berlin (Bullock, 1962, p. 104; Kershaw, 2001a, pp. 203–7; Shirer, 1960, p. 92). Hitler, Rohm and their allies prepared ultra-nationalist paramilitaries to support any march or, if nothing happened, to seize the initiative. The latter plan became the more likely as the Bavarian government hesitated. At a meeting in a Munich beer hall on the night of 8 November 1923 addressed by Kahr, Goering and a squad of stormtroopers burst in and seized control. Hitler fired a shot in the air and proclaimed that revolution had begun. He announced that a new government would be formed in Bavaria and one in Berlin under Hitler and Ludendorff as army commander (Kershaw, 2001a, p. 207). Ludendorff was highly displeased at having been hijacked by the Nazis but did not denounce them. But when Hitler left the beer hall to help the stormtroopers win over troops at the army engineers' barracks, the Bavarian state officials escaped and reported to German state radio that the putsch had failed. Hitler had failed to ensure that the Bavarian leadership was kept under lock and key. The Bavarian government now used loyal Bavarian regiments to put down the putsch – 16 Nazis were killed. Rohm and Hitler were arrested.

The trial of the coup leaders started in Munich on 26 February 1924. Hitler used it assiduously to promote his ideology and attack the government, gaining nationwide publicity, as the trial was reported by all the main national newspapers. Ludendorff and Rohm were among the accused alongside Hitler, but from the beginning, he dominated the courtroom – there was no attempt to stop him speaking or interrogating witnesses. His opening statement lasted four hours (Shirer, 1960, p. 103). He proclaimed that, 'I alone bear responsibility. But am not a criminal because of that. If today I stand here as a revolutionary, it is as a revolutionary against revolution. There is no such thing as high treason against the traitors of 1918' (Shirer, 1960, pp. 103–4). Through daily coverage of the trial in the newspapers, Hitler became identified with resistance to the government and portrayed himself as one prepared to take responsibility and suffer for his actions on behalf of Germany. His court performances and then the publication of *Mein Kampf*, written in Landsberg prison, achieved what the coup had failed to achieve – to make him a national political figure with a growing reputation. In his final speech from the dock, he made little pretence about his ultimate political ambitions:

> Believe me, I do not regard the acquisition of a minister's portfolio as a thing worth striving for. I do not hold it worthy of a great man to endeavour to go down in history just by becoming a minister [...] I wanted to become the destroyer of Marxism.

I am going to achieve this task [...] The man who is born to be a dictator is not compelled; he wills it. He is not driven forward, but drives himself. There is nothing immodest about this [...] the man who feels called upon to govern a people has no right to say: If you want me or summon me, I will cooperate. No, it is his duty to step forward.

(cited by Bullock, 1952, p. 117)

The trial ended with Hitler's imprisonment for five years – of which he served under nine months. The Nazi Party had been dissolved by the government on 9 November 1923 because of the coup attempt. Hitler did not call on his allies to form a new party – clearly not wanting one formed while he couldn't actively lead it.

Hitler's time in prison didn't damage his long-term political career despite the dislocation and fragmentation of the national socialists, which persisted for some years after his release. Imprisonment gave him the time to marshal his political thoughts and publish them as *Mein Kampf*. This work set out his approach to party organization, propaganda, to the failures of those who 'sold' Germany at Versailles and, in particular, his racial theories about the Germans and the evil threat posed by the intertwined threats of the Jews and Marxism to Germany's future greatness. The book was to sell well but not spectacularly between 1925 and 1933; but sales rocketed after 1933, when Hitler became Chancellor.

Mein Kampf expanded on views that Hitler had expounded in speeches and his long court statements. A fierce German nationalism was to the fore, which promised to restore Germany to the front rank of powerful nations. The key to this resurgence would be the uniting of all Germans – many of whom lived outside Germany's borders in Poland, Austria and Czechoslovakia. Hitler also posited a new type of state that eschewed traditional ideas of liberal democracy, eliminated all traces of Marxism and was based on German racial purity. A strong strain of anti-Semitism had been present in manifestations of Hitler's ideology up to this time, but he now developed it further alongside the primacy of German/Aryan racial purity. The blame for the defeat in the world war was placed on the Jews and their Marxist allies, 'with their unqualified capacity for falsehood [...] From time immemorial, however, the Jews have known better than any others how falsehoods and calumny can be exploited. Is not their very existence founded on one great lie, namely, that they are a religious community, whereas in reality they are a race?' (Hitler, 1988, p. 213). He goes on to attack Jews for poisoning German blood while preserving the male bloodlines of his 'racial stock'. He says that when Christians take Jews as wives, the union produces 'mongrels' (Hitler, 1988, p. 286).

Parliamentary democracy is attacked by Hitler as the embodiment of Jewish influence in politics. The Jewish 'control' of the press is lambasted as the way that Jews undermine Germany while protecting their own business and racial interests. Through the press, powerful Jews attack 'all men of character who refuse to fall into line with the Jewish effort to obtain control over the State or who appear dangerous to Jews merely because of their superior intelligence'. In the same passage, Hitler goes on to dwell on the demonic character, as he depicts it, of the Jews:

> Since the Jew is not the object of aggression but the aggressor himself, he considers as his enemies not only those who attack him but also those who may be capable of resisting him. The means which he employs to break people of this kind, who may show themselves decent and upright, are not the open means generally used in honourable conflict, but falsehood and calumny.

> He will stop at nothing. His utterly low-down conduct is so appalling that one really cannot be surprised if in the imagination of our people the Jew is pictured as the incarnation of Satan and the symbol of evil.
>
> (Hitler, 1988, pp. 294–5)

Hitler was to use these extreme and mythical images of the Jews to appeal to underlying elements of anti-Semitism among sections of German society. These sentiments were particularly strong among the lower-middle and working classes, some of whom saw themselves as disadvantaged by the emancipation of the Jews in the 19th century and the alleged strength of the Jews in business and retail. This was the very audience – the mass of the lower-middle and working classes – that Hitler's nationalist, racist ideology appealed to. As Kettenacker puts it, 'Hitler was basically the mouthpiece of the lower middle class' and for Hitler and those on whose behalf he claimed to speak 'the Jew typified everything the war veteran had learned to loathe, the profiteering bourgeois capitalist who made a fortune from the war, as well as the left-wing journalist' (Kettenacker, 1983, pp. 11 and 14). Hitler built up a simple, consistent picture of Germany's ills and laid them all at the door of the Jews.

The existing, underlying strain of anti-Semitism or at least suspicion of the Jews in German nationalism was something that Hitler and the Nazis (especially Streicher, Rosenberg, Ley, Goering, Himmler and later Goebbels) could exploit and repeat over and over again. Without accepting every aspect of Goldhagen's depiction of Germans as *Hitler's Willing Executioners*, he has a strong argument when he points to 'the corpus of German anti-Semitic literature in the 19th and 20th centuries – with its wild and hallucinatory accounts of the nature of Jews, their virtually limitless power, and their responsibility for nearly every harm that has fallen the world' (Goldhagen, 1996, p. 28). As both Kershaw and Goldhagen point out, the anti-Jewish discourse was so prevalent that once Nazi propaganda had pushed it to the fore, 'to be an anti-Semite in Hitler's Germany was so commonplace as to go practically unnoticed' (Goldhagen, 1996, p. 32; Kershaw, 1983, p. 370).

Nazi propaganda developed a circular argument by which the Jews were behind every misfortune – Jews could be attacked as the hidden menace, the evil puppeteers pulling the strings or wires of national or international opponents of Nazism and every example of opposition to or criticism of the Nazis or any setback could be lamented and then found to be the work of the Jews. 'Hitler's propaganda was one of pure hatred which was all the more effective because it was directed not against anonymous forces but against the Jew as the personally responsible and recognisable perpetrator' and this message, couched in strong and direct language, which was common in Bavaria, was 'most favourably received by the half-educated yet self-righteous lower middle class, such as artisans, shopkeepers, low grade employees and civil servants' (Kettenacker, 1983, pp. 14–5). Kershaw takes a similar view, arguing that: 'The Jew was clearly the number one hate target for Nazi propaganda [...] propaganda could depend upon the pre-existence of extensive latent anti-Jewish feeling for its campaigns [...] Prejudice against Jews derived in no small measure from ignorance' as Jews did not constitute a significant part of the population and many Germans had little, if any, contact with them. Germans suffering privation and feeling humiliated after the war needed a scapegoat and Jews could serve that purpose. But for most Germans, "the Jew" was seldom equated with a real, living person'. But achieving this took time and Nazi propaganda wasn't always successful, which was perhaps one reason despite the acceptability of anti-Semitism and the prevalence of Nazi propaganda, that propaganda did not lead to a hugely successful response when the Nazis called boycotts of Jewish businesses, and germans weren't convinced that racial purity was more important than price (Kershaw, 1983, pp. 190–1).

The image of the 'Jew' was a potent one in Nazi discourse and Goldhagen has a point when he contends that:

> identifying Jews with evil, defining them as violators of the sacred and as being opposed to the fundamental good towards which people ought to strive, demonizes them [...] Much that is good becomes defined in opposition to Jews and, in turn, comes to depend upon maintaining this conception of Jews [...] It becomes difficult for them [anti-Semites] to see the Jews' actions, even their existence, other than as desecration and defilement.
>
> (Goldhagen, 1996, p. 38)

This was the aim of the consistent, simple and constantly repeated anti-Semitism of the Nazis. Hitler posited the image of a resurgent, powerful Germany with the sacred duty of advancing German interests and protecting European civilization against that of evil, scheming international Jewry – 'the Jews were the cement for this myth, first in the political battle within Germany and then on the international plane' (Herf, 2006, p. 2).

Hitler was intent on building German anti-Semitism into active hatred and to go beyond just demonization of the Jews to bring about their elimination from German national life. He wrote that:

Hatred is more lasting than mere aversion. And the driving force which has brought the most tremendous revolutions on this earth has never been a body of scientific teaching which has gained power over the masses, but always a devotion which has inspired them, and often a kind of hysteria which has urged them to action. Whoever wishes to win over the sole of the masses must know the key that will open the door to their hearts [...]

(Hitler, 1988, p. 307)

Following the failure of the putsch, Hitler realised that to fight his enemy and to seize power he needed the support of the army – he had not won it and they had opposed his attempt to seize power. He needed to win them over and to do so he would have to develop at least a veneer of legality and not be seen to be antagonistic towards the military establishment (Kershaw, 2001a, p. 218). He would also need to curb the paramilitary side of the movement and Rohm's power, if he was to become the leader and unifier of Bavaria's multiplicity of nationalist paramilitary groups.

From prison to power

Following his release on parole from Landsberg on 20 December 1924, Hitler set about rebuilding the party and establishing a national, rather than Bavarian, platform for his political ambitions. In prison he had not just sharpened his anti-Jewish and anti-Bolshevik opinions, his ideas now also incorporated a belief that Germany could not cooperate with communist Russia – his Russia policy combined a conviction that sooner or later, 'Jewish-Bolshevism' would seek to overrun Germany with an expansionist philosophy that saw the needed living-space for Germans in the east.

The Nazi movement and the Volkischer parties were in disarray and weak in early 1925. Hitler began to mend fences with the more conventional and influential right-wing groups in Bavaria, such as the Bavarian People's Party. He needed some form of reconciliation with the Bavarian establishment in order to have the suspension of the Nazi Party lifted and to start publishing *Volkischer Beobachter* again. On 26 February, *Volkischer Beobachter* reappeared with an editorial from Hitler on the party's new beginning and new tasks. The next day he held a meeting in the Burgerbraukeller, scene of the putsch, and used it to reclaim his leadership of the national socialist movement and to emphasize that the fight against the Jewish-Marxist alliance continued. His performance showed that he had lost none of his powers of whipping up an audience, and immediately afterwards he was banned from public speaking in Bavaria and soon after in several other German states. The Bavarian ban was only lifted in May 1927 – this was a real obstacle for a leader so dependent on his voice and presence.

Although the party now began to have a greater geographical spread, improvements in the economy and the weakening of the party in 1924 meant that the period up to the depression in 1929 were 'lean years for Adolf Hitler and the Nazi movement' (Shirer, 1960, p. 149). Hitler's stock among the lower-middle classes fell as their economic lot improved and their grievances diminished. His speaking ban also held him back, while party organizer Gregor Strasser, on whom there was no ban and who had the advantage of being an elected member of the Reichstag, took on an ever more important role along with his brother Otto, who edited his brother's newspaper, *Berliner Arbeitszeitung*. Their anti-capitalism and desire to nationalize industry while breaking up large country estates was not to Hitler's liking, as he was still trying to woo big business and landowners (Bullock, 1952, p. 136). The Strassers brought Josef Goebbels into the party, who became Gregor Strasser's secretary and was manager of the party's Rheinland-Nord Gau (district). At first close to the Strassers, he soon became 'an unconditional follower of Hitler' (Bullock, 1962, p. 23). From early on, Goebbels, like Hitler, found that his power and appeal lay in addressing meetings and winning over the audience with his rhetoric and appeals to emotion and instinct.

The first few years after his release from prison saw Hitler fighting and defeating the Strassers for control of the party and direction of its ideology. He then took steps to cement his own power, by ensuring the primacy of the Munich party leadership over the national movement. Goebbels rapidly gained influence within the party and with Hitler, soon becoming the leading propaganda strategist. In 1927, he established his own weekly newspaper, *Der Angriff (The Attack)*, one of whose roles was to counter the press owned by Gregor and Otto Strasser and to develop his own pro-Hitler propaganda stream. While Nazi propaganda was concentrated in the printed media and through speeches at rallies and public meetings, Goebbels was increasingly aware of the power that radio could have for a movement that owned or controlled stations. He wrote in his diary on 14 December 1925, 'Radio! Radio! Radio in the house! The German with his radio will forget about his occupation and his fatherland! Radio! The modern instrument to create philistines! Everything at home! The philistine's ideal!'(Goebbels, 1962, p. 54). Like Hitler, Goebbels had a low opinion of the audiences to which he spoke. For him, it mattered little if the audience were philistines as long as he could win them over, influence them and get them to accept and act on what he said. This made radio a tool that he hankered to control and use. He believed that if radio could so influence people, it could be used as the primary tool for Nazi propaganda to be transmitted into every home, saturating the population with the Nazi message.

In May 1927, Bavaria lifted the ban on Hitler speaking in public – Prussia followed suit in September 1928. This enabled Hitler to use his main weapon again – his voice – and to utilize to good effect the theatrical/militaristic rallies with torchlight march-pasts by massed ranks of stormtroopers. At the first 'Party day' in Nuremberg in August 1927, 30,000 SA paraded in front of Nazi leaders – this indicated that despite low national support, the 'activist core of mainly dedicated fanatics was relatively large' (Kershaw, 2001a, p. 259). Party membership rose steadily, too, from 27,000 in 1925 to 178,000 in 1929 (Bullock, 1962, p. 141). The significant size of the SA and party membership ensured income from party dues but also gave Hitler funds and manpower to campaign, put on shows of strength and intimidate opponents through weight of numbers and the appearance of discipline.

In November 1928, Goebbels was made party propaganda head as part of Hitler's determination to make this the spearhead of the party. This followed his elevation to Party Gauleiter for Berlin and his election to the Reichstag as one of the party's 12 members in May 1928 – the election result was a severe disappointment for Hitler. Having control of the Berlin section of the party, now as head of propaganda and as publisher and editor of *Der Angriff*, Goebbels was able to given free reign to his skills in propagandizing. He published endless attacks on Jews, including SA songs with lines like, 'Only when the Jews are bleeding, only then shall we be free' (cited by Reuth, 1993, p. 102).

The Nazi Party was at this time struggling to break into the front ranks of right-wing parties in Germany and to establish, SA violence notwithstanding, a greater air of respectability. The party received a huge boost following the Wall Street Crash in November 1929. The recovery of the mid-1920s became the deep depression of 1929 and the early 1930s, with unemployment soaring – it reached 3.39 million in January 1930. This again created fertile ground for Nazi propaganda and recruitment. Hitler was able to give public speeches once more and used the growing party and SA membership to ensure that meetings were packed with a core of fanatical supporters to build up the atmosphere to an emotional pitch that became infectious. He would never arrive at a venue until it was full – his entry delayed to increase anticipation. When he spoke, there was:

> A pause at the beginning to allow the tension to mount; a low-key, even hesitant, start; undulations and variations of dictions, not melodious certainly, but vivid and highly expressive; almost staccato bursts of sentences, followed by well-timed *rallentando* to expose the emphasis of a critical point; theatrical use of the hands as the speech rose in crescendo; sarcastic wit aimed at opponents; all were devices carefully nurtured to maximize effect.
>
> (Kershaw, 2001a, p. 280)

Hitler was able to rouse crowds to the point of hysteria and his meetings and rallies helped build support and get across simple, oft-repeated messages whether about Versailles, reparations or the Jewish-Bolshevik conspiracy. Once in power, speeches at rallies, in the Reichstag or at other meetings were broadcast live or recorded and repeated frequently on national and local radio. What Hitler proved useless at, though, was recording speeches or talks in the studio. Without the audience and the build-up, he lacked impact. He also wrote regular pieces for *Volkischer Beobachter*, again sticking to a few basic themes. Between his release from prison and 1927, anti-Semitism was very much to the fore – in February 1927, he wrote in the paper that 'The Jew remains the world enemy, and his weapon, Marxism, a plague on mankind' (cited by Kershaw, 2001a, p. 288). As with much of Hitler's ideology, there was no clear set of policies or outcomes identified in his anti-Semitic tirades. At this stage, there was no direct talk of eliminating Jews from German national life, let alone extermination – his rants were about the evil of the Jews, their threat to Germany and Europe. After 1927 and into the depression, anti-Semitism lost its prominence and anti-Bolshevism, reuniting Germans and finding living-space for Germans came more to the fore along with the need to expunge the war guilt admission, end reparations and reject the conditions imposed on Germany at Versailles – limits on the armed forces, demilitarization of the Rhineland and the loss of the Saar.

The depression period saw open street warfare between the Nazis and the communists against the backdrop of economic stagnation, the failures of businesses and mass unemployment. Skilled propagandists like Hitler and Goebbels had little trouble in laying this all at the door of the politicians who had signed at Versailles and at the door of the international Jewish-Bolshevik-capitalist conspiracy. To many Germans, the simplistic Nazi answer of doing away with the post-war republic, with Versailles and breaking the power of Jews, Bolsheviks and bankers seemed an easy and convenient answer to their problems. It appealed to those losing their small businesses, struggling to survive on earnings subject to constant devaluation or those forced into unemployment.

While the Nazis engaged in street fighting and broke up opponents' meetings, the thrust of the party was now more political and aimed at getting mass support and votes while not alienating the business or military elite. To get those votes, as Shirer points out from the basis of his experience as an American news correspondent in Europe between 1926 and 1941 (much of that in Berlin), 'Hitler only had to take advantage of the times, which once more, as the Thirties began, saw the German people plunged into despair; to obtain the support of those in power he had to convince them that only he could rescue Germany from its disastrous predicament' (Shirer, 1960, p. 171). Nazi propaganda – now under the combined direction of Hitler and Goebbels – concentrated on anti-socialist and anti-Marxist rhetoric. German social democracy and communism were the chief enemies and the Nazis emphasized images of a Germany wrecked by Marxism with only the Nazis standing between Germany and a communist-led descent into total disaster. These themes were used to gain the support of the masses but also to convince industrialists and the army high command that the Nazis were allies in the fight against Marxism.

With Reichstag elections on the cards in September 1930, Goebbels produced a campaign entitled *Freedom and Bread* that culminated in a huge rally at the Berlin Sportpalast on 10 September (four days before the election). Hitler spoke for an hour and gave what he termed his manifesto to the German People, in which he said the slogan for election day must be 'Strike at those who have bankrupted our old parties! Destroy those who would undermine our national unity! Away with those responsible for our degeneration!' (cited by Reuth, 1993, p. 120). Two days after the Berlin meeting, Hitler spoke at a rally in Breslau and the party set up loudspeakers outside the meeting hall so that those who could not get in could still hear Hitler – a forerunner of the nationwide broadcasting of Nazi leaders' speeches as a mainstay of radio propaganda. This well-organized hard-hitting and simply expounded campaign was increasingly popular and was backed up by the use of the SA to harass opponents and break up their meetings and by a dynamic organization that sent agitators to every corner of the country. Speeches concentrated on the state of Germany, the crimes of those in government, the evils of the social democratic/socialist parties of the Weimar Republic, and on *lebensraum*; the anti-Semitism of the early and mid-1920s was largely shelved.

The elections were a huge success for the party – it gained 107 seats nationally and increased its percentage of the vote to 18.3 per cent, becoming the second largest party in the Reichstag. It increased its vote in Berlin tenfold to 395,000, but was only the third largest party in the capital after the Communists and Social Democrats. The Communists had increased their share of the vote and most of the Nazi gains came at the expense of parties in the centre and on the right. Party membership continued to grow; by January 1931, the SA movement (including the SS) numbered around 100,000 – within a year, it trebled.

The election success meant that Hitler and the Nazis were front page news across Germany and even began to be reported internationally – the British reactionary and right-wing *Daily Mail*, welcoming the rise of national socialism as a defence against Bolshevism and Soviet Russia (*Daily Mail*, 24 September 1930) – something picked up on as proof of Nazi legitimacy by *Volkischer Beobachter*. Despite the size of the Nazi group in the Reichstag, Chancellor Heinrich Bruning refused to offer them a place in his coalition government. Hitler continued to court major industrialists – there was a notable success when steel magnate Fritz Thyssen joined the party in December 1931 and there were growing indications that large numbers of the German officer corps had Nazi sympathies (Bullock, 1952, pp. 175 and 179).

With increasing membership, resources and organizational expertise, the Nazis could stage huge and intimidating public rallies. In Braunschweig, in October 1931, Hitler took the salute from 104,000 SA and SS members at a huge paramilitary rally. This combination of growing voter support and the potential for extra-parliamentary activity put the Nazis in pole position as the economy continued to deteriorate and the shifting coalition governments kept coming apart at the seams. The party put particular stress on campaigning in Berlin and Prussia – Goebbels wrote in *Der Angriff* that whoever was in control in Prussia would control Germany. He set about to beat the communists in Berlin to get the working-class vote. During a metalworkers' strike, he tried to outdo the communists in attacking capitalism but blamed the evils of capitalism on Jewish 'stock-exchange hyenas' (Reuth, 1993, p. 122).

The German political crisis began to come to a head when the Reichstag was faced with a vote to extend the term in office of President Paul von Hindenburg. The main parties could not agree on a candidate if an election was to be held for president and Bruning wanted to extend the presidential term. Hitler refused and then Goebbels announced Hitler's candidacy for the post at a Sportspalast rally. Hitler's challenge to the old but revered general led to a massive Nazi propaganda campaign. During a 12 city tour to promote his candidacy, *Volkischer Beobachter* claimed he had spoken to a total of half a million voters. The result was a disappointment for the Nazis – Hitler came second with 30 per cent, ahead of communist candidate Thalmann with 17 per cent but behind Hindenburg with 49 per cent. This result necessitated a second round. The Nazis put even more effort into this, with Hitler flying around Germany to give 20 major speeches to over a million voters (Kershaw, 2001a, p. 363). Hitler increased his share to almost 37 per cent but Hindenburg won an outright victory.

German politics were in stalemate and the Nazis were not powerful enough to break it. To a great extent it was broken for them by sympathizers in the military and by the elevation to national importance of General Kurt von Schleicher, the head of the Reichswehr Ministerial Office – effectively the political voice of the army. Hitler was negotiating with von Schleicher, who wanted to topple Bruning and develop a military-style authoritarian government with army and Nazi support. Bruning was forced to resign on 30 May 1932. He was replaced as Chancellor by Franz von Papen. Elections were set for 31 July. The SA was unbanned by the new government.

The political tension, legalization of the SA and the vehemence of the conflict between the Nazis and Communists led to an extremely violent election campaign with over 100 people killed during June and July. The Nazi campaign particularly aimed at destroying what remained of centrist and right-wing parties attracting middle and lower-middle class voters. Mass rallies and parades were again the order of the day, but films and gramophone recordings of an 'appeal to the nation' by Hitler were also distributed

(Kershaw, 2001a, p. 369). During the campaign, Goebbels had been permitted to broadcast on the radio – following a dispute with the Ministry of Information, which said that his planned speech 'went beyond the bounds of what is usual and permissible on the radio' (cited by Reuth, 1993, p. 150).

The elections made the Nazis the largest party in the Reichstag with 230 seats, 37.4 per cent of the vote and a total national vote of over 13.7 million – with their nearest rivals the Social Democrats receiving just 8 million (Bullock, 1962, p. 217; Kershaw, 2001a, p. 369). Writing in his diary on 1 August, Goebbels lamented that 'so we can't get an absolute majority this way. All right: take the other path'; the next day, he wrote of the need to get power to 'exterminate Marxism [...] Something must happen. The time for opposition is over' (Kershaw, 2001a, p. 370; Reuth, 1993, p. 151). Hitler started negotiations with von Schleicher to find a path to power with military support – von Schleicher and military leaders were prepared to consider this, believing that even if he was appointed Chancellor, Hitler would be under their control. Hitler thought he had a deal that would see him appointed Chancellor, but it was vetoed by President Hindenburg. Further political crises followed and Hitler was under pressure from Rohm and the SA to end his concentration on elections and conventional politics. Hitler resisted and retained control of the party, further marginalizing the Strassers and Rohm. The crisis necessitated new elections in November.

In many ways, the elections were a political disaster for the Nazis. There was a low turnout and the party lost 2 million votes and 34 seats – falling to 196 in the Reichstag, with its percentage of the vote going down from 37.4 to 33. More political manoeuvring followed in which Hitler was unable to attain the post of Chancellor on his own terms and von Schleicher was appointed. Hitler now turned to attacking the weak von Schleicher government. He issued a party memorandum demanding total loyalty and total adherence to the aim of mobilizing the nation to achieve a National Socialist victory. Above all, he demanded an all-out propaganda fight to inculcate the ideas of the Nazis in all Germans.

The von Schleicher government was doomed from the start and political negotiations involving Hitler, Hindenburg, von Papen and other right-wing leaders continued. After much haggling, it was agreed that Hitler would be chancellor, von Papen vice-chancellor and Reich commissioner for Prussia, the foreign, finance and posts ministers from the Schleicher cabinet were retained in post, the Nazi Frick became interior minister and Goering became deputy in the Prussian Interior Ministry, effectively giving him control over the police in Prussia. Goebbels, though not yet named as propaganda minister, seized the opportunity and, with the help of new Interior Minister Frick, bullied German national radio and the local *lender* radio stations into carrying the events of the day on 30 January when the new cabinet and Hitler as Chancellor were presented to the president, followed by a Nazi torchlight procession through Berlin. Goering and Goebbels gave speeches and Goebbels was able to have interviews broadcast with party members pretending to be ordinary citizens praising Hitler and the new start for Germany (Reuth, 1993, p. 164).

Propaganda in power

Hitler was able, despite his lack of a majority and the suspicions of his partners in government, to move swiftly during his first six months in office to destroy civil liberties, establish a propaganda ministry that would control the press, culture, art and all key areas of ideas and entertainment, sideline the Reichstag, ban trades unions and suppress political parties (Kershaw, 2001a, p. 435). Some of these actions met with the approval of many Germans but importantly of the business leaders and army high command, who were viscerally opposed to socialism and communism and welcomed the suppression of parties of the left. Many ordinary Germans were sick of the inadequacies of politicians and seemed willing to accept the destruction of a failed republican democracy and give all power to someone proclaiming his right to rule from a sense of destiny and mission.

Hitler's first substantive move was to get Hindenburg to dissolve the Reichstag, with elections set for 5 March 1933. This was to be an election to confirm the new government and enable it to pass an enabling act that would permit it to rule without needing the consent of the Reichstag. Immediately, a decree came into force restricting press freedom and other measures to stop the Communists organizing to fight the Nazis. The Nazis could now dominate the campaign – using their own newspapers and with almost unfettered access to the radio. Goebbels used this access to the full and, in his own writings, emphasizes how he was able to use the national radio network in February and March 1933 to get Hitler's and his own voice regularly on air. He says that with radio at his disposal,

> we shall achieve a masterpiece of propaganda [...] we decide that [during the campaign] the Leader is to speak in all towns having their own broadcasting station. We transmit the broadcast to the entire people and give listeners a clear idea of all that occurs at our meetings [...] I shall try to convey the magical atmosphere of our huge demonstrations.
>
> (Goebbels, 1940, p. 211)

The Nazi propaganda head, despite having no formal powers in this regard, ensured that 'hardly an evening passed without an election speech on every station, and those speeches took up the entire evening's programming. Hitler spoke only in cities with radio stations' (Reuth, 1993, p. 166). As he was to do for much of the next 12 years, Goebbels would set the scene for Hitler's broadcast rally speeches, 'with a narrative full of escalating superlatives, describing the feverish tension in the crowd, the vastness of the gathering, the loss of individual isolation in the mass of the people' (ibid.).

The methods used by Goebbels and Hitler were a classic approach to make the individual part of the mass. As Ellul identified:

> Any modern propaganda will, first of all, address itself at one and the same time to the individual and to the masses. It cannot separate the two elements [...] the individual never is considered as an individual, but always in terms of what he has common with others, such as his motivation, his feelings, or his myths. He is reduced to an average; and, except for a small percentage, action based on averages is effectual.
>
> (Ellul, 1973, pp. 6–7)

Nazi propaganda was aimed at the lowest common denominator and attempted to instil the same fears, emotions and myths in the mass of Germans – the individual German always had to be made to see him or herself just part of the mass of Germans. Goebbels's ability to run the propaganda campaign was enhanced by a donation of one million marks from a group of leading industrialists.

With the police increasingly under Nazi control, the powers of the state were in hand for the next phase of repression, the pretext for which was the burning down of the Reichstag building on the night of 27 February. Conveniently, a Dutch man with alleged Communist connections, Marinus van der Lubbe, was found wandering near the building and confessed to setting fire to the building. Whether or not he really set fire to the building, it was used as a pretext by the Nazis to convince von Papen and Hindenburg that this was the first act in a Communist uprising. Frick, as interior minister, now drew up the emergency decree 'For the Protection of People and State', which took away the civil liberties of the Weimar constitution in one act – freedom of speech and association, freedom of the press, and the privacy of posts and telecommunications (Bullock, 1962, p. 263; Kershaw, 2001a, p. 459). Hindenburg signed the decree into law on 28 February.

'Armed with these all-embracing powers, Hitler and Goering were in a position to take any action they pleased against their opponents' (Bullock, 1962, pp. 263–4). The powers were immediately in use with Goering's police, the SA and SS detaining, beating, torturing and killing Communists, Social Democrats, trades unionists and left-wing intellectuals. By mid-April, in Prussia 25,000 leftists had been taken into what was termed 'protective custody' (Kershaw, 2001a, p. 460). Many Germans, worried by the economy and political instability and taken in by the Nazis' anti-socialist propaganda and accusations over the Reichstag fire, were willing to accept or even support the measures and the persecution of the left.

This all led up to the elections on 5 March – with Hitler now telling Germans that he and Hindenburg were standing hand-in-hand to save Germany. But the results were far from overwhelming and, while the Nazis increased their share of the vote – 17,277,230 votes out of 39.3 million,

43.9 per cent – they still were well short of a majority. They had 288 of 647 Reichstag seats. Their allies in the right-wing nationalist parties received 8 per cent, giving a combined (nearly) 52 per cent. But the Socialists and Communists had a combined total of just over 30 per cent. Needless to say, Goebbels in his diary proclaimed it a 'glorious triumph' (Bullock, 1962, p. 265; Kershaw, 2001a, p. 461). But it was hardly a triumph in the propaganda sense, given the banning of most left-wing papers after the Reichstag fire, Nazi access to radio and the ability to use it to broadcast all of Hitler's election rallies and speeches – it showed the limits of propaganda in getting more than acquiescence or acceptance.

The Nazis rapidly drew all the reins of power into their hands – particularly those of state violence and repression, massively supplemented by the SA, SS and SD (the Nazi security police). Nazi stormtroopers carried out waves of attacks against leftists and Jewish targets with impunity – despite complaints from Hindenburg directly to Hitler. Alongside the repressive powers, the Nazis now had full control of state propaganda through the national and *lender* radio network. On 13 March, Goebbels was appointed a minister and the next day, Hindenburg swore him in as Reich Minister for Popular Enlightenment and Propaganda – giving him sweeping powers over all aspects of the media, arts, culture, entertainment and aspects of education. Control over radio, film, theatre and the press were removed from the Interior Ministry and handed over to Goebbels. The stage was set for the two-pronged Nazi domination strategy of propaganda and naked physical power to destroy opponents and threaten waverers.

Two days after becoming a minister, Goebbels said that his aim was to get the German people 'to think uniformly, react uniformly, and to place themselves body and soul at the disposal of the government' (cited by Reuth, 1993, p. 172). Addressing press representatives on 15 March, he said:

> I see the establishment of this new Ministry of Popular Enlightenment and Propaganda as a revolutionary act of government because the new government has no intention of abandoning people to their own devices and locking them up in an airless room [...] The task of the press cannot be merely to inform, rather the press has above and beyond that the much greater task of instructing [...] It is not enough to reconcile people more or less to our regimen, to move them towards a position of neutrality toward us, we want rather to work on people until they are addicted to us, until they realise, in the ideological sense as well, that what is happening now in Germany not only must be accepted, but can be accepted.
>
> (cited by Taylor, 1983, pp. 35–6)

Germans were to get a constant, repetitive diet of propaganda in the press, on the radio and in film, theatre and arts, to ram home the Nazi message. Goebbels wanted acceptance but also an addiction so that people accepted and acted upon what they were told. They would be told what was what and not given the opportunity to make up their own minds or read/hear other opinions or versions of events.

The Reichstag opened on 23 March, with the Enabling Law at the top of the agenda – this would give the government the power for four years to enact laws without needing approval from the Reichstag, the right to depart from the constitution and to conclude treaties with foreign states. Laws could be drafted by the Chancellor and come into effect on the day after their publication. The hall in which the parliament met was hung with swastika flags and members had to walk into the hall through a guard of black-shirted SS members. Hitler promised the Reichstag that the government would only use the powers,

> in so far as they are essential for carrying out vitally necessary measures [...] The Government offers to the parties of the Reichstag the opportunity for friendly cooperation. But it is equally prepared to go ahead in the face of their refusal and of the hostilities which will result from that refusal. It is for you, gentlemen of the Reichstag, to decide between war and peace.
>
> (cited by Bullock, 1952, p. 269)

When the Social Democrat leader spoke against, Hitler told him that the star of Germany was in the ascendant, 'yours is about to disappear, your death-knell has sounded' (Bullock, 1952, p. 270). With several of his party Reichstag members already in detention (along with 81 Communist deputies), he could have little doubt about Hitler's seriousness. The other parties wilted in the face of the onslaught and the bill was passed by 441 to 94 votes – giving Hitler powers that would even enable him to bypass the president. Practically every area of public life and every political or social institution was now brought under Nazi control under what was called the *Gleischchaltung* or coordination.

The entrenchment of Nazi power was nowhere faster than in the Ministry of Popular Enlightenment and Propaganda. In his speech to representatives of the press on 15 March, Goebbels said that the ministry had the role of being the 'living contact between the national Government as the expression of the popular will and the people itself [...] I see the first task of this new ministry as establishing a coordination between the Government and the whole people' (Goebbels, 1993a, p. 174). He went on to elaborate his positive view of the role of propaganda and the role of the propagandist:

> the propagandist must not just know the soul of the people in general but must also understand the secret swings of the popular soul from one side to another. The propagandist must understand how to speak not only to the people in their totality but also to individual sections of the

population: to the worker, the peasant, the middle class [...] The propagandist must always be in a position to speak to people in the language that they understand.

(Goebbels, 1993a, p. 175)

He stressed that this was not a task to be assessed by aesthetes but on results – propaganda was a means to an end and not an end in itself. The press was to be utilized by the Ministry and the party 'to place the nation firmly behind the idea of the National Revolution' (ibid.). While criticism would be allowed, he said, 'you should not lose sight of the Government's interest' (Goebbels, 1993a, p. 179).

When he met the press for the first time as minister, he also set out the absolute rule – that all propaganda must be centralized, it must instruct and not just inform, and that it must speak with one voice. This last aim, though was never quite to be achieved. Hitler's system of rule had overlapping areas of responsibility and control between party and state bodies, between the Chancellery and other ministries, thereby blurring clear lines of command – there was to be constant conflict between Goebbels and Hitler's press chief for the party, Otto Dietrich, with Max Amman as head of the Reich Press Chamber also having a role in the direction of newspapers and periodicals (Kallis, 2008, pp. 8 and 27). Goebbels was never entirely satisfied with newspaper output and frequently criticized it as insipid or unfocused. He saw it as a less valuable and reliable instrument than radio.

When it came to instituting control, the left opposition press was not a problem for the Nazis. The order for the protection of the state put in place immediately after the Reichstag fire enabled them to close more than 230 socialist, communist and other left-wing publications – in mid-1933 a law for the expropriation of hostile and subversive people's property allowed them to be fully taken over and either closed or turned into Nazi organs. In October 1933, Goebbels presented the draft law on the press, known as the Editors' Law, giving control of content to newspaper editors and also placing party papers under government control – editors of course all being controlled from the centre and appointed and sacked by the party or ministry rather than by publishers or even local Gau leaders.

When Hitler came to power there were 4703 newspapers in Germany representing a variety of interests and political views. By the end of 1934, the Nazi party had direct control or ownership of 436 papers and, through the ministry and Reich press organs controlled the rest (Zeman, 1964, p. 43). Over time, the Nazi party publishing house, Eher Verlag, gained direct or indirect control over much of the printed media (it owned two thirds of the German press by the outbreak of war in 1939), those working in the press were closely controlled and Goebbels ministry controlled the flow of news and therefore newspaper content through the state-controlled German

News Agency and through the ministry's daily press briefings and directives to editors (Welch, 1993, pp. 43–4).

But it was radio that was to become the centre piece of daily propaganda and to be the means, along with some Nazi papers (especially Streicher's violently and obscenely anti-Semitic *Der Sturmer*), of inciting hatred of Jews, gypsies and, when it suited Nazi policy, Russians, Poles, Slavs generally, and capitalists (or plutocrats as they came to be called). Radio could harness not only the propaganda content that Goebbels and Hitler desired but the power of the human voice – such an effective weapon in the Nazis' rise to power. Goebbels wrote that with radio at his disposal, propaganda would be irresistible and that 'as an instrument for propaganda on a large scale, the efficacy or radio has not yet been sufficiently appreciated [. . .] All the better, we shall have to explore the possibilities.' He added that radio would be crucial in the ability to fight 'the Jewish gutter press' (Goebbels, 1940, p. 214 and 212).

The Nazi takeover of radio broadcasting was simpler than the press. The country's first radio transmissions were made in 1915 but German radio didn't really develop into a national means of communication until at least five years after the end of the war. In 1925, the government had instituted state regulation through the Reich Radio Company (*Reichsrundfunkgesellschaft* – RRG). The Ministry of Posts owned 51 per cent of the company and appointed a Radio Commissioner to oversee broadcasting; nine regional/*lender* radio companies owned the remaining 49 per cent (Welch, 1993, p. 38). The RRG had control over the Wireless News Agency, which selected and distributed news features for regional broadcasters, but the level of control was not great and Bergmeier and Lotz described radio as 'a loosely knit network of financially independent regional companies' with the RRG 'exercising a limited control over the regional stations'; the national body had little say over programme content and the government had only 'marginal political influence' over radio (Bergmeier and Lotz, 1997, p. 4). It was only during von Papen's period as chancellor that radio was fully nationalized and he instituted a daily, hour-long programme produced in Berlin called the *Voice of the Reich* to broadcast the government's views on major issues (Bergmeier and Lotz, 1997, p. 5).

Radio was clearly going to be of primary importance in Goebbels's propaganda campaigns. He had little knowledge of how radio worked other than its ability to transmit the power and emotion of the voice and to reach into peoples' homes so that the voices of Hitler, Goebbels and other Nazi potentates would reach audiences nationally every time they gave a major speech. Kallis gets the value of this perfectly when he writes:

> In terms of communication potential, it was both more versatile than the press, capable of reaching audiences across the Reich and beyond, and less flexible, when compared to the diversification of press on the

basis of a national, regional and local division of labour. As a device of totalitarian integration and manipulation, broadcasting had significant potential, being far easier to coordinate and then regulate, centrally.

(Kallis, 2008, p. 31)

Radio also had the advantage of being broadcast across the day, giving endless opportunities to tweak the content if it was not what had been demanded at the Propaganda Ministry's morning meetings. It could also react faster than the press to breaking events and could harness live events in a way that the press couldn't.

Goebbels put reliable Nazis in senior positions and prepared to restructure the national radio network to ensure central control – output nationally and in each *lender* did not have to be identical but propaganda messages had to be uniform and all radio stations had to be singing from the same hymn sheet when it came to the repetition and consistency of propaganda over time. An important figure appointed in 1933 by Goebbels was Eugen Hadamovsky. When the RRG was reorganized in July 1933 as a central-ized network run from Berlin with the regional stations obeying its diktat, Hadamovksy was appointed director of broadcasting and Reich transmitter leader. A Nazi supporter and then member from the 1920s, he had fixed up the giant PA systems for Hitler's rallies. Alongside him as chief radio com-mentator was Wulf Bley (a leading member of the SA). During the year in which he was appointed, Bley wrote a pamphlet entitled *National Education and Radio Reform in Germany,* in which he argued that, 'The German radio under National Socialist auspices must become the clearest and most direct instrument for educating and restructuring the German nation' (cited by Bergmeier and Lotz, 1997, p. 6).

In 1933, Hadamovsky wrote a whole book on propaganda and national power, dedicated to Goebbels. In it, he said:

> The real effect of a word or sound carried by radio is much deeper than that, say of a newspaper or other piece of writing that must be inter-preted before it is understood. Radio broadcasting works directly, without that bridge of thought, and has, therefore, greater effectiveness than the printed page [...]

(Hadamovsky, 1933, chapter 4)

Hadamovsky and Goebbels absolutely believed in the mass character of radio and its role in ensuring that the individual always saw him or herself as part of the mass and reacted to propaganda in that way (ibid.) The new radio head saw the way that the broadcasting on content on radio could be less ambiguous or subject to interpretation than the printed word in newspapers:

> The spoken word allows the listener much less freedom of thought [...] The radio can work like a newspaper, but with more immediacy,

versatility, depth, and impressiveness [...] For the first time in history, radio gives us the chance to reach millions of people with daily and hourly influences. The old and young, workers, farmers, soldiers, and officers, men and women, sit before the apparatus, listening [...] what counts the most is not what one has carried home in black and white, but rather the spoken words that come with all their suggestive urgency from the radio speaker [...] in this generation of mass movements, he wants to join a mass of those who sound the same, feel the same, and think the same. They desire for unity, for identity with a large community, triumphs over individualism [...] In it, he feels sheltered from lies and deceptions, defended from all attacks on his mental stability [...] The radio must be political [...] It belongs in authorized hands [...]

(Hadamovsky, 1933, chapter 4)

In his speech to representatives of radio stations on 25 March, Goebbels took a very similar line. He stated bluntly that 'the age of individualism was finally destroyed and replaced by an age of national community feeling' when the Nazi-led government was sworn in and that radio would now be conquered by the Nazi revolution (Goebbels, 1993b, p. 183). He went on:

We make no bones about the fact that the radio belongs to us and to no one else. And we will place the radio in the service of our ideology, and no other ideology will find expression here [...] The Ministry for Propaganda has the task of effecting a spiritual mobilisation in Germany [...] I am placing a major responsibility in your hands, for you have in your possession the most modern instrument in existence for influencing the masses. By means of this instrument you are the creators of public opinion. If you carry this out well, we shall win over the people [...]

(Goebbels, 1993b, pp. 183–4)

Goebbels attained full control over radio through a Hitler decree of 30 June 1993, which said that as Reich minister for Popular Enlightenment and Propaganda he was 'responsible for all influences on the intellectual life of the nation; public relations for the State, and the economy, for instructing the domestic and foreign public about them, and for the administration of all the institutions serving these purposes' (cited by Welch, 1993, p. 39). Hitler also wrote to the Reich governors making clear that Goebbels and not they had control over the regional radio stations.

Goebbels worked for a year to hammer the old system into a centralized one – which was finally formed on 1 April 1934 as the Reich Radio Company, with the nine regional stations just branches of the national one. Goebbels ensured control over news content through the German Wireless Service – a branch of the press department of the Propaganda Ministry, headed by Hans

Fritzsche. The service supplied news material for all radio stations. Fritzsche had only joined the Nazi Party in May 1933, but gained Goebbels's trust and was head of German radio news until 1938, when he became head of the press department of the ministry. He was to become an effective and, by Nazi standards, sophisticated radio broadcaster and from 1942–45 was head of the ministry's radio department. Prior to and during the war, Fritzsche's commentaries were broadcast on a regular, at times almost daily, basis. As Bergmeier and Lotz note, 'his commentaries were marked by an absence of the crude lies and polemics so common to most of his colleagues. Instead, he "analysed" the political situation with an irony and intelligence that appealed to many listeners and delivered his broadcasts with rare skill and urbanity' (Bergmeier and Lotz, 1997, p. 17).

In January 1933, Germany had 4,300,000 radio owners registered with the Postal Ministry, at that stage responsible for radio. Hadamovsky wrote in 1933 that the total estimated number of listeners was 20,000,000 out of a total population of 64,776,000; he said there were about 66.5 registered radio receivers per 1000 of the population (Hadamovsky, 1933, chapter 4). Goebbels wanted to increase the numbers of listeners massively and, in May 1933, German manufacturers started producing 100,000 cheap radios – known as *Volsempfanger* (people's receiver). They were subsidized by the state to make them affordable to poorer workers. Cheap and easy to produce, they were limited to frequencies broadcasting RRG stations – they could not to pick up foreign broadcasts. Goebbels wanted a radio set in every home. By January 1938, radio ownership had jumped to 8.2 million with a corresponding massive increase in numbers of listeners (Bergmeier and Lotz, 1997, pp. 8–9; Welch, 1993, pp. 41–2). By a huge effort, with war looming, ownership was pushed up to 15.3 million in July 1939 and 16 million in 1941 (Kris and Speier, 1944, p. 51).

To ensure not just that people owned radio sets but that they listened to them for important speeches, Goebbels and Hadamovsky encouraged the development of community listening. Prior to 1933, the Nazis had gained control of the Federation of German Radio Participants and, within a year of its establishment, the National Socialists undertook a drive within the federation and established about 3000 radio listening rooms around the entire nation, united under the leadership of radio wardens in the National Socialist Federation (Hadamovsky, 1933, chapter 4). Now local party branches were encouraged to ensure that people listened to speeches by leaders and important commentaries or news announcements. Communal listening (aided by setting up loudspeakers in public squares, factories, offices, schools and restaurants) was important to the Nazis as part of their attempt to wear away at individualism and make listening to the radio the nearest equivalent to attending Nazi rallies (Kris and Speier, 1944, pp. 51–2; Welch, 1993, p. 42). Radio wardens were appointed by the party to encourage listening, to channel back comments and criticisms of programming but also, especially during the war, to find out who was listening to foreign stations and report them (Kris and Speier, 1944, pp. 51–2).

Through these methods, radio became an important and everyday part of most peoples' lives and the primary channel for getting the Nazi message into practically every home. In 1935, for example, it is estimated that Hitler's speeches regularly reached an audience of 56 million people. Signature tunes were introduced for particular party leaders – Hitler's speeches were preceded by his favourite march, the *Badenweiler;* when Goebbels broadcast his annual eulogy on Hitler's birthday, the broadcast would be preceded by Wagner's *Meistersinger Overture;* Hitler's annual Heroes' Day speech was introduced by Beethoven's *Eroica.*

Despite the level of control established and the consistent, repetitive messages pumped out, radio did not always have the desired effect. Right at the start of Nazi rule, the party launched a boycott of Jewish businesses as its first part of a concerted offensive against Germany's Jews and criticism of Nazi anti-Semitism by Jewish groups abroad. In a memorandum sent to all party organizations, Goebbels called for 1 April 1933 to be the start of a boycott – he said, 'you performed the miracle of overthrowing the November state in a single attack; you will solve this second assignment in similar fashion. Let International Jewry be put on notice [. . .] National Socialists! Saturday, at the stroke of ten, the Jews will find out whom they've declared war on' (cited by Reuth, 1993, p. 179). Streicher was heavily involved in the boycott, as was his paper *Der Stürmer.* On the day of the boycott, he gave a speech at the Berlin Lustgarten on the subject of the 'atrocities of world Jewry'. This was broadcast on all German radio stations. He attacked the Jews for dragging Germany through the mire and encouraging their fellows in Britain and the USA to criticize the Nazis, warning that the National Socialists would now call the Jews to account (ibid.).

After a disappointing reaction, Hitler limited the boycott to just one day, but warned that it would be reinstituted the next week if what he claimed was Jewish agitation against Germany did not stop. The boycott, despite the propaganda, was less than a success – with many Jewish shops closing for the day, anyway. Many shoppers ignored SA men standing outside Jewish shops exhorting people not to use them; many Nazis used the boycott as an excuse to loot Jewish businesses. Party and radio propaganda clearly had its limits in prompting action and manipulating the population.

The failure of the boycott led the Nazis to institute anti-Semitism as state, rather than just party, policy. Moves were set in train, with the accompanying press and radio propaganda, to progressively purge the civil service and professions of Jews and political enemies. The Law for the Restoration of the Professional Civil Service was promulgated on 7 April 1933, and, though it lacked a clear definition of Jewish or Aryan, it was used to sack Jews from their posts. Laws stopping Jews entering the legal profession, stopping Jewish doctors treating patients with national insurance, and limits on the number of Jewish children allowed in schools were all passed the same month (Bullock, 1962, p. 270; Kershaw, 2001a, pp. 474–5). Goebbels wrote during this period that the sins of the Jews would not be forgotten and that German soldiers would rise from their graves in Flanders and Poland against the Jews and their libels against Germany (cited by Reuth, 1993, p. 179).

Propaganda now became part German daily life – whether on the radio, in the newspapers, in film, art or at meetings or rallies. The output of propaganda was matched by growing repression but also surveillance of public mood and reactions – not only were there the radio wardens but also the Gestapo, the SD security police, local party cells and local government institutions were all involved in assessing public opinion and feeding back on the response to propaganda and policies. The SD alone had, by 1939, 3000 full-time and some 50,000 part-time agents. Success of a particular radio or other propaganda campaign relied not just on whether the content or delivery were good but was dependent on the extent to which it reflected an accurate awareness of how the public already felt about an issue and on 'the prevailing opinions and prejudices of the German people' (Welch, 1993, p. 59). Goebbels and Hitler did not try to change people's opinions, they sought to work on existing beliefs, prejudices and feelings. As Kallis correctly points out, the 'active complicity or even passive consensus of the audience cannot be taken for granted, even in putatively "totalitarian" systems where individual issues become related to a one-dimensional world view'; the playing on existing feelings, exploitation of widely held beliefs or myths was one thing, but the replacement of existing views with a 'revolutionary idea or outlook is a slow process' (Kallis, 2008, p. 4).

The themes that dominated Nazi propaganda output in the years between gaining power and the outbreak of the war were Hitler's variants and developments of traditional lines of right-wing, nationalist and Volkischer thought in Germany – '(1) appeal to national unity based on the principle "The community before the individual" [...] (2) the need for racial purity; (3) a hatred of enemies which increasingly centred on Jews and Bolsheviks; and (4) charismatic leadership' (Welch, 1993, p. 60). Anti-Bolshevik and anti-socialist rhetoric was very much to the fore during the destruction of the trades unions and the formation of the German Labour Front, led by Dr Robert Ley – the front brought together workers and employers and was sold as part of the creation of a community to replace old class or socio-economic divisions. This idea – espoused on radio and in leaders' speeches and the press – was a core aspect of the Nazi aim of creating a continuous sense of *Volksgemeinschaft* (national community) and ensuring social conformity. A 'new series of public rituals to celebrate important days in the Nazi calendar' was created, which 'national comrades' were expected to attend (Welch, 1993, p. 72). Radio broadcasts encouraging participation and relaying marches, music, speeches and ceremonies were all part of the process of enforcing conformity.

Intrinsic to *Volksgemeinschaft* was racial purity and the campaign against the Jews and others identified as *untermenschen* (inferior races or even sub-humans – not racially pure or Aryan). 'Racial teaching within the education system, and propaganda in general, preached hatred of Jews and Slavs and proclaimed the superiority of the so-called Aryan races' (Welch, 1993, p. 83). Hitler in *Mein Kampf*, and he and Nazi leaders in speeches and their published writings in the 1920s and 1930s, had concentrated particularly on the threat posed by the Jews, an inferior and parasitical race in Nazi parlance, and the need to save Germany from their power and 'influence over politics, the economy and society' (Herf, 2006, p. 2). Hitler summed it up in a speech as early as April 1920, when he told a Nationalist meeting,

> We don't want to be emotional anti-Semites who seek to create a mood for pogroms. Rather, we are driven by a pitiless and fierce determination to attack the evil at its roots and to exterminate it root and branch. Every means is justified to reach our goal, even if it means we have to make a pact with the devil.
>
> (cited by Herf, 2006, p. 2)

Nazi anti-Semitism did not as a rule encourage individual or spontaneous attacks. The campaign was to involve legal measures, social, political and economic exclusion and, when the conditions of war and conquest made it possible, forced emigration and extermination. The latter point was mentioned periodically in Hitler's speeches, though never spelled out in. Hitler made his hatred of the Jews part of everyday discourse on the radio, in newspapers and in the speeches and activities of party members.

One of the main characteristics of this discourse was the use of the mirror image or reverse image approach. Germany was presented as vulnerable to or threatened by domestic and international Jewry in alliance with Bolshevism and capitalism or plutocracy:

> the propaganda of the Nazi party and Nazi regime presented Hitler and Germany as merely responding to the initiatives, injustices, and threats of others. It was a propaganda that trumpeted innocence and self-righteous indignation and turned the power relations between Germany and the Jews upside down: Germany was the innocent victim; Jewry was all powerful.
>
> (Herf, 2006, p. 4)

For Hitler, the Jews became eternal scapegoats:

> the Jew was manipulated to fulfil a psychological need for Germany, Nazi propaganda simply used a historical predisposition of the audience towards an anti-Semitic explanation for Germany's cultural, economic and political grievances [...] an important negative function of

anti-Semitic propaganda was to divert the population from the economic
and social measures that the regime had promised but failed to deliver

(Welch, 1993, p. 92)

though it is hard to assess just how effective anti-Semitic propaganda was
and Welch notes that there is increasing questioning of its overall efficacy.
But one area in which it did seem to succeed was 'in the advancing deper-
sonalization of the Jew which accompanied the progressive elimination of
Jews from German society and their reduction to little more than an abstract
symbol. The result was the creation of a fatal degree of indifference rather
than dynamic hatred of the Jews', the latter having already been instilled in
active Nazi supporters' (Kershaw, 1983, p. 191).

Anti-Semitism was less prominent in propaganda at the end of 1933 and
in 1934 (perhaps partly as a result of the disappointing reaction to the boycott of April 1933), when the regime was distracted by the consequences
of the walk-out from disarmament talks in Geneva and the following election and plebiscite. This was the period of Hindenburg's illness and death,
and the brutal retribution against Rohm, Strasser, Schleicher, 'untrustwor-
thy' elements in the SA and other right-wing opponents or 'traitors' in the
Night of the Long Knives.

The walk out from the October 1933 disarmament talks was in line with
the Nazis' and the army's opposition to limits imposed on Germany's armed
forces at Versailles. On 14 October, Hitler announced over radio the dissolu-
tion of the Reichstag with elections set for 12 November. The election was
effectively a plebiscite for Hitler and the Nazis – including on the withdrawal
from the arms talks and from the League of Nations. The thrust of the radio,
press and speaking campaign before the vote was on Hitler and his role as
Fuhrer. The voting paper said simply:

Do you, German man, and you, German woman, approve this policy of
your Reich government, and are you ready to declare it to be the expression of your own view, and your own will, and solemnly give it your
allegiance' – the implication was that the Reich government and Hitler
were synonymous.

(cited by Kershaw, 2001a, p. 495)

The propaganda before the vote stressed Hitler's role as the saviour of
Germany and as the man to rescue Germany and the army from the prison
of the Versailles conditions. Hitler's speeches around this period, broadcast
and printed in the now sycophantic press, concentrated on the injustices
meted out to Germany after the First World War and of the continuation
of injustice and of the distinction between winners and losers in 1918 (Bullock, 1962, p. 321). Goebbels and other leaders concentrated much of their
speechmaking and broadcasting on the importance of Hitler as the Leader.

The result was a 95.1 per cent vote for Hitler's decision on the arms talks in the plebiscite and a 92.1 per cent vote for the Nazi list for the Reichstag (Kershaw, 2001a, p. 495; Shirer, 1960, p. 265). Soon after the vote, Hitler appeared to allay European fears of a resurgent Germany when he negotiated and signed a ten-year non-aggression pact with Poland, renouncing the use of force but not giving up Germany's aim of ending the separation of the bulk of Germany from East Prussia by the Polish Corridor or of recovering the port of Danzig. The conclusion of the pact was announced shortly before the anniversary of Hitler's appointment as Chancellor. The agreement also recognized the growing role of propaganda in inter-state relations, including a clause on the mutual cessation of hostile broadcasts.

On 30 January 1934, in an address repeatedly broadcast and even more repetitively commented upon on German radio, Hitler told the Reichstag on the anniversary of his appointment as Chancellor that Germany could look back on a year of unparalleled achievement (Shirer, 1960, p. 266). But there was a problem looming large for the Nazis – the power, attempts to retain independence and uncoordinated violence of the SA. In the months following Hitler's accession to power, the SA and its head, Rohm, had acted in a way that emphasized a lack of discipline and unwillingness just to be an instrument of Nazi power. Rohm had said, in a speech of May 1933, that for the SA the task of completing the National Socialist revolution 'still lies before it' (Evans, 2006, p. 21). Hitler did not appreciate Rohm making decisions and public statements about what was or was not part of the revolution. The next month, the SA undertook a week of violence in Berlin against Social Democrat supporters. The Nazis were now carrying out their own state-sanctified repression against opponents and did not want the SA taking things into its own hands. Hitler believed that the SA had outlived its purpose and was becoming a destabilizing factor, particularly in relations with the army high command (Kershaw, 2001a, p. 499). In August 1933, Goering rescinded the order in Prussia that gave the SA auxiliary police powers and other states followed suit. There were at the time increasing complaints from pro-Nazi groups of the loutish and uncontrolled behaviour of the SA – with industrialists and municipal leaders complaining to Nazi leaders about the effects of SA attacks.

It came to a head in late June 1934 when Hitler decided to act to undercut the threat of an army takeover. As Hindenburg's health declined in mid-year, Hitler cancelled planned SA exercises and in late May ordered SA members to go on leave for a month. At the end of June, Hitler summoned SA leaders to Bad Wiessee in Bavaria, where Hitler, his SS bodyguards and a squad of police arrested Rohm and several senior SA leaders. Rohm was told to commit suicide; when he defied the order, he was shot. Across Germany, SA leaders and other perceived opponents were arrested – many were shot and others taken to concentration camps (Evans, 2006, pp. 32–3). General von Schleicher and his wife were both shot by the SS. Gregor Strasser was arrested and shot.

Two weeks later, Hitler openly spoke of the purge in a Reichstag speech on 13 July broadcast nationwide by Goebbels's radio stations. He accused those killed of being traitors and suggested that they had received the backing of the French. The Führer also attacked the morals of Rohm and other SA leaders renowned for their debauchery and said that they were all part of a conspiracy to overthrow the new Reich that involved those who believed in permanent revolution and upper-class 'drones' (Evans, 2006, p. 37; Shirer, 1960, pp. 280–1). In an indication of Hitler's confidence in his reaffirmed power, Hitler told the Reichstag that:

> I gave the order to shoot those parties mainly responsible for this treason [...] The nation should know that no one can threaten its existence [...] and escape unpunished! And every person should know for all time that if he raises his hand to strike out the State, certain death will be his lot.
>
> (Evans, 2006, pp. 37–8)

The purge and Germany's acceptance of it so strengthened Hitler that when Hindenburg died on 2 August 1934, he announced to the nation that the post of president would die with him and henceforth, Hitler would be Führer and Reich chancellor, inheriting presidential powers – this was confirmed in another plebiscite on 19 August. The day before Hindenburg died, Hitler obtained the signatures of his cabinet (including von Blomberg on behalf of the army) making the Reich chancellor the supreme commander of the German armed forces (Evans, 2006, pp. 42–3; Kershaw, 2001a, pp. 524–5).

If Hitler was increasingly secure in power, the methods used to achieve this, the propaganda aimed at and the organization of Nazi groups in neighbouring states with German minorities led to increasing foreign suspicion of Hitler. Even fascist Italy, which Hitler visited as his first foreign trip as leader in 1934, was suspicious of his intentions. Foreign concern increased hugely when, on 25 July 1934, a group of Austrian Nazis (members of the SS) tried to overthrow the government of Chancellor Dolfuss. Dolfuss had banned the party the previous month. They shot the chancellor, seized a radio station and broadcast a statement saying that the government had resigned – but they got little support, even from Nazis in the Austrian army and police, and the putsch failed within hours. Hitler tried to smooth things over by appointing former Chancellor von Papen as ambassador to Austria.

The only foreign policy advance for Hitler at this time came in the Saarland territory in the western Rhineland – an advance that owed much to the power of radio. At the peace talks in 1919, the area had been mandated to France under the League of Nations but with the provision that a referendum would be held after 15 years to determine whether the area would stay with France or be re-incorporated into Germany. The territory was predominantly German-speaking and most wanted unity with Germany rather than to become a German-speaking minority in France (Evans, 2006,

p. 623). Goebbels organized a radio campaign with coordinated broadcasts aimed at the population – he also set up a special office to coordinate both broadcasts and the distribution of cheap radios that would receive German broadcasts (Bergmeier and Lotz, 1997, p. 23; Hale, 1975, p. 2). The campaign was named by Goebbels 'Home to the Reich' and it viciously attacked all those who advocated that the Saar remain a League of Nations mandated territory as lackeys of Jewish Bolshevism (cited by Reuth, 1993, p. 203). The campaign started a year before the vote. A special team led by a Saar journalist office approved every broadcast to or about the Saar before it went out. The local Nazi party in the Saar was active in propagandizing and in intimidating any group opposed to reunification – Social Democratic Party meetings were broken up and people told that the vote would not be wholly secret and that those who voted no would end up in concentration camps (Evans, 2006, p. 625). Again, this was the dovetailing of propaganda and the threat of violence.

A programme about the Saar was broadcast every week on Wednesdays throughout Germany and 6 May 1934 was named the Day of the Saar – all radio output that day was devoted to the Saar and even the church services, music and radio dramas broadcast had Saar connections (Zeman, 1964, p. 107). In the final hours of 1934, all German radio stations broadcast a programme entitled *115 – in thirteen days – the Saar Returns Home*. Between January 1934 and January 1935, 4000 radio sets had been distributed in the Saar and the radio audience boosted from 28,000 to 40,000, while Nazi listeners' associations had been established to hold meetings at which key broadcasts were listened to communally. Because of this, Zeman concludes that 'there can be no doubt that broadcasting played the decisive role in the success of the National Socialist campaign. The Germans were of course unlikely to lose in the plebiscite; but they would never have won by such an overwhelming margin without an effective propaganda campaign' (Zeman, 1964, p. 108). The result of the plebiscite was nearly 91 per cent in favour of becoming part of Nazi Germany. The reincorporation of the Saar into Germany was a massive boost to Hitler's standing at home and the effectiveness of the radio output an affirmation for Goebbels of what he could achieve through the medium. The Saar victory put Hitler in a stronger position than ever to start arguing for rearmament, the scrapping of the Versailles limitations on the German army and the ban on an air force.

On 16 March 1935, Hitler announced that Germany had an air force, was reintroducing conscription and would increase the armed forces to over 500,000 men (five times the Versailles limit). Hitler told foreign diplomats about the decisions at a meeting the same day – drawing immediate protests from the French and British ambassadors. The Nazis rushed out special editions of newspapers to report Hitler's announcements. The American newspaper and radio correspondent, William Shirer, was in Berlin when the announcement was made and reported open celebration and rejoicing in the streets. He said that there was no doubt about the support of most Germans for the measures (Shirer, 1960, p. 351).

The British, French and Italians condemned the move and made a point of stressing their support for the independence of Austria. On 21 May, Hitler addressed the Reichstag (and by radio the bulk of the nation) and for the benefit of his international critics and domestic audience said that Germany wanted peace. Lacking the histrionics of many of his performances, the speech exuded tolerance and conciliation while sounding confident and more statesmanlike than usual (Shirer, 1960, p. 353). Hitler stressed that Germany had no wish to annexe or incorporate Austria into Germany.

Growing confidence internationally was accompanied by clear moves domestically to deal with Germany's Jewish population. Although in 1934 there had been little government-sponsored violence, Jews continued to experience frequent harassment by party members and the SA. But the government now moved to codify anti-Semitism and translate into law Hitler's promises to remove Jews from German public life. At a marathon party rally at Nuremberg in September 1935, Hitler and Goebbels launched a combined attack on Jews and Bolshevism. Hitler used his speech at the rally (as usual broadcast live across Germany – and shown as newsreels in cinemas and put together in Leni Reifenstahl's film, *Triumph of the Will*) to announce the promulgation of the law for the Protection of German Blood and German Honour – this denied Jews German citizenship, and forbade marriage or sexual relations between Germans and Jews. Hitler justified this in his speech to the rally on 15 September arguing that it was 'exclusively Jewish elements that emerge as agitators of conflicts between peoples and of their inner disintegration', adding that complaints from Jewish groups in the USA and Europe over Nazi policies towards the Jews confirmed the correctness of his anti-Jewish stance and proposed laws (cited by Herf, 2006, p. 41).

Goebbels also spoke, attacking Jews and linking them inextricably with anti-Bolshevism. In a speech entitled 'Communism Without a Mask', the propaganda minister said that Bolshevism was Jewry's declaration of war against culture, which would bring about 'the absolute destruction' of Western civilization in the interests of a 'rootless and nomadic international clique of conspirators' (ibid.). Bolshevism was, he went on, run by 'the international sub-human forces under the leadership of the Jews' (cited by Reuth, 1993, p. 205). He said that the Soviet Union was ruled by 'a small, terrorist, mostly Jewish minority' and that Germany was the only defence for Europe against this Jewish threat. Bolshevism, he promised, would be eradicated by attacking it at its roots in Jewish culture (Herf, 2006, p. 42).

The ground for the rally speeches and the Nuremberg Laws, as the anti-Jewish legislation became known, had been prepared during 1935 by Goebbels in regular radio broadcasts in which he accused the Jews and Bolsheviks of preparing for 'the extermination of peoples and states' and because of which Jewry and Bolshevism had to be crushed. As Herf points out, Goebbels increasingly used words like 'extermination' and 'destruction' in his description of the plans of the Bolshevik-Jewish conspiracy against mankind (Herf, 2006, p. 42); and then these began to be used by him, Hitler and other Nazi leaders in their demands that this conspiracy be crushed. Using the 'world conspiracy', 'destruction' and 'extermination' frames for stories about Bolshevism and Jewry and always representing Jews and Bolsheviks (later adding US and British plutocrats to the mix) as evil, sub-human and an eternal threat to German and European civilization, the Nazi propagandists through constant repetition of these themes, established as a normal part of their political and social discourse the image of the Jew as a threat that must be eradicated. The method or nature of this eradication was not clearly set out, but the intent was clear.

In successive party rallies in Nuremberg in September 1936 and again in 1937, broadcast live and repeated regularly over the days after the rallies, Hitler returned to the alleged dominance of the Jews in political and economic life outside Germany and their conspiracies against Germany and against European civilization; in 1936, the attacks on Jews focused on Bolshevism's aim of exterminating racial purity and civilization and replacing it with Jewish hegemony (Herf, 2006, p. 42). The link between Bolshevism and Jewry was constantly reinforced in these speeches, regular radio and press pieces by Goebbels and other leaders and in film, art and other forms of communication. *Der Stürmer* maintained its regular output of anti-Jewish bile with a constant stream of sensationalist sexual, criminal, violent or other allegations about the Jews; and grotesque cartoons caricaturing Jews, reducing them to evil, lecherous, grasping monsters, living representations of 'depravity' (Bytwerk, 2001, p. 32). They were vilified as parasites, as a disease. By 1935, the newspaper had a readership of 500,000 a week and the publishers also produced anti-Semitic children's books and pseudo-scientific works on the 'Jewish question'.

At the Nuremberg Rally in September 1937, Hitler made one of his strongest anti-Semitic attacks for two years and appeared to threaten the total exclusion of Jews from business and economic life. He said that the Jews had been responsible for Germany's economic woes and the curse of unemployment for seven million Germans at the height of the depression – a clever combination of general anti-Jewish propaganda with specific charges that would resonate with Germans who had lost their jobs or businesses during the economic crisis.

The major attack on Jews prior to the outbreak of war came in November 1938, following the shooting of a German diplomat, Ernst von Rath, in Paris by a Polish Jewish refugee. Within hours of the shooting and before von Rath had died, Goebbels's ministry had instructed the German News Agency to give great prominence to the incident and instructed newspaper and radio editors: 'In your commentaries you will point out that the Jewish plot must have the most unfortunate results for the Jews as well as for foreign

Jews in Germany' (cited by Bramsted, 1965, p. 385). The diplomat died on 9 November and Hitler heard about it just as he was about to speak at a commemoration of the beer hall putsch anniversary. He left the meeting without speaking, but Goebbels gave a speech that his biographer Reuth describes as 'a hate-filled tirade against "international Jewry" ' (Reuth, 1993, p. 240).

Local party leaders, especially those under Goebbels's control in Berlin, were ordered to get their members to carry out attacks on Jews and Jewish property. The resulting violence, known as *Kristallnacht* because of the amount of glass smashed in attacks on Jewish businesses and homes, was an orgy of violence that lasted for two days until 10 November, when the party and government brought it to an end. During the height of the violence, Goebbels had to explain to a concerned Hitler why the violence should be allowed to continue and he wrote in his diary on 9 November that 'the Jews should for once feel the anger of the people,' though this was anger whipped up by him and organized by party officials, not a spontaneous outbreak of anti-Jewish violence by ordinary Germans or even violence encouraged by propaganda. It was violence organized by the party and encouraged and sanctified by propaganda on the radio and in the press.

Over the two days about 100 Jews were killed, countless more beaten and over 20,000–30,000 Jews were detained and sent to the Dachau, Buchenwald or Oranienberg concentration camps. Once the violence was over, Goebbels sought to minimize coverage in the press and told foreign journalists on 10 November that reports of destruction, looting and violence against Jews were 'filthy lies' and not a Jew had been harmed (ibid.). The violence was followed by measures to exclude Jews from the economy and to place responsibility for Jewish affairs directly under the control of the SS, 'whose leaders linked war, expansion, and eradication of Jewry' (Kershaw, 2001b, p. 130). Himmler had told top SS leaders in early November 1938, prior to *Kristallnacht*, that in the coming years Germany would be engaged in critical conflicts:

> It is not only the struggle of the nations [...] but it is the ideological struggle (*weltanschauliche*) of the entire Jewry, freemasonry, Marxism, and churches of the world. These forces – of which I presume the Jews to be the driving spirit, the origin of all the negatives – are clear that if Germany and Italy are not annihilated, *they* will be annihilated (*vernichtet warden*). That is a simple conclusion. In Germany the Jew cannot hold out. This is a question of years. We will drive them out more and more with an unprecedented ruthlessness [...]
>
> (cited by Kershaw, 2001b, p. 130)

For Goebbels, the task was to provide the propaganda campaign to gain the support or at least acquiescence of Germans and to encourage the active participation in this annihilation by those military and other forces earmarked to eliminate Jews – the anti-Jewish campaign was gaining momentum and had to be justified by a continuous discourse of hatred and dehumanization. Kershaw believes that by this time, 'For Hitler too, the connection between the war he knew was coming and the destruction of Europe's Jews was now beginning to take concrete shape' (Kershaw, 2001b, p. 130). On 22 November, measures were announced levying a 20 per cent reparations payment on Jewish business for the destruction wrought by the Nazis, enforcing the Aryanization of a any remaining businesses in Jewish hands, banning Jews from attending cultural events, bans on Jewish children attending schools and Heydrich was instructed by Goering to start planning and carrying out the removal of all Jews from the Reich. In April 1938, Goebbels recorded in his diary a meeting with Hitler at which they had discussed forcing all Jews out of Berlin and eventually out of the whole of Germany – Goebbels suggested at this stage that Poland or Romania should be asked to take them, though he also floated the idea of sending all Jews to Madagascar (Kershaw, 2001b, p. 134) – an idea that was to surface periodically over the coming years prior to the final decision on complete extermination.

During 1937 and 1938, apart from the Nuremberg speeches, Hitler avoided making too many anti-Semitic speeches. He was concentrating at this stage on achieving his immediate European goals of annexing Austria and the Sudetenland and preparing for expansion into the rest of Czechoslovakia and then war with Poland. In May 1935, Hitler had signed and promulgated in secret the Reich Defence Law, which charged Minister of Economics Schact to make economic preparations for war. The same day, Hitler addressed the Reichstag and professed his desire for peace and rejection of war. He talked of states needing to give their energies to 'wiser purposes' than war (cited by Bullock, 1952, p. 335). It was a classic case of someone talking peace while preparing for and planning war. The German nation had to be told that peace was the priority. Whatever his aims and his fantasies about the world, Hitler knew that the Germans did not want war and would not willingly support him in the initiation of war.

Hitler wanted to maintain an image of reasonableness in Europe – hoping to avoid war until Germany was fully prepared and to convince Germans that if war took place he would not be seen as responsible. His global image had been boosted by the propaganda success of the 1936 Olympics. As Shirer, who reported on the Olympics from Berlin, writes, the August games 'afforded the Nazis a golden opportunity to impress the world with the achievements of the Third Reich, and they made the most of it' – most visitors were impressed by the organization and lavish nature of the games (Shirer, 1960, p. 290). Signs banning Jews from shops, hotels, beer halls and places of entertainment were taken down for the duration of the games. The Nazi propaganda machine made the most of this event – presenting it as another legitimization of the Third Reich and of Hitler's vision for Germany.

Hitler tried to maintain an image of reasonableness and cooperation as he set about expansion in 1938. The radio coverage within Germany of the growing crisis in Europe over Austria and then the Sudetenland portrayed Hitler and Germany as paragons of reason and peace and tried consistently to place all blame for conflicts or tension on countries opposed to the rise of the new Germany (and behind them, of course, the Jewish-Marxist-capitalist conspiracy). Even though the announcement of rearmament and the remilitarization of the Rhineland (using the Franco-Soviet treaty as a pretext) had progressed with less international opposition than many in Germany feared and with no military response from Britain or France, many in the government and the army were anxious about possible responses to further German moves. Hitler moved to allay fears of his intentions towards Austria – something preventing closer relations with fascist Italy. The Austro-German Agreement was signed on 11 July 1936 and on the face of things eased tensions – the agreement recognized Austrian sovereignty and promised non-interference in each other's affairs but did bind Austria to a foreign policy that was in line with its status as 'a German state' (Bullock, 1952, p. 348).

Germany and Italy cooperated in assisting Franco's fascists during the Spanish Civil War – both providing arms and combatants (notably the German Condor Legion air unit – enabling German airmen to practise modern warfare using newly developed Messerschmitt and Heinkel aircraft. The legion was infamous for its bombing of civilian towns such as Durango and Guernica. By late 1936, Mussolini was referring openly to the importance of the Rome-Berlin Axis (Evans, 2006, p. 641).

Having destroyed or outmanoeuvred his enemies internally and started the process of rearming and planning for a war economy, Hitler could turn in earnest to one of the basic Nazi aims, of having all Germans in one Germany. Austria would be first on the list, followed by the Sudetenland and the recovery of the Polish Corridor. In the summer of 1937, Hitler moved to bring the Austrian Nazi party under his control by appointing a close adviser to run it, and, after a meeting he held with Lord Halifax, convinced himself of British unwillingness to take action to defend Austrian independence; Halifax even intimated that Britain would not strongly object to changes to boundaries with Czechoslovakia or Poland to deal with the Sudeten German issue and Danzig (Kershaw, 2001b, p. 66).

German propaganda for the domestic and Austrian audiences concentrated on slogans like *Ein Volk, ein Reich, ein Fuhrer* – stressing unity of all Germans (Welch, 1993, p. 12). German propaganda was so successful that, in 1934, before the attempted Nazi coup and the assassination of Dolfuss, Austria had attempted to jam German broadcasts that were inciting Austrians against their government and in favour of the Nazis (Hale, 1975, p. 136). Nazis in Austria provided information on events and feelings in Austria that were invaluable to radio broadcasters in developing effective propaganda in favour of union (Zeman, 1973, p. 123). As German pressure for Anschluss with Austria grew and Hitler was trying to intimidate the Austrian Chancellor Schuschnigg, Goebbels carefully orchestrated a campaign, principally on radio and benefitting from the success in the Saar, to promote a mood in Austria in favour of Anschluss and a mood in Germany supporting the campaign against the Austrian government's resistance – Goebbels tried to ensure that the barrage of criticism of Schuschnigg was not so extreme that it could be interpreted as a general attack on Austrians, as Germany wanted their support (Zeman, 1973, pp. 140–1). After a period of intense political pressure and threats, Hitler obtained the resignation of Chancellor Schuschnigg and his replacement with a Nazi, Seyys-Inquart. Germany then simply marched in and effected a union of the two countries.

German troops crossed the Austrian border at 5.30 am on 12 March and, at midday, German and Austrian radios both broadcast a proclamation by Hitler and read by Goebbels that a 'true plebiscite' on Austria's future would be held soon. On 13 March, Hitler had Wilhelm Stuckart of the German Interior Ministry (who drafted the anti-Jewish Nuremberg Laws) draw up the Law for the Reunion of Austria with the German Reich, which Hitler signed that evening making Austria a German province; the Austrian army then swore an oath of loyalty to Hitler (Evans, 2006, p. 653; Kershaw, 2001b, pp. 80–1).

In his speech to the Reichstag on 18 March, Hitler signalled that the action in Austria presaged further action to bring the German diaspora in Europe back into the German fold. He spoke of the 'brutal violation of countless millions of German racial comrades' across Europe but was targeting Czechoslovakia and then Poland – in April, he held secret meetings with leaders of the Sudeten German Party, a Nazi-backed movement claiming to represent the German minority there (Evans, 2006, p. 664). A plebiscite was held in Austria and Germany on the union. It was preceded by the usual propaganda barrage on radio, in the newspapers and through speeches by Hitler at public meetings (6 out of 14 were held in Austria). The SS and Heydrich's SD were active in Austria before the vote detaining or eliminating opponents of the Nazis. The result was 99.08 per cent approval in Germany and 99.75 per cent in Austria (Evans, 2006, p. 655; Kershaw, 2001b, p. 82). The effects of the union were swift in terms of incorporation of the economy into Germany's and then the application of the Nuremberg Laws to Austria – leading to the sacking of Jews from the civil service and their banning from the professions. Austrian Nazis systematically looted Jewish property and in the first five months of rule 23,000 Jewish businesses were forced to close, their assets generally being seized by the Nazis. The Austrian branch of the stormtroopers instituted a wave of terror against prominent Jews – these stormtroopers were later brought under control by Heydrich and the SS as Hitler did not appreciate chaotic oppression. But a more organized persecution was also being carried out, with Jews forced out of Vienna, foreign Jews deported and Jews in provinces bordering Czechoslovakia and Hungary forced across the border – though many were then refused admission. By November 1938, 5,000 Jews had been deported.

The German minority in Czechoslovakia enjoyed full civil and political rights in what was one of Europe's most liberal and democratic states. They had guaranteed rights as individual citizens, though there were no specific collective/community rights for Germans or for other ethnic minorities (Ukrainians, Croatians, Hungarians, Poles and Romanians). The first stirrings of German nationalism there came during the economic depression in the early 1930s, when Germans seemed to be particularly badly affected and had a very high rate of unemployment. As Germany recovered from recession and the Nazis launched their policies to restore Germany's power and prestige, it was not surprising that many Sudeten Germans began to look to Germany for their economic salvation. They, like other Germans in neighbouring countries, were targeted by the Propaganda Ministry in broadcasts aimed at Eastern Europe. These sought not only to laud Hitler and the achievements of the new Reich but to create a sense of German nationality and a desire to be part of a resurgent Germany. Prior to and during the Austrian crisis, Goebbels was careful not to allow the German press and radio to attack Czechoslovakia, to avoid alarm in Europe over German intentions. This prohibition of criticism of the Czech government was lifted in June 1938 as Goebbels was made party to Hitler's plans to absorb the Sudetenland (Reuth, 1993, p. 235).

During the Sudeten crisis, Goebbels encountered a setback – Ribbentrop as the new foreign minister established his own foreign press and broadcasting division in his ministry, which was to be a cause of rage and resentment for Goebbels and a lasting source of inter-ministerial conflict (Zeman, 1973, p. 59). This added to the problems that Goebbels was encountering with Otto Dietrich, appointed by Hitler in 1937 as state secretary for the press in the Propaganda Ministry in addition to his role as party press chief. Dietrich was responsible for the press rather than radio and was in theory subordinate to Goebbels, but he effectively became Hitler's press supremo, briefing him daily on what was in the newspapers (Bergmeier and Lotz, 1997, p. 178). These competing and conflicting lines of authority may not have made Goebbels's life easy and contributed to factionalism and failures in coordination of policy, but they fitted perfectly with Hitler's modus operandi in his highly individual and charismatic form of government.

Notwithstanding this factionalism, Goebbels still directed the thrust of propaganda and had total control over radio. He was a key player, therefore, in the Sudeten crisis and the build-up to war. His job was not just to explain and garner support for the policy towards Sudetenland but also to allay German fears of war and blame any fears he could not still on the Jewish-Bolshevik-capitalist conspiracy and their puppets. In 1938, he was at odds with Dietrich over what he saw as the gloomy mood in Germany partly caused by the fear of war that could be detected, he claimed, in newspaper reporting (Reuth, 1993, p. 235). Hitler had so far been able to play on his successes as bloodless victories, but this wouldn't last and Goebbels was getting regular reports from Heydrich's SD about widespread fear of and opposition to another war among Germans. At the end of 1938, following the Anschluss and the Czech crisis, the SD reported a war psychosis and people being 'serious and depressed' – people had been particularly alarmed when Czechoslovakia announced the mobilization of its armed forces in May 1938 in the face of the increasing Nazi threat (cited by Kershaw, 1987, p. 133).

Hitler was continually briefing Goebbels on his plans for Czechoslovakia and Goebbels had been convinced by him that Germany was ready for war should Britain choose to oppose an attack on the Czechs. The minister had already established coordination with the Wehrmacht so that journalists from the ministry would accompany German armies and ensure that the propaganda effort was fully part of wars fought by Germany. And war was now a distinct possibility, Hitler made clear at the 1938 Nuremberg rally, when he told his audience in the stadium and on the radio that he would no longer stand idly by to watch with patience 'the continued oppression of our fellow Germans' in Czechoslovakia' (Reuth, 1993, p. 238).

Hitler was clearly intent on going beyond just the revision of Versailles, by redrawing the map of Europe to meet his pan-German and expansionist objectives. Czechoslovakia had a large and restive German minority but would also be a valuable economic asset with its raw materials and its thriving armaments industry. For the German audience, the mistreatment of Germans was to be the key card played in the propaganda game to convince a population anxious about war that tough action and an aggressive diplomatic stance were necessary – it was a version of the centuries-old use of atrocity stories to stoke resentment, fear or hatred in order to elicit support for active participation against an identified target or to create hatred of the 'other'.

Radio propaganda over the Sudetenland question was part of a campaign called *Heimkehr ins Reich* (Return Home to the Reich) which had also been the title for the output urging union with Austria. The campaign gained in intensity during the summer of 1938 and involved ever more ridiculous accusations of Czech atrocities against German-speakers. Kershaw says that this propaganda, however false in its basic premise, 'was not without effect, and that it was widely felt that Germany was justified in assisting the "repressed" Sudeten population'; but even if there was support for the policy, there was not support for war to achieve its aims and, as the crisis persisted, so the anxiety about war increased (Kershaw, 1987, p. 133).

The crisis developed over the spring and summer of 1938 as Hitler's rhetoric against the Czechs and their treatment of German-speakers became more extreme. Hitler intended to pressure the Prague to negotiate the detachment of the area from Czechoslovakia. On 21 April, Hitler ordered

General Keitel to draw up plans for military action against the Czechs, though he said Germany would not attack unless developments in the country or favourable international circumstances presented themselves (Kershaw, 2001a, p. 97). The crisis came when German troop movements near the Czech border in mid-May led to mobilization of the Czech army – the combination of mounting anti-Czech propaganda and the movement of large numbers of troops convinced Prague that Hitler was about to invade. The British and French expressed serious concern – Keitel reassured the British that these were just military exercises. This happened the weekend that Keitel gave Hitler the plans for a German invasion. These included a section on propaganda warfare, which stated that it 'must on the one hand intimidate the Czechs by means of threats and wear down their power of resistance; on the other hand it must give the national minorities indications as to how to support our military operations and influence the neutrals in our favour' (cited by Shirer, 1960, p. 443).

As a result of the heightened state of tension, the British Foreign Secretary Lord Halifax instructed Ambassador Henderson to tell Ribbentrop that a German attack against the Czechs would lead to French military action, though clearly not a British response (Kershaw, 2001a, p. 99). Hitler was furious. He was intent on dismembering Czechoslovakia and on occupying the Sudetenland militarily by mid-October 1938. In a speech to the Reichstag in January 1939, Hitler said that by the end of May 1938, he had decided to prepare for military action to take place on 2 October and that the Western defences must be built up to deter a French response (cited by Shirer, 1960, p. 447).

Hitler's determination to send his troops into the Sudetenland whatever the cost was such that he was able to push through his policy and succeed in the face of dithering and fearful French and British governments and a resistant Czech government devoid of allies willing to support its independence. The series of meetings in September with Chamberlain and then Chamberlain, Daladier and Mussolini resulted in Hitler getting his way and forcing the Czech evacuation of the Sudetenland and getting the nod for German military occupation. The diplomatic and military manoeuvring was accompanied by an increasingly shrill and almost hysterical propaganda campaign that repeated ad nauseam the accusations that the Czechs were oppressing and committing atrocities against the Sudeten Germans.

At the party rallies in Nuremberg in the second week of September, German leaders hammered home their message to the nation about the Sudetenland issue. Hitler, in his speech on 12 September, stopped short of declaring war but, as Shirer (who was present) reports, it was 'brutal and bombastic, and dripping with venom against the Czech state and especially against the Czech President' (Shirer, 1960, p. 469).

On 30 September, Hitler, Chamberlain, Mussolini and Daladier signed the Munich agreement, which allowed German occupation and was the death knell for Czechoslovakia. Despite Hitler's promise that this was his last territorial demand in Europe, the agreement cleared the way for the later destruction of the whole country and seemed to convince Hitler that Britain and France would not intervene if his expansion was eastwards. On 2 October, as planned all along by Hitler, German troops occupied the Sudetenland and for the propaganda newsreels crowds of cheering Sudeten Germans had been gathered to give flowers to the troops and cheer them on their way – an important aspect of propaganda was to both present the Germans as welcomed liberators and to stress the absence of conflict to justify the action to the domestic and international audiences.

The final dismemberment of Czechoslovakia happened in early 1939 as separatist movements in Slovakia and Ruthenia fomented by the Germans (and in Ruthenia's case the Hungarians as well) weakened the Czech state further. Slovakia, urged on by Germany, declared independence on 14 March. A day later the new Czech president, Emil Hacha (who had replaced Benes in October), was summoned to Berlin and forced to surrender, agreeing in the joint communique on the meeting to place the 'fate of the Czech people and the country in the hands of the Fuhrer of the German Reich' (cited by Shirer, 1960, p. 546). On 15 March at 6am German troops occupied Bohemia and Moravia and on 16 March placed 'independent Slovakia' under German protection.

In the latter stages of the Czech crisis, Goebbels's propaganda task was to build up German self-confidence in the wake of the Anschluss, the occupation of the Sudetenland and then of Bohemia and Moravia. He had to use these bloodless successes to convince Germans of the power of the armed forces and gain their acceptance for the use of violence in achieving further gains in the east – these centred on Memel and the Polish Corridor.

Addressing the Reichstag on the sixth anniversary of his accession to power, he spoke openly of 'extending the *lebensraum* of our people' (Reuth, 1993, p. 244). But this speech was more remarkable for its open threat of annihilation of the Jews and his accusations of a Jewish plot to exterminate the German people. As usual, the speech was broadcast live across Germany and commented upon repeatedly in the following days – in fact part of the speech was to be referred to and repeated on radio and in print regularly over the next few years – especially when Goebbels gave speeches or wrote and broadcast his regular editorials for the *Das Reich* publication (founded in May 1940). In the two-hour speech, Hitler said that the 'Jewish world enemy' had been defeated in Germany but was now confronting and threatening Germany from abroad. He said that international Jewry wanted revenge on Germany and to satisfy its hunger for profit. He said that the Jews were trying to use their financial strength, control of the Western press and political influence to drive 'millions among the masses of people into a conflict that is utterly senseless for them and serves only Jewish interests' (cited by Herf,

2006, p. 52). He then turned to prophecy and threat – a threat he was to attempt to carry out:

> Europe cannot find peace until the Jewish question has been solved. [...] One thing I should like to say on this day which may be memorable for others as well as for us Germans. In the course of my life I have very often been a prophet and have usually been ridiculed for it. At the time of my struggle for power it was in the first instance the Jewish people who only greeted with laughter my prophecies that I would someday take over the leadership of the state and the entire people of Germany and then, among other things, also bring the Jewish problem to its solution. I believe that this hollow laughter of Jewry in Germany has already stuck in its throat. I want today to be a prophet again: if the international Jewish financiers in and outside Europe should succeed in plunging the nations once more into a world war, then the result will not be the Bolshevization of the earth, and thus the victory of Jewry, but the annihilation of the Jewish race in Europe.
>
> (Herf, 2006, p. 52; UWE, 1998)

The thrust of Hitler's speech was that the Jews were forcing war on Europe to destroy Germany, that Hitler and Germany did not want war, but if they were forced into war, that war would only end with the extermination of the Jews in Europe. This theme was take up in march by a 'Jewish expert', Dr Rudolf Urban, in the 21 March edition of *Die Judenfrage* (*The Jewish Question* – a bi-weekly anti-Semitic publication of the Nazi party that was produced from 1937 to 1943 and circulated among party functionaries, Propaganda Ministry staff and to newspapers and universities), in which he justified the invasion of the rump Czechsolovakia as something forced on Germany by the machinations of world Jewry – Germany simply could not have tolerated any longer 'a stronghold of Jewry and Bolshevism' on its borders as the Czech government had totally failed to end the threat posed by these two linked evils (cited by Herf, 2006, p. 54). At around the same time, in a short pamphlet entitled *Who WantsWar?*, Goebbels said that fear of war was being fostered in London, Paris and New York by Jewish circles. He accused the American President Roosevelt of being dominated by a circle of Jewish advisers (this was to become a constant theme in attacks on the USA and Roosevelt). He went on, echoing Hitler, to say that 'if one dark hour war should 1 day break out in Europe, this cry must resound over our whole part of the earth. The Jews are guilty. They want war, and they are doing everything in their power to drive the people into it' (Goebbels, 1982).

   In the first seven months of 1939, this anti-Semitic propaganda became the constant theme in radio commentaries, the press and Nazi leaders' speeches. At first peppered with attacks on Bolshevism, this aspect of the propaganda stopped in May when Goebbels was instructed to halt press and radio polemics against the Soviet Union and Bolshevism (Reuth, 1993, p. 251) – this was in the lead up to the signing of the Molotov-Ribbentrop Non-Aggression Pact between Germany and the Soviet Union in August 1939. From being part of the world Jewish conspiracy and ever-present in Nazi propaganda, Soviet Bolshevism now became the ghost at the feast. Until the 1941 invasion of the USSR, it disappeared from broadcast or written propaganda – an indication of the ability of Goebbels and the press chiefs to control content. The non-aggression treaty included commitments to avoid propaganda attacks on each other. The Soviet-German agreement followed the May Axis military pact with Italy – something that strengthened Germany's diplomatic and military position. In April, citing Polish intransigence over Danzig and the Polish Corridor and alleging Polish aggressive intent, Hitler had renounced with non-aggression pact with Poland and, on the same day, the naval agreement with Britain, accusing the latter of allying itself with Poland to encircle Germany.

During the summer of 1939, Hitler went on the offensive over Danzig and the Polish Corridor. He sought to convince the German people that his intentions were peaceful but those of Poland were not and that Poland was, like the Czechs before it, oppressing the German minority. The implication was that the bloodless victories over Austria and the Czechs could be repeated. Despite the increasingly violent rhetoric from leading Nazis about the Jews and their attempts to foment war, the mood in Germany was more confident than in 1938 and there wasn't the same fear of war (Kershaw, 1987, p. 141).

The propaganda campaign that preceded the invasion of Poland mirrored the earlier one against Czechoslovakia – the rights of the Germans in the semi-autonomous free city of Danzig and in the west of Poland were highlighted and atrocity stories involving Polish police and state persecution of and brutality against Germans abounded. For the domestic audience, the stress was on Polish inhumanity and brutality and the iniquity of East Prussia being cut off from the rest of Germany. But reports by the SD and other organizations on popular opinion in Germany at this time indicated that:

> the desire for peace is stronger than for war [...] there is agreement with the solution of the Danzig question only if this proceeds with the same swift and bloodless fashion as the previous annexations in the east [...] Enthusiasm [for war] such as there was in 1914 cannot be reckoned with today.
>
> (cited by Kershaw, 1987, pp. 142–3)

The propaganda war against Poland continued unabated with a mounting series of radio reports and commentaries on Polish atrocities and aggressive intent. Throughout the last week of August, the German Home Service broadcast daily reports of these atrocities and of allegations that Poland was preparing for war against Germany – on 30 August, German domestic radio and broadcasts for listeners abroad warned of an imminent attack on Danzig by the Polish army and said there was an atmosphere of 'war fever' in Poland (German Home and Foreign Services in German, 30 August 1939). The non-aggression pact with the USSR in late August was used as a means of demonstrating Germany's desire for peace to a population scared of war.

In the last days of August, Hitler was trying to manoeuvre Britain into accepting German action against Poland, but Britain said it would not renounce its guarantees to Poland in the event of an attack. Germany, for its part, reaffirmed that it was demanding the return of Danzig to Germany and a plebiscite in the Polish Corridor – neither of which were acceptable to Poland. At 9 pm on 31 August, German radio broadcast Hitler's 16 point proposal to Poland. But just 90 minutes later German Home Service was reporting violations of the frontier at Danzig by Polish troops and an attack on the German radio station at Gleiwitz at Upper Silesia. The attacks were not by Polish forces – they were carried out by Heydrich's SS forces dressed in Polish uniforms and the bodies of those said to have been killed were dead concentration camp inmates (Kershaw, 2001a, p. 221).

On 1 September, German troops invaded Poland and by the afternoon the army high command reports were being broadcast to the effect that objectives were being achieved with only slight resistance. Hitler issued a proclamation to the army that was widely broadcast and reported:

> Poland has refused my offer for a friendly settlement of our relation. Instead she has taken up arms. The Germans in Poland have been victims of bloody terror, hunted from house to house. A series of frontier violations that a Great power cannot accept, proves that Poland is not willing to respect Reich frontiers. To put an end to this foolhardy situation, I am left with no other means than from now on opposing force to force [...]

> (cited by Shirer, broadcast from Berlin 1 September 1939 in Shirer, 1999, p. 69)

Shirer reported in his broadcasts from Berlin in the early days of September the gloomy atmosphere and the barrage of German radio and newspaper propaganda putting the blame for war on Poland, Britain and France – and behind them the Jews. He emphasizes that the organized and consistent German propaganda did not engender any enthusiasm for war (Shirer, 1999, pp. 68–77). As both Kershaw and Kallis point out, German propaganda failed to develop support for war or even a consensus that war was necessary; in fact there was a manifest opposition to war. What was more successful was the convincing of many Germans that the war was unavoidable and had been forced on Germany (Kallis, 2008, p. 72; Kershaw, 1983, p. 186).

Britain issued an ultimatum that Germany must assure Britain by 11am on 3 September that it was prepared to end its military action against Poland

and withdraw its forces or a state of war would exist. No assurance was supplied and so Chamberlain announced over the radio that Britain was at war with Germany – the French declaration of war followed that afternoon. Hitler used the declarations of war and the alleged Polish aggression against Germany to try to demonstrate to the German people that he had been forced into war by others and had not initiated the conflict. German radio broadcast commentaries saying that Jewish financiers had caused the war, that they controlled the Polish government and had pushed Britain and France into declaring war (German Home Service, 1 September; also broadcast on German Foreign Service in Polish).

German propaganda now developed a much more strongly anti-Western stance and portrayed Britain, France and Poland as warmongers in juxtaposition to the 'peaceful German Reich' (Kallis, 2008, pp. 72–3) British plutocracy took the place of Soviet Bolshevism as the ally of international Jewry. Goebbels wrote just after the outbreak of war that Germany 'did not want war. England inflicted it upon us. English plutocracy forced it on us [...] They [Germany and it allies] will one day deal a terrible blow to the capitalist plutocrats who are the cause of their misery' (cited by Kallis, 2008, p. 73). Interestingly, throughout the war, German propaganda against Britain concentrated on the guilt of the plutocrats and the Jews, the brutality of British bombing raids and the warmongering of Churchill, but the propaganda against Britain lacked the racial hatred aimed at the Poles, Russians, Slavs generally and the Jews. The impression given was that the Nazi leadership still saw the British as people with whom they could eventually find agreement rather than as implacable enemies of Germany. On 23 October, the Reich Press Office issued a directive on attacking Jews in England, stressing the need to emphasize the influence of Jews over the British upper classes and plutocrats, to stress any comments by British people or the British press critical of the Jews and to avoid direct attacks against the English people (Herf, 2006, p. 63). Directives were to become a regular part of the life of the German media – from the Reich Press Office, at Goebbels's daily editorial conferences and from the Ministry of Propaganda's Office of Anti-Semitic Action.

Wartime propaganda and the discourse of extermination

Almost immediately war started, German domestic radio started broadcasting reports from the front, the high command, Führer headquarters communiques and commentaries on both the military and political situations. The radio on 1 September also broadcast a proclamation that listening to foreign radio stations was illegal and punishable by imprisonment, while spreading news broadcast by foreign stations was punishable by death – radio wardens would play a key role along with the SD in rooting out those who were listening to foreign radio. A stream of propaganda blaming the Jews was now to be found across German domestic and foreign radio output – broadcasts in French on 7 September appealed to French troops to refuse to fight in a war that had been started by the Jews, pointing out that British War Minister Leslie Hore-Belisha was Jewish and was 'mobilizing British and French soldiers to fight for world Jewry's profits'. Hore-Belisha, who remained in post until 1940, was a regular target for anti-Semitic attacks on German radio – frequently being described in offensive terms as 'this fat negroid Jew' (German Home Service, 25 October 1939). The same broadcast told German listeners that British soldiers sang a song with the words – 'We are led by a Jew, we are fed by a Jew and we are clothed by a Jew'. Eden and Churchill were constantly derided on German radio as 'friends of the Jews'. On 7 November, German Home Service said that Chamberlain had been harnessed by the Jews to their cart and that British soldiers would become cannon fodder for Jewish interests in a war started by Jews because of Germany's willingness to stand up to Jews and their conspiracies.

German domestic propaganda attacked British plutocrats, the world Jewish conspiracy and also vilified Germans Jews, who were blamed for the defeat in the First World War, for profiteering and for Germany's humiliation in 1918. The anti-Semitic propaganda was multifaceted and constant. Atrocity stories about the Poles continued to be used to justify the invasion; German radio reported on 18 September that Poles had killed German civilians in Warsaw by throwing them from the windows of high buildings. The Poles were increasingly described as sub-human as part of a discourse of dehumanization that was used to justify brutality against them. Goebbels writes in his diary on 10 October that he agreed with Hitler's view that Poles were 'more like animals than human beings, completely primitive, stupid and amorphous' (Goebbels, 1982, p. 16). German radio was quick to point out the numbers of Jews in Poland, saying on 19 September that Warsaw was 'crowded with Jews and full of smells and vermin'. The theme of insanitary, unhealthy conditions in Jewish areas and the picture of Jews as parasites, vermin and sub-human were consistently perpetrated and used to justify the removal of Jews from Germany and the campaign of evacuation of Jews from all occupied areas to concentration camps, labour camps and ghettoes.

Where possible, German domestic radio would find comments from newspapers or radio stations around Europe that were anti-Jewish to try to prove that hatred and suspicion of the Jews was widespread in Europe. Anti-Jewish comments in the British conservative newspaper, the *Daily Mail*, were frequently repeated by the German media – though as the war progressed and the paper became very patriotic it was denounced by German radio as having fallen into the hands of the Jews (German Home Service, 15 November 1939). German soldiers – real or invented – were frequently quoted describing the squalor of Poland and blaming it on the Jews; one being quoted in November in extracts from a war diary as saying the Jews oppressed the Poles and were 'guilty of every crime' in Poland (German Home Service,

8 November 1939). Commenting on radio on 10 November on the bomb that exploded at the Munich beer hall on the night of the commemoration of the putsch, which had been intended to kill Hitler, Hans Fritzsche said there could be only one culprit – the plutocratic English Jew.

Domestic radio output was a mix of narrow, carefully written and highly propagandistic news (always with a slant and often concealing more than it revealed); communiques from the front or from Hitler's headquarters; political, social and military commentaries extolling the virtues of the Fuhrer, the armed forces and the Nazi programme and deriding or dehumanizing their opponents; and, as wartime radio monitor at the BBC (and later art historian) Ernst Gombrich wrote on the basis of his monitoring of German radio throughout the war, the centre pieces:

> were the carefully managed relays of Hitler's or Goebbels's speeches which were invariably held in front of responsive and well-drilled audiences. People were encouraged to listen in groups in factories and barracks, for the idea of the hearer alone in the privacy of his room and capable even to switch off was anathema to this theory.
>
> (Gombrich, 1970, p. 4)

There were nine news bulletins daily along with commentaries given by key performers such as Hans Fritzsche and feature reports with outside broadcasts from the war front or the home front. There was a considerable amount of entertainment programming provided, including martial and classical music and light entertainment. Output was carefully planned and the intention was to make the listener feel part of a great national endeavour, 'to make the listener feel that he or she was living through great times and stirring events and that the radio provided him with the privilege of witnessing history in the making' (Gombrich, 1970, p. 5). The overall theme, Gombrich says, was of 'World history as seen from Germany [...] the fulfilment of a destiny, the redeeming of a promise [...] the reborn nation would triumph over enemies and decadent warmongers in the West [...]' and defeat Bolshevism and the ultimate enemy, 'the Jew' (Gombrich, 1970, pp. 6–7). Victories were celebrated and the armed forces made into heroes, but on radio, in the newspapers and in newsreels for the cinema, there was a clear policy from Goebbels's directives to avoid images or descriptions that would arouse horror, revulsion or disgust with war. Defeats were rarely reported promptly or in full detail.

At the end of 1939 and beginning of 1940 – the period referred to in Britain as the phoney war – little of military substance happened but radio propaganda to the home audience in Germany was on the offensive to convince it that the British and French were fighting on behalf of Jews and to make profits for Jewish financiers. One 'propaganda talk' (as it was openly called) on 20 November 1939 said that France was beset by crime, by 'Jewish fraud,

Jewish swindles, Jewish murders, Jewish chefs du cabinet, and a Jewish journalist representing the government [...] a conglomeration of Jewish criminality and impudence'. This was the tenor of commentaries on an almost daily basis at this stage of the war.

The records of the daily conferences at the Propaganda Ministry show the instructions given by Goebbels or Fritzsche for particular topics or campaigns to be highlighted – for example on 8 November 1939, the radio and press editors were told to compile material on Jewish infiltration of the British press (Boelcke, 1967, p. 4). In December, the meeting was told by Goebbels that no coverage was to be given of British hints that they might discuss a peaceful settlement (Boelcke, 1967, p. 7). On 18 December, Goebbels made it clear that the scuttling of the German battleship *Graf Spee* in the River Plate near Uruguay after being damaged by British cruisers was not to be reported as 'bald fact' and that false propaganda reports were to be put out about the use of poison gas by the British to cover the embarrassment of her loss (Boelcke, 1967, p. 9). Radio reports about the event were suitably economical with the truth or, as in the case of the repeated and inaccurate reports of the sinking of the British aircraft carrier *Ark Royal,* were complete falsifications. With the latter story, after several reports that the boat had been sunk, it turned up in Cape Town and Goebbels asked the naval representative at the press briefing what should be said about this. In a risky rejoinder, the naval representative replied, 'I am afraid I can't make any suggestion on this subject, Herr Reichsminister; after all, the *Ark Royal* was sunk by the Ministry for Propaganda and not by us' (ibid.).

In early 1940, mass executions of Jews in Poland had begun. Reports had been published in the foreign press and Goebbels told the ministerial press conference on 27 January 1940 that this had to be refuted and the German media had to go on the offensive to prevent these reported atrocities from getting wide currency (Boelcke, 1967, p. 17). Within a month of the invasion of Poland, Himmler as Reichsführer of the SS, had been appointed settlement commissar for the east with responsibility for the deportation of Poles, Jews and Gypsies to the 'foreign-speaking Gau' to the east of the areas of Poland that were deemed German provinces. Heydrich was put in charge of the deportation programme, which involved the 'evacuation' of all Jews from Germany to the east (Kershaw, 2001a, p. 244). Very soon after the occupation of Poland, militias had been set up, under SS auspices, staffed by ethnic Germans from captured areas. They were soon involved in the execution of captured Poles and Jews. Hitler wanted no assimilation of Poles with Germans – Goebbels says in his diaries that Hitler's view was that the Poles were animals and their 'dirtiness is unimaginable' – something which was conveyed in propaganda to the German people (Goebbels, 1982, p. 16).

During 1940, propaganda concentrated on continuing to dehumanize the defeated Poles and the Jews and to blame the war with Britain and France on the machinations of Jews. Goebbels said in a speech on German Home

Service on 16 June that Hitler's diplomatic genius in forging the pact with the Soviet Union meant this would not be a war on two fronts but that it would be a war clearly understood as a 'Jewish war' against the Jews who had started the war. Clearly, it was felt that the message still had to be rammed home that the Jews alone were responsible for the war and that Germany was an innocent party, forced into war but now determined to defeat once and for all the Jewish enemy.

Recording in his diary on 17 October 1939 his discussions with Hitler about the work on the propaganda film *Der Ewige Jude (The Eternal Jew)*, Goebbels says that Hitler was very interested and goes on to give his reactions to the clips of film of the Jewish ghetto to be used in it – 'Never seen anything like it. Scenes so horrific and brutal in their explicitness that one's blood runs cold. One shudders at such barbarism. This Jewry must be eliminated' (Goebbels, 1982, p. 23). At this stage, the progress towards the policy of extermination was becoming clearer – Jews were being deported to occupied areas outside the Reich along with gypsies and other undesirables and there incarcerated in concentration camps or murdered in increasing numbers along with the Poles. On 5 April, Goebbels addressed leading editors and the chiefs of the Berlin offices of the foreign press and said that the principle of continuous repetition of propaganda slogans once issued 'must be kept up at all costs; the papers had to address themselves to the broad masses and not to any narrow elite. News without comment must not be published; this meant that each report must be presented as a commentary' (cited by Boelcke, 1967, p. 29).

In the spring and summer of 1940, Germany stepped up the military side of the war with the invasion of Norway and Denmark, then the Netherlands and Belgium, followed by France. As the German army advanced into France, German radio kept up a stream of front reports and commentaries, stressing the nobility of the German forces when compared with the French, who had drafted in colonial troops from Africa – these were described in ghastly racist fashion by radio correspondent Heinz Laubenthal on German Home Service: 'Animal is too honorific a name for these monsters in human shape, with their bloated lips, far-protruding teeth, flattened noses and matted hair' (cited by Gombrich, 1970, p. 8). Racist caricatures of ethnic groups deemed sub-human by the Nazis (black Africans, Jews, Slavs or gypsies) were part of the dehumanization process by which the German army and public were desensitized to the brutality shown towards them.

Goebbels wrote in his diary on 21 June that Hitler had phoned him to report the surrender of France. Goebbels said that the disgrace of 1918 had been extinguished. He then wrote a few days later that he was preparing a 'big programme of celebrations for the radio' in which the entire German people would be involved (Goebbels, 1982, p. 123). On 24 June, Hitler proclaimed the end of the war in the west. Goebbels, at his daily conference on 28 June, ordered that propaganda should now concentrate on

Britain, stressing constantly that Britain wanted this war and would now get what it wanted. He said that the media should not suggest that Germany wanted to destroy the British Empire but should concentrate on defeating the 'war criminals' running the country' (Boelcke, 1967, p. 62). The attacks on Churchill (now prime minister) and other British leaders constantly accused them of being the tools of the Jews (see BBC Monitoring transcripts of German Home Service broadcasts from late 1939 onwards for a host of examples).

The next war propaganda campaign was concerned with the air war against Britain. During the Battle of Britain, Hadamovsky went on bombing raids and filed radio reports, such as that on German Home Service on 11 September 1940, in which he described London as being illuminated by fire and said 'we see the blazing metropoles of England, the centre of plutocrats and slave holders, the capital of world enemy number one'. Goebbels later ordered a stop to this sort of reporting, as he thought Germans would not believe endless reports about a blazing London (Gombrich, 1970, p. 9). When British air raids against Berlin and other German towns took place, the media were ordered to project a sense of outrage but to be accurate about any detail reported – Goebbels's daily conference was told on 23 August that 'the Reich Propaganda offices are to be reminded once more that local reports about air raids must be in conformity with the facts. It is nonsense to distort facts which have taken place in front of everybody's eyes' (Boelcke, 1967, pp. 81–2). When a raid on Berlin hit a hospital, Goebbels ordered that this was to be 'thoroughly exploited' by German radio and it was alleged that the British had targeted a children's hospital (Gombrich, 1970, p. 10). On 20 September, German Home Service said that 'murder upon murder is the password of the British warmongers. Churchill is letting loose his armies against the civilian population of Germany. With typical British brutality he makes them attack places marked with the Red Cross [...] It is Churchill's aim to exterminate German women and children.'

During this period, the daily editorial conferences were being fed a stream of reports – though not for broadcast – of the expulsion of Jews from Vienna and Berlin. The meeting on 6 September 1940 was told that 60,000 Jews would be removed from Berlin over a period of four months and the remaining 12,000 would be gone a month after that. On 17 September, Goebbels told the conference that when the war ended, the Jews would all be removed to Madagascar – this policy and Goebbels's interest in it was raised periodically at the meetings and in his diaries up until early 1942, when the policy was dropped as the 'final solution' programme was put into effect following the invasion of the USSR and the Wannsee Conference on the extermination of the Jews on 20 January 1942.

Throughout the remainder of 1940 and into 1941, propaganda broadcasts stressed the evil of the British warmongers and their obedience to the dictates of the Jewish-plutocrat conspiracy against Germany. By the closing months of the year, Hitler had given up indefinitely his plans for invasion of Britain and signed the directive of 18 December 1940 on the preparation for the invasion of the Soviet Union. In North Africa, the British were in the process of defeating Italian forces – something which led Goebbels to note in his diary on 11 December that, 'our fascist allies are turning into a real mill-stone around out neck'. Goebbels seems unaware at this time, through not having been taken into Hitler's confidence, that he intended to pursue a war against Russia without first having defeated Britain (Reuth, 1993, p. 282).

From the end of 1940 to March 1941, Hitler concentrated heavily on the planning for what was to be Operation Barabarossa – trying to fight against the doubts of his military commanders about what could be achieved. At the same time, he had to commit German troops to North Africa, Greece and the Balkans after the ill-planned and poorly implemented Italian invasion. Alongside these military tasks, considerable resources were being put into the deportation of Jews from Germany, Austria and western Poland and the expulsion of three quarters of a million Poles from the west of the country.

The deportation of the Jews was part of what was now being called by Eichmann (Heydrich's right-hand man) the 'final solution project' under which, 'in accordance with the will of the Fuhrer, the Jewish question within the part of Europe ruled or controlled by Germany is after the war to be subjected to a final solution' (Kershaw, 2001a, p. 352). The plan to rid German-controlled areas of Jews was variously referred to as final evacuation or the final solution. No explicit mention was made of extermination, though Himmler did tell senior SS officers in January 1941 that, after the invasion of Russia, the Slav population of the east would have to be reduced by 30 million (Kershaw, 2001a, p. 353).

On 30 March, Hitler addressed 200 senior Wehrmacht officers at the Reich Chancellery and spelled out his expectations for the coming war with the USSR. This would be the war to crush Bolshevism and Hitler made it clear that Communist officials, commissars and Soviet secret police personnel were to be liquidated. On 31 May, the final preparations for Operation Barbarossa were underway. Goebbels wrote that the entire state and military apparatus was being mobilized and a careful camouflage exercise was being implemented to hide it. The Propaganda Ministry was to play up the threat of invasion from England and fourteen army divisions were moved westwards to give this credibility (Goebbels, 1982, p. 390). The stream of anti-Jewish propaganda was maintained, too, with attacks on the former War Minister Hore-Belisha for trying to fix up 'a typically Jewish deal' with Washington aimed against Germany and then a description of him as 'a son of the ghetto' and as a 'small and dirty Jew' (German Home Service, 7 and 11 June 1940). There was a particular focus on the USA and the power of Jewish financiers there in this bout of propaganda. In his *Das Reich* article broadcast on 14 June, Goebbels did not address major issues of the day but talked about the problems of pleasing all radio listeners – admitting that in wartime the needs of the war and the broadcast or communiques, reports from the front and other material limited what else could be put in programmes.

At 5.30 am on 22 June, German radio broadcast fanfares by Liszt and then Goebbels read out Hitler's proclamation to the German people announcing the start of the war with the Soviet Union. It was justified as the only defence against the Jewish-Bolshevik plot to destroy Germany and the whole of European civilization. This was accompanied by a declaration by Ribbentrop that faced with the aggression of the Soviet government, Germany 'has taken defensive military measures' (German Home Service, 22 June 1941). Later in the day, the radio said that Germany had uncovered a British-Bolshevik conspiracy and on 'a scale unprecedented in the world, the German armed forces started on their march against the Bolshevik traitors of the Kremlin'. The thrust of radio and newspaper propaganda over the following days – accompanying the optimistic front reports that described the rapid advance of the Germans and the collapse of the Soviet defences in many areas – was that the Soviet Union had betrayed Europe by planning to stab Germany in the back as it was fighting 'plutocratic England'; the 'double-crossing intrigue of the Jewish Bolshevist leaders in the Kremlin' had led to the German actions (German Home Service, 22 June 1941). The propaganda plot read like a poor crime novel, full of simplistic, unbelievable and emotional accusations. Despite the propaganda onslaught to come about the barbarian, Asiatic Slavs, initial broadcast commentaries spoke of the plight of the Russian people under the 'Jewish-Marxists' who 'sucked the blood of this gigantic country'. Full-scale attacks now resumed on the Jewish-plutocratic-Bolshevik alliance. The USA was not forgotten in the attacks and one 'Topic of the Day' commentary on 24 June told Germans that American Jewish capitalists had financed the Russian Revolution. Listeners were told repeatedly that they were part of a great crusade to save Europe from the Jewish-Bolshevik threat.

Within days of the invasion, there were reports emerging of the killing of large numbers of civilians by the advancing armies and of other atrocities. Fritzsche broadcast a riposte on 28 June saying, in typical reverse propaganda style, that these accusations were only being made to cover up the atrocities committed by the Soviets, these commentaries were supplemented with eye-witness reports from German soldiers describing the atrocities committed by the Soviet government against their own population – particularly in areas inhabited by non-Russians, such as the Ukraine and the Baltic states. Some of the commentaries referred back to Hitler's 1939 Reichstag speech warning that if the Jews started a war, they would be annihilated. The 'Topic of the Day' on German Home Service on 10 July said openly that 'The Jew wanted war. He will lose it, and Europe will be rid of a 1000 year old pest.'

The battle against the Soviets and the Jews was being increasingly referred to as a 'battle of annihilation' (German Home Service, 28 July 1941). Russian prisoners were described as little more than beasts – one Front Report in mid-August talking of 'this procession of misery and ugliness cannot be imagined. Base and criminal faces prevail in this assembly of races and race mixtures.' The debasement of the captured enemy again provided a frame for viewing the Slavs as less than human and therefore not deserving of the same human respect as the Germans – ideologically and psychologically paving the wave for the killing by execution, gas chambers or starvation of countless Soviet prisoners of war.

The depictions of Soviet prisoners and descriptions of life in the Soviet Union were part of the propaganda discourse established and reinforced daily at the conference at the Propaganda Ministry. On 5 July, the minutes of the meeting state that the press and radio must show how by

> means of their diabolical system of Bolshevism, the Jews have cast the people of the Soviet Union into this unspeakable condition of deepest human misery [...] It will therefore be the task of the German press [including radio] to present these views in an effective campaign of enlightenment [...] A particular role will have to be played by an impressive juxtaposition of inhuman conditions in the Soviet Union on the one hand and the social progress, the high cultural standard and the health *Lebensfraude* of the working man in National Socialist Germany – newspapers are told to have contrasting pictures of the German worker and the bestialized Bolshevik types.
>
> (Boelcke, 1967, p. 178)

In one of his first major speeches after the invasion of the USSR, Hitler launched the annual Winter Relief Campaign with a speech in Berlin, broadcast live on German Home Service on 3 October, in which he justified the invasion of the Soviet Union as necessary to overthrow the conspiracy of 'democrats, Jews and freemasons' that had thrown Europe into war in 1939. He went on to refer to the Russians as the 'Mongols of Genghis Khan'; the alleged Asiatic and barbaric nature of the Slavic enemy became a regular theme in anti-Soviet propaganda. In his *Das Reich* editorial broadcast on 14 November 1941, Goebbels returns to the responsibility of the Jews for starting the war and refers to Hitler's prophecy on 30 January 1939 that if they started a world war then the result would not be their victory but 'the annihilation of the Jewish race in Europe, [which] is now being fulfilled'. He said that:

> the Jews are experiencing a fate which is hard but more than deserved. Sympathy or pity have no place here. World Jewry, when instigating this war, estimated the power at its disposal quite wrongly, and is now undergoing a gradual process of annihilation [...] It is now perishing according to its own law.

The article and subsequent broadcast on German Home Service concluded by saying that the task of dealing with the 'parasitical race' was that of the government and he warned people not to take things into their own hands but 'everyone has the duty to appreciate the measures of the state against the Jews, to stand up for these measures against anybody'. A week later in a speech at Berlin University, reportedly widely on the radio, Goebbels repeated Hitler's prophecy of the annihilation of the Jews. At the time of these broadcasts, the mass killing of Jews was taking place and being accelerated so that the rate of annihilation was far from gradual.

The invasion of the Soviet Union hastened the extermination process that started after the invasion of Poland and the deportation of Jews from Germany and Austria. These measures, with the encouragement of Hitler and the SS leadership, were 'pushing German policy towards the Jews strongly in the direction of genocide. The preparations for the "war of annihilation" with the Soviet Union marked [...] a "quantum jump" into genocide' (Kershaw, 2008, p. 67). The *Einsatzgruppen* (SS death squads operating in German-occupied Eastern Europe and pushing into the USSR in the wake of the invasion) continued in an uncoordinated way the work of killing Jews and other 'undesirables' begun in Poland; but in August 1941 they were ordered by Himmler that there was to be 'a drastic extension of the slaughter to all Jews, irrespective of age or sex' (ibid.). In November, Goering, who was in charge of the forced emigration of Jews from Germany, commissioned Head of Reich Security Heydrich to complete the preparations for the 'complete solution of the Jewish question within the German sphere of influence in Europe' (IMT, 1949, XXVI, pp. 266–7). Heydrich set these preparations in motion, drawing representatives of all the major institutions involved together at the Wannsee Conference on 20 January 1942, where protocols were drawn up for the extermination of the Jews in German-controlled Europe, with gas chambers at camps like Auschwitz to replace shootings by the SS or gassing using carbon monoxide from truck exhausts.

As these preparations continued and the rate of killings of Jews, Poles, Russians and others increased, the German public and armed forces through the radio and the press (and of course on film, at exhibitions, in Nazi art and through the education system) were bombarded with descriptions, images and exhortations about the sub-human nature of the Jews and Slavs and of the responsibility of the Jews for the war. Goebbels recorded in his diary on 19 August 1941, that Hitler's prophecy of annihilation 'is coming to pass in these weeks and months with an almost eerily graceful certainty. In the East, the Jews are paying for it. In Germany they have already in part paid for it, and in the future they will have to pay still more' (cited by Herf, 2006, p. 116). Millions of Germans in local administration, the party machine, the railways, the police, the army and the SS were involved in the deportation, incarceration and killing of the Jews and it was hardly a secret, despite not being spoken of openly. The Soviet media reported mass killings by the Germans in occupied Soviet territory and on 17 December 1942, Foreign Secretary Anthony Eden told the House of Commons that Jews were being killed in huge numbers by the Germans in occupied Eastern Europe.

As war dragged on in the east into 1942 and then on into the next winter, the war propaganda had increasingly, as Goebbels pointed out at the daily conferences, to call on the 'fortitude inherent in the German people [...] People must be made to realise that our thesis of the superiority of the German people over the Russians must now be put to the test since we cannot otherwise maintain our fundamental claims' (Boelcke, 1967, p. 198). Front Reports and the daily Fuhrer HQ communiques became more guarded and careful as there were fewer victories to report and setbacks were rarely reported factually, often with a spin that tried to make retreats or defeats appear like clever tactical manoeuvres. Major disasters were misreported or reported very late with the maximum of camouflage.

The Japanese attack on Pearl Harbour on 7 December 1941 and Germany's subsequent declaration of war on the USA announced by Hitler in the Reichstag on 11 December, led to an even greater outpouring of anti-Jewish bile. The declaration of war attacked the Jews and the alliance of Jewry, US capitalism, British plutocracy and Jewish-Bolshevism in the Soviet Union, likening the Russians to the Asiatic hordes of Attila the Hun (German Home Service, 11 December 1940). Now the attacks came in full spate, though again (as in the case of anti-British propaganda) lacking the hatred of the Americans per se rather than their war-mongering leaders. The German people were told that the British and American people never found out the truth of what was going on or why they were at war because of Jewish control of the press by 'Roosevelt's and Churchill's news Jews' (German Home Service, 13 December 1940). In his New Year proclamation, read on radio by Goebbels, Hitler attacked the Jews once more saying that the war being fought by Britain and the USA was not for democracy as they claimed but for Jewish capitalism and Jewish Bolshevism. The annual speech by Hitler on the anniversary of his appointment as chancellor, in January 1942, again concentrated largely on threats against the Jews – just ten days after the Wannsee conference to plan the final solution. Hitler said that Germany's Jewish enemies were now suffering 'a shipwreck' and he repeated that the war would end with the wiping out either of the Jews in Europe or the German nation (German Home Service, 30 January 1942).

As the war in North Africa and the east continued and the overall outlook was not so optimistic militarily, Goebbels carried out a reorganization of the balance of programming and, on 20 February 1942, it was announced that there would be an increase in light entertainment programmes. In the broadcast on 6 March of his *Das Reich* editorial, the propaganda minister reminded Germans that they were involved in a total war and that 'to lose this war would mean the end of our Reich' – an indication of the growing realism in commentary and the need to prepare Germans for even more sacrifice and for a long and painful war.

Hitler's Reichstag speech on 26 April, broadcast live, reminded Germans that it was the Jews who had been responsible for the defeat in 1918, that it was the Jews who 'carried the Bolshevik infection' and were 'the war-mongers in the ranks of the plutocracies' and had dragged Britain and the USA into the war. He warned that 'death will come' to those fighting for Jewish world domination. A few days later, Nazi Labour Head Robert Ley used May Day to attack satanic Bolshevism and remind Germans that it was the Nazis who had rescued May Day from the Jewish poison of Bolshevism and its 'bestial methods' of domination (German Home Service, 1 May 1942). Later in May, Goebbels told his daily conference that the German people should be told about the hatred of Britain and the USA, directed by the Jews, against the Germans and the annihilation of the German people that would be the fate if the war was lost – but he warned against giving too much detail of Western plans for Germany at the end of the war as this would 'merely have an overall depressing effect' (cited by Boelcke, 1967, p. 238). In August, Goebbels instructed the media to print more attacks on Jewish agitation in enemy countries to coincide with the increased pace of evacuations of Jews from Berlin to the east (Boelcke, 1967, p. 268).

The daily conferences at this time are ever more concerned with how to counter British, American and Russian statements that German offensive military strength had been exhausted – though now German propaganda would be increasingly fighting against the mounting tide of events, with only a few minor victories, like the capture of Tobruk, to celebrate (Boelcke, 1967, p. 244). By July, Goebbels was already warning journalists to stop reporting any stories about the difficulties of fighting in Russia during the last winter, as 'if this subject were now to be discussed, the public would no longer feel that sense of relief as at the end of winter, when it's all over and done with, but would feel anxious about what the coming winter would bring in terms of sacrifices, hardships and demands' (Boelcke, 1967, p. 253–6).

In August, the siege of Stalingrad began. Front Report and communiques from Hitler's headquarters mentioned the city practically every day, stressing that it was only a matter of time before it fell to the Germans. In a speech at the Sportpalast on 30 September, Hitler tried to hit a positive note, telling his live and radio audience that the perils of the previous winter had been surmounted, that Stalingrad would soon be taken and he then went on to repeat his prophecy about the annihilation of the Jews and say that he was right to say that the Jews would be annihilated (German Home Service, 30 September 1942). In his speech to veteran party militants on the anniversary of the beer hall putsch on 9 November, Hitler had nothing to say of the increasingly unfavourable situation in North Africa, of which his audience was now aware, and relied on hackneyed attacks on Roosevelt and Churchill and then fell back on his Jewish annihilation prophecy once more (German Home Service, 7 November 1942).

There was further bad news for the German war effort in mid-month when the Soviet winter offensive began and Soviet forces broke the German-Romanian line north and west of Stalingrad. By 23 November, Goebbels had to tell the daily conference that Paulus's army had been surrounded – the German public were not told until 16 January 1943 that this encirclement had taken place. The battle reports broadcast on German radio between late November and mid-January tried to give a picture of solid defence and successful counter-offensives against the Red Army. Over the next few weeks, there were regular reports of 'fruitless' Soviet attacks, 'hard defensive battles' and 'heroic counter-offensives' (see, for example, German Home Service, 12 December 1942). The defeat in North Africa was by mid-December being reported as 'Rommel's masterly withdrawal from El Alamein', a victory for the 'fluid warfare practised by Rommel' (Front Report on German Home Service, 15 December 1942). On 18 December, amid the worsening military situation, Hans Fritzsche broadcast a riposte to what he said were false atrocity allegations against Germany, especially Eden's speech to parliament. Fritzsche denounced the accusations as a sign of Britain's failing morale.

In his Christmas radio address broadcast on 24 December, Goebbels called on Germans to be aware of the need for the subordination of all else to the war effort. Hitler's New Year proclamation on the radio, read out by an announcer, reminded Germans that it was the 'Jewish wire-pullers' who had caused Germany's defeat in 1918 and he returned once more to the theme that having launched the war to exterminate Germany, the Jews would find that it was they who would be exterminated in the conflict (German Home Service, 1 January 1943). In early January, military commentaries avoided the topic of Stalingrad and there were fewer Front Reports from there. But by the last two weeks of the month, German war reports admitted encirclement and told of Soviet attacks on all fronts at Stalingrad. Between 22 January and 2 February, German defences were breached and Paulus, promoted to Field Marshal by Hitler on 30 January, negotiated the surrender of the Sixth Army and the end of the battle for Stalingrad. For the first time, Hitler failed to make a speech on the anniversary of his coming to power and Goebbels read a proclamation by the Führer over the radio from a rally at the Sportpalast – much of the speech concentrated on fighting world Jewry, which was described as 'the ferment of decomposition of nations and states [...] and it will be as long as nations do not find the strength to rid themselves of this germ of disease' (German Home Service, 30 January 1943). The propaganda minister made no direct reference to the scale of the disaster in the east, referring only to the unimaginable ferocity of the fighting and the need for the German people to embark on total war.

In a talk on the radio on 2 February, Fritzsche admitted that the last German bastion at Stalingrad had been overwhelmed, suggesting a glorious last ditch defence rather than the surrender of a field marshal and hundreds of thousands of troops. A communique from the Führer headquarters on 3 February said that the battle at Stalingrad was over and army 'loyal to their oath to the last breath [...] under the exemplary leadership of Field Marshal Paulus' had succumbed to superior numbers. This version was diametrically opposed to Hitler's fury that Paulus had betrayed him and Germany and that he should have killed himself (Kershaw, 2001b, p. 550). A series of political talks and commentaries over the next few days emphasized that there could be no middle course between German and European culture and Jewish Bolshevism and demanded resistance to the threat from 'Mongolized Russia' (German Home Service, 4 February 1943). Goebbels *Das Reich* editorial after the defeat said that Stalingrad had been Europe's advance guard in resisting the threat from the steppes of the 'Asiatic flood'.

By the time that Germans began to understand the enormity of the defeat suffered at Stalingrad, Goebbels had been given plenipotentiary powers to direct the 'total war' and this was to become the dominant theme in his speeches over the remaining years of the war. On 18 February, Goebbels made his keynote speech about total war to a carefully coached audience of party members at the Sportpalast in Berlin. The audience was whipped up to constantly chant and shout in support of what Goebbels had to say, so that the radio audience could have no doubt about the fervour of the reception for his words – he was interrupted over 200 times during the speech by his cheering and clapping audience (Welch, 1993, p. 140). He told his audience not to ask how things like Stalingrad happened but to see that history would prove that they were not in vain. He said the most important task now was to fight 'eastern Bolshevism which had subjected almost two million to the Jewish terror and which was preparing for a war of aggression against Europe'. Goebbels repeated the images of Jews being like infectious diseases and said that Germany alone was standing against this contagion and it was necessary to combat it through 'complete and radical exter [here he corrects himself], elimination of Jewry [this is followed by loud applause and chants of Out with the Jews]' (German Home Service, 18 February 1943).

At the daily conferences on the days following the speech, it was made clear by the minister that full exploitation was to be made in propaganda of the speech and the concept of total war. Throughout February and March 1943, radio carried a stream of commentaries on the threat of Jewish-backed Bolshevism. The needs of total war were to include the war against the Jews – in February and March Goebbels, as Gauleiter of Berlin, was almost frenetic in his efforts to clear Berlin of Jews and believed that he had more or less achieved this by mid-March, something his biographer says the propaganda minister considered his 'greatest political achievement' (Reuth, 1993, p. 318).

From April 1943, a major anti-Bolshevik and anti-Jewish campaign was conducted following the discovery of the remains of thousands of Polish officers and soldiers in the Katyn forest in Poland. The killings were blamed on the Jewish-Bolshevik secret police – throughout April and May 1943, German radio presented the massacre as a specifically Jewish crime using terms such as the 'Jewish slaughter' and the 'Jewish mass murder at Katyn'. The message to Germans was resist the Jewish-Bolshevik forces or your fate will be the same as those who died at Katyn. In his speech on the fourth anniversary of the German Labour Front, Dr Ley concentrated on attacking the Jews. The BBC Monitor who transcribed and translated the speech on German Home Service on 3 May 1943 describes Ley as screaming at points during his speech that the Jews must and will be destroyed and saying 'we will not abandon the struggle until the last Jew in Europe has been destroyed', leaving little doubt as to how he saw the objectives of the war.

Despite the increasingly unfavourable military outlook, the shortages of manpower and the continuing Soviet advances, there was no let-up in the campaign to kill the Jews. Speaking to a meeting of SS officers in Posen on 4 October, Himmler was frank about the 'Jewish evacuation programme, the extermination of the Jewish people [...] a glorious page in our history' (cited by Kershaw, 2001a, p. 604). Jews were still being transported to camps such as Auschwitz-Birkenau, Treblinka, Belzec and Chelmno; those ghettoes which still existed in Eastern Europe were being emptied; and the extermination programme using gas chambers was being carried out on an industrial basis. It should not be forgotten that at the Majdanek extermination camp Soviet prisoners of war were killed alongside Jews and other inmates – of 235,000 people of 50 nationalities killed there between mid-1942 and the autumn of 1943, 120,000 were Jews (Herf, 2006, p. 139). Soviet prisoners of war, Poles, gypsies and other nationalities were killed in the camps alongside the Jews. None of this was reported by the German media – the destruction of Jewish ghettoes in Poland, the deportations of Jews from Greece, Italy and other occupied areas, the construction of gas chambers and crematoria never happened as far as German reporting was concerned. While Goebbels's diary entries, some of his speeches and those of Hitler, as well as records of Himmler's meetings with SS commanders, all show a knowledge and close involvement in the whole extermination campaign, as Herf points out there is no 'paper trail that would indicate the state of their detailed knowledge' of the final solution (Herf, 2006, p. 233).

As the military situation worsened, Hitler became less and less visible to the German people and major speeches were left to Goebbels and other leaders. The initial radio reporting of the D-Day landings on 6 June 1944 presented them as though they were a piece of everyday news (German Home Service, 6 June 1944). Fritzsche broadcast a commentary that day that just repeated the message that whatever happened, German military victory was inevitable. There were no major speeches or announcements by Nazi leaders – even Goebbels. The minutes of his daily conferences collected by Boelcke end well before 6 June and so there is no record of how he instructed the Propaganda Ministry and radio/press editors to react. He seemed more concerned, to judge by his diary entries, with the success of the Soviet offensive against German Army Group Centre in late June. One of the lines of propaganda pursued by German radio and the press after the invasion was to revert to the Jewish angle – saying that only 'human vultures, Jewish dealers in death' would benefit from the invasion (German Home Service, 8 June 1944). But even Hitler's headquarters could not totally avoid the facts and on 10 June admitted that the invasion force had been reinforced and allied troops were mounting ever heavier attacks on German defences inland from the beaches. The attempt on Hitler's life on 20 July 1944 took a little more explaining – Hitler spoke on the radio at one in the morning after the attempt and said Germans should not blame the army and promised that the guilty would be punished (German Home Service, 21 July 1944). Over the next few months, much of the commentary and Goebbels's editorials concentrated on ramming home the total war message or lauding the performance of the V-1 and then V-2 rockets used to bombard British cities.

Hitler's New Year speech was broadcast on 1 January but contained nothing but the usual attacks on the world Jewish conspiracy and a promise that national socialism would rebuild what had been destroyed. In the New Year, propaganda output contained increasing accusations of atrocities committed by the Soviet army – many undoubtedly based on the brutal revenge exacted by the advancing forces but as usual it was hard to unravel the truth from falsehoods designed to scare the German people into greater resistance. The atrocity accusations were accompanied by the assertion that 'the Jews are ruling everywhere' in the territories captured by the Soviet army and that 'the Jewish OGPU [Soviet secret police] are carrying out executions and sending children to the USSR in sealed carriages' (German Home Service, 9 January 1945).

In the remaining months of the war, fear and atrocity propaganda mixed with unrealistic hopes pinned on new weapons and then a brief period of hysterical optimism after the death of Roosevelt dominated radio and other propaganda. Goebbels was even more prominent and Hitler yet more reclusive and absent from the lives of Germans – he issued a proclamation to the armed forces on 11 March 1945, which Goebbels read over the radio, calling on Germans to resist the Jewish alliance of capitalism and Bolshevism. In his penultimate *Das Reich* editorial written on 14 April, Goebbels warned of the 'bloodthirsty and vengeful enemy in east and west' and on Hitler's birthday, 20 April, he broadcast on the home service to rant against Germany's enemies and their 'mania for destruction and a diabolical rage for annihilation'. He accused Jewry of going all out for its 'Satanic aim of world destruction'.

On 30 April, as the Reich Chancellery in Berlin came under Soviet artillery fire and serious resistance was all but at an end, Hitler committed suicide. Goebbels and his family followed suit the next day. The designated heir to the Reich, Admiral Doenitz announced on radio on 1 May that Hitler was dead and that it was his task to save the German people from destruction. Between that date and the radio announcement of Germany's surrender on 7 May, radio broadcasts tried to deny strenuously reports from the British and US forces of the discoveries of concentration and extermination camps – saying that these accusations were the work of 'Jewish propagandists'. The Nazi delusion that all could be blamed on the Jews persisted until the bitter end.

5
Rwanda: Genocide, Hate Radio and the Power of the Broadcast Word

> They will be throwing themselves into the mouth of the hyena and committing suicide. They will all be Exterminated and none will live to tell the disastrous story. Let them come, the Rwandans are waiting for them with machetes.
>
> (Comments by Rwandan Prime Minister Jean Kambanda broadcast by Radio Televison Libre des Mille Collines (RTLM), 12 April 1994)

> The Chamber finds that RTLM broadcasts engaged in ethnic Stereotyping in a manner that promoted contempt and hatred for the Tutsi population. RTLM broadcasts called on listeners to seek out and take up arms against the enemy [...] These broadcasts called explicitly for the extermination of the Tutsi ethnic group.
>
> (International Criminal Tribunal for Rwanda (ICTR) Verdict on RTLM and *Kangura* journalists, nahimana, p. 283)

Note on sources

Unlike the previous case study of Nazi Germany, this one of Rwandan radio broadcasts before and during the genocide cannot make extensive references to a wealth of transcript material. Whereas Nazi radio was monitored and transcripts published by the British Broadcasting Corporation (BBC) Monitoring Service, this was not the case with RTLM. This station, which became the dominant broadcaster in the year before and during the genocide, was not widely or systematically monitored. Its broadcasting range prevented the BBC Monitoring Service station in Nairobi and the American Foreign Broadcast Information Service station in Kinshasa from picking up its programmes and they did not have in place monitoring capabilities in the Kinyarwanda language (interviews with Greenway and Harmes).

Some transcript material is available from the documentation of the 'media trial' at the International Criminal Tribunal for Rwanda and online at the University of Texas collection, but it is very limited; the ICTR, for example, has released translations of just 34 Kinyarwanda broadcasts (Straus, 2007, p. 623). There is also the written testimony of the head of United Nations (UN) peacekeeping forces in Rwanda and of journalists and academics who covered or studied the genocide, which has provided accounts and dates of broadcasts and this is also used, though with care because of the problems of verifying the accuracy of some of the accounts. It has, for example, proved impossible to verify that a broadcast was made by RTLM calling on Hutus to kill more Tutsis because 'the graves are not yet full', which became the title of a book about the genocide (Berkeley, 2002).

This case study uses the transcripts available, supplementing them with the accounts of those involved in the events and in reporting or studying them. This involves analysis of the transcript material that is available (in terms of the framing and representation of events and their participants), but also exposition and interpretation of the huge quantity of secondary material and the proceedings of the ICTR in Arusha, Tanzania. Of particular use have been the works of Gulseth (2004), the Thompson collection (2007), Prunier (2008), the analysis published by Kellow and Steeves (1998) and the challenging and provocative work of Straus (2006 and 2007).

Introduction

Between 6 April and 19 July 1994, Hutu militants, militias, ordinary Hutu civilians, the Rwandan army and the police killed between 500,000 and 800,000 people. Estimates by leading researchers of the genocide (Prunier, 2008, p. 265) have put the figure at 800,000–850,000, while the leading sceptic and questioner of widely accepted details of the genocide, Scott Straus, argues for the lower figure (Straus, 2006, p. 51). There is unlikely ever to be a thoroughly accurate figure as many bodies were dumped in rivers, others were buried in remote graves and the mass movements of people before and during the genocide mean that accurate censuses are not available to set levels for the pre and post-genocide populations. Extensive argument over numbers is like a morbid version of the theological arguments over the number of angels on a pinhead. What is abundantly clear is that a massive proportion of Rwanda's Tutsi population were killed along with tens of thousands of Hutus opposed to the militant Hutu Power ideology of the planners and leaders of the genocide. The genocide was carried out with haste but with evident organization and with the media, especially vernacular radio, playing a prominent role.

The genocide was not a sudden event. Rwanda and neighbouring Burundi, both of which have a mix of Hutu and Tutsi citizens, had since the dying years of Belgian colonialism suffered frequent and bloody outbreaks of violence between the two communities marked by horrific massacres, waves of refugees moving within and beyond the borders of the countries and periodic bouts of guerrilla warfare. They were not stable, well-ruled polities governed according to the rule of law and with equality of all citizens.

The two main population groups, the majority Hutu and the minority Tutsi, had co-existed within the Great Lakes region covering Rwanda, Burundi, parts of eastern Congo and southern Uganda for many centuries, developing a complex and highly hierarchical society. The constantly developing and evolving social, political and economic structures in Rwanda and the balance of power between the communities were altered by German and Belgian colonialism and then later by the poorly managed decolonization process. The result was negative in its consequences and helped develop the communal conflict and suspicions that formed the foundations for frequent bouts of violence and mass killings between 1959 and 1994, and then for the genocide in 1994.

The course of the genocide and the role of the media before and during the killings can only be understood through placing it in the context of the historical development of Hutu-Tutsi relations, the effects of colonialism and decolonization, and the development of the political dynamics and the discourse of Hutu dominance and Tutsi resistance over decades of independence. The following sections look at key aspects of the history of colonial and independent Rwanda, the development of a political culture dominated by hierarchy, hegemony and obedience and the evolution of a language of political discourse that stressed the primacy of identity. The history of the genocide and the role of the media, notably radio, is set out and examined to identify the key factors in the role and behaviour of the media as part of the machinery of mass murder. The intention is not to write a new history of the genocide and its causes, but to identify clearly the role played in it by radio and the particular characteristics of radio output that made it the most oft repeated example of broadcast incitement of hatred and murder.

Colonial myth-making and the creation of Tutsi hegemony

Rwanda is a mountainous country with a very high density of population and resulting competition for cultivable land. It has long been known, and from it comes the name of the 'hate radio' station, as the land of a thousand hills (*mille collines*). It has high rainfall and is suitable for agricultural cultivation, but the mountainous nature of the terrain makes this arduous with hillsides painstakingly terraced to provide farming land on all but the steepest and most heavily forested slopes. Human habitation has traditionally been on hillsides rather than in valleys, with the hilltops the abodes of the elites.

The 20th century saw a huge growth in the population – from 1.59 million in 1934 to 7.12 million in 1989, with population density rising from an index of 61 people per square kilometre in 1989 to 270 per square kilometre in 1989 (Prunier, 1997, p. 4). The population is, in practice, even more densely packed together because of the terrain and terracing of the hills – leading to practical density of people to arable land of 380 per square kilometre in 1989. As can be seen, a key element in conflict between the Hutu and Tutsi was control of land. Over time, the exact percentages have fluctuated slightly but the population split was 85 per cent Hutu, 14 per cent Tutsi and 1 per cent Twa.

The history of settlement and the development of hierarchical structures of government is a contested one. There are few accounts of the pre-colonial history of Rwanda that are reliable and are not coloured either by colonial distortions, misunderstandings or misrepresentations of the nature of the pre-imperialist society. The task of establishing an accurate picture is made more difficult by attempts at revisionism by Hutu intellectuals and historians, who constructed an account of pre-colonial society based almost purely on the concept 'segregation and violence' perpetrated against the Hutu agriculturalists by Tutsi pastoralists occupying positions of absolute dominance (Berry and Berry, 2001, p. 5). The colonial and revisionist accounts of history used the terms 'tribe' or 'ethnic group' to describe the Hutu, Tutsi and Twa. And, as the ever sharp Straus observes, 'Tribe offers understanding without history. Tribe can explain Africa in a way that disregards how countries were put together, how leaders and parties have governed, and how economies and institutions shape behavior' (Straus, 2006, p. 17).

There are fundamental problems in using the word 'tribe' in delineating communities in Rwanda and also the question of how its use or applicability compares with that of the term 'ethnic'. Tribe and its derivatives – tribesman, tribal, tribalism, tribalist and so forth – have been at the core of European descriptions of Africa for centuries. The word itself is derived from the Latin *tribus*. Of key importance in the modern usage of the word is the link with concepts of primordialism or primitiveness. In his accounts of the civil wars in Rome and the Gallic and African wars, Julius Caesar refers repeatedly to the 'Roman people' and to the 'tribes' of Gaul and Germany or to the 'barbarian tribe' of the Albici, and to 'the Lusitanians and other barbarian tribes' (Caesar, 1976, pp. 53–4 and 58; 2006, p. 27). The importance of Roman history and Latin in teaching at schools and universities for the upper and privileged middle classes in 19th-century Europe introduced the term, with all its connotations of primitivism, to the cohorts of soon-to-be colonizers and colonial administrators. Colonialism took the concept of tribe and applied it, designating people as belonging to tribes and even inventing tribes where there existed only loose communities (Davidson, 1992, p. 100; Somerville, 2009, p. 536).

It was only in the decades following the end of colonialism in Africa that the use of the term began to be questioned. Archie Mafeje was prominent in the rebellion against the use of tribe and tribalism within anthropology and political science. He pointed to the ubiquity of the term in describing Africa and its inadequacy in describing the diversity of African societal and political forms prior to colonialism – something key to the over-simplification and distortion of reality that was to occur with profound societal consequences in Rwanda. Mafeje argued that:

> European colonialism, like any epoch, brought with it certain ways of reconstructing the African reality. It regarded African societies as particularly tribal. This approach produced certain blinkers or ideological predispositions which made it difficult for those associated with the system to view these societies in any other light.
>
> (Mafeje, 1971, p. 253)

In Rwanda, the reconstruction of reality and the imposition of a colonial version of the relationship between the Hutu and Tutsi communities had profound and incendiary consequences. At the time of the arrival of the Europeans, Rwanda was a hierarchical kingdom ruled by a Tutsi king (*mwami*) with a structure under him dominated by a Tutsi aristocracy, but within a system where Hutus could occupy major positions within society. Power was based on lineage but also on control of resources. Tutsis were predominantly pastoralists and 'the herding of cattle had more than just economic significance; the ownership of cows was not only an important status symbol but it was an essential ingredient in the traditional socio-political systems of Rwanda and Burundi', according to Lemarchand (1970, p. 15). The Hutu were mainly cultivators of the land and had a lower social status. But the divisions were not hermetically sealed and Hutu could own cattle and raise their status, and there were also poor Tutsi farmers. The Rwandan population was 'linguistically and culturally homogenous' and, while divided into three groups (Tutsi, Hutu and Twa), they 'had none of the characteristics of tribes, which are micro-nations. They shared the same Bantu language, lived side by side with each other without any "Hutuland" or "Tutsiland" and often intermarried' (Prunier, 2008, p. 5).

The ethnic and geographic origins of the Hutu and Tutsi are far from clear. Anthropologists and historians of the pre-colonial era have yet to provide a coherent account of the settlement patterns or migration routes of Rwandans. Lemarchand has suggested that the Tutsi pastoralists established their dominance after moving into the territory of present-day Rwanda through a mixture of conquest and assimilation, though he also questions just how different ethnically they were from the Hutu, given the sharing of a common language with no evidence of either group having been forced to assimilate linguistically (Lemarchand, 1970, pp. 18–19).

Physical differences attributed to the two groups have been used by colonialists and the politically motivated elites and intellectuals of each community to posit a history of ethnic difference and to support the contentious narrative of Tutsi origins in Ethiopia and of Tutsi conquest and subjugation of the Hutu. The Tutsi are often tall and thin, while Hutu are more often short and stocky, though whether this denotes differing ethnic origins or just the effects of differing physical activity and lineage patterns over centuries is not clear. In the eyes of the colonizers, this spoke of widely differing origins. Belgian administrators portrayed the Tutsi as aristocratic, having 'nothing of the negro [...] His features are very fine [...] Gifted with a vivacious intelligence [...] he is a natural-born leader'; while the Hutu 'display very typical Bantu features [...] a wide nose and enormous lips They are extroverts who [...] lead simple life' (accounts of Rwandans by Belgian administrators recorded in reports of the Ministry for the Colonies cited by Prunier, 2008, p. 6).

These very simplistic and racist descriptions were taken by the colonizers as universally applicable to all Tutsi and Hutu and they developed from them a basic categorization that the Tutsi were born to lead and were aristocrats by right of conquest of the Hutu inhabitants, who were by their very nature peasants and helots. But the societal structure in place when colonial rule was imposed was far more complex. The Tutsi were clearly dominant and had developed a complex structure of rule involving political, societal and economic hegemony including forms of clientism, in which ownership and utilization of cattle and land helped maintain the Tutsi elite in a position of power.

The mwami was the source and symbol of Tutsi rule and he ruled through a structure with divisions between chiefs responsible for ruling people and commanding armies (chiefs of men – *mutwale wa ingabo*), those with responsibility for cattle (chiefs of pastures – *mutwale wa inka*) and chiefs who governed areas of land (chief of the landholdings – *mutwale wa buttaka*) and were responsible for distributing land for cultivation and for taxing landholders or users; peasant farmers had the use of land but not the ownership, which was ultimately invested in the mwami (Prunier, 2008, p. 11). Occupancy of these positions was in the gift of the mwami (Lemarchand, 1970, p. 27). Army and cattle chiefs were almost always Tutsis, while land chiefs could be either Tutsi or Hutu. As cultivators, the Hutu gained access to the land through the land chiefs and so their point of contact with the system was frequently through a Hutu chief.

While the Hutu were clearly at a lower social level than the Tutsi, there were no absolute institutional obstacles, rather than economic ones, to Hutu becoming cattle-owners and so improving their lot economically and socially. A Hutu who:

> made his way up the social ladder should ipso facto be assimilated into the Tutsi caste and henceforth regarded as Tutsi – a Tutsi was a patron and a Hutu a client; a Hutu could not be a patron, but if he developed the wealth or social standing to wield patronage he had effectively become part of the Tutsi hierarchy.

> (Lemarchand, 1970, pp. 38–9)

There was no concept of innate superiority because of race or place of origin, this was a myth developed by the Germans and Belgians and later the Tutsi elite under colonial rule – then of course used in a different form by Hutu intellectuals to justify revolt against the mwami and to support the concept of Hutu Power (Mamdani, 2002, p. 79).

The right to rule of the Tutsi mwami and the hierarchical system under him had the status 'of a divinely ordained social structure in which each individual was assigned a specific caste and each caste a specific rank' (Lemarchand, 1970, p. 33). It should be noted, though, that this system was not universal throughout Rwanda at the time of colonization. Several Hutu communities lived beyond the rule of the Tutsi and the mwami – notably in the north, north-west and south-west of the country. President Juvenal Habyarimana and the group around him, who were to become the planners and leaders of the genocide, were mainly from the north-western area that was only brought under Tutsi hegemony with the assistance of the colonial administration – some of these areas were still under Hutu rule until well into the 20th century (Prunier, 1997, p. 19).

The role of the Belgian colonial administration in assisting the spread of Tutsi hegemony followed the pattern developed by the Germans before the First World War. Colonial control involved considerable indirect rule, with power being retained by the mwami and his chiefs under Belgian tutelage. The Belgians stripped the Hutu of what little role they had in the chiefly system and gave ever more power to the Tutsi – including access to education, opportunities for entry into the priesthood and Catholic hierarchy, and military assistance and administrative backing for the expansion and entrenchment of Tutsi societal dominance. This took place in the mid-1920s and resulted in the removal of the vast majority of Hutu chiefs from their positions and the filling of all vacancies with Tutsi – so that the vast majority of Hutu were now directly governed by Tutsi chiefs (Mamdani, 2002, p. 34). In 1929, the system of people, cattle and land chiefs was streamlined into one with a single all-powerful chief – this meant fewer chiefs and clearer lines of authority. More significantly, a system of communal labour known as *ubuletwa*, which was controlled by the chiefs and had been an accepted, if not liked, part of the traditional structures of rule and economic relationships, was transformed into a far more exploitative form of forced labour totally under Tutsi control.

Land tenancy and grazing contracts between rich patrons and clients began to change as the Belgians conducted land reforms and alienated land from traditional users (especially in the former Hutu-controlled areas in the north-west and south-west). As these changes were often mediated through the agency of Tutsi chiefs and elites, they became another symbol of growing Tutsi exploitation of the Hutu (Prunier, 2008, pp. 27–9). This whole period of Belgian rule transformed Hutu-Tutsi relations and created 'Tutsi and Hutu identities evocative of colonial power and colonial subjugation – and not just local power relations – colonialism made them more volatile than ever in history' (Mamdani, 2002, p. 74).

In 1933, the Belgians introduced identity cards that clearly listed a person as either Tutsi or Hutu. Lacking any clear historical, linguistic or scientific method for ascribing ethnic identity, the Belgian authorities used ownership of ten cattle as the measure for who was a Tutsi – itself a clear negation of any idea of ethnic differences between the two groups; identity became a function of cattle wealth (Mamdani, 2002, pp. 98–9; Ndayambaje and Mutabarika, 2001, p. 32). From then onwards, 'tribal identity' became hereditary, so entrenching and institutionalizing the concept of inherited superiority or inferiority. Within this system, the discourse of societal relationships was very much of master and servant – no longer even patron and client – with little or no opportunity for the Hutu to progress socially or even economically. The pre-colonial social structures and beliefs underlying them had hardly been egalitarian, but the colonially constructed Tutsi hegemony had shed the element of porousness and there was a loss of the space for the agents within the system to be able to negotiate their role in it. Belgian power, as Mamdani puts it, 'turned Hamitic racial supremacy from an ideology into an institutional fact by making it the basis of changes in political, social and cultural relations. The institutions underpinning racial ideology were created in the decade from 1927 to 1936' (Mamdani, 2002, p. 88).

For their part, a large proportion of the Hutu seemed to accept, albeit grudgingly, this racial superiority. There seemed to many, as Lemarchand concludes, a natural order to this and a habit of passive if sullen obedience developed with a parallel attitude that suggestions of change and greater equality for Hutus somehow 'violated some basic cultural norms' (Lemarchand, 1970, pp. 43–4). There developed an ever greater resentment of Tutsi dominance but alongside it a fear of trying to challenge the system, supported as it was by the Belgians. The few Hutus able to gain access to education were insecure and increasingly suspicious of both the Tutsi and the Belgians. This suspicion and insecurity built up and, when released, manifested itself in outbreaks of unchecked aggression against the Tutsi.

The Hutu revolution, the Belgian volte face and independence

Following the Second World War, the UN took over supervision of the government of all the mandated territories – of which Rwanda was one. It renamed them trusteeships and charged mandated powers like Belgium with moving towards independence and ensuring development and fair treatment of the populations of the territories. A Trusteeship Council was set up consisting of representatives of the five permanent members of the UN Security Council. The Trusteeship Council sent periodic missions to trust territories and they and UN members (notably the independent states of Asia and Africa) began to exert pressure for progressive change and the preparation of territories for independence. The Belgians were slow to react to growing evidence of Hutu resentment, to pressure from the UN and were out of step with the growing climate of world opinion in favour of progress towards independence for colonies.

These developments and the rising, very vocal tide of nationalism across Africa fuelled further the resentment and a sense of injustice among Hutu elites in Rwanda. In the 1950s, the few educated Hutu, those who most immediately felt the exclusion of Hutu from social or economic advancement, began to call openly for change and to set up Hutu organizations aimed at achieving changes in the status of the majority of the population. At the forefront was a desire for the recognition of the equality and rights of educated Hutus. This was accompanied by changes in the attitude of the Church – from effectively excluding all but a tiny minority of Hutu, the Church began to express doubts about the inequalities of the existing system and to talk of raising the status of the Hutu (Linden, 1977, p. 97). There was particular sympathy for the Hutu among younger clergy. The Swiss-born Bishop of Rwanda in the 1950s, Monsignor Perraudin, came to support the cause of Hutu equality and worked closely with one of the leading Hutu campaigners, Gregoire Kayibanda.

Kayibanda was one of the small Hutu elite, who were becoming increasingly vocal in opposition to Tutsi hegemony and to Belgian use of the Tutsi elite to rule the Hutu. He was fortunate enough to attend the seminary of Nyakibanda, which in turn enabled him to become a teacher at Classe Institute near Kigali. He was active in Hutu and wider Rwandan cultural organizations and became secretary of the Rwandan Literary Committee and the Belgian-Rwandan Friendship Society. In 1954, Kayibanda was appointed editor of the Catholic journal *l'AMI*. He also became editor-in-chief of the Catholic periodical *Kinyamateka*, and personal secretary to the bishop, Monseigneur Perraudin. He used his position in the Church and access to the bishop to argue the case for Hutu rights and attract the backing of the Church and win supporters (Prunier, 1997, p. 45).

The slow rise of the Hutu elite, their gradual appointment to positions of authority or influence in the economy, the Church and as teachers, gave them a little more confidence in dealing with the Tutsi. Although there were gradual measures by the Belgians to improve the position of the Hutu, by 1959 only 1 out of 82 chiefs was Hutu and 50 out of 1100 sub-chiefs; on newly established advisory councils, Hutu had 6 per cent of seats with 19.3 per cent of seats on lower councils. But the Hutu continued to organize. Cultural associations, cooperatives, mutual societies and clan organizations began to form – with the clear aim of developing institutions and pressing for Hutu rights and for the diminution of Tutsi power. The clan organizations were chiefly among the northern and north-western Hutu groups (notably the Bakiga clans in the north-west), who had most recently been brought under Tutsi control.

As the Hutu elite became more organized, it received increasingly vocal backing from sections of the Catholic Church. In 1956, in a stridently political public statement, Bishop Perraudin said that the Hutu should overthrow and chase into exile the Tutsi elite – a chillingly prophetic statement that showed the switch in support but also the continuing idea of the Tutsis as some form of external force (Ndayambaje and Mutabarika, 2001, p. 37). The church's volte face was matched by a slower but nonetheless clear change in official Belgian policy and the beginnings of greater equality for the Hutu. Visits by members of the UN Trusteeship Council in the 1950s and their critical reports about inequality, injustice and the wrongs of the Belgian-enhanced Tutsi supremacy both encouraged Hutu resistance and helped pushed the Belgians into raising their status. Church support was moving from the vocal to the financial, with funds going to Hutu groups, as well as Hutu leaders like Kayibanda being appointed to edit Church publications with the freedom to use them to promote the Hutu cause (Lemarchand, 1970, p. 108).

The big leap forward in the development of the Hutu ideology of revolt came in March 1957 with the publication and propagation of what became known as the Bahutu Manifesto. Drafted by a nine Hutu intellectuals, including Kayibanda, the manifesto highlighted what it called 'the social aspect of the racial problem' and demanded 'reforms in favour of the Muhutu population subjected to the Hamite monopoly on other races which had inhabited the country earlier and in greater numbers' (Sebahara, 1998). It stated that, 'The problem is basically that of the political monopoly of one race, the Mututsi. In the present circumstances, this political monopoly is tuned into an economic and social monopoly [. . .] [and] a cultural monopoly, which condemns the desperate Bahutu to be forever subaltern workers' (cited by James, 2008, p. 92).

The ideology set out in the manifesto took on and developed the Belgian-inspired ethnic view, keenly adopted by sections of the Tutsi elite, that the Tutsi were a separate, possibly Hamitic race from Egypt or Ethiopia, which had migrated to Rwanda, conquered the Hutu and subjected them to Tutsi hegemony on the basis of an assumed ethnic superiority (Lemarchand, 1970, p. 152; Mamdani, 2002, pp. 103–4; Sebahara, 1998). The rather artificial colonial/Tutsi ethnic/racial superiority construct had backfired and now had the effect of fuelling a racially based ideology of Hutu revolt that would in the short term fire rebellion against the 'outsider' and in the long term would become part of the ideological discourse of Hutu power, and the generation of even greater suspicion and hatred of the Tutsi. Hutu political movements now began to form. The dominant group around Kayibanda followed the tenets of the manifesto and formed the Hutu Social Movement, which then became the first major Hutu political movement, Parmehutu – the Party of the Hutu Emancipation Movement. This was the largest and most influential movement and through Kayibanda's Church links had the effective support of Bishop Perraudin and material support from the Church.

The rise of the Hutu movements and the shift in Belgian attitudes did not go unnoticed by the Tutsi elite. In 1957, ahead of a planned visit by the UN Trusteeship Council, a document was produced by Tutsi leaders in the name of the mwami and the Rwandan people calling on the Belgians to transfer government power to the mwami and his council. This was an attempt to outflank Hutu activism and to get the UN to back very rapid decolonization before the Hutu could persuade the Belgian to replace the Tutsi elite with a Hutu one. In the late 1950s, members of the pro-monarchist Tutsi elite formed the Rwandan National Union (UNAR), while more moderate Tutsis willing to cooperate more with Hutu groups established the Rwandan Democratic Rally (Rader). Hutu political leaders stressed that they wanted an end to minority rule and for power to be transferred to the majority (but clearly they intended it to be Hutu rule with the exclusion from politics of the Tutsi minority, rather than a more representative system in which the Tutsi still had some political role) and said that only this could bring democracy. The reaction of the Tutsi elite was shrill and was a reflection, Mamdani cogently argues, of the beliefs of an elite that had accepted completely the colonial racial myth and 'who were bent on defending colonial privilege as a time-tested tradition' and by so doing retaining Tutsi hegemony in an independent Rwanda (Mamdani, 2002, p. 118).

A letter was published by hard-line members of the Tutsi elite close to the mwami stating that the Hutu could never enjoy equality and fraternity with the Tutsi because the supreme ancestor, Kigiwa, had made the Hutu subordinate; the letter went on to argue that the Tutsi ruled by right of conquest as 'our kings conquered the land of the Hutu, killed their "little" kings and thus subjugated the Hutu; how can they now pretend to be our brothers?' (cited by Mamdani, 2002, p. 118). This Tutsi view showed a lack of understanding of the Hutu proclamations about democracy for all Rwandans – Hutu activists intended 'democracy' to mean Hutu majority rule and subordination of the Tutsi, not equality and fraternity. The effect of the Tutsi declarations and appeals for rapid independence was heightened by UN calls for Belgium to set a date for independence – this pushed the Hutu political leaders and groups to accelerate their political activity. Leaders like Kayibanda realized that accepting the UN-desired pace of change would favour Tutsi dominance in an independent Rwanda if nothing was done immediately to change the balance of political, social and economic power between Hutu and Tutsi in favour of the majority.

The event that led to the first major outbreak of violence between the two communities developed from the death of the mwami on 28 July 1959 and the appointment by members of the royal court of a weak successor whom the elite believed they could manipulate. Following the death, Kayibanda openly proclaimed Parmehutu as a political movement renaming it MDR-Parmehutu (MDR standing for Rwandan Democratic Movement). It had the majority of its support in the Gitarama and Ruhengeri regions (gaining some support from the north-western Hutu clans). It now only needed one incident to release the violent tensions seething beneath the surface. That incident came on 1 November 1959, when Dominique Mbonyumutwa, a Hutu sub-chief and Parmehutu activist was attacked and badly beaten by a group of Tutsi militants belonging to UNAR. Rumours rapidly circulated that he had been killed and Parmehutu mobilized thousands of Hutu to carry out revenge attacks against the Tutsi – this was not just an attack on UNAR but on the Tutsi elite and the chiefs who exercised its powers at local and regional level. Hutu gangs killed many Tutsis and burned Tutsi homes 'without making any distinction between high-lineage Tutsi and ordinary *"petit Tutsis"* ' (Prunier, 1997, p. 49). Estimates of the numbers killed vary, but most put the figure around 200–300, most of them Tutsi, though with some Hutu victims of Tutsi reprisals organized by UNAR (Mamdani, 2002, p. 123; Prunier, 2008, p. 49).

The Tutsi elite and UNAR tried to resist, but while the Belgians did little to stop Hutu attacks, they obstructed Tutsi retaliation. A state of emergency was imposed and the Belgians appointed an officer of the colonial Force Publique in Congo, Colonel Guy Logiest, to take charge of security and effectively run the territory. He immediately made clear that his sympathies were with the Hutu and that Tutsi elite domination was a threat to public order. To the satisfaction of the Hutu movements, he started replacing Tutsi chiefs and sub-chiefs with Hutu (Mamdani, 2002, pp. 123–4). Logiest took charge of the political evolution of Rwanda in the years leading up to independence and, writing over 25 years later, he was unrepentant about his decision to fully support Hutu action to overthrow Tutsi dominance:

> Some among my assistants thought I was wrong in being so partial against the Tutsi and that I was leading Rwanda on a road towards democratisation whose end was distant and uncertain [...] Today, twenty-five years later, I ask myself what was it made me act with such resolution. It was without doubt the will to give people back their dignity. And it was just as much the desire to [...] expose the duplicity of a basically oppressive and unjust aristocracy.
>
> (Logiest memoir cited by Prunier, 1997, p. 49)

By assisting the destruction of the Tutsi aristocracy, Logiest and the Belgians failed to give support or protection to ordinary Tutsi and set the precedent for mass violence, with Hutu perpetrators allowed to act with impunity. The killings and the support of newly appointed Hutu chiefs for the revolution, meant that although the violence subsided somewhat, Hutu groups were able to proceed with their aim of driving the Tutsi from many areas, seizing their land and killing Tutsi leaders who resisted. Tutsi reprisals made the

Hutu even more determined to destroy Tutsi power, but also fuelled Hutu insecurity – there was a real anxiety among the Hutu that there would be a massive Tutsi backlash and it was this 'anxiety that fed hatred of the Tutsis that was prevalent everywhere' (Ndayambaje and Mutabarika, 2001, p. 41).

The fear and the insecurity turned the violence from something aimed against the Tutsi monarchy and chiefs into 'a xenophobic radicalization of the Hutu revolt' so that it became broadly anti-Tutsi (Lemarchand, 1970, p. 166). In the period between November 1959 and mid-1960, 21 Tutsi chiefs and 332 sub-chiefs were killed, arrested by the security forces or forced to resign in the face of local Hutu hostility (Lemarchand, 1970, p. 173). The killings, violent attacks and the failure of the authorities to stop the violence caused over 130,000 Tutsis to flee Rwanda – mainly to Uganda or Tanzania.

In this atmosphere of fear, violence and growing Hutu ascendancy, communal elections were held in the middle of 1960. With Tutsi chiefs ousted and voting on an individual basis rather than conducted communally through the chiefs, Hutu parties dominated. The structural changes and the elections saw chiefs and sub-chiefs replaced by mayors, burgomasters and communal councillors. Between 26 June and 30 July 1960, 229 burgomasters and 3125 councillors were voted in. The traditional structures had been swept away, with mayors and burgomasters in place of chiefs and communes run by elected councils instead of sub-chiefs. The voting was dominated by Parmehutu – the most radical and organized Hutu group. It returned 2390 councillors: Apromosa (a more moderate Hutu party) won 233, Rader 209 and UNAR 56, with 237 independents elected. Of the 229 burgomasters, 160 were from Parmehutu and only 19 were Tutsi (Prunier, 1997, pp. 51–2).

To prevent further interference and to get round criticism of the slow speed of decolonization, an administrative coup was carried out by Kayibanda and his supporters, with the backing of Logiest and the Belgian government. On 28 January 1960, a meeting of burgomasters and communal councillors was called in Kayibanda's home territory of Gitarama – Parmehutu bussed in thousands of its supporters to ensure no backsliding. Kayibanda had prepared in advance a declaration of independence, which was adopted by acclamation by the elected officials present. A provisional government was set up under Hutu control. The Belgians accepted the verdict and legislative elections were set for 25 September.

In the run up to and immediately after the election, there was further anti-Tutsi violence, with over 150 Tutsi killed, thousands of houses burned and 22,000 people displaced, many of them fleeing to Uganda. The election was an overwhelming victory for Parmehutu – Kayibanda's party received 78 per cent of the vote and UNAR 17 per cent. The UN had little choice but to accept this, though the Trusteeship Council gave a scathing opinion of what had happened: 'The developments of the last 18 months have brought about the racial dictatorship of one party [...] An oppressive system has been replaced by another one [...] It is quite possible that some day we will witness violent reactions on the part of the Tutsi' (UN Trusteeship Commission, 1961). The UN had clearly adopted the colonial/Tutsi myth of racial conflict – which also served Kayibanda's purposes. Between the legislative election and independence on 1 July 1962, small groups of Tutsi rebels carried out attacks in Rwanda from bases inside Uganda. These attacks, often against Hutu civilians as well as government targets, brought immediate and massive retaliation. The Tutsi fighters became known by the Hutu as *inyenzi* (the Kinyarwanda name for cockroaches). This became the label for all Tutsi fighters and was often used indiscriminately to mean Tutsi generally. The killing of cockroaches became almost a national duty for Hutu.

From independence to the genocide: the development of a discourse of dominance

The First Republic in Rwanda, with Kayibanda elected president, was a Hutu state with racially based hegemony of the majority over the minority (Gulseth, 2004, p. 12). An ideology and language of politics developed that was the reverse of the colonially encouraged Tutsi superiority discourse – now the Tutsi were excluded because they were labelled as outsiders who had subjugated the majority by force and who must now be permanently excluded from power on the basis of their racial identity. Between independence on 1 July 1962 and the end of the decade, the racial discourse became even more dominant in politics and Tutsis were progressively excluded from politics, administration and denied educational or other opportunities. The Hutu elite's use of racist ideology to exclude the Tutsi was given impetus in July 1963 by raids into northern Rwanda by Tutsi guerrillas based in Uganda and later by guerrillas based around Kivu in the conflict-ridden eastern Congo.

In December 1963, a raid into the Bugesera region of Rwanda by Tutsi led to a government-encouraged pogrom in the area against resident Tutsi. Lemarchand estimates that 10,000 Tutsi were killed and that in the weeks that followed 'Rwanda lived through an unprecedented orgy of violence of murder' targeted against Tutsi (Lemarchand, 1970, pp. 216–9). The final death toll is unknown, though Mamdani puts it between 10,000 and 14,000 (Mamdani, 2002, pp. 130–1). Tens of thousands of Tutsis fled Rwanda – many of them joining the guerrillas and thereby increasing Hutu apprehension of a backlash to come from the feared *inyenzi*. Fear, suspicion and dehumanization of the Tutsi as *inyenzi* or covert supporters of the guerrillas became part of the everyday language of politics. Tutsi leaders within Rwanda were harassed, imprisoned or even executed and UNAR was eventually banned by the government in 1969. The propagation of the racial ideology of Hutu rule was stepped up by the government and Parmehutu through government pronouncements, public meetings, the government-run Radio Rwanda station (the sole legal broadcaster) and government-run newspapers.

Radio Rwanda was particularly important, as the government used it to broadcast frequent warnings for Hutus to be alert to incursions by Tutsi. During the December 1963 raids, the Hutu prefect of the Gikongoro region, Andre Nkeremugaba, summed up what was becoming the core of Hutu power ideology when he told burgomasters and councillors from his prefecture, 'We are expected to defend ourselves. The only way to go about it is to paralyse the Tutsi. How? They must be killed' (Lemarchand, 1970, pp. 223–4). He and other local officials (with central government backing) urged local Hutu armed with pangas, clubs and spears to kill the Tutsi to stop them supporting incursions. As Lemarchand acutely concludes, 'popular participation in violence created a kind of collective catharsis through which years of pent-up hatred seemed to find an outlet' – a hatred deriving from subjugation but carefully nurtured and developed by the ruling elite (ibid.). There was little international interest in events in Rwanda but on 10 February 1964, in one of the rare international comments on the killings, Vatican Radio described them as the most terrible and systematic genocide since the genocide of the Jews by Hitler.

The events of 1963, by creating greater fear among ordinary Hutu of Tutsi invasions, increased the credibility of racially based pronouncements by Hutu elites and increased the animosity of Tutsi in exile. It became clear that Tutsi would only be tolerated if they kept completely out of politics and accepted their subjugation passively. The imposition of an ideology of racial difference was complete – with the Tutsi defined and identified on official identity cards as a separate race, and treated as barely tolerated aliens.

Relatively few Hutu benefitted materially from the new hegemony. Economic problems and the insularity of the Parmehutu elite around Kayibanda meant that many Hutu peasants were hardly better off than under Belgian and Tutsi rule. By the early 1970s, this led to demonstrations by students and young Hutu demanding even more discrimination in favour of the majority group. The demonstrations were accompanied by outbreaks of violence against Tutsi civilians. By this time, Kayibanda was increasingly autocratic in his rule but also increasingly distant – rarely appearing in public. A recluse in his palace (Prunier, 2008, p. 60), he tried to use anti-Tutsi feeling resulting from the lack of development and as a result of recent massacres of Hutu by the Tutsi military regime in Burundi to rally the Hutu to support his increasingly enfeebled rule. He encouraged the rigid enforcement of racial quotas to exclude the Tutsi in order to promote Hutus. He charged the army chief, Juvenal Habyarimana, with establishing Committees of Public Safety to keep watch on the Tutsi. There were a few killings and a further round of mass emigration of Tutsis in 1972 and early 1973, but this time it did little to bolster Kayibanda's power.

These problems and the effective exclusion of the Hutu elite from the north-west from positions of power in favour of those close to the president, led to the coup of 5 July 1973. This was led by one of the few northerners to retain power, Major-General Juvenal Habyarimana. He was supported by officers and elites from the north who felt they had been marginalized – the northern elite group were known as the *abakonde*. Kayibanda was kept in detention until his death on 15 December 1976. Habyarimana replaced Parmehutu elites with his supporters, with northerners and particularly the *abakonde* group from the north-west. By the time of the invasion of northern Rwanda by the Tutsi-led Rwandan Patriotic Front (RPF) in October 1990, Hutu from the north-west held a near monopoly of senior positions within the government, the army and the economy (Straus, 2006, p. 23). The new leader also set about replacing the racially based ideology with a less severe one based more on ethnic rather than racial differences – the Tutsi were not accorded equality, but it did mean that the extreme racialism was dropped and it was conceded that the Tutsi were a Rwandan ethnic group with limited rights of participation and education according to their representation in the overall population. This was intended to reduce the growing tensions and outbreaks of violence caused by the strict imposition of racial identities and the labelling of the Tutsi as an alien race (Ndayambire and Mutabarika, 2001, pp. 42–3). Habyarimana diminished discrimination but retained limits on Tutsi advancement through a system of regional and ethnic quotas in education, the civil service and other areas of employment (Newbury, 1992, pp. 198–9; Straus, 2006, p. 23).

One thing that didn't change under Habryarimana, was the level of central government control exerted right down to local level and the continuation of forms of compulsory communal labour. Habyarimana retained control over the most minor local appointment to ensure that his supporters retained power and surveillance both over the Tutsi and of former supporters of Kayibanda. The new regime continued to exclude Tutsis from the higher positions in local and central government, education, the civil service and the army. Not a single Tutsi burgomaster or prefect was appointed under Habyarimana and there was only one Tutsi officer in the army, two Tutsi members of parliament (MPs) in the national assembly and one Tutsi cabinet minister. But in education, the quota system wasn't as strict as under Kayibanda and more than 9 per cent of school and university students were Tutsi (9 per cent being the official figure given for the proportion of Tutsi in the population as a whole).

In 1974, Habyarimana created his own political party to replace Parmehutu and entrench the new government as the sole force in Rwandan politics. It was called the Revolutionary Movement for National Development (MRND) and changed the constitution to make Rwanda a one-party state – Parmehutu was no longer legal. The MRND was dominated by the north-western elites. In line with the tradition of tight control over all aspects of life, all Rwandans were required to be members of the party. All burgomasters and prefects had to come from the ranks of established party cadres (Prunier, 2008, p. 76). The government carried out administrative reforms to clearly designate who controlled what. Appointments were carefully controlled to ensure maximum obedience and so local administration units served as efficient transmission belts for directives from above. They also ensured that information on potential sources of unrest could be gathered quickly and dealt with through the hierarchy. The system was also used to exact communal labour. As Mamdani notes, this system of tight local control was key to the rapid organization and implementation of the genocide and the mobilization of ordinary Rwandans as executioners on a mass scale in 1994 (Mamdani, 2002, p. 144). Administrative control went alongside a small but tightly organized army and a rigidly controlled state broadcast and print media system, overseen by Office Rwandais d'Information (ORINFOR – the government-run body that ran the press and radio broadcasting).

The existing identity card system for all Rwandans was also tightened up, with ethnic origin and place of residence included on the cards. These had to be produced on demand, particularly when travelling outside the holder's home region. Travel was not encouraged nor was internal migration – authorization had to be granted by the authorities for people to move residence. Rwanda in the 1970s and 1980s 'was probably the most controlled state in the world outside' the communist bloc (Melvern, 2000, p. 25; Prunier, 2008, p. 77).

The late 1970s and 1980s were periods of relative peace in Rwanda, with little violence – partly a result of the rigid control exercised through the party, administration and army and partly a result of relative prosperity, with high coffee and tin prices on the world market bringing in increased income. When the author visited Rwanda in October 1988, Rwandan Tutsis told him that, while they were hardly free and equal, they were at least now safer than under Kayibanda. Habyarimana's tightly run regime enjoyed close relations with the Mobutu regime in Zaire and received strong aid and military support from France. In the 1980s, Paris had overtaken Brussels as Rwanda's main backer – particularly in terms of military training and support. Rwanda's relations with neighbouring Burundi were poor – Burundi was ruled by a Tutsi military elite prone to carrying out massacres of educated Hutu when they felt threatened by the majority population. But this picture was soon to change. Economic decline, due to adverse weather and to a decline in coffee and tin prices, led to greater worsening poverty. There was growing resentment of the communal labour demands of the administration – theoretically no more than two days a month but frequently double that. The historical overcrowding and land shortages now became extreme, as an expanding population was faced with falling income and no surplus land to increase export crop or food production.

The fall in export income affected the prosperity of those immediately around Habyarimana, and competition increased for means of extracting personal wealth. The main conflict occurred between government and party leaders from the tight-knit group around the president's wife Agathe and her extended family and clan members, and those of the elite outside this group. Madame Habyarimana was the descendant of Hutu chiefs from the north-west and her marriage to Habyarimana had extended his support network in the region. This group was known as 'le clan de Madame' or the *akazu* (Kinyarwandan for 'little house'). It had strong influence over the president and was strongly represented in government and in the higher echelons of the army. Members of the group supported the president's policies but had a tougher attitude towards the Tutsi, as was soon to emerge.

To make matters worse, a wave of demonstrations in support of democracy was sweeping sub-Saharan Africa. Donors, international organizations and traditional supporters like the French were putting pressure on Habyarimana (as they were on other African leaders) to democratize and move away from one-party systems. In this atmosphere, there was growing feeling among educated Rwandans outside the tight circle of the ruling elite that political reform was long overdue. These elite groups included many Hutu from central and southern Rwanda who felt excluded under Habyarimana. Some were old Parmehutu-style politicians with a continuing suspicion of the Tutsi, others had a more inclusive approach to politics and were willing to work with Tutsi if this would lead to more equitable participation in government. Under pressure, in September 1990 Habryarimana set up a commission to look at political reform.

Before any serious consideration could be given to the political structures, an invasion of northern Rwanda by the Tutsi-dominated RPF and its army, the RPA, changed everything. The RPF was the main exile movement and was based in Uganda. Its leading members included many who had been, or whose parents had been, forced into exile in anti-Tutsi violence after 1959. The main leaders, Fred Rwigyema, Paul Kagame and Adam Wasswa, were all exiles who had fought for and gained senior positions in Ugandan leader Yoweri Museveni's National Resistance Army (NRA) during its fight for power in the 1980s. Rwigyema had risen to be Commander of the NRA and Minister of Defence.

Once Museveni was entrenched in power, the presence of large numbers of Tutsi exiles in the army and government became a political embarrassment and in November 1989, Rwigyema and other leading Tustis lost their posts. This spurred them on to use the RPF to force change in Rwanda. The RPF's primary aim was to bring about the return of Rwandan exiles to their home country with guarantees of their safety – and they were prepared to use the military force that the veterans of the Ugandan war offered. Their longer-term political aims were not clear and while the RPF claimed to represent all Rwandans, it was clearly Tutsi-led and made up largely of Tutsi exiles and their descendants. The 2500-strong RPA army that invaded on 1 October 1990 was led by officers and non-commanding officers (NCOs) who had combat experience in the NRA and the Ugandan army. They were well-armed, some of the arms having been simply taken from the Ugandan army. It posed a serious threat to Habyarimana and his 5200 strong army, the Rwandan Armed Forces, FAR.

The RPF invasion enjoyed the element of surprise and was initially successful. In the opening days of the invasion, with little serious resistance from the Rwandan army, they advanced some 60 kilometres into the country. Then disaster struck the RPF. In a short period of time, Fred Rwigyema and two senior officers, Majors Banyingana and Bunyenyezi, were killed. There has been speculation that internal dissension led to the killing of Rwigyema, but the fast-moving nature of the offensive and the close combat control exercised by the officers seems a much more realistic account (Prunier, 2008, pp. 94–6). The RPF was pushed back towards the Ugandan border once the Rwandan army recovered from the initial shock and took advantage of the command vacuum. But the RPF did not fracture and Major (later to be Major-General) Paul Kagame returned from a training course in the USA and took command.

After the initial shock of the invasion, the government reacted with a three-pronged strategy of internal repression and propaganda against opponents, a military offensive and a diplomatic push to gain backing for the fight against the RPF. Within days of the invasion, the government had arrested over 13,000 suspected opponents – most of them Tutsis (Straus, 2006, p. 25). Many of them disappeared and may have been killed soon after the invasion or during the genocide. The regime also moved away from its marginally gentler approach to the Tutsis and, as Gulseth observes, started to 're-racialize' them, with the militant group around the *akazu* taking a major role in this and in the formation of the group of Hutu supremacists that came to be known as Hutu Power (Gulseth, 2004, p. 12).

The propaganda was conducted through government-controlled newspapers, by government and local government leaders at public meetings from national to local level, and particularly through Radio Rwanda, the government's national radio station. Radio Rwanda was the only legal station in Rwanda and it was used to give the government version of events and to issue directives to the population. Under Kayibanda, the racial approach to Hutu dominance was the key factor of the discourse in politics and in the government-controlled media when it came to the Tutsi – there would be upsurges in anti-Tutsi rhetoric during periods of insurgency by Tutsi exiles. Habyarimana toned down the rhetoric a little and dropped the racial aspect largely, but the message was still there that the Hutus were in control and the Tutsis should know their place.

The upsurge in demands for an end to the one-party state and for greater political freedom, a freedom that would also give freedom for Tutsis to engage in politics, led to a different political environment for the media and different demands on government propaganda. As Chretien points out, first:

the propaganda is set within a traditional socio-racial policy that had been refined for a generation. Second, changes within Rwanda's political and social conditions in the generation since independence meant that, after 1990, the sense of belonging among the Hutu was no longer the sole factor leading to political mobilization

and so the propaganda discourse had to be developed and became 'a tool for disqualifying all opponents and for uniting the Hutu masses around the so-called Hutu Power movement, thus facilitating recruitment and expansion' of the drive for Hutu supremacy and regime stability (Chretien, IDRC). For the president, retention of power for him and the elite surrounding him was paramount. He was intent on using all instruments, including the media, to achieve this. The wider Hutu elite around him, and especially the *akazu* and other northern elites, both wanted to fight off challenges from other Hutu factions and from those advocating a more inclusive approach to politics. But most importantly, the elite wanted to entrench Hutu dominance to an extent that, RPF or no RPF, Tutsis would never be in a position to challenge it. To achieve this, they wanted a return to naked Hutu supremacy and to tell the population that all Tutsi were *inyenzi* and were suspect. This wing of the Hutu elite wanted a violent response to the invasion and not just in terms of the counter-offensive by the Hutu army.

The Hutu backlash following the invasion was not long in coming. On 8 October, Radio Rwanda broadcast a statement by Foreign Minister Casimir Bizimungu, warning 'this terrorist organization [the RPF] has as its only aim the establishment of a minority regime embodying feudalism with a modern outlook. The Rwandan people will not agree to reverse history, leading the nation's dynamic forces back to feudal drudgery and enslavement' (BBC, SWB). The message was clear, the RPF was intent on taking Rwanda back to minority Tutsi rule and subordination and exploitation of the Hutu – news reports, commentary and speeches broadcast on or reported by the radio and government-run media were now framed in this way. Everything said about the conflict would be about the threat of Tutsi hegemony and Hutu subjugation.

The RPF and, very quickly, all Tutsis would be represented as the enemy, a threat and as traitors. This framing and representation was intended to both set a long-term agenda for Hutu of all-out opposition to the RPF and vigilance against the Tutsi threat and then to justify or encourage participation in attacks on the Tutsi. A UN report on killings in Rwanda between 1990 and 1993, written by UN special rapporteur on Rwanda, Bacre Waly Ndiaye, concluded that the result of the RPF attack 'and of a policy of deliberately targeted government propaganda was that all Tutsi inside the country were collectively labelled accomplices of the RPF' (United Nations Educational, Scientific and Cultural Organization (UNESCO), 1993, p. 12). Ndiaye said that a violent propaganda campaign started immediately after the RPF invasion and 'soon escalated beyond rhetoric' (UNESCO, 1993, pp. 25–6). Evidence of this was the speeches and directives by local leaders in the town of Kibilira in Gisenyi prefecture, which:

> instructed Hutus their communal work duty for the month would consist of fighting their Tutsi neighbours, with whom they had lived at peace for at least 15 years. The Hutus went to work with singing and drumming, and the slaughter lasted 3 days; some three hundred and fifty Tutsis were killed.
>
> (Gourevitch, 1998, p. 84)

None of the victims was ever proved to be an RPF soldier. Asked about the killings at a press conference, Habyarimana denied that any civilians had been killed saying, 'Civilians? Why should we kill civilians if they are not involved in the fighting? There is no revolt. Everybody is obeying' (Prunier, 2008, p. 110).

The regime used other methods, too, to encourage hatred of the Tutsi. On 4 and 5 October, the Rwandan army staged a gun battle in Kigali – there were no casualties but Radio Rwanda reported that it was a terror attack by the RPF and couched it in terms to generate fear and hatred (Article XIX, 1996, pp. 25–6). The attack and the alleged threat it posed to the regime was used in the government's diplomatic strategy to exaggerate the RPF threat and elicit military support from France, Belgium and Mobutu's Zaire. France had sent 150 troops to Kigali immediately after the RPF invasion (to protect French nationals and the airport). The French force was increased to 600 following the Kigali 'attack'. On 15 October, Habyarimana made a speech (broadcast on radio) accusing all Tutsi of being accomplices of the RPF and saying that the RPF launched its attack in the knowledge that it would receive support from Tutsi within Rwanda. He called the attack diabolic and said enemy arms caches had been found in the capital. In his radio address he called on Rwandans to participate in the defence of the nation, asking them to be ever alert for enemies (BBC, SWB). The speech said that the international media was being duped by RPF and Tutsi lies – these falsehoods were 'systematic lies which we can only describe as diabolic' (ibid.). The president told Rwandans that Tutsis were the accomplices of the RPF, adding that 'In order to prepare an attack of such a scale there needed to be people who could be trusted. Rwandans of the same ethnic group were the obvious choice' (cited by Article XIX, 1996, p. 26).

Habyarimana had already said in a statement reported by Radio Rwanda on 11 October that during the Kigali 'attack', the RPF had disguised themselves as civilians. From the time of the invasion onwards, exhortations by the president against the RPF, Tutsis in general and his critics among Hutu politicians became almost daily features of radio output and were broadcast just prior to major news bulletins (Des Forges, 2002, p. 238). The use of the Radio Rwanda was particularly important as, for a large proportion of Rwandans, broadcasting in their own language 'was the only medium they had access to, given the high illiteracy level and the small percentage of the population which could understand French and English on international radio stations' (Article XIX, 1996, p. 28). Radio Rwanda, which from the first day of the RPF invasion, presented news as part of a strategy to galvanize resistance and create suspicion about the Tutsi population, was the government voice and a source of both one-sided reporting and exhortation to vigilance and action. There developed other Hutu propaganda outlets that played an even more extreme role in the war against the RPF and the demonization of the Tutsi. Prior to the establishment of RTLM in 1993, the chief voice of Hutu Power was the Kinyarwanda newspaper *Kangura* (the translation of which is 'wake him up'). It had been established in May 1990 at the instigation of Agathe Habyarimana and her *akazu* acolytes as the media opened up and critical, anti-MRND voices began to be heard in the press. The editor was Hassan Ngeze (later to be tried and convicted of crimes relating to genocide by the ICTR). Ngeze, later to become prominent in the extreme Hutu Coalition pour la Défense de la République (CDR), made *Kangura* into a virulently anti-Tutsi publication that incited hatred and violence. For a fortnightly paper in a country with limited literacy (approximately 66 per cent in 1994 and higher among men than women), *Kangura* sold well; Ngeze claimed a circulation of 10,000 for most issues and 30,000 for particularly popular ones (Higiro, 2007, p. 81).

In the view of the Rwandan historian Marcel Kabanda, *Kangura* 'exhorted the Bahutu to understand that the Tutsi were first and foremost an enemy and that they should break all ties with them' and treat them as a perpetual threat to Hutu 'democracy' (Kabanda, 2007, p. 62). In the way that *Der Sturmer* had called for a racially pure Germany purged of Jews, *Kangura* called for the destruction of a Rwandan society in which Hutu and Tutsi coexisted for 'one that would supposedly be authentic and pure' (Ibid.). Tutsis might remain in Rwanda but not as accepted parts of society and forever under surveillance. It was a throwback to the most extreme, racial elements of the 1957 Bahutu Manifesto and the racialization of Hutu-Tutsi relations once more, but with an even more violent edge. Just as RTLM, the Coalition for the Defence of the Republic (CDR) and Hutu Power were to do in the following years, *Kangura* set out to wake Hutu up from what the growing Hutu supremacist movement saw as the complacent sleep of recent years, during which the Tutsi threat had been downplayed. The harking back to the Hutu revolution was often made evident in words and pictures – the cover of the December 1993 issue of *Kangura* has the headline, 'Tutsi: Race of God' and to the left of it a page-length picture of a panga, while the other text on the page asks, 'Which weapons are we going to use to beat the cockroaches for good?'

Just as Habyarimana tried to use the RPF invasion to unite Hutu and prevent the rise of political groups that could threaten his hold on power, so the supremacists wanted to use the invasion to reinstate racial images of the Tutsi and incite Hutu hatred of all Tutsi. These ideas began to be propagated vigorously and used to advance the cause of militant Hutu supremacism and exclusion or, ultimately, expulsion or extermination of the Tutsi. There was the implication in what the proponents of this ideology said that Habyarimana had gone soft on the Tutsis and on moderate Hutu politicians, to whom he was about to accord the right to their own political parties and newspapers.

The discourse developed by Ngeze and his backers in the newspaper was one of historical revisionism and consistent demonization of the Tutsi. It repeatedly told its audience not to forget the reasons and principles of the 1959 Hutu revolution and the attempts by the Tutsi to prevent it. An edition shortly after the RPF invasion exhorted readers to:

> Remember also, at the beginning of November 1959, the Batutsi provoked inter-ethnic massacres in trying to eliminate the Hutu elite who were call-ing for democracy and social justice [...] Since the revolution of 1959, the Batutsi haven't for one moment relinquished the notion of reconquer-ing power in Rwanda, of exterminating intellectuals and of dominating Hutu farmers [...] The war declared against Rwanda in October 1990 is undoubtedly aimed at achieving what the Batutsi had attempted to accomplish through guerrilla warfare and terrorism.
>
> (cited by Kabanda, 2007, p. 64)

A clear pattern of framing and representation emerged – one even more extreme than that put out by the president and government on Radio Rwanda, in MRND publications and at public meetings. The message from the developing Hutu Power movement was that the current war must be seen as a seamless continuation of Tutsi yearning for hegemony and the subjugation of the Hutu and that the Tutsi will stop at nothing, includ-ing massacring Hutu, to achieve this. The outlook was encapsulated in the publication by *Kangura* in December 1990 of the Hutu Ten Command-ments to support the doctrine of 'militant Hutu purity' (Gourevitch, 1998, pp. 86–7).

The Ten Commandments according to *Kangura*:

1. Every Hutu should know that a Tutsi woman, whoever she is, works for the interest of her Tutsi ethnic group. As a result, we shall con-sider a traitor any Hutu who marries a Tutsi woman befriends a Tutsi woman employs a Tutsi woman as a secretary or a concubine.
2. Every Hutu should know that our Hutu daughters are more suitable and conscientious in their role as woman, wife and mother of the family. Are they not beautiful, good secretaries and more honest?
3. Hutu women, be vigilant and try to bring your husbands, brothers and sons back to reason.

4. Every Hutu should know that every Tutsi is dishonest in business. His only aim is the supremacy of his ethnic group. As a result, any Hutu who does the following is a traitor:

   makes a partnership with Tutsi in business

   invests his money or the government's money in a Tutsi enterprise

   lends or borrows money from a Tutsi

   gives favours to Tutsi in business (obtaining import licenses, bank loans, construction sites, public markets, etc.).

5. All strategic positions, political, administrative, economic, military and security should be entrusted only to Hutu.

6. The education sector (school pupils, students, teachers) must be majority Hutu.

7. The Rwandan Armed Forces should be exclusively Hutu. The experience of the October 1990 war has taught us a lesson. No member of the military shall marry a Tutsi.

8. The Hutu should stop having mercy on the Tutsi.

9. The Hutu, wherever they are, must have unity and solidarity and be concerned with the fate of their Hutu brothers. The Hutu inside and outside Rwanda must constantly look for friends and allies for the Hutu cause, starting with their Hutu brothers.

   They must constantly counteract Tutsi propaganda.

   The Hutu must be firm and vigilant against their common Tutsi enemy.

10. The Social Revolution of 1959, the Referendum of 1961, and the Hutu Ideology, must be taught to every Hutu at every level. Every Hutu must spread this ideology widely. Any Hutu who persecutes his brother Hutu for having read, spread, and taught this ideology is a traitor.

(printed in full in Berry and Berry, 2001, pp. 113–5)

The message could not be clearer, the Tutsi are the enemy and should be excluded from the life of Hutus and from control of all major aspects of political, social and economic activity in Rwanda – there was a chilling reminder in the commandments, and the ideology of Hutu racial power that lay behind them, of the German Nuremburg Laws for the Protection of German Blood and Honour.

The newspaper and its supporters sought to set an agenda of hatred and willingness to kill or drive out all Tutsis to protect the future of the Hutu. It was more extreme in its message than government propaganda, but at times that wasn't far behind. On 22 November 1990, Radio Rwanda told listeners that they had to harden themselves to resist the RPF and their Tutsi accomplices, 'since their goal is to exterminate and enslave us, we must not feel any mercy towards them' (BBC, SWB). Between 1990 and 1994, the station regularly broadcast such warnings and also regular accusations of atrocities by the RPF against civilians.

In December 1990, Ferdinand Nahimana (a Hutu historian and keen prop-agator of ideas of Hutu Power) became director of the Rwandan office of Information, ORINFOR, and ensured that the government radio output took a consistently anti-Tutsi line. One of the best studies of the media during the genocide says that under Nahimana, Radio Rwanda's output became more virulently anti-Tutsi and even more distorted in its reporting (Article XIX, 1996, pp. 28–9). He was also keen to use propaganda and distortions to convince Rwanda's international allies of the need to support the govern-ment military support against the RPF. In January 1991, he gave an interview to Radio France International claiming that the RPF forces included Libyan commandos and volunteers for other Arab countries – this at a time when Paris had been at war by proxy with Libya in Chad (Somerville, 1990, pp. 61–82).

After he took command of the RPF, Kagame regrouped the demoralized rebels in the Virunga mountain area on the border with Uganda. With the tacit backing of Uganda, Kagame was able to recruit more fighters from the Tutsi exiles in Zaire and Uganda and to get financial support from the Tutsi diaspora in Europe and North America. A number of exiled Hutu also joined the group, though it remained a predominantly Tutsi force, with those who had lived in Uganda in the majority. On 23 January 1991, the RPF attacked Ruhengeri and its prison – freeing over 1000 inmates, many of whom were political detainees. They held the town for a day, recruited many of the pris-oners and captured stocks of arms and ammunition. They then withdrew back into the mountains, having given a clear indication that they were still a force to be reckoned with. The government response was to accuse the RPF of killing large numbers of civilians in Ruhengeri. Radio Rwanda reported a few months later that an eyewitness had told them that the RPF soldiers had all been under the influence of drugs and had killed hundreds of civilians at the town and prison (Radio Rwanda, 28 April 1991, BBC, SWB). There was no evidence that civilians had been killed. As in Germany, Yugoslavia and back as far as the Crusades and Thirty Years' War, allegations of enemy atrocities were a potent weapon to create fear and loathing for the enemy – there is also here an element of the mirror technique where one's own intentions and actions are reflected on to the enemy to deflect attention.

As the war built in intensity and alongside it the government's propaganda offensive, so the political environment in Rwanda changed. The initial moves towards ending one-party rule and legalizing opposition parties con-tinued under pressure from domestic political groups and Rwanda's foreign donors. In March 1991, the president had been pushed into allowing first the registration of legal opposition parties in March 1991. On 28 April 1991, the MRND congress followed Habyarimana's lead and agreed to change party statutes to recognize other parties and permit the development of a multi-party system.

A plethora of parties emerged with a mass of acronyms – the main ones were the Republican Demoratic Movement (MDR – Parmehutu reborn), the Liberal Party (PL), the Social Democratic Party (PSD) and the Christian Democrat Party (PDC). The ruling MRND added democratic and another D to its initials but did little else to adapt to an evolving political landscape. It was committed to retaining power and to Hutu hegemony. The other parties were Hutu-based and varied in their approach to Hutu-Tusi relations – the MDR being essentially the inheritors of Kayibanda's political legacy. Alongside the open political activity, there was the growth of the Hutu Power movement – in March 1992 this was to manifest itself in the formation of the CDR. The CDR represented Hutu Power supporters increasingly worried that Habyarimana was giving too much to the opposition parties and foreign pressure – it later became very critical of his willingness to compromise during the long drawn out Arusha peace process with the RPF. The CDR, its militia and the *Interahamwe* militia (the armed wing of the MRND, but which was more extreme than the party) became the public manifestations of Hutu supremacism. Prunier, not unreasonably, refers to the CDR as being on 'the lunatic fringes of radical Hutu extremism [...] it was from these political circles that the founders of RTLM were drawn' (Prunier, 2008, pp. 128–9).

Hutu Power was more than ever concerned with maintaining the rule of those Hutus (mainly northerners) committed to excluding the Tutsi from power and opposing any Hutu groups seen as being soft on the Tutsi. It sought to use the war to increase fear of the Tutsi and paranoia among Hutus about the threat they posed. It was not hard for Hutu hegemonists to use the war to raise the spectre of Tutsi resurgence and the threat of a return to subservience and enslavement for the Hutu. As Mamdani contends, 'the growing appeal of Hutu Power propaganda among the Hutu masses was in direct proportion to the spreading conviction that the real aim of the RPF was not rights for all Rwandans but power for the Tutsi' (Mamdani, 2002, p. 191). This message came in speeches by Habyarimana, his ministers, local officials and Radio Rwanda and even more vehemently from those Hutu Power proponents in or on the edge of the ruling elite and from *Kangura*.

Propaganda was accompanied by the growing organization of Rwandans into local defence groups and militias. The government launched a civil defence programme in 1990, involving the establishment of local patrols organized by commune or prefecture officials and armed with traditional weapons like pangas and clubs. As the government purchased more weapons from abroad, firearms were distributed to local officials and to army reservists (Des Forges, 1999, pp. 106–7). Roadblocks were set up to tighten the already strict controls over movement and to check the ID cards or travellers. The communal labour demanded of Rwandans now involved civil defence and vigilance against internal enemies – which effectively meant harassment and surveillance of all Tutsis.

As the war continued, Hutu Power politicians from the MRND and the more militant CDR established, trained and armed militias with the assistance of army and police commanders. The largest militia was the *Interahamwe*, which began its existence as the MRND youth wing (Straus, 2006, p. 26) – following a pattern in one party states across Africa in which the youth wing is the street-fighting strike force of the ruling party. The name meant, 'we work together' but could also mean 'we fight together' – during attacks on Tutsis prior to and during the genocide, 'work' was often used as a euphemism for killing Tutsis. The CDR had its own militia, known as *Impuzamugambi*, 'those with a single purpose' (Melvern, 2004, p. 51). The militias, led or backed by local officials, central government and the army, were to become the spearhead for attacks on Tutsis and leaders of the genocide. The presence of militias was to be a key factor in localities in deciding how extensive the killing was and how many local civilians joined in (Straus, 2006, p. 27). The militias demanded participation as a national duty or as communal labour, with the use of intimidation, threats of violence and even the killing of Hutus who did not take part in patrols, roadblocks or killings.

As political reform progressed, though without inspiring any great hope of real accountability and democratic choice, the war dragged on. The RPF was active in carrying out guerrilla warfare in the north, which the Rwandan army was unable to suppress. The insecurity there led to a wave of Hutu refugees (around 100,000) heading south. If the RPF hoped that all Rwandans would flock to it as an alternative to Harbyarimana, it was disappointed and Hutus did not join its fight. Perhaps influenced by government and Hutu hegemonist propaganda, they fled, fearing for the lives. By early 1992, the RPF was strong and well-armed enough to push slowly south. During 1991, as the war continued there was a series of massacres of Tutsis at Kanama, Rwerere and Gisenye – estimates put the numbers of Tutsi civilians killed at the behest of local burgomasters or MRND officials at between 300 and 1000. In March 1992, a series of mass killings took place at Bugesera in eastern Rwanda. The killings of local Tutsi by Rwandan soldiers, the *Interahamwe* and local civilians followed a broadcast by Radio Rwanda on 3 March 1992 (BBC, SWB) alleging that a human rights group in Nairobi had issued a statement warning that Tutsis in Bugesera were planning to kill their Hutu neighbours. It claimed that the RPF offensive would move into a new phase involving assassinations and the destruction of property and the use of foreign African and Arab agents. The report was broadcast five times. It was later found to have been written by civil servants and that the unnamed human rights group was a total invention. The report was followed on the radio by a communique from ORINFOR director Nahimana, which urged listeners to beware of the dangers at hand and to take preventative action. He told listeners to annihilate these Machiavellian plans of the enemy '*inyenzi-inkontanyi*' (cited by Article XIX, 1996, p. 37).

In late November 1991, Hassan Ngeze, the editor of *Kangura*, had been to Bugesera and organized the distribution of violently anti-Tutsi leaflets warning of the threat they posed to the local Hutu (Article XIX, 1996, p. 36). His work was built on by the radio and by Hutu militants. As Alison des Forges says, 'Local officials built on the radio announcement to convince Hutu that they needed to protect themselves by attacking first' (Des Forges, 2007, p. 42). Hundreds of Tutsi civilians and some opposition supporters were killed – the toll reached 277 and 15,000 people fled the area. What the massacre demonstrated was not the power of radio alone to direct killings (something rightly questioned by Straus in his critical studies of the influence of radio – see Straus, 2007), but the importance of radio combined with control of armed force and administrative power. The dovetailing of violent, hate-inspired propaganda with the resources to command and carry out killings was at the heart of the ability of Hutu militants to carry out massacres quickly and with impunity both prior to and during the genocide. At this stage of the conflict, there were signs that monitoring and reporting of massacres had an effect in halting them. In his report for the UN, Ndiaye said that killings had stopped when journalists and human rights groups had brought them to national and international attention. In his recommendations, he said that some system of monitoring and reporting outbreaks of violence could help contain or prevent them (UNESCO, 1993, pp. 14–16).

Radio Rwanda still remained firmly in government hands in 1990 and 1991, even though it had agreed under pressure in late 1991 to allow opposition parties 15 minutes air time each a week (Gulseth, 2004, p. 53). This followed demonstrations by thousands of opposition supporters against government control of the media. Ferdinand Nahimana continued to run ORINFOR and ensured that apart from the time allotted to the other parties, the news and commentary output was firmly anti-Tutsi. One of the pieces of evidence brought forward by the ICTR against Nahimana during his trial on genocide charges was that he had used his position at ORINFOR to direct a propaganda campaign against Tutsis. In relation to Bugesera, he was identified as having ordered the broadcasting of the fake report and the communique inciting the population to 'annihilate' *inyenzi* plots and by implication those identified as *inyenzi* (ICTR, Nahimana).

Hutu Power influence over radio output was weakened soon after the massacres. On 14 March 1992, Habyarimana – to the horror of the *akazu* and other militant Hutu elites – signed an agreement with opposition parties on the formation of a coalition government. The post of prime minister was allotted to the MDR party but the MRND retained 9 out of 20 ministerial posts – crucially including defence, the interior and the civil service. The new government had some executive power but could not seriously challenge Habryarimana or MRND control of the national or local administrative machinery, the security forces and militias. The new cabinet was sworn in on 14 April 1992. Dismas Nsengiyaremye became prime minister and another

MDR leader, Boniface Ngulinzira, became foreign minister. But there was change, and change that worried the Hutu supremacists. The new education minister, Agathe Uwilingiyimana (MDR), immediately ended the quota system that limited Tutsi access to education. The government also acted on the media and Ferdinand Nahimana was sacked as ORINFOR director. Des Forges believes he was removed from ORINFOR as a direct result of domestic and international complaints over the broadcast about Bugesera – the Radio Rwanda announcer who made the broadcast, Jean-Baptiste Bamwanga, was also sacked (Des Forges, 1999, pp. 68–70; 2002, p. 239). The episode demonstrated not only the power of radio combined with the means to order and carry out violence, but also an awareness on the part of the opposition parties and elements of the international community concerned with Rwanda about the use of the media to propagate hatred and violence.

The sacking of Nahimana, though perhaps a move in the right direction didn't give the power-sharing government real control. The minister of information was Pascal Ndengejebo of the PSD (Social Democratic Party) but the interim director of ORINFOR was Prospere Musemabweli, an MRND supporter who thwarted the minister's attempts to stop the media taking a balanced approach. With ORINFOR and Radio Rwanda staffed by MRND loyalists who would still take the Hutu supremacist line on every issue, there was little chance of change. The three key Radio Rwanda executives (all of whom were to move to RTLM) were Jean-Baptiste Bamwanga, the editor-in-chief of radio news; Joseph Serugendo, head of technical services; and Froduald Ntawulkura, head of programmes (Article XIX, 1996, p. 48). The national station continued to be blatantly biased and broadcast regular and false reports of atrocities by the RPF while denying air time to human rights groups reporting killings by Hutus (ibid.). The only real alternative to Radio Rwanda was the RPF's Radio Muhabura (set up in 1991 and first monitored by the BBC's Monitoring Service unit in Nairobi in mid-1992, according to Greenaway, interview 2009), which could be heard over much of the north, west and centre of the country. It broadcast the RPF's version of the news and was heavily propagandistic – though it espoused a vision of a future Rwanda entirely ignoring ethnicity. But it was said to be 'dull and propagandistic' in its style and so tedious that even RPF soldiers were said to prefer listening to RTLM when it was established because it was more lively (Li, 2007, pp. 96–7).

The Nsengiyaremye government did try to get rid of the worst local leaders and prefects and also tried to break up the powerful Service Centrale de Rensignements (SCR) secret service organization. It split this between four ministries to reduce its power, but it still operated as one unit clandestinely and worked closely with death squads known as Zero Network – this was a combined civil-military organization formed from soldiers and MRND militia members and led by *akazu* members including Agathe Habyarimana's three brothers, Alphonse Ntirivamunda (Habyarimana's son-in-law), and Colonel Theoneste Bagosora, the cabinet director of the Defence Ministry and a prime mover in the Hutu Power movement (Prunier, 2008, pp. 46 and 168–9).

The new government started talks with the RPF in Kampala on 24 May 1992, with Foreign Minister Boniface Ngulinzira leading the delegation from Kigali. Habyarimana was prepared, under international pressure, to let the talks proceed and a second round was held in Paris. But the MRND (with the president's acquiescence or implicit support) held protests in Kigali and other towns against the talks. There were also several minor army mutinies – notably in the *akazu* and Hutu Power strongholds of Gisenyi and Ruhengeri – where local Hutu officials supported the mutineers and did nothing to stop troops going on the rampage and killing 27 civilians (Prunier, 2008, p. 150). Against this background, the government delegation continued the talks with the rebels and a ceasefire agreement was signed in Paris on 6 July 1992 – the RPF agreed to halt all violence on 14 July. Peace talks aimed at finding a long-term solution then started in the Tanzanian town of Arusha. But the ceasefire did not last and, following accusations by the RPF that the government was not abiding by it and was killing innocent civilians, the RPF launched a new offensive in February 1993. They advanced further south into Rwanda and reached within striking distance of Kigali before being halted by the Rwandans.

The military were becoming increasingly suspicious of Habyarimana's intentions and established their own commission, led by Deogratias Nsabimana, to develop ways of combating the RPF and Tutsis 'on the battlefield, in politics and in the media' (cited by Article XIX, 1996, p. 38). On 21 September, the commission published a reported defining the enemy as 'Tutsi inside or outside the country, who are extremists and nostalgic for power, who have never recognised [...] the realities of the Social revolution of 1959, and who want to take power in Rwanda by any means, including by force' (ibid.). In practice, the definition of the enemy came to be all Tutsis.

The targeting of all Tutsis was evident in a speech made at an MRND rally in Kabaya, Gisenyi prefecture, on 22 November 1992 by Dr Leon Mugesera, vice-president of the MRND in Gisenyi. He called on his audience to be vigilant and to meet violence with even greater violence. He said that the gospel for the movement had to be that you returned one slap with two fatal ones. Mugesera voiced the feelings of many MRND leaders about the new government when he said that they had interfered with Rwanda's defences and this needed to be punished with 'nothing less than death'. This was the clearest indication from Hutu militants that Hutu politicians who did not take the right line on racial/ethnic issues would be considered collaborators. The speech went on to call all Tutsi *inyenzi* and called for the extermination of any Tutsi thought to be providing recruits or support for the RPF. Adopting biblical language that he knew would be understood by his audience, Mugesera demanded of the Hutu that 'we ourselves will take care of massacring these gangs of thugs. You know it says in the Gospel that the snake comes to bite you and, if you let it stay, you are the one who will perish' (Article XIX, 1996, pp. 39–40). As with the content of pieces in *Kangura* and the later thrust of RTLM broadcasts, Mugesera dwelt on the threat posed to Hutu by the Tutsi and their need to protect themselves through violence and through pre-emptive action against 'the snake'.

In a chilling prediction of scenes from the 1994 genocide, the MRND leader told his audience that, in 1959, a mistake had been made by letting Tutsis escape abroad and that next time 'we will send you home [to Ethiopia] via Nyaborongo [river in western Rwanda flowing north towards the Nile] on an express trip' (ibid.). During the genocide, Rwanda's rivers were to be choked with corpses of genocide victims. Despite the attempts of the new government to control the media more closely, Mugesera's speech was broadcast by Radio Rwanda (Des Forges, 1999, pp. 85–6) – including his words that 'know that the person whose throat you do not cut now will be the one who will cut yours'. In 1994, Mugesera's words were to be repeated regularly by RTLM.

The Arusha talks made slow progress and it took months after the renewal of the RPF offensive for agreement to be reached on a new ceasefire. The Arusha Accords were signed in Tanzania on 4 August 1993 – they established a new ceasefire and set out the process for forming a new broad-based government incorporating RPF ministers along with representatives of the five parties in the existing coalition – MRND and RPF were to have five posts, MDR four (including that of prime minister), PSD and PL three each and the Christian Democratic Party one. Despite the signing of the agreement, the new government never functioned properly, as the MRND dragged out negotiations on the distribution of portfolios and appointment of ministers. The accords also provided for the rapid deployment of a 2500 strong UN force – the UN Assistance Mission to Rwanda (UNAMIR) led by Major-General Romeo Dallaire of the Canadian army.

The ceasefire and the accords were not welcome developments for most MRND members or for the groups involved in the Hutu Power movement. The army was fearful of the plans for a merger with the RPF to form a single unified Rwandan force, while the elite Presidential Guard opposed the clause in the agreement that planned a new republican guard elite force made up of it and elite RPF forces. Although Habyarimana's broadcast to the nation on Radio Rwanda on 17 August distanced him from the negotiating team in Arusha and promised his supporters 'that the Rwandan people can rest assured that all the precautions have been taken to ensure that individual actions do not lead our country into an adventure it would not like' (BBC, SWB), hard-liners were suspicious of his intentions and anti-Arusha demonstrations broke out in the Hutu and *akuza* strongholds of Gisnehyi and Ruhengeri. In the month before the accords were signed, Agathe Uwilingiyimana had succeeded Nsengiyaremye as prime minister at the head of a new cabinet with a mandate from the president to sign the accords. Among her first actions was to get rid of the interim head of ORINFOR and replace him with Jean-Marie Vianney Higiro, who was expected to free the media of MRND control.

RTLM – the voice of hatred and incitement

By the signing of the accords, a new weapon had been forged by Hutu militants – Radio Television Libre des Mille Collines (RTLM). Perhaps seeing the writing on the wall for Radio Rwanda under a broad-based government and under any peace accords, former ORINFOR head Nahimana, Joseph Serugendo and Jean-Bosco Barayagwiza of the militant CDR movement had started in late 1992 to plan the establishment of an 'independent' radio station. Supported by the Hutu Power elite and the *akazu*, they raised funds and in November Nahimana and Serugendo (the technical chief at Radio Rwanda and a senior *Interahamwe* member) travelled to Brussels to buy broadcasting equipment (Melvern, 2004, p. 53). In May 1991, *Kangura* had announced that a new radio station would start broadcasting that year, probably from Gisenyi (Article XIX, 1996, p. 71). Nothing came of this but Nahimana, Barayagwiza and Ngeze were involved in planning to launch a station funded by politicians and businessmen close to the *akazu* and Hutu Power. The preparations gained pace in April 1992 when Nahimana was removed as ORINFOR head and the opposition parties were able to get air time on Radio Rwanda. This is not to suggest that the media had been liberalized totally by this move. Radio Rwanda remained under the effective tutelage of the MRND and papers like *Kangura* and a number of publications linked to the MRND and the CDR propagated the Hutu hegemonist line. Papers had been set up by the new parties, but movement restrictions (always part of the Rwandan administrative regime but tightened up after October 1990) were used to prevent journalists, other than those recognized as friendly to the ruling Hutu elite, from being able to report on alleged RPF attacks and atrocities or ones carried out by government forces or Hutu militias. Yet, the extremist Hutus, ever more suspicious of Habyarimana, wanted their own voice. The CDR arranged a mass protest rally in Kigali to protest against the talks with the RPF, the new ORINFOR management and the changes at Radio Rwanda.

The fundraising took some time, but on 8 April 1993, RTLM Societe Anonyme was formally registered as a company with 50 shareholders (all of them closely linked with the Hutu Power network and *akazu*). The ICTR found evidence that the bank account set up to pay for RTLM operations was used to pay for the importing of weapons for the militias connected with it (ICTR, Nahimana, section 5:9). With imported equipment, a power supply (directly from the generators at the Presidential Office), access to transmitters of its own and logistical and transmission assistance from Radio Rwanda (ICTR, Nahimana, section 6:4), it began to broadcast on 7 July 1993.

Under Rwandan media law it was required to have a formal contract with the Ministry of Information, but because of its connections with the MRND and CDR militants, senior military officers and militant Hutu members of the government, it was able to start broadcasting without a contract, which was only signed on 30 October 1993 (Des Forges, 2007, pp. 44–5). The station was theoretically an independent, commercial organization but it had such strong connections with the CDR, senior government and military officials and the *akazu* that it had a semi-official status and was the creature of Hutu political elites (Article XIX, 1996, pp. 70–1). Many senior RTLM staff and shareholders were closely connected with the government – Telesphore Bizimungu was director-general of the Ministry of Planning and Jean-Bosco Barayagwiza was director of political affairs in the Foreign Affairs Ministry, while Joseph Serugendo remained Head of Technical Services at ORINFOR while running the technical side of RTLM's operations. According to Richard Carver, author of the Article XIX examination of the media and genocide in Rwanda, 'a significant number' of RTLM shareholders were members of the post-April 94 interim government and some, like Transport Minister Andre Ntagerura, were indicted by the ICTR for their roles in planning and executing the genocide – the ICTR acquitted him despite his major role in events after 6 April 1994 (Article XIX, 1996, p. 74).

While it was clearly intended from the start to be the voice of Hutu Power, the station took a populist, lively and relaxed approach to broadcasting. Radio Rwanda had not had to think about fighting for an audience or attracting listeners – as for most of its existence it had a monopoly over domestic broadcasting. Muhabura was a dull and very obviously political station. RTLM set out to grab the audience and keep them listening because they enjoyed the music, comment and lively talk shows. This mix was informal and its journalists became known for their humour and wit as well as their extreme views and incitement of hatred (Des Forges, 2007, pp. 44–5; Li, 2007, p. 97). It would intersperse this entertaining style with exhortations to action and with enough interviews or broadcasts by Hutu figures in positions of authority to be able to harness its popularity to become the ideal vehicle for Hutu propaganda and to be a medium that could both influence and try to direct the actions of its listeners.

RTLM was staffed by professionals, many of whom had worked for Radio Rwanda or MRND-linked newspapers. The most popular presenter was Kantano Habimana – an excitable but also exciting broadcaster who was able to talk to the audience in language they could understand (Li, 2007, p. 98). He developed a rapport with the audience that engendered trust in what he said. The main political editor and editor-in-chief at the station was Gaspar Gahigi, a member of the MRND Central Committee and editor of the MRND paper *Umurwanashyaka*. Other major broadcasters were Noel Hitimana, an experienced and popular presenter who had been required to leave Radio Rwanda because of his excessive drinking; Ananie Nkurunziza, a former intelligence officer, who had been editor of the newspaper *Intera*, owned by Network Zero member Seraphim Rwabukumba; Valerie Bemeriki, an experienced journalist who had worked for the *Interahamwe* newspaper; and Georges Ruggiu, a Belgian with no journalistic background, who broadcast on RTLM's programmes in French. They were all committed to the Hutu cause.

Initially, the RTLM transmissions were heard in Kigali, Bugesera to the south and Kibungo to the east. In January 1994, a transmitter was set up on Mount Muhe in Gisenyi prefecture, which enabled it to reach that area and Ruhengeri to the north. Des Forges made a close study of the role of RTLM and believes that it could be heard in most of the country, with the exception of Butare in the south and Gisenyi town itself (Des Forges, 2007, p. 53), The reach of the radio has been disputed by Straus, who has taken the valuable but sometimes exaggerated role of questioner of accepted wisdom on the genocide and on RTLM. His hypothetical calculations of the range contend that it was limited to areas immediately around Kigali and Mount Muhe (Straus, 2007, pp. 617–20), though he admits the he doesn't know the actual range. But accounts from human rights groups, journalists working in Rwanda (including journalists working for the BBC and in direct touch with the author at the time of the genocide) and the head of the UNAMIR force all suggest that it was very widely heard, even if it did not have 100 per cent coverage. The ICTR established that the station received its power supply from the Presidential Office and was able to use Radio Rwanda technical facilities and logistical help to make its broadcasts. Because there was no concerted monitoring inside or outside Rwanda, it is impossible to give exact details of the reach, but the weight of evidence from those in the country suggests that much of the population was able to hear the station.

Starting its broadcasts as the negotiations in Arusha reached fruition, it is hardly surprising that initial comment broadcast on the station was highly critical of the accords and of the non-MRND members of the government who negotiated it. The Foreign Minister Boniface Ngulinzira was a particular target of RTLM (ICTR, Nahimana, section 5:12) and, when he was killed in the first week of the genocide on 11 April 1994, RTLM broadcast that 'we have exterminated all RPF accomplices. Mr Boniface Ngulinzira will no longer go to Arusha to sell the country to the RPF. The peace accords are nothing but scraps of paper as our father Habyarimana had predicted' (broadcast cited by ICTR, Nahimana, section 5:12). Such broadcasts made clear the station's political stance and its unashamed support for the killing of those deemed accomplices of the RPF. During 1993, according to the evidence presented by the prosecution at the Nahimana trial, Ferdinand Nahimana had a meeting in Kigali with *Interahamwe* leaders where lists of Tutsis to be killed were prepared – well in advance of the death of Habyarimana and the commencement of the genocide – a key indication of the pre-planned nature of the killings and of RTLM's close involvement in the planning as well as the propagation of genocide.

In the nine months that RTLM was broadcasting prior to the genocide, the station consistently set an agenda of suspicion and hatred of the Tutsi. As one witness at the trial of Nahimana and Barayagwiza said, 'what RTLM did was to pour petrol – to spread petrol throughout the country little by little, so that one day it would be able to set fire to the whole country' (ICTR, 2003b, p. 33). Soon after broadcasts started, a general meeting of RTLM shareholders took place at which the phrase 'No chance for the Tutsi' was oft repeated – this was picked up as a front page headline in July 1993 by *Kangura* in an edition praising the formation and role of RTLM, according to ICTR prosecutor Simone Monasebian (2007, pp. 309–10). Human rights groups and foreign diplomats soon became aware of the station and its extreme output. But they didn't all see it as important or as a threat – the Canadian Ambassador in Rwanda at the time, Lucie Edwards, was quoted by Article XIX as saying that,

> The question of Radio Milles Collines propaganda is a difficult one. There were so many genuinely silly things being said on the station, so many obvious lies, that it was hard to take it seriously. It was like relying on the *National Enquirer* to determine your policy on outer space.
>
> (Article XIX, 1996, p. 84)

But the station's output wasn't silly, it was a consistent diet of atrocity stories about the RPF, slanders against Tutsi and opposition Hutu politicians and the propagation of hatred of the Tutsi in general. The virulence of the broadcast content became more exaggerated after the killing on 21 October 1993 of first Hutu president, Melchior Ndadaye, by extreme elements in the Tutsi-dominated Burundian army as part of an army coup to overthrow the first elected Hutu-led government. Ndadaye was bayonetted to death. There followed reprisal attacks on Tutsis by the Hutu Frodebu movement and then massacres of tens of thousands of Hutus by the Tutsi army – an estimated 50,000 people died in the violence that followed the coup and 300,000 Hutu fled the country (most entering Rwanda). RTLM reported his killing and the massacres and broadcast a series of commentaries warning that this is what the Tutsi intended for Hutus in Rwanda – the broadcasts and comments by presenters left little doubt that they were advocating pre-emptive violence against Rwanda's Tutsi population. The period was marked by an increase in attacks on Tutsi civilians in Rwanda (Prunier, 2008, p. 203). Burundi experienced its own problems with hate media, which have been chronicled by Frere, with newspapers and to a lesser extent radio contributing to 'a political discourse of division and hate through the use of rhetoric that reinforced stereotypes and fear of the "Other" and a sense of imminent threat' (Frere, 2007, p. 15). In his testimony at the ICTR, Ferdinand Nahimana admitted that after the Burundi violence RTLM became openly a Hutu Power station advocating extreme action against Tutsis (ICTR, transcript of proceedings on 23 September 2002, pp. 105–8).

There are unfortunately few transcripts or tapes of broadcasts available from this period. At the ICTR in Arusha, some evidence was provided by notes kept by officials in the Ministry of Information who were trying to monitor RTLM. The trial transcripts show that broadcasts were heard that called on Hutus to prove to Tutsis that they are strong and that 'you Hutus must be on the look-out. You might meet the fate of the ones in Burundi'. The officials noted that Kantano Habimana and Noel Hitimana were the broadcasters who issued the warnings (Monasebian, 2007, p. 310). As a result of the heightened anti-Tutsi incitement in RTLM's output, the ORINFOR head Jean Marie Vianney Higiro, Information Minister Faustin Rucogoza and Francois Xavier Nsanzuwera of the Kigali state prosecutor's office (all Hutus from opposition parties) tried to bring RTLM to heel. The minister visited and wrote to RTLM to point out that the broadcasts violated Rwanda's media laws, the Arusha Accords and the contract signed by RTLM and the Ministry of Information allowing the station to broadcast (ICTR, Nahimana, section 33). Rucogoza met both Nahimana, as RTLM director, and Baraygwiza to press home the point that the station must stop broadcasting such incitement. They appeared to be contrite and said that mistakes had been made, but then Rucogoza became a target for RTLM verbal attacks. A Hutu Power statement was read out the day Rucogoza wrote to RTLM, accusing the minister of 'evil intentions'; the reading of the statement was followed by comments by the announcer whipping up revulsion against Tutsis and saying that 'bloodthirsty Tutsi dog-eaters' had murdered and mutilated Ndadaye (Monasebian, 2007, pp. 310–11) – the minister and his family were all killed on the first day of the genocide (ICTR, Nahimana, section 33). The continuation of RTLM invective against Tutsis and moderate Hutus led to Nahimana, Barayagwiza and Felicien Kabuga (a businessman and Network Zero member who was a major shareholder and RTLM president) being summoned to the Ministry of Information. Rucogoza, according to the ICTR hearing transcripts, told them that they were broadcasting unsubstantiated reports of killings by the RPF, irresponsible comment and material that was causing ethnic divisions. But the Ministry was powerless to compel RTLM to tone down its reporting and comment and the output became even more vitriolic (ICTR, 2003b, pp. 159–60). On the day of the meeting, the Belgian ambassador told his government that RTLM had called for the assassination of Prime Minister Agathe Uwilingyimana and Prime Minister-designate Faustin Twagiramungu (Monasebian, 2007, p. 312).

In November 1993, the first UNAMIR troops arrived in Kigali. Their commander, Romeo Dallaire, and a small reconnaissance group had first visited Rwanda in mid-August and Dalllaire had been guardedly optimistic that his mission could succeed in assisting demobilization and the formation of a joint army from the Rwandan army and RPF, but was aware of how under-resourced his force would be. Prior to the arrival of a Belgian contingent of the UN force, RTLM started a campaign against the UN and the Belgian role (Dallaire, 2004, p. 101). As the UN forces started to be deployed, the 600-strong RPF battalion to be stationed in Kigali under the Arusha Accords also arrived in the capital. The next month, Kagame, Pasteur Bizimungu and other RPF leaders visited Kigali. But there was no progress on implementing the Arusha agreement on a broad-based government including the RPF and led by Twagiramungu. Instead, there was increasing tension and the RTLM rhetoric was helping give 'an increasingly violent tone to political discourse', according to the UN force head General Romeo Dallaire (Dallaire, 2004, p. 123). Dallaire was already getting information from informants within the *Interahamwe* that the militia was training young men across the country and that lists were being drawn up of the Tutsis in every commune – 'Jean-Pierre [the informant] suspected that these lists were being made so that, when the time came, the Tutsis, or the *Inyenzi* as Rwandan hate radio called them – the word means cockroaches in Kinyarwanda – could easily be rounded up and exterminated' (Dallaire, 2004, p. 142).

In late 1993 and early 1994, anti-Tutsi broadcasts were so common on RTLM that they had become routine. One angle they took up was that the Tutsis had grabbed all Rwanda's wealth and controlled the economy – this theme was repeated repeatedly on 17, 20 and 21 December 1993, with one Tutsi businessman, Charles Shamukiga, singled out for invective. With the Rwandan economy in decline, this propaganda was effective in turning poor Hutus against their neighbours. As the human rights activist Alison des Forges testified at the ICTR, this copied the anti-Semitic propaganda of the Nazis in accusing the Jews of grabbing all Germany's wealth. What made it even more pernicious was the suggestion in much of the propaganda that when the Tutsis had been wiped out, their wealth would belong to Hutus. Des Forges said that as soon as the genocide began 'the fields of the Tutsis were allocated almost immediately [...] Other kinds of property was allocated as well. I'm thinking particularly of the contents of the small traders' booths at the open-air market in Butare, which were distributed to people who had participated in attacking Tutsi' (Des Forges at ICTR, 22 May 2002). The singling out of particular businessmen frequently meant that they were liable for attack. Shamukiga, named in a number of RTLM attacks, was killed by the Presidential Guard on 7 April 1994. After his attempts to control RTLM, Higiro of ORINFOR became a target of their verbal attacks and, in a broadcast of 7 January 1994, he was warned that if he continued criticizing RTLM the Hutus would rise up against him – Higiro was able to flee Rwanda after Habyarimana's death.

In some of his broadcasts prior to the genocide, Kantano Habimana admitted that he was being criticized for heating up the atmosphere. His reply in an RTLM broadcast on 21 January 1994 was:

all I am doing is explaining events as they unfold. Each and every event calls for commentary […] I have nothing against Tutsis […] I am Hutu, but I have nothing against Tutsis. However, given the current political situation, I have the duty to explain and say, 'Beware! The Tutsis are trying to appropriate the Hutus property by force or trickery'. However, my remarks do not in any way imply hatred for the Tutsis.

(ICTR, 2003b)

In other broadcasts around this time and leading up to the genocide, RTLM repeatedly said that the RPF was the enemy and the RPF and the Tutsis were the same (ICTR, 2003b).

In February 1994, there was a spate of inter-party violence between supporters of various Hutu parties in Kigali, leading to the deaths of opposition figures and of senior members of the CDR. By this time the CDR, extreme Hutus within the MRND and in some of the smaller parties were working together openly as Hutu Power – with an agenda increasingly divergent from that of Habyarimana. The *Interahamwe* and the CDR militia worked closely together. Hutu Power leaders, especially businessmen like Kabuga, were importing huge quantities of pangas to be used as weapons – these were distributed to militia members and supporters of the movement. They were clearly not designed to be used to fight the well-armed RPF. In the wake of the Kigali violence, Hutu Power supporters and Hutu militias launched attacks on supporters of opposition parties and at least 70 died in Kigali. RTLM said that the violence was being carried out by the RPF, which it accused of breaking the ceasefire. The radio urged Kigali residents to search out and attack RPF personnel and supporters in Kigali (Des Forges, 2002, p. 241).

RTLM did not try to be a comprehensive news service but rather was a vicious variant of the sort of opinionated talk shows becoming popular in the USA and Europe. The presenters would have guests or comments from people who phoned in and long unstructured commentaries by one or two of the presenters on a variety of subjects. The style was lively, colloquial and totally unrestrained. Hitimana was frequently drunk on air and this became a standing joke that seemed to endear him to the audience. Editor-in-chief Gahigi was correct when he said in March 1994 that people, especially the young, were bored with Radio Rwanda's formal and outmoded language. Prunier accurately described the character of the station in his account of the genocide:

while fiercely loyal to the Hutu cause, it was only conditionally loyal to President Habyarimana. In its own way it was effective. It knew how to use street slang, obscene jokes and good music to push its racist message. During the genocide, it became what one listener called 'a vampire radio' openly calling for more blood and massacres.

(Prunier, 2008, p. 189)

The station appealed particularly to young, poor, unemployed and usually poorly educated Hutu youths, who appreciated the street language and the strong, basic opinions expressed (Article XIX, 1996, p. 86).

In February 1994, Information Minister Rucogoza called Nahimana, Barayagwiza and Kabuga in again and told them that the press should support democracy and not set one ethnic group against another. The answer was threats against the minister and accusations that he was *inyenzi* and the statement that RTLM would 'continue to give time to anyone who would come to testify about Tutsi tricks and their Hutu accomplices' (Monasebian, 2007, p. 316). Monasebian says that a witness at the ICTR hearing said that when he delivered a report of the meeting to Barayagwiza at the Foreign Ministry, the latter threw it in his face and accused him of being an accomplice of the RPF (Monasebian, 2007, p. 317).

Human rights campaigner Joseph Matata produced a document on ethnic massacres, which described violations by the *Interahamwe*, in Kanzenze commune, in the Bugesera region. RTLM denounced Matata as a RPF agent and, from late November onwards, he was denounced approximately once a week by RTLM, which accused him of hating the military and people from the north. When Matata's group published a report on an incident in Taba, Gitarama préfecture, in which 17 schoolchildren were killed in a grenade attack, Silas Kubwimana, a local businessman and alleged financial supporter of the militias in that area, informed RTLM broadcasters of the report and asked them to denounce the human rights activist (Article XIX, 1996, pp. 94–5). Matata received open threats from the militias and local officials in his home area in Kibungo prefecture; he fled to Kigali, from where he continued to denounce killings by the militias. RTLM's close relationship with Hutu militias and Network Zero meant that its denunciations were not mere words and named individuals were in danger. Article XIX spoke to the journalist Sixbert Musangamfura, who told them:

> I listened to it [RTLM] constantly because every time RTLM alluded to someone, you were sure to see the *Interahamwe* head out shortly afterwards. Also, people who were prudent absolutely needed to listen to this station in case they were mention. [If this happened], you knew you had to change your address that day.
>
> (Article XIX, 1996, pp. 95–6)

The threats also spread to journalists working for international broadcasters. On 24 December 1993, the BBC's Swahili Service stringer Ali Yusuf Mugenzi was accused by Kantano Habimana on air of having reported for the BBC that RTLM was owned by CDR supporters. Habimana warned him, 'Tell him [Mugenzi] to come here. This is not a CDR station.' Mugenzi knew that such a statement could be a death warrant. He repeatedly telephoned the radio station and asked its broadcasters to change what they had said about him, saying that he now feared attack. Two days later, RTLM finally retracted the statement. Mugenzi survived, escaped Rwanda and became head of the BBC's Great Lakes (Kinyarwanda service) after the genocide (Harmes interview, 2009; see also Article XIX, 1996, pp. 95–6).

Shortly before Habyarimana's death, Noel Hitimana launched a vicious verbal attack on the independent journalist Joseph Mudatsikira, effectively threatening that he would be killed: 'if you die first as everyone has been speaking about you, it is not like dying like a sheep, without having been spoken of. When we have spoken about you, you have effectively been spoken of' (cited by Article XIX, 1996, p. 93). The chilling message was clear, as was the use of the term 'spoken of' to suggest that those spoken of by RTLM were targets. Mudatsikira died during the genocide, but the circumstances of his death are not known. There is, though, an uncanny match between those threatened by RTLM and those who died in the genocide – perhaps more than a coincidence given the reported role of RTLM's prime movers in drawing up lists of Tutsis in each commune along with the *Interahamwe* and others who were to lead the genocide.

In the lead up to 6 April, RTLM continued its campaign against ministers of the interim government seen as opponents. Minister of Information Rucogoza was a regular target. On 18 March, Kantano Habimana attacked him on the grounds that he had been trying to get RTLM closed down. More ominously, Alphonse Nkubito (the chief prosecutor in Kigali) filed a complaint against the station after it accused him of plotting to kill the president – the report was broadcast shortly after Nkubito survived a grenade attack. Accused of being responsible for reading out the accusation, Kantano Habimana used the 'I was only following orders' defence and said that Ferdinand Nahimana had told him to read out a telegram accusing Nkubito. Every time the prosecutor's office summoned RTLM staff over complaints, the radio reported it on air with the names of people in the prosecutor's office mentioned in a tone that did not bode well for the future' (Monasebian, 2007, p. 318; see also, ICTR, 2003b).

On 30 March, the station broadcast another report suggesting that Tutsis in Bugasera were planning to kill all the Hutus there – a chilling echo of the Radio Rwanda broadcast before the 1992 massacre. In the same broadcast, Valerie Bemeriki 'called for violence and shooting on the spot' (Monasebian, 2007, p. 319). Direct calls for violence were increasing during this period on RTLM. After the killing of a senior CDR member in Kigali, the radio identified a number of people, including a Tutsi doctor, that they held responsible with the clear message that they should be killed (ICTR, 2003b; Monsebian, 2007, p. 320). On 2 April, RTLM broadcast threats against Prime Minister Uwilingiyimana and the head of the Supreme Court, Joseph Kavaruganda, calling them both traitors and saying that they should be afraid as they had betrayed the people (ICTR, 2003b). The next day, the threats against Tutsis became even more blatant. The station said that RPF accomplices should be named – and went on to broadcast the following, using the term *inkontanyis* for RPF members and supporters: [People] have sent RTLM a list of persons who are accomplices of *Inkontanyis*. Those persons are the following: Mr Sebucinganda of Butete in Kidaho commune, Ms Laurencia Kura, wife of Gakenyeri, living in Butete sector, The Counsellor of Butete sector is also an accomplice of *Inkontanyis'* (Monasebian, 2007, p. 321). Another aspect of RTLM output in the days before the start of the genocide was the increasing playing of anti-Tutsi songs by a popular Hutu musician, Simon Bikindi. There were also death threats against taxi drivers in Kigali who took suspected RPF supporters or members of the RPF battalion in Kigali in their taxis – 'we warn you, those who drive the taxis [...] if they [the *Interhamwe*] rip them in to little pieces, they should not claim that they had not been warned' (Article XIX, 1996, p. 96).

In the last week before Habyarimana's death and the start of the genocide, both RTLM and other Hutu Power media warned of a coming bloodbath in Rwanda and accused the RPF of intending to break the ceasefire. In February, Ngeze wrote in *Kangura* that Habyarimana would soon be shot by the RPF. In the opening days of April, RTLM said that the RPF were about to attack again and people should be vigilant. The radio warned specifically that its agents had told the station that 'on 3rd, the 4th, and the 5th, there will be a little something here in Kigali City. And also on 7th and the 8th [...] you will hear the sound of bullets or grenades explode [...] But I hope that the Rwandan armed forces are on alert' (Article XIX, 1996, pp. 100–1). Oddly, the date on which Habyarimana was killed, 6 April, is missing from the list. The radio went on to say that the 'little something' was a distraction before what it called the *simusiga* (the first attack). This word would be used repeatedly by RTLM to describe the events of the genocide period. These warnings said that the bloodshed would be great and mocked the RPF leadership by saying that, 'You cannot pick up spilled blood. Blood can be spilled but it cannot be picked up. Ha Heeee [said in a menacing tone]. [...] We will have news about all that' (cited by Article XIX, 1996, p. 101).

The radio also broadcast an unambiguous warning to Habyarimana – who was due in Tanzania for talks with regional leaders about the delays in implementing the Arusha Accords. RTLM said that the nation would not tolerate a leader without popular support and

> the day when the people stand up and no longer want you and when they hate you [...] from the bottom of their hearts, when you make them nauseous [...] I wonder how you will escape? How can you get out? You cannot govern someone who does not want you. That is impossible. And even Habyarimana himself, if the citizens no longer wanted him, he would no longer be able to enter his office. It is impossible.

> (ibid.)

On 6 April, Habyarimana flew to Dar es Salaam – there he was to meet the presidents of Burundi (Cyprien Ntaryamira), of Uganda (Yoweri Museveni) and of Tanzania, (Ali Hassan Mwinyi) plus Kenyan Vice-President George Saitoti. The meeting was to discuss developments in Burundi following Ntaryamira's assumption of the presidency in the wake of the coup attempt and murder of Ndadaye, but it developed into a long critique by Mwinyi and Museveni of Habyarimana's failure to implement the Arusha Accords – even Ntaryamira (a Burundian Hutu) joined in the criticism. The presidents demanded that he honour the agreements he signed. Habyarimana left Dar es Salaam that evening in his presidential jet, accompanied by Ntaryamira.

Death of a president – the genocide begins

The events of the night of 6 April are still the subject of much dispute. Habyarimana's aircraft was shot down as it came in to land at Kigali. It was shot down at about 8.30 pm. That much is agreed, beyond that there are numerous theories and accusations about the shooting down of the plane. There are four basic versions: (1) The plane was downed by the RPF, who wanted to kill Habyarimana and restart the war; (2) The plane was shot down by soldiers (perhaps from the Presidential Guard) on the orders of the leaders of the Hutu Power movement who felt that Habyarimana was selling out the Hutus – his assassination could then be used as the pretext to launch genocidal attacks on the Tutsi; (3) French soldiers from the small contingent left in Rwanda after the main force departed in December 2003 shot down the plane to assist the Hutu militants and prevent Habyarimana reaching a deal with the RPF that would not be in French interests; (4) The plane was downed by Belgian members of UNAMIR, the Belgians allegedly having decided to back the RPF.

The answer as to who shot down the plane will never be known. Although the version of events blaming the French was broken by a leading Belgian journalist who knew Rwanda well, Collette Braeckman (Braeckman, 2007), it seems a little far-fetched. The French were very quick to blame the RPF (without much evidence) and a French inquiry reported in 2004 that the RPF were responsible for the assassination of the president, though without clear and convincing evidence. The French desire to blame Kagame and the RPF seems to be based on suspicion of the RPF's links with Uganda and its closer relations with Anglophone rather than Francophone Africa. It is perhaps also a post-hoc attempt to justify French support for the Hutus, which persisted throughout most of the period of the genocide. There is no convincing evidence that French troops were involved.

Blaming the Belgians seems an unlikely theory, as Prunier has pointed out (Prunier, 2008, p. 214). The theory emerged from Hutu groups and Habyarimana loyalists. The only circumstantial evidence supporting this version of events is that the ground-to-air missile which destroyed the plane could have been fired from an area regularly patrolled by the Belgian UNAMIR force – though also by the Presidential Guard. This version of events suited Hutu militants who opposed the Belgian presence, especially after the killing of the ten Belgian UNAMIR soldiers.

The interpretation that says the RPF was responsible has always been supported by the French government and is the one opted for by Straus – ever keen to question the widely accepted versions of events in Rwanda and to put up new, contentious theories of what happened (Straus, 2006, p. 45). His argument is that not only did the French inquiry blame the RPF, but also that RPF dissidents have said it was planned and ordered by Kagame. He extrapolates that 'the Tutsi rebels would have desired a clean military victory rather than a negotiated political settlement [...] [and]the RPF opted for a lightning strike and quick offensive' (ibid.). If Straus is right then, as he admits himself, the RPF made a huge miscalculation that led to the mass killing of its core support base. This version also ignores that it put in severe danger the isolated RPF battalion in Kigali and RPF officials in the capital. Furthermore, the RPF offensive following Habyarimana's death only came two days after the assassination when it was clear that Hutu militants were killing opposition politicians and large numbers of Tutsis. If Kagame was such a clever strategist, he would have prepared his forces for an immediate offensive as soon as the plane was down, to take full advantage of any interruption in the change of command and any struggle for power among the dead president's subordinates. And, as Prunier argues cogently, the RPF had negotiated a good deal at Arusha and in April 1994 it was not in their interests to kill Habyarimana; he was already a 'political corpse' who split the Hutu politically and so fractured the opposition to the RPF (Prunier, 2008, p. 220).

Although there is no decisive evidence to support the theory that it was Hutu hard-liners who killed Habyarimana, it is the theory that most closely fits the facts and is for that reason the most widely accepted. Ever since the signing of Arusha Accords and the opening up of the political system, hardliners had become increasingly critical and suspicious of the president. They thought he was giving too much away to both the RPF and the moderate Hutu opposition. *Kangura* and RTLM were openly critical of his policies. The radio had warned in advance of events to come in Kigali in early April that would be followed by bloodshed – preparing the listeners for the bloodshed that followed the president's death. This version of the events of 6 April is now strongly supported by a more extensive French investigation, which sent forensic science and ballistic experts to Kigali to examine the scene of the crash. They concluded that the Habyarimana plane had been shot down by a ground-to-air missile fired from the Presidential Guard camp. The BBC and other media outlets reported on 10 January 2012 that a Paris court had concluded on the basis of the new investigation that the missile was shot from a distance of up to 1 kilometre (more than half a mile) away from the plane, which was about to land at Kigali airport. At the time, this area was held by a unit of the Rwandan army's elite Presidential Guard. The court quoted the experts team as saying that it would have been very difficult for forces loyal to Mr Kagame to have been in this area and to have shot down the plane. They concluded that it would have been much easier for Habyarimana's troops or French troops, both of which were in the area, to launch the missile.

The importing of pangas and the arming of militias and Hutu Power supporters with weapons suitable for killing unarmed civilians but not for resisting the RPF, also points to preparations by Hutu Power for the mass killing of civilians rather than preparations to fight off a renewed RPF offensive. The speed of the Hutu hard-line reaction to the killing and the launching of targeted attacks alongside the general assault on Tutsis point to careful planning of all out attacks on Tutsis and Hutu moderates to follow immediately on the announcement of the killing of the president. *Interahamwe* roadblocks were in place within 45 minutes of the plane going down. When I, editing that night's BBC World Service *Newshour* programme from London, got the first reports of the president's death, they were followed very quickly by news of the roadblocks and of shooting from news agencies and BBC African Service reporters in Kigali. Within hours of the death, RTLM was broadcasting calls for vengeance, the militias were at work in Kigali and the Presidential Guard (whose commander, Colonel Mpiranya, and former commander, Colonel Leonard Nkundiye, were coordinators and planners of the countrywide genocide) was already at work seeking out the prime minister and other senior opposition figures in the government to kill them. As Prunier observes, this was not spontaneity, 'everything went ahead with the precision of a well-rehearsed drill' (Prunier, 2008, p. 224).

Whether or not you accept the version of events that the murder and genocide were planned together and both executed by Hutu militants, it is clear that the response in military, militia and civilian Hutu terms was swift and organized. Roadblocks were in place in less than an hour, militias were mobilized and the army, gendarmerie and Presidential Guard were swift to hunt down and kill priority targets – though a few Rwandan army units loyal to the president rather than the hard-liners did try briefly to stop the killings; the army commander-in-chief, Colonel Marcel Gatsinzi, was not involved in Hutu Power's plans and his troops clashed with the Presidential Guard on 7 and 8 April, though he joined the anti-Tutsi attacks when the RPF reacted to the killings with a new offensive (Prunier, 2008, p. 229).

Within the first 24 hours, Prime Minister Uwilingiyimana was killed along with her ten-man Belgian UNAMIR protection force; Information Minister Rucogoza was killed; Boniface Ngulinzira, who negotiated the Arusha Accords was killed; businessman Charles Shamukiga – so vilified by RTLM, was killed, though leader of the Liberal Party, the PSD. Faustin Twagiramungu, the prime minister-designate, so often attacked and threatened with death in print and on the airwaves, escaped and took refuge with UNAMIR forces. The UNAMIR commander, Romeo Dallaire, has given a full account of events after the plane came down – noting the role played by hard-liners like Theoneste Bagosora in the organization of the genocide and the new Hutu government. He has written that, within a few hours of the death of the president, he was getting reports that the Presidential Guard, gendarmerie and *Interahamwe* were going from house to house in Kigali with lists of names of those to be killed. He also details how UNAMIR forces were kept out of Kigali city centre on the night of 6 and 7 April by roadblocks manned by heavily armed troops and militiamen. They had been specifically instructed not to let UNAMIR forces through the roadblocks and to fire on them if they tried to force a way through (Dallaire, 2004, pp. 231, 234–5).

Those being killed were Tutsis – who were killed because of their identity rather than any allegiance they might or might not have had – and moderate Hutus known to be members or supporters of the opposition parties. Many in Kigali were killed because they looked prosperous and were not clearly part of the Hutu movements – many of the Tutsi in Kigali were well educated and were in business or in white-collar jobs – making them obvious targets for the poor, young militia members (Prunier, 2008, p. 232). As the killing proceeded, Bagosora and others formed a Committee for Public Salvation, which put together a new government under Jean Kambanda (from the Hutu Power wing of the MDR) and including Hutu militants from several of the major parties. While the government said it was intent on stopping violence and looting, reopening talks with the RPF and helping people displaced by the violence, it did nothing to stop the army and militias. Neither did the French troops flown in as part of Operation Amaryllis – purportedly to evacuate French and other foreign nationals but also to create safe zones around the airport and other key areas to prevent them falling into RPF hands.

As the militias and army went into action, RTLM was ready with a stream of increasingly violent rhetoric to support, mobilize and encourage killing, but also to justify, even sanctify, it as the duty of every Hutu. RTLM was the first to broadcast the news of the president's death – at 9.00 pm, half an hour after the plane was shot down. This was a very fast turnaround given the confusion that follows such an event – suggesting that the station was ready for this piece of news. Radio Rwanda did not report the event until the next morning. RTLM's line straightaway was that the RPF helped by UNAMIR's Belgian troops were responsible for killing Habyarimana (Article XIX, 1996, p. 109; Gourevitch, 1998, p. 111). From then on, RTLM content included frequent exhortations to join the genocide couched in the language of the calls for communal labour – Hutus were ordered to 'go to work', 'clear the bush', 'go clean' and were told, following the killing of the ten UNAMIR soldiers on the first day of the genocide, 'to each his own Belgian' (ICTR, Nahimana, section 6:7). On 7 April, according to Gourevitch, RTLM broadcast the threat that 'you *inyenzi* must know you are made of flesh. We won't let you kill. We will kill you' (Gourevitch, 1998, p. 114). RTLM was the first media outlet to announce the formation of the new government and to call on people to support it. On 8 April, Bemeriki and Hitimana sneeringly said that no one could find any of the members of the old government from the opposition parties. It was said in a way that implied knowledge that they had been killed. When they referred to the prime minister, they followed her name up with the comment that, 'people have said that she has answered the call by God' (Article XIX, 1996, p. 110).

As the genocide progressed, RTLM did urge not only participation and eternal suspicion of the Tutsis, but also information on where to find *inyenzi* and their sympathizers. On 10 April, Bemeriki and Hitimana made broadcasts inciting militias to search the Kadafi mosque in Nyamirambo, Kigali, and to find certain named people hiding there and eliminate them. There was an attack on the mosque within hours and a number of Tutsis were taken from the building and killed (ICTR, Nahimana, section 6:15). No doubt instructions went out to army units and militias to carry out attacks, but there is no denying the strong element of coincidence between the radio broadcast and the attack. On another occasion, Bemeriki read out the names, addresses, jobs and nicknames of 13 people and urged listeners to track them down (Melvern, 2000, pp. 155–6). The new prime minister, Jean Kambanda, made a number of broadcasts on RTLM, telling the population to search out the enemy, which meant those 'who do not share our opinion' – and search out meant search and destroy, it did not mean search out and gently show them the error of their ways. On 12 April, he used a broadcast on RTLM to warn Tutsis that if they attack, 'They will be throwing themselves into the mouth of the hyena and committing suicide. They will all be exterminated and none will live to tell the disastrous story. Let them come, the Rwandans are waiting for them with machetes.'

Another coincidence of broadcast and attack has been cited by Philippe Gaillard, the chief delegate of the International Committee of the Red Cross in Rwanda. He had been accused by RTLM – when he tried to intervene to protect injured victims of attacks – of being Belgian. He contacted the station and proved he was Swiss, so RTLM broadcast a report saying Gaillard was too intelligent and brave to be Belgian. Soon after this, he organized a convoy to take 100 wounded from Kigali to a hospital 40 kilometres away. RTLM was given information about the convoy and broadcast a report that RPF supporters were hiding in the lorries. The convoy was stopped at a convoy by the *Interahamwe*. Gaiilard managed to speak to contacts in the army; RTLM then issued a denial that there were RPF in the convoy and it was allowed to move on by the militia (Malvern, 2000, p. 156). This is a very telling indication of the role that RTLM played in directing militia actions. It is not, of course, evidence that RTLM was the prime source of motivation or instructions for the genocide but is strong evidence of the effects of radio and its ability to shape events in particular circumstances.

Atrocity stories were used by RTLM to scare their audience and convince them of the need to kill or be killed. One broadcast said that Tutsi soldiers were devils who killed their victims by 'extracting various organs [...] for example, by taking the heart, the liver, the stomach [...] the cruelty of the inyenzi is incurable, the cruelty of the inyenzi can only be cured by their total extermination' (Aticle XIX, 1996, p. 112). This was one of the few open references to the need for total extermination, though Tutsi were constantly referred to as 'evil incarnate, a direct menace to the entire Rwandan population, and to all humanity'. Most of RTLM's incitement amounted to identification of specific enemies to be sought out along with their location, reports of alleged RPF atrocities and the systematic advocacy of 'the killings of Tutsis by identifying them with the RPF', though the broadcasts often referred to the struggle as the 'final war' or 'a final confrontation with bloodthirsty monsters'; some of the broadcasts included accusations of cannibalism (ibid.).

The violence of the language, the framing of the reports and commentaries during the genocide period and the representation of the Tutsi as monsters, a never-ending threat, as cannibals and as the incarnation of evil clearly indicated to the audience that the threat was total and the solution had to be a total one. In the available transcript material, there is no room for doubt about the content and the intent of the broadcasts. Over the long term, they set an agenda of fear and hatred of the Tutsi, represented them as totally alien, as a threat to all Hutu and as vermin to be eradicated. This is summed up in an RTLM broadcast of 4 June 1994, in the latter stages of the genocide, when Kantano Habimana told his audience, 'They should all stand up so that we kill the *inkotanyi* and exterminate them [...] the reason we will exterminate them is that they belong to one ethnic group. Look at the person's height and his physical appearance. Just look at his small nose and then break it' (ICTR, Nahimana, section 27). This broadcast was cited in the ICTR's judgement in December 2003 on Nahimana, Barayagwiza and Ngeze, which stated that,

> The Chamber finds that RTLM broadcasts engaged in ethnic stereotyping in a manner that promoted contempt and hatred for the Tutsi population. RTLM broadcasts called on listeners to seek out and take up arms against the enemy. The enemy was identified as the RPF, the *inkotanyi*, the *inyenzi*, and their accomplices, all of whom were effectively equated with the Tutsi ethnic group by the broadcasts. After 6 April 1994, the virulence and intensity of RTLM broadcasts propagating ethnic Hatred and calling for violence increased. These broadcasts called explicitly for the extermination of the Tutsi ethnic group.
>
> (ICTR, 2003b, section 25)

The ICTR rulings in December 2003 further found that RTLM had paved the way for genocide and that it didn't just indirectly engage in incitement through equating Tutsi with the enemy, preaching hatred and contempt but it also directly advocated extermination and

> both before and after April 6, 1994, RTLM broadcast the names of Tutsi individuals and their families, as well as Hutu political opponents. In some cases, these people were subsequently killed, the Chamber finds that to varying degrees their deaths were causally linked to the broad cast of their names.
>
> (ICTR, 2003b, section 25)

RTLM was able to continue broadcasting throughout the genocide. At one stage an RPF attack took it off air briefly, but until the fall of Kigali in mid-July, RTLM was able to continue to broadcast. It experienced its greatest problems in late June 1994, when the French sent more troops into Rwanda as part of Operation Turquoise. At first, RTLM welcomed the troops as it was expected that France would continue its policy of supporting the Hutus and opposing the RPF and there were signs that the French would create safe zones that were still Hutu-controlled and beyond the reach of the RPF advance. But the international awareness of the genocide and growing criticism of French support for the Hutus led to a change in policy. The arriving French troops, to the horror of the extremists, began protecting Tutsis and destroyed at least one of RTLM's transmitters (Des Forges, 2007, p. 51). A little earlier, the US State Department had considered attempts at jamming broadcasts but had dropped the idea in the belief that it was not legal and would constitute an attack on freedom of speech enshrined in international conventions. RTLM was driven from Kigali by the RPF but continued broadcasting from a mobile transmitter and told Hutus to flee from the RPF – contributing to the huge exodus of Hutus to the Goma region of Zaire. In August, according to des Forges, the USA again considered jamming the broadcasts but by then the jamming equipment the French forces had taken to Rwanda was unavailable and the plan came to nothing (Des Forges, 2007, p. 53). RTLM continued broadcasting sporadically between August and October 1994, when it finally disappeared.

In less than 18 months of broadcasting, RTLM had become notorious, as the ICTR media trial and trial of Ruggiu were to reveal in huge detail, for its racist, violent and hate-filled messages. It embodied the ideology of Hutu supremacism and the desire to maintain hegemony if necessary through extermination of the 'other', the Tutsis. There is little doubt, even from the relatively small number of transcripts available, of the nature of the content and of the intent that it revealed. Mary Kimani, in her analysis of RTLM transcripts, has catalogued that just over 40 per cent of broadcast content contained attacks on the RPF and allegations of RPF atrocities or incited the listeners to fight and kill Tutsis, 9 per cent called for the extermination of the Tutsis, another 7 per cent that Tutsis were deviants, that they killed Habyarimana or that massacring them was justified. Only 13 per cent had no inflammatory content (Kimani, 2007, p. 118). She also notes that the majority of broadcasts – 74 per cent – were made solely by RTLM broadcasters and were not comments from government, army or militia officials; 89 per cent of the broadcasts were made or introduced by Habimana, Bemereiki, Gahigi, Nkurunziza, Ruggiu or Hitimana. The great concentration of output in the hands of a few broadcasters, all committed to hatred of the Tutsi and incitement to violence, indicates the way that the station set out to be the voice of Hutu extremism and to propagate hatred and incitement against the Tutsi and against moderate Hutus. There were no alternative views represented among the main broadcasters. Kimani concludes, very reasonably, that:

> RTLM told its listeners that the only way to avoid what was coming was for everyone to look out for the 'enemy in their midst' and work with the authorities to ensure the extermination of the RPA [military wing of the RPF] and all its accomplices. It was a fait accompli – kill or be killed.
>
> (Kimani, 2007, p. 123)

RTLM – did hate broadcasting cause the genocide?

One of the key arguments since the genocide and the 'media' trial of Nahimana, Brayagwiza, Ngeze and the separate trial of Ruggiu, has been over the effects of RTLM (and to a lesser extent *Kangura*) before and during the genocide. These centre on the extent to which the propaganda and incitement they contained acted to cause or worsen the genocide and whether a causal link can be found between broadcasts and the acts of killing and the intention of both Hutu individuals and Hutus as a group to carry out genocide.

Once the output of RTLM and its link with the genocide became widely known and began to be reported and researched, the horror that journalists and a form of communication thought to be a positive development tool could be used to incite and even direct genocide led to a spate of articles about the radio and genocide. Some made a very clear link between radio and killing suggesting, though without a detailed relating of broadcasts to events, that the key tools in the genocide were the panga (machete) and the radio – arguing that without radio the genocide might not have happened or at least not as quickly as it did. There was often an unspoken and perhaps at times even unintended implication that if RTLM had not existed then the genocide would not have happened. This clearly could not be backed up by evidence – though such a conclusion was rarely put down in those terms. Writers like Samantha Power fall into this category, with her statement that 'killers in Rwanda often carried a machete in one hand and a radio transistor in the other' (Power, 2001, p. 89). This view was also taken by the ICTR in its judgement in the Nahimana, Barayagwiza and Ngeze trial. The verdict stated that radios and weapons like pangas were the 'two key objects' to be seen at roadblocks and in the hands of the militia – implying the direct link between the two (ICTR, 2003a, p. 283). Misser and Jaumain, writing in *Index on Censorship* talked of 'death by radio' (Misser and Jaumain, 1994, pp. 72–4) and the term 'radio machete' was used regularly during the media trial in Arusha.

Not all writers on the subject implied such a strong connection. Darryl Li, for example, makes clear the power of RTLM as a source of propaganda and information but enters the caveat that radio did not have such a strong effect that it directly caused the genocide – he says that from his research,

> a broad theme emerges of radio implicating rather than manipulating its listeners, informing but not determining their choices. In its various aspects, RTLM's activities intertwined with Rwandan's efforts to make sense of and navigate the world in which they lived during such difficult times. Radio served as a medium through which Rwandans experienced and enacted the genocide, its broadcasts reverberating in the thoughts and actions of millions of people, both participant and witnesses, alongside and at times in opposition to other social forces based on coercion, interest or fear.
>
> (Li, 2007, p. 105)

The most sceptical voice on radio and the genocide is that of Straus. He rightly questions the view that radio was the reason for the onset of genocide but rather inaccurately portrays 'the conventional wisdom on hate radio' as taking the view that hate radio accounted for the start of the genocide and for the 'participation of most perpetrators' (Straus, 2007, p. 611). But he sets up a straw man in saying this, as none of the commentators quoted above take such a view that is so hard-line and impossible to authenticate. Certainly, there is a lack of precision in some accounts with little reference to actual content of broadcasts or relating of broadcasts to actual violence, but none of them put the entire blame for the genocide or the willingness of so many Hutus to kill on radio broadcasts alone. Some of Straus's arguments fall by the wayside as he is knocking down a theory that was never seriously propounded. It is hard to argue with his view that 'hate radio constituted one dimension by which hard-liners achieved dominance and were able to persuade individuals to join attacks against Tutsi civilians' (Straus, 2007, p. 632), but on the other hand it is impossible to disentangle the complex web of radio propaganda, exhortations at public meetings and the effects of a strongly ordered and controlled society under the hegemony of first a government and then a Hutu supremacist movement that had the manpower, means and will to enforce its word. Given that, his contention that

'To the extent radio mattered, it had a second-order impact' (ibid.) is not supportable.

In his account of RTLM, Straus admits that it set an agenda for racism, hatred of the Tutsi and for the extermination of the Tutsi and that on occasions there is clear evidence that RTLM broadcasts about specific people and specific locations were followed rapidly by attacks, strongly indicating a causal link (Straus, 2007, p. 620). This suggests far more than a second-order impact but very much a primary impact as part of a complex mixture of custom, government control of people's lives, peer pressure, fear of persecution and propaganda. On the basis of his own interviews with genocidaires, Straus says that 'First, radio broadcasts communicated the intent and instructions of authorities. Second, radio broadcasts reinforced messages that authorities communicated in person. And, third, radio broadcasts framed the political crisis: broadcasts categorized Tutsis as "the enemy" or as inyenzi' (Straus, 2007, p. 630).

This role in communicating intent and instructions, reinforcing messages given in other ways and framing the whole political crisis indicates a very major impact on the way that Rwandans viewed the events leading up to and after the killing of Habyarimana and to their preparedness (willingly or under coercion) to engage in genocide. Hate radio in the form of RTLM broadcasts (and to a lesser extent in the early 1990s in the form of Radio Rwanda broadcasts) played the role of the promoter of Hutu supremacism, the purveyor of extreme racist imaging of the Tutsi and the inciter of hatred and violence. Radio did this in a number of ways:

1. As Kellow and Steeves have identified, 'the role and influence of the media cannot be divorced from the historical, cultural and political-economic environments in which they function' (Kellow and Steeves, 1998, p. 107). RTLM adopted and utilized the Hutu supremacism ideas that first surfaced in the late 1950s in the Bahutu Manifesto, were developed and applied as government policy by Kayibanda and Parmehutu, gained currency again after the 1990 invasion by the RPF and were part of the daily outlook on life of many Hutu. RTLM took an existing set of ideas that were deeply ingrained – even if not acted upon or even consciously acknowledged in daily life – and worked them into an ideology and active policy of hatred and violence. There was no invention of a new ideology but rather the evolution of existing, known and largely unchallenged ideas of Tutsi malevolence and the need for the Hutu to be aware and prepared to act in defence of themselves and their livelihoods.

2. RTLM and *Kangura* played the role prior to the genocide of agenda setting. The political situation, the 'plight' of the Hutu and the Tutsi 'threat' were framed in such a way as to provide the prism through which Hutus were told to view their world. Throughout their coverage, RTLM and Kangura promoted clear images of the Tutsi, a strong causal interpretation

of events as they unfolded putting them in the context of an ineluctable conflict between Hutu and Tutsi, and constantly reinforced the Hutu Power line that only through exterminating the Tutsi could the Hutu be free of peril.

3. The agenda set by broadcasts was then translated into exhortations to action, backed up by the repressive machinery of the state and of the Hutu militias. As in National Socialist Germany, there was a complex interplay between propaganda, peer pressure and coercion. This is not to deny the agency of individual Rwandans – clearly not all took part in the genocide. But those that did took part either because they thoroughly believed in the Hutu Power ideology, were convinced by the constantly reinforced argument that it was kill or be killed, feared to be different from their peers or were directly coerced into action by the threat that those who did not kill would themselves be killed.

4. Radio had particular power in Rwanda, and much of the rest of Africa, because of high rates of illiteracy, logistical and economic obstacles to the distribution and purchasing of newspapers, and the relative cheapness of radios and batteries. Radio ownership in Rwanda was reasonably high – one radio to every thirteen Rwandans – and it was an immediately accessible media wherever there was a signal. Under colonialism and then under Kayibanda and Habyarimana, radio had been the voice of authority and the government in what has been demonstrated to be a highly ordered state. RTLM inherited that authority by using familiar Radio Rwanda broadcasters but made the message even more powerful by using simpler but more effective forms of broadcasting that mixed music, humour, comment and exhortation in an accessible format using language that appealed to and was familiar to the mass of Rwandans. This amplified the effect of what was being said, made it more palatable and trusted.

5. There were few if any alternative voices to be heard. Radio Rwanda declined in importance after RTLM inception but did not offer an alternative account of unfolding events, while Muhabura was dull, propagandistic and hardly listened to by its own side. Newspapers were more varied but not as accessible to the mass of people, while foreign radio stations broadcast in French but not Kinyarwanda.

6. As Kellow and Steeves argue:

> In sum, this study suggests that the strong establishment of media dependency for political information, alongside media's agenda-setting and framing roles, and absence of alternative voices, can set the stage for unusually powerful propaganda campaigns. Such campaigns, in turn, may spark extreme fear and mass panic with catastrophic outcomes, even genocide.

(Kellow and Steeves, 1998)

RTLM was not the cause or the sole influence on the genocide and on those taking part, but it played a powerful role in combination with historical, social, political, economic and military factors that led to the genocide. No one factor can easily be teased out, they act in combination with the influence of particular factor varying according to circumstance. The discourse of hatred on RTLM was inextricably bound up with the development of Hutu-Tutsi relations over centuries and over the development and use as a political, social and economic tool of a discourse of Tutsi 'otherness' and Hutu identity in the five decades leading up to 1994.

The ICTR verdicts

On 3 December 2003, the ICTR in Arusha gave its unanimous verdicts in the media trial – the accused were Ferdinand Nahimana, Jean-Bosco Barayagwiza and Hassan Ngeze. The court found Ferdinand Nahimana guilty of conspiracy to commit genocide; guilty of genocide; of direct and public incitement to commit genocide; not guilty of complicity in genocide; guilty of crimes against humanity (persecution); guilty of crimes against humanity (extermination); not guilty of crimes against humanity (murder).

The Chamber found Jean-Bosco Baraygwiza guilty of conspiracy to commit genocide; guilty of genocide; not guilty of complicity in genocide; guilty of direct and public incitement to commit genocide; guilty of crimes against humanity (extermination); guilty of crimes against humanity (murder); guilty of crimes against humanity (persecution); not guilty of serious violations of Article 3 Common to the Geneva Conventions and of Additional Protocol II. Hassan Ngeze was found guilty of conspiracy to commit genocide; guilty of genocide; not guilty of complicity in genocide; guilty of direct and public incitement to commit genocide; not guilty of crimes against humanity (murder); guilty of crimes against humanity (persecution); guilty of crimes against humanity (extermination).

Nahimana was sentenced to life imprisonment, as was Ngeze; Baraygwiza received a sentence of 35 years minus time served.

The ICTR verdict stated that:

RTLM broadcasting was a drumbeat, calling listeners to take action against the enemy and enemy accomplices, equated with the Tutsi population [...] The nature of radio transmission made RTLM particularly dangerous and harmful, as did the breadth of its reach [...] Unlike print media, radio is immediately present and active. The power of the human voice, heard by the Chamber when the broadcast tapes were played in Kinyarwanda, adds a quality and a dimension beyond language to the message conveyed. Radio heightened the sense of fear, the sense of danger and the sense of urgency giving rise to the need for action by listeners.

These conclusions were applied in the cases of Nahimana and Barayagwiza for their roles at RTLM, while Ngeze's conviction related particularly to *Kangura* (ICTR, 2003a, section 99).

However, in November 2007, the ICTR appeal court gave its verdict on the appeals by the three and reduced their sentences, re-ruling the original judges for 'not drawing a clear line between hate speech and incitement to commit genocide' (Benesch, 2008, p. 489). Issuing its decision on 28 November 2008, the tribunal affirmed the charge of 'direct and public incitement to commit genocide' for Ngeze and Nahimana. The judges reversed the finding of guilt on this charge against Barayagwiza, ruling that only RTLM broadcasts made after April 6, 1994 (when the genocide began), constituted 'direct and public incitement to commit genocide' and that by then Barayagwiza no longer exercised control over the employees or output of the radio station. Barayagwiza was still found guilty of instigating the perpetration of acts of genocide and crimes against humanity. Because of the reversal of some charges against the three defendants, the judges lowered the defendants' sentences: Nahimana's from life to 30 years, Negeze's from life to 35 years, and Barayagwiza's from 35 to 32 years (United States Holocaust Memorial Museum, USHMM, website).

When it came to the case of George Ruggiu, he at first pleaded not guilty and then changed his plea to guilty of direct and public incitement to commit genocide and crimes against humanity (persecution). The Chamber said that, in considering the verdict, it examined legal precedents related to the crime of persecution, including the judgement on Julius Streicher. In that case, the International Military Tribunal at Nuremberg held that as publisher of the anti-Semitic weekly newspaper *Der Stürmer*, Streicher had incited the German population to actively persecute the Jewish people and that Streicher's incitement to murder and extermination at the time when Jews in the east clearly constituted persecution on political and racial grounds (ICTR, Ruggiu). The Chamber said that the Streicher case was particularly relevant to Ruggiu's, 'since the accused, like Streicher, infected peoples' minds with ethnic hatred and persecution' (ibid.). The Ruggiu judgement was that he had responsibility for 'direct and public radio broadcasts all aimed at singling out and attacking the Tutsi ethnic group and Belgians on discriminatory grounds, by depriving them of the fundamental rights to life, liberty and basic humanity enjoyed by members of wider society. The deprivation of these rights can be said to have as its aim the death and removal of those persons from the society in which they live alongside the perpetrators, or eventually even from humanity itself' (ibid.).

Accepting his guilty pleas, the ICTR Chamber found Georges Ruggiu guilty of the crime of direct and public incitement to commit genocide and of crime against humanity (persecution)

The court transcript of the verdict says that

> the accused acknowledges that the widespread use of the term 'Inyenzi' conferred the de facto meaning of 'persons to be killed'. Within the context of the civil war in 1994, the term 'Inyenzi' became synonymous with the term 'Tutsi'. The accused acknowledges that the word 'Inyenzi', as used in a socio-political context, came to designate the Tutsis as 'persons to be killed'.
>
> (ibid.)

It further said that he:

> admits that as part of the move to appeal for, or encourage, 'civil defence', he made a public broadcast to the population on several occasions to 'go to work'. The phrase 'go to work' is a literal translation of the Rwandan expression that Phocas Habimana, Manager of the RTLM, expressly instructed the accused to use during his broadcasts. With time, this expression came to clearly signify 'go fight against members of the RPF and their accomplices'. With the passage of time, the expression came to mean, 'go kill the Tutsis and Hutu political opponents of the interim government'.
>
> (ibid.)

The court also noted that Ruggiu admitted that RTLM broadcasts incited young Rwandans, Interahamwe militiamen and soldiers to engage in armed conflict against the 'enemy' and its accomplices and to kill and inflict serious bodily and mental harm on Tutsis and moderate Hutus and that he admitted that 'that RTLM broadcasters, managerial and editorial staff bear full responsibility for the 1994 massacre of Tutsis and Hutu opposition party members' (ibid.). Ruggiu was sentenced to 20 years imprisonment, less time already served.

On 14 December 2009, the BBC reported that Valerie Bemeriki had been found guilty of inciting, planning and complicity in murder and genocide. During the trial, Valerie Bemeriki admitted to inciting violence and said that in one broadcast, she told her listeners: 'Do not kill those cockroaches with a bullet – cut them to pieces with a machete.' She was sentenced to life imprisonment.

None of the other major broadcasters – Habimana, Hitimana, Gahigi or Njurunziza have been brought to justice. Gahigi always denied that RTLM incited hatred or genocide and in an interview with Article XIX in Goma, Zaire, soon after the genocide, he said that there was an ethnic problem and that 'if RTLM had not said it, would this have prevented the problem from existing'. He went on to Say that RTLM was criticized because it spoke of taboo subjects like ethnicity. Article XIX also spoke to a lesser RTLM broadcaster, Emmanuel Rucogoza, who denied incitement and said 'this radio tells the truth and the truth hurts' (Article XIX, 1996, pp. 142–3).

6

Kenya: Political Violence, the Media and the Role of Vernacular Radio Stations

In late December 2007, violence broke out in Nairobi, Kisumu and the Rift Valley in Kenya in protest against the results of the presidential election. There was a widespread belief among members and leaders of opposition parties, subsequently confirmed by election monitors from the European Union (EU) and the Commonwealth, that the results were fraudulent and that Mwai Kibaki had not been re-elected and should not have been sworn in for a second term as president. The violence lasted for nearly four months, between 1200 and 1500 people died and over 660,000 were displaced from their homes and localities.

What started as demonstrations by the main opposition movement and its supporters became widespread and in places violent, with the police and security forces reacting with lethal force. The unrest, clearly sparked by the election, rapidly took on the appearance of an ethnic struggle between the Luo and Kalenjin supporters of Raila Odinga and the Orange Democratic Movement (ODM) and the mainly Kikuyu supporters or perceived supporters of Kibaki's Party of National Unity (PNU). As the conflict escalated, the planned and organized nature of many of the attacks on particular communities became clear – this was not a totally spontaneous outburst of anger, but carefully orchestrated violence with clear political and economic objectives. This is not to say that as the violence took hold there were not spontaneous outbreaks, but there is strong evidence of pre-planning, of the arming and training of groups from different communities and the direction by political leaders of much of the violence. The level of direction believed to have been involved is such that four prominent Kenyans from the ODM and PNU, including a leading radio editor and presenter, have been indicted by the International Criminal Court (ICC) charged with playing leading roles in the organization of the violence and will stand trial in The Hague in 2012. Those under indictment are William Ruto (leading ODM member in 2007–08 and subsequently a minister in the coalition government), Joshua arap Sang (ODM supporter and head of operations and leading broadcaster with the

Kalenjin language radio station Kass FM), Uhuru Kenyatta (PNU member in 2007–08 and key Kikuyu ally of President Kibaki) and Francis Muthaura (Kibaki ally and head of the civil service) (House of Commons Library, 2011, p. 1). They were all charged with crimes against humanity relating to their suspected role in the violence – including murder, forcible transfers of population and persecution. Sang's indictment included reference to his role as a radio presenter. The ICC indictment read as follows:

> As early as December 2006, WILLIAM SAMOEI RUTO ('RUTO') [...] of the Orange Democratic Movement ('ODM') political party, began preparing a criminal plan to attack those identified as supporters of the Party of National Unity ('PNU').1 JOSHUA ARAP SANG ('SANG'), a prominent ODM supporter, was a crucial part of the plan, using his radio program to collect supporters and provide signals to members of the plan on when and where to attack. To reach their goal, RUTO [...] and SANG coordinated a series of actors and institutions to establish a network, using it to implement an organizational policy to commit crimes. Their two goals were: (1) to gain power in the Rift Valley Province, Kenya ('Rift Valley'), and ultimately in the Republic of Kenya, and (2) to punish and expel from the Rift Valley those perceived to support the PNU (collectively referred to as 'PNU supporters').
>
> (ICC, 15 December 2010, p. 4)

The indictments indicated not only a perceived level of organization of the violence but also that radio played a role in it. This was the first direct indictment of a journalist by an international legal entity since the charges and convictions of the journalists and executive of Radio-Television Libre des Mille Collines and *Kangura* newspaper following the Rwandan genocide.

The Rwanda angle is particularly pertinent as within a few weeks of the outbreak of violence in Kenya, the situation there had spawned comparisons with the 1994 genocide in Rwanda. Kenyan politicians on both sides of the electoral divide exchanged accusations of genocide and ethnic cleansing, with little concern for the facts, their own roles in the events or the consequences for Kenya.

The genocide/ethnic cleansing theme was taken up by many Western and Kenyan journalists and by media monitors – there were worrying comparisons being made by Kenyans and foreign observers alike with the 1994 genocide in Rwanda. Part of this comparison involved warnings that politicians and community leaders were engaged in inciting ethnic and community hatred with a view to encouraging violence, and that hate radio was operating in Kenya and was at least partly to blame for inter-communal violence and the inflaming of suspicion, fear and hatred between ethnic groups. Human rights organisations, media monitors, politicians and commentators all pointed to the role of the media, and vernacular radio stations in particular, in inciting violence, contempt and ethnic hatred (see, for example, Integrated Regional Information Networks (IRIN), 27 January 2008).

The major accusation against a number of radio stations broadcasting to the Kalenjin, Luo and Kikuyu communities in their own languages was that they were deliberately and knowingly increasing ethnic suspicion, directly advocating violence against 'others' and disseminating messages of hatred and incitement. The Inter Press Service (IPS) immediately drew a comparison with Rwanda and the well-documented role of hate radio during the 1994 genocide:

> The media was partly blamed for the Rwandan genocide 14 years ago which left nearly one million people dead in 100 days. 'Kill the Inkotanyi [cockroaches]!' a local radio station urged its listeners at the time. '30 Days in Words and Pictures: Media Response in Kenya During the Election Crisis' – a workshop organised here last week by California-based media advocacy group Internews – enabled media professionals to conduct a 'self-audit' of the role local media played in the post-election violence. The audit revealed that media – especially vernacular radio stations – might be partly to blame for the on-going violence sparked off by the announcement of Mwai Kibaki as winner of the Dec. 27 elections.
>
> (IPS, 2 February 2008)

Some experienced media observers, who had been monitoring Kenyan radio during the elections and the violence, were more cautious but still drew parallels with Rwanda and suggested that Kenya could move towards a situation in which radio stations acted like the infamous Radio-Television Libre de Mille Collines (RTLM) in Rwanda. Caesar Handa, the director of Strategic Public Relations Research, which produced media monitoring reports for the UN Development Programme (UNDP), said that, 'we did not reach the Radio Mille Collines level, but we were not very far from it' (British Broadcasting Corporation (BBC) World Service Trust, April 2008, p. 5) – a chilling image. Handa confirmed this view in an exchange of emails with the author in 2009.

But how accurate is this portrayal of the violence in Kenya and of the role of radio in spreading hate and inciting violence? In looking at these questions, this chapter examines the political/social environment that gave rise to the violence, locate it in the historical context of political violence in Kenya in recent decades and in the language of political discourse in Kenyan politics, and examine the behaviour of the Kenyan media and particularly vernacular radio during the elections and the ensuing violence in terms of dissemination of fear, hatred and incitement to murder. These topics form the social and political context of the media and broadcasting and, without them, examination of the content and the intent of the broadcasts would be very shallow.

Research limitations and methodology

Documenting hate broadcasting in Kenya during the 2007–08 violence and the 2005 and 2010 referendum campaigns has proved a less than exact science. Due to the absence of a large body of transcripts of vernacular radio, the analysis is primarily qualitative rather than quantitative. The radio stations identified as broadcasting incitement were not monitored by the main source of radio monitoring for East Africa, the BBC Monitoring Service's Nairobi monitoring unit. There was some monitoring by independent consultants such as Caesar Handa, but there is a dearth of transcript material. Much of the analysis of radio output from the vernacular stations is based on the few transcripts available, supplemented by interviews carried out by the author, reports on the violence from official bodies (notably Kriegler) and human rights organizations.

This is not ideal. Detailed analysis of transcripts would enable a more searching inquiry into agenda setting, framing and representation within the broadcast content. Another drawback in carrying out the research, as can be seen from interview material, has been the unwillingness of those working for vernacular radio stations to discuss in detail the content of broadcasts or the ownership and political affiliations of stations because of the ICC investigations and indictments. A final obstacle to research has been the wariness of Kenyan journalists, media organizations and ordinary Kenyans to discuss aspects of the violence and the roles of senior politicians. There remains a considerable climate of fear when it comes to assessing or discussing responsibility for the violence. The author was consulted by the ICC during the drawing up of the indictments and advised that the lack of transcript material made any assessment of the culpability of broadcasters, like Sang, almost impossible to assess. Sang, himself, denies any role in hate broadcasting or incitement – he has said this consistently both before and since the indictment (Sang interview with author, February 2010).

In an ideal world, focus groups would have been used to assess audience reaction to broadcasts, but both the climate of secrecy and fear and the lack of transcripts to put before groups prevented this. Kenyan politics is continuing as usual in the wake of the 2010 referendum on the constitution (which also saw examples of violence, hate speech and intimidation) with jockeying for political advantage and the making and breaking of alliances; there is considerable underlying tension and apprehension over the run-up to the 2013 elections. Journalists and media trainers working to improve vernacular and community radio told the author, under conditions of anonymity, that there was still a climate of fear and harassment among journalists in this sector – journalists who did not toe the line within their communities had been threatened. Some of those interviewed said that if bribery or the danger of losing one's job did not work, then threats along the lines of 'we know where you and your family live' would be used to stop reporting of issues or stories that political leaders did not want broadcast (interviews in Nairobi, February 2010).

The political context: shifting alliances and violence

The 2007 presidential and parliamentary elections were a contest between two main political rivals, the incumbent president, Mwai Kibaki, and his Party, the PNU, and the opposition coalition, the ODM, led by Raila Odinga. Kalonzo Musyoka of the smaller ODM-Kenya also fought the presidential election and a total of 20 parties put up candidates for parliament. Campaigning and political discourse during the campaign were harsh, bitter and often violent. The bitterness of the campaign had its roots in Kenya's developing political culture and, on a personal level, in events following the previous election.

During the 2002 election, which saw long-time President Daniel arap Moi's favoured candidate, Uhuru Kenyatta, defeated, Kibaki and Odinga led the National Rainbow Coalition (NRC). This consisted of politicians from a variety of parties, politicians and communities opposed to Moi. The pre-election deal between them fell apart as the conservative Kibaki used the presidency to entrench his power and favour his closest allies at the expense of his alliance partners. By the time of a constitutional reform referendum in 2005, Odinga had become a fierce critic of Kibaki. The referendum was the result of a tortuous process of constitutional reform. Kibaki and Odinga had agreed to institute this reform – long called for by many politicians in Kenya – when they took power. Odinga believed that Kibaki had agreed to a diminution of presidential powers and the creation of the post of prime minister with extensive executive powers – a post that he expected to hold himself.

Reform proved hard to agree and it was two tortuous years before a draft was agreed, based on a reduction in presidential powers and the creation of the post of prime minister. Kibaki was not happy with this and changed the draft prior to the November referendum. This resulted in a fiercely fought and violent referendum campaign (in which hundreds died and tens of thousands were displaced by violence). Odinga forged an alliance of groups from Luo, Luahya and Kalenjin communities and political leaders, in direct opposition to Kibaki and his allies. Odinga was successful and Kibaki's draft was voted down, with the 'No' vote registering 57 per cent of the vote. Kibaki dissolved his cabinet, appointing a new one drawn from the 'Yes' camp, irrevocably splitting the alliance that had defeated Moi. The violence of the referendum campaign in the Rift Valley, Kisumu and Mombasa, and the bitterness of the campaigning, was a foretaste of what was to come in 2007.

The Kriegler report (commissioned after the 2007–08 violence by the Kenyan government and the international mediators who negotiated a political compromize between Kibaki and Odinga, and chaired by the South African judge, Justice Johann Kriegler) reported that the passions that developed during the referendum campaign had maintained political discourse at a high pitch leading up to the 2007 election campaign, which was characterized by 'robust language occasionally lapsing into ethnic hate speech and deteriorating into violence' (Kriegler, 2008, p. 1).

In addition to the controversy and bitterness over the referendum, Kibaki's incumbency saw none of the redistribution of land, wealth or solving of historical land and other grievances that Odinga's supporters had hoped for when they joined together with him to form the National Rainbow Coalition. The president was seen by many Kenyans as ruling for the benefit of a small group of politicians and businessmen, who became known as the Mount Kenya Mafia. This group was perceived by other communities – notably the Luo and Kalenjin – as working solely for the benefit of a small Kikuyu/Kiamba elite who were closely allied to Kibaki and who gained from access to wealth, government contracts and political patronage (Anderson, Royal African Society website, 2008b).

As the 2007 elections approached, Odinga used the 'No' alliance of the referendum to put together a coalition of politicians who supported a populist agenda based on poverty reduction, the settlement of land and economic grievances dating back to colonial land seizures and a revisiting of constitutional issues (including a commitment to consider devolution of power to provinces – something that particularly appealed to Kalenjin and Masaai political leaders). For once, there were not only personality issues between 'big men' to the fore in the election but also serious political and economic issues.

The president's economic policies were seen by many Kenyans outside the political and business elite as benefitting the rich and further impoverishing and marginalizing the poor (Rodrigues, 2008). There was even criticism within the Kikuyu community of the corruption surrounding what was called Kibaki's Mount Kenya Mafia. This dissatisfaction among poor Kikuyu manifested itself in the growing power of a criminal gang/sect known as Mungiki. This group ran protection rackets and carried out violent extortion in poor urban areas, recruiting from among poor, badly educated and unemployed Kikuyu youths and using oathing ceremonies reminiscent of the Kikuyu-based Mau Mau anti-colonial movement of the 1950s. The group came into conflict with the government and, in the years running up to the 2007 election, there were outbreaks of violence in slum areas between the police and sect members – many police were killed and Mungiki members frequently killed policemen and left their bodies displayed prominently in slum areas or by major roads. The government and paramilitary police struck back and Nic Cheeseman believes that, just months before the elections, up to 500 suspected Mungiki were killed by government security forces in the slums of Nairobi – part of an estimated 600 people who died between the start of the election campaigning in October 2007 and the vote at the end of December (Cheeseman, 2008, p. 170).

Despite this bitter struggle between the sect and the police prior to the elections, Mungiki became available as the paid thugs for Kikuyu politicians during the elections. Part of the ICC investigation into supporters of the PNU involved establishing links between senior PNU officials and Mungiki. Uhuru Kenyatta was identified by the ICC as a key link between the PNU and the sect Kenyatta, according to the ICC pre-trial documents:

> allegedly exercised over the Mungiki a control that amounted to the "control over the organisation" and his contribution to the implementation of the common plan was essential.

More specifically, Kenyatta allegedly:

> (1) organised and facilitated, on several occasions, meetings between powerful pro-PNU figures and representatives of the Mungiki, thus making possible the very conception of the common plan referred to above; (2) supervised the preparation and coordination of the Mungiki in advance of the attack; (3) contributed money towards the retaliatory attack perpetrated by the Mungiki in the Rift Valley.
>
> (ICC, 8 April 2011)

The relationship between politicians and criminals or loosely organized gangs of poor and unemployed youths has been a growing facet of Kenyan politics since the end of the one-party system and the dilution of the monopoly of state power by the ruling party from independence up to the early 1990s – there was a growing 'informalization' of political violence. There were no permanent alliances involved here, as Branch and Cheeseman point out, but shifting relationships based on money, mutual benefit of gangs and political barons and common community/ethnic identity – the latter not specifically a result of ethnic animosities but because gangs were recruited locally in the political strongholds/heartlands of powerbrokers and politicians (Branch and Cheeseman, 2009, p. 15).

In terms of their support bases, Odinga had Luo support and the support of younger, poorer Kenyans, particularly in Nairobi slums like Kibera. His forging of alliances was assisted by a struggle for power within the political elite in the Rift Valley, the results of which enabled him to gain the backing of the most powerful political factions in the Rift Valley from among Kalenjin and Masaai communities. It was not a foregone conclusion that the Kalenjin and Masaai would opt to support Odinga against Kibaki. As Lynch has described (Lynch, 2008, pp. 542–3), the Kalenjin community has usually voted en masse for the same party in a particular election – though not for the same party in successive elections. The Kalenjin supported Moi's Kenya African Democratic Union (KADU) in 1963 and the Kenyan African National Union (KANU), by then led by Moi, in 1992, 1997 and 2002 (in 2002 Moi

was barred by the constitution from running for a third term and supported Uhuru Kenyatta as the KANU candidate, though Moi was still the
pre-eminent Kalenjin political leader). In 2002, Kalenjin leaders supported
Moi against both Kibaki and Odinga.

The Rift Valley political changes in 2007 were the result of a number of
factors, including generational struggle and dissatisfaction with the benefits to the mass of people in the Rift of decades of Moi rule. Competition
for Kalenjin backing was between Moi and a group led by a younger politician, William Ruto. Ruto was a former KANU member of parliament (MP)
and minister under Moi. Ruto won the struggle and threw Kalenjin support
behind Odinga and the ODM. Ruto had become a powerful force among
the Kalenjin, appealing to the poor, who had not benefited under Moi, and
those who wanted the restitution of land claimed as Kalenjin and to prevent
Kikuyu ascendancy. One must also note that while restitution of lost land
was an issue for most Kalenjin, some of the Kalenjin and Masaai elite who
had benefited materially from Moi's rule, were afraid that a Kibaki government would investigate land acquisitions and financial dealings that were
the fruits of the abuse of position.

Ruto threw his weight and that of the majority of the Kalenjin behind
Odinga and the ODM – he was a key member of the coalition, the chief
organizer in the Rift for the ODM and has been indicted by the ICC on
suspicion of preparing a plan for violence against political opponents, of
organizing killings and the forced displacement of communities. Whether
or not the ICC is able to prove these charges, it is undeniable that Ruto and
his supporters threw their support behind the ODM.

What Ruto and his Kalenjin and Masaai allies wanted was for a future
Odinga-led government to settle land issues in the Rift Valley and move
towards devolution of power away from the central government in Nairobi –
a process known as *majimboism* and long vilified by successive governing
elite groups. In the 1960s and 1970s, President Kenyatta, his supporters
and those enjoying the fruits of government power depicted majimboism as
being ethnically/tribally based and a threat to national unity. They attacked
the process as backward, divisive and anti-Kenyan. Kenyatta had successfully co-opted the pro-federalist, Kalenjin leader, Daniel arap Moi, and his
supporters into government in 1964, thereby undercutting the federalists in
the 1960s and rendering them marginal to mainstream politics.

The issue was largely dormant in mainstream politics during most of the
Moi period, as previously pro-federalist politicians from the predominantly
Kalenjin Rift Valley and from Masaai areas had their hands on the levers of
power and sources of patronage; to use the popular Kenyan expression for
the nature of power and wealth, it was their turn 'to eat'. They did not then
want any dilution of their power through regionalism. Devolution of power
only became a major political issue again when demands for multi-party
rule from Moi's opponents put him under political pressure. Moi and his
supporters in KANU revived ideas of federalism – again it was political

leaders in the Rift Valley who wanted to follow this route. The devolution of power to regional/provincial bodies, notably in the Rift Valley, was seen by Kalenjin leaders as a possible way of preserving their power bases and sources of economic wealth and political patronage in the face of threats to their monopoly control of national politics represented by multi-party rule (Klopp, p. 484). Devolution became a central plank of the ODM campaign, though with Odinga trying to avoid being tarred with the brush of a simplistic majimboism, with its connotations for some Kenyans of ethnic separatism and even ethnic cleansing. Moi's Kalenjin supporters had been widely accused of carrying out ethnic cleansing in the Rift Valley under the guise of majimboism in the 1990s, a period which saw over 2000 deaths and 500,000 displaced in land conflicts in the Rift (Mueller, 2008, p. 191).

The political aspects of this approach to competitive politics were bound up with grievances over land ownership and occupation dating back to land seizures by white settlers during the colonial period and subsequent politically motivated resettlement schemes after independence. Resettlement schemes launched by Kenyatta were perceived by the Kalenjin to have benefited Kikuyu and Kisii migrants into the Rift Valley rather than the Kalenjin or Masaai, who claimed original ownership of the land (Human Rights Watch (HRW), 2008, p. 5). In the 1990s and 2002, the question of land and the grievances of the Masaai and Kalenjin became key rallying points for politicians allied with Moi and against what were seen as Kikuyu-led or influenced parties/coalitions established as one-party rule was abolished. These issues were exploited repeatedly during the 1992, 1997 and 2002 elections, with varying degrees of success, but always with elements of whipped-up anti-outsider feeling and the threat or actual use of violence (see, for example, HRW, 2008; Klopp, pp. 485–91; Lonsdale, 2008, p. 308). This pattern was repeated in the 2005 referendum campaign.

During the 2007 election campaign, beginning in November, violence was frequent and serious and was accompanied by the effective barring of politicians and party supporters from one alliance from areas that were the strongholds of opposing parties. Election monitors, who were highly critical of the fairness of the elections and the vote count, pointed to the inability, for example, of the ODM or ODM-Kenya to campaign in pro-PNU areas of Central Province. Similarly it was impossible for the PNU to campaign safely or effectively in areas of the Rift Valley and Nyanza province (European union Election Observers, EUEO, 2008, p. 8). Politicians or activists campaigning in opposition territory were liable to be physically attacked and have their rallies or meetings broken up by opposition supporters or paid thugs.

Kenya has experienced serious outbreaks of politically motivated violence at each of the elections from 1992 onwards (1992 marking the resumption of multi-party elections after a gap of 29 years), during the attempted coup against President Daniel arap Moi by Kenyan Air Force officers in 1982 and during the 2005 referendum campaign. Violence has also

punctuated disputes over land ownership, political patronage and historical grievances derived from the upheavals of the colonial period (for more
detailed examinations of these issues, see Berman, 1990; HRW, 2008; Klopp,
2001; Lynch, 2008). But the ferocity, rapid escalation and scale of the violence after the 2007 election took many Kenyans and international observers
by surprise, shattering myths of Kenya as an essentially politically stable
country (*Guardian*, 31 December 2007, *Financial Times*, 29 December 2007
and *Independent*, 6 January 2008 all have variants on the 'haven of stability
descends into violent chaos' approach to reporting the violence).

Politicians intent on maintaining or extending their power and privileges
or struggling to challenge the powers of local or national rivals used a variety of instruments to strengthen their own power bases and utilized violence
and hate propaganda against opponents and their real, perceived or potential supporters (HRW, 2008). They created an atmosphere in which they
could mobilize supporters to carry out violent attacks against opponents and
in which their supporters would, on occasion, react spontaneously to events,
having been incited to expect threats of fraud from their opponents. There
was a substantial escalation of violence following the announcement of the
presidential results and accusations by losing candidate, Raila Odinga of the
Orange Democratic Movement, that the count in the presidential election
had been fraudulent – accusations backed up by reports from the international observers, notably the European Union monitors (EUEO, 2008).

The initial form of unrest was mass demonstrations by ODM supporters in Nyanza province, the Rift Valley and slums like Kibera in Nairobi.
There had been no widespread or sustained violence in the areas affected
prior to the start of the election campaign. The protests by ODM supporters in the Kibera slum near Nairobi, the Rift Valley and Nyanza province
drew a swift and brutal response from the police acting under orders from
the Kibaki government and PNU leaders, with many fatalities resulting from
police use of extreme force and live ammunition to combat demonstrations
(HRW, 2008, pp. 27–30). But the unrest generated by the ODM, the police
response and then the reaction by PNU supporters appeared to take on a life
of its own and rapidly came to resemble ethnic warfare – notably between
Luo/Kalenjin supporters on the one hand and Kikuyu/Kisii supporters of the
PNU on the other.

The growing violence and mounting deaths were interpreted by many
politicians in Kenya (for their own mercenary purposes) and by the Kenyan
and international media as ethnic or 'tribal' violence that was a spontaneous reaction to the election result but that had its roots in historical and
primordial tribal hatreds. Powerful politicians who were using political violence as an instrument – whether ODM leaders using it to force a recount
or rerun of the election, or PNU leaders using violence to protect their less
than fair election victory – wanted the violence to be seen as spontaneous,
ethnic or 'tribal' violence to mask their own organizing roles (Anderson,
Prospect, 2008a) and to use the 'tribal' aspect as a propaganda stick with

which to beat their opponents. Close examination of the violence shows that however spontaneous some initial demonstrations were, the escalation and proliferation of violence was to a great extent orchestrated by politicians and showed significant planning (HRW, 2008). For journalists, the ethnic or tribal explanation was a convenient, lazy and value-laden shorthand that absolved them of the need to go into complex explanations of the intricacies of Kenyan politics and generally fitted in with their assumptions about ethnic/tribal African politics (Somerville, 2009). Certainly, in some cases, local communities or party supporters reacted spontaneously to suspected threats or to the heavy-handed suppression of demonstrations by the police, but there is no evidence that some form of traditional, 'tribal' animosity existed between communities in the sense that was often reported in the international media (see the argument presented in Somerville, 2009).

There was violence between communities from different linguistic/cultural/ethnic traditions but it was very clearly politically based and, as the ICC contends in its indictments and as the Kriegler reported demonstrated (ICC, 2011; Kriegler, 2008), the violence was political and much of it was meticulously planned and financed by political leaders. The spontaneous element grew out of the responses of demonstrators to police violence and to the fear generated by the conflict and the violence of the rhetoric used by politicians, community leaders and, at times, a few broadcasters – though the latter must be viewed carefully without jumping to conclusions about Rwandan-style incitement.

There are major problems with the tribal hatred approach. The Kalenjin shifted their political allegiances, at times supporting Moi and his allies, at others Kibaki and Odinga. And, prior to colonization, there was no such group as the Kalenjin per se. The 'tribe' brings together 'a number of subgroups administered as separate tribes during the colonial period' (Lynch, 2008, p. 542). The term 'Kalenjin', first used in the late 1950s, was a creation of the colonial period though not directly of the colonizing power, when it suited nascent political leaders from within the groups (including Nandi, Kipsigis and Tugen) that now make up the Kalenjin, to bring together those communities sharing common linguistic roots and inhabiting a particular area within the Rift Valley and surrounding regions. The new identity was accepted by the colonial authorities for greater ease of administration and with a view, perhaps, as Lynch argues, of creating a bulwark against growing Luo and Kikuyu nationalism (Lynch, 2007, chapter 1); political leaders from the communities now comprising the Kalenjin gained by becoming part of a larger population group and a wider support base.

The important factor that needs emphasizing about the shifting alliances and the political allegiances of Kenya's groups is that there is no long history of sustained ethnic conflict between specific groups. Both before and during the early colonial period, there was coexistence between different communities, intermarriage and trade (Berman, 1990, p. 49; Klopp, 2001 pp. 487–9;). Conflict occurred over water, grazing or cattle, but it happened alongside the other communal interactions noted above. It was colonial occupation, the seizure of land and the creation by the British colonial authorities of reserves for 'tribes' that created 'tribes' in specific areas with potentially conflicting interests, landless peasants and developed a desire to reclaim land taken from various communities. Land reclamation became a serious issue for displaced communities and failure to address it was the cause of serious and lasting grievance for some of them. This created or sustained suspicion or competition between communities and was endlessly exploited by greedy or ambitious politicians. There is no evidence of sustained and lasting animosity, let alone violence, between ethnic groups.

Post-independence land resettlement schemes only enhanced the grievances of non-Kikuyu communities. The perception became ingrained, especially among the Kalenjin and Masaai, that 'outsiders' had gained at the expense of indigenous communities creating a level of suspicion and political/community competition that had not previously existed. This was fertile ground for politicians willing to incite ethnic conflict for political advantage. Their ability to do this was enhanced, according to Martin Gitau, the head of the Kenyan Journalists' Association, and Dennis Ole Itumbi, editor of the 'Fountain Post' blog in Kenya, because as a general rule Kenyans of one particular community tend to vote en masse for the candidate seen as representing their community in elections (interviews with Gitau and Itumbi, 10 February 2010, Nairobi). Alliances shifted as a result of the political opportunities perceived by political leaders, not as a result of established ethnic alliances or conflict. It was an exaggerated form of clientism, with the 'big men' of politics using patronage and other methods to take their communities with them.

The failure of Kenyatta and then Moi to deal with land ownership and related problems meant that, for many poor or landless Kenyans, the competitive elections from 1992 onwards became opportunities to seek redress. This rendered poor, rural Kenyans susceptible to politicians keen to exploit these issues to build local political and electoral support. As the BBC's experienced Africa correspondent, Mark Doyle, wrote:

> ahead of and during the 2007 elections 'politicians from all ethnic groups [...] had been preparing the ground for trouble in the wake of the elections because they know that "land clashes", as they are known in Kenya, always flare up around polling time' and can be manipulated to serve the interests of the politicians.
>
> (Doyle, 2008)

Political parties were of less intrinsic importance in Kenya than in Western Europe or the USA, for example, and generally served not as aggregators of individuals with shared political beliefs or interests but as means for politicians to build the machinery, resources, local, regional and national support to win power. Kenyan parties have always been shifting coalitions of politicians seeking power and election to office. There was a slight difference in 2007 in that Odinga was more clearly radical and populist than Kibaki and so issues rather than just personalities were involved. Odinga was trying hard to appeal beyond ethnic community, particularly to the poor and the young who felt that they had gained nothing from economic growth or decades of independence. He had had massive support in his home province, Nyanza, and in the Rift Valley, where Ruto and his allies had taken the support base that had underpinned Moi for decades and built a Kalenjin following based on expectations of a solution to land grievances and hopes of some form of federalism. Kibaki's PNU was based on alliances more reminiscent of the days of Kenyatta, with the Kikuyu at the centre, and support from smaller communities outside the Rift Valley and Nyanza, along with the backing of declining politicians like Moi. The incumbent president was viscerally opposed to Odinga's radical populism and was unwilling to seriously contemplate a major redistribution of land or wealth or a diminution of central control through federalism or a reduction in presidential powers. The mix of competing approaches to major issues like land and the personal rivalries combined with huge economic/social inequality and major grievances among key communities to provide a wealth of combustible material that only needed a spark to ignite substantial conflict. Behind it all was a deep well of frustration, anger and deprivation among poor Kenyans of all communities; grievances that could be exploited to build votes, intimidate opponents or fight an unwanted election result.

When the voting was over and initial results emerged from the electoral commission, the ODM was ahead in the parliamentary vote and Raila Odinga had a marginal lead that some opinion polls in Kenya suggested had stretched to a million votes. The Kenyan *Nation* newspaper, normally a supporter of incumbent governments, went as far as to report on 29 December that 'bar any force majeure, Mr Rail Odinga is poised to win the presidency'. Delays in announcing the result of the presidential vote and rumours of fraud within the electoral commission led to protests by Odinga supporters and the violent and lethal reaction from the police. The announcement of the victory by Kibaki drew immediate accusations of cheating from the ODM and expressions of concern over the veracity of the count from independent observers. The initial violence was a direct result of anger over the delays in the count and then over the result. The violence continued until the signing of a political agreement by Kibaki and Odinga at the end of February.

Political violence with an ethnic face

Although it was the violence between ethnic groups that dominated reports of the three months of crisis, it must be noted that in the opening days, the most serious violence was from the Kenyan police and was directed against ODM demonstrators. Attacks by supporters of one party from one community against perceived supporters of their opponents among alien communities escalated and caused hundreds of deaths, but police violence principally against ODM supporters was constant (HRW, 2008, p. 4). It became clear that during and after the election campaign, leaders and party activists on both sides utilized local grievances, ethnic stereotypes, insults and fear of 'others' to mobilize votes, boost attendance at rallies, mobilize demonstrators and eventually involve people in intimidation and direct violence against opponents. But some violence was spontaneous and a certain gruesome tit-for-tat pattern emerged in some areas beyond the control of political leaders.

The violence took on the appearance of ethnic conflict, especially in the Rift Valley. Kalenjin and Masaai gangs were used by ODM politicians and by local grandees to attack their political opponents and to achieve through violence and threats the destabilizing of the government and, at least in the short term, reoccupation of land claimed as Kalenjin or Masaai. The level of planning of violence is set out, though with large redacted sections, in the indictments release by the ICC on 10 December 2010 against the six leading politicians and public figures. As David Anderson has pointed out, the ODM was prepared before the election results were announced to cry foul and had 'laid plans for a campaign of civil unrest' (Anderson, 2008a and b). It is no surprise that 'the worst violence has occurred in areas where it is easy to mobilise thuggery, such as the slums of Nairobi and in places where there is a long history of animosity between neighbouring communities such as the resettlement schemes of the Rift Valley' (Anderson, 2008a). But Anderson is clear in his view that this animosity and the resulting ethnic violence is 'not rooted in any deep-seated ethnic hatred, although no one would deny that as this crisis has mounted, growing fear and latterly, a lust for vengeance has driven a wedge between communities' (Anderson, 2008b).

The reactions of politicians to the post-election violence did nothing to cool tempers or discourage violence. In inciting violence, Kalenjin politicians in the ODM used the lure of getting land back and fear tactics – they said that if Kibaki remained in power, local communities would be under threat, would lose more land and come under the control of outsiders like the Kikuyu. The demonstrations and violence sparked off by the fraudulent election was used by these leaders to pursue long-term underlying aims of their own. These aims involved the seizure of land and the ejection, effectively ethnic cleansing, of opposing communities. Despite repeated use of the term by Kenyan politicians for their own, self-serving ends, there was and still is no compelling evidence that genocide was part of the equation.

In their in-depth report on the violence, HRW pointed out that the failure of successive Kenyan governments to address grievances had intensified community animosity leading to serious ethnic divisions, that politicians who had organized and funded political violence during previous elections had never been brought to book, and concluded that, 'this violence is the outcome of decades of political manipulation of ethnic tensions, and of impunity intertwined with longstanding grievances over land, corruption, inequality and other issues' (HRW, 2008, pp. 2–3). The report added that the ODM had built a coalition 'based on the widespread perception that the Kibaki government had entrenched tribalism and governed in the interests of the Kikuyu community' (HRW, 2008, pp. 4–5). As already seen in the ICC indictments detailed above, Uhuru Kenyatta and others in the PNU camp, are accused of having made their own preparations ahead of the election results for political violence and had militias prepared, co-opting the Mungiki sect as a strike force (ICC, 8 April 2011).

The organized violence against target communities was matched by substantial and consistent vilification of opponents by political leaders on a national, regional and local basis. Ethnic stereotypes were widely utilized to denigrate opponents. Raila Odinga and his Luo supporters were repeatedly ridiculed for being just 'boys' – a play on the different rituals for the progression from boyhood to manhood among Kenya's different groups. The Kikuyu practise circumcision, the Luo don't. There was racist, obscene and offensive campaigning on this issue by PNU leaders and supporters. The circumcision motif had been used by Kibaki supporters during the 2005 referendum campaign and was used extensively to denigrate ODM politicians and supporters in 2007 – even to the extent of calling for them to be forcibly circumcized (Kenyan National Human Rights Commission (KNCHR), 2006, p. 45 and 2007; and Warungu, 2008). ODM politicians and propaganda concentrated far more on land issues, alleged corruption, Kikuyu tribalism and the dangers of Kikuyu hegemony to other groups. In such a situation, the media was bound to become part of the problem even if they only reported political rhetoric.

The media, political hate speech and radio's role in incitement

Elections are always a testing time for the media, even in societies with established, varied and well-regulated media. In Kenya, political debate and elections take place in a difficult and potentially hostile environment for the media and journalists. During the period of one-party rule under Kenyatta and Moi, there was limited political debate and, despite a variety of newspapers with diverse ownership, there was a strong authoritarian tradition, which meant that while the Kenyan press was not as directly censored or repressed as that in many African states, it served as an instrument of the government with considerable self-censorship and a major emphasis on the actions and pronouncements of the president and his senior ministers (Heath, 1997, pp. 44–5). The state-funded public service radio and TV (the Kenya Broadcasting Corporation (KBC)) was subject to government control and acted as the voice of the government, and, to a great extent, still does today.

As one-party rule came to an end, the self-censorship and the authoritarian attitude of government weakened but the opening up of the press and broadcasting was a slow and far from easy process – as the author can testify from personal experience, having been arrested, briefly detained and then deported from Kenya for trying to enter the country in February 1991 to make a BBC radio documentary on the mounting pressure for an end to one-party rule.

After 1992 and the formal legalization of a multiplicity of political parties, the press became less tightly controlled but was polarized. The two main papers: the *Nation*, owned by the Agha Khan; and the *Standard*, formerly owned by the Lonrho multinational based in London, were seen as the two main voices of government and opposition. The *Standard* is now viewed as an opposition newspaper – when Lonrho sold the newspaper, the first chairman of the new *Standard* board was Mark Too, a close relative of Moi and the paper is now regarded as part of the Moi family's business empire (Loughran, 2010, p. 237). Similarly, most media-aware Kenyans believe that controversial Kalenjin leader William Ruto is behind the Kalenjin radio station Kass FM and that Uhuru Kenyatta is behind K24 TV and Kameme FM radio. Senior journalists and executives at Kass and Kameme deny the links with Ruto and Kenyatta (author's interviews with Joshua arap Sang and Macharia Wamugi, February 2010) but journalists and media monitors have little doubt about who controls these stations (interview with Itumbi, Gitau, Jooste and Rambaud, Nairobi, February 2010).

During the 2007–08 elections, it was considered that the press and broadcast media was relatively free to reflect the political debates (EUEO, 2008, pp. 1–2) as it had been during the 2005 referendum campaign and, to a lesser extent because of Moi's incumbency, in 2002. But observers felt strongly that the media failed to provide equitable coverage of the political leaders and parties. Internews, an American-based non-governmental organization (NGO) working in Kenya to help train journalists, believes that the picture is mixed and that extensive coverage was given of the campaign by the print media, but that there were, as there are for example in Britain during elections, clear preferences expressed or implied for particular candidates or parties. There was also a clear need for better training for journalists to cover the intricacies, controversies and politically sensitive issues arising during elections (interviews with Rambaud and Jooste, Nairobi, 17 February 2010). The state-owned KBC was criticized heavily by EU election monitors for failing 'to fulfil even its minimal legal obligation as a public service broadcaster [...] its coverage demonstrating high degree of bias in favour of the Party of National Unity (PNU) coalition' (EUEO, 2007, p. 2).

A study commissioned by the United Nations Development Programme (UNDP) found that 'even though the leading newspapers, television and radio stations were not very biased for or against any of the candidates, there were discernable preferences shown by the tilt they gave in favour of or against candidates and their campaign issues'. The report also noted that vernacular FM radio stations showed clear preferences for the candidates and parties 'whom they perceived to be the choice of their listeners' (UNDP, 2008). The behaviour of the vernacular stations gave rise to accusations (see in detail below) that they were acting as hate radio broadcasters.

Observers of the Kenyan media felt that the mainstream press and broadcasting organisations did not incite hatred but failed to prevent the dissemination of party propaganda and the violent rhetoric of many political leaders, and they failed 'to live up to professional and ethical standards' (BBC World Service Trust (WST), 2008, p. 2). Some Kenyan journalists went further in their criticism at a workshop in Nairobi in January 2008, accusing the print and broadcast media of being willing to put money ahead of responsibility by 'accepting and conveying paid-for hate material' which could have incited the audience at a time of tension (IPS News, 2008).

The general thrust of comment on the media – leaving aside the vernacular stations for the time being – was that while Kenya had a relatively free press by African standards, there was a lack of professionalism and training that would enable journalists to effectively cover political controversy, conflict and elections and a vulnerability because of a lack of viable media laws and legal protection for journalists. This rendered the media and journalists vulnerable to politicians wishing to intimidate or manipulate them. The BBC WST, in its report on the media and the elections, made clear the political and commercial pressures and constraints that affected the independence and integrity of the media and highlighted the need for the strengthening of the freedom of the press, the removal of political and economic constraints and the creation of an environment in which journalists could do their work in safety and free from pressure or intimidation (BBC WST, 2008).

The level of interference by the government was obvious, too. The EU monitors explicitly criticized the ejection of all but a chosen few 'trusted' journalists and organisations from the venue in which the hurried announcement of Kibaki's victory was made and emphasized the lack of media freedom resulting from the order by Kibaki's internal security minister 'to suspend all live broadcasts, seriously infringing the rights of the media to report without undue state interference' (EUEO, 2008, p. 1). While the Kenyan government argued that the live ban was to prevent broadcasting of film of violence that could provoke further conflict, the ban gave KBC (under government control) a monopoly on TV and radio reporting. What was even more interesting is that journalists in Nairobi told the author in 2010 that the film crew and outside broadcast unit that filmed the ceremony for broadcast on KBC were from the station that owned K24 television and Kameme FM, and were closely linked with Kibaki lieutenant Uhuru Kenyatta.

As the violence increased, the limitations and failures of the mainstream and government media gave commercial and vernacular stations greater credibility when they broadcast accounts of events or statements by political leaders that contradicted the official position, which was widely believed to be inaccurate. This led to a very skewed and chaotic media environment after the elections. The commercial sector in broadcasting has low standards of editorial control, untrained staff and little experience and, as Maina has cogently argued about the emerging private sector, 'The private broadcasters, while seeming to take the duty of informing the public seriously, exhibit a tendency towards bias, and almost every channel can be identified with a political party or personality' (Maina, 2006, p. 9).

The UNDP report on the media is even more forthright about bias in reporting the violence after the 2007 elections: 'The coverage of the post-election violence by the media brought to the fore the entrenched political divisions as various media houses took obvious positions for or against the status quo' (UNDP, 2008). As the violence escalated from demonstrations about the results by the ODM and an extreme police response to clearly orchestrated violence against specific targets with an increasingly ethnic character (even though this paper argues that the causal factors were political, social and economic rather than primarily ethnic), the partiality of the media became part of the problem.

The mongoose and the chickens and the beasts from the West – incitement to hatred in political rhetoric

Kenyan politicians have routinely used local grievances to set communities at each other's throats and used language designed to denigrate and dehumanize their opponents. In the period from independence to 1991, Kenya was a *de facto* and later *de jure* one-party state in which the media was not free to report and in which politicians in power had free rein to physically or verbally harass opponents or critics. As the pressure built for multi-party politics, the language of political discourse emanating first from Moi and his supporters within KANU and then spreading throughout the competing political elites was one of insult, threat and accusations, which ranged from corruption, through ethnic supremacism, to ethnic cleansing, murder and genocide. Substantive policy issues or even the political or administrative capabilities of individuals or parties were not at the heart of political debate, incendiary personal diatribes and the denigration of personalities, parties and whole communities were. The denigration of communities or ethnically based stereotyping were not an everyday part of political discourse. They were there in the background and not taken hugely seriously most of the time, but came to the forefront at times of tension or during elections.

In the early 1990s, Moi and his ministers used the rhetoric of fear to oppose multi-partyism, claiming that it would destroy unity and lead to fragmentation. They threatened multi-party advocates and at public meetings called on KANU supporters to 'oppose selfish troublemakers' and 'some regime supporters themselves appeared to advocate violence against political dissidents, publicly urging citizens to cut off the fingers of multi-party advocates, and to arm themselves with *rungu* (knobbed sticks) and spears to crush opponents of one-party rule' (Haugerud, 1997, pp. 76–7).

This political discourse of violent rhetoric and the dehumanization or denigration of opponents became dominant during elections, periods of political tension and in land disputes after 1992. Much of the language used was extreme and called openly for violence and killing, even though it is not clear that speakers realistically expected their audiences to follow the instructions rather than treating them as symbolically strong statements of contempt for opponents. During the bitter and violent 2005 referendum campaign, a pro-Kibaki local council leader in the Tatu area told his audience at a 'Yes' rally that, 'Raila [Odinga, the 'No' campaign leader] the monster should be hit on the head and killed so as not to destabilize the Kibaki government'; at another 'Yes' rally, energy minister and Kibaki stalwart Simeon Nyachae demanded that 'those who are not circumcised [Luos like Odinga] should be taken for circumcision ceremony'; at a 'No' rally pro-Odinga MP Joe Khaimi said that critics of Odinga should be lynched (KNHCR, 2006, pp. 30–3).

The circumcision insult was used frequently during 2005 and 2007 about Odinga and his Luo supporters and, during violence in both campaigns, forcible circumcision of Luo by Kibaki supporters was an horrific part of the political violence. The stereotype of the Luo as 'boys' and therefore inferior was a theme in the 'Yes' campaign led by Kibaki and his supporters among the Kikuyu community and was taken up again by PNU leaders and supporters in 2007–08. It was a motif used to denigrate Odinga and his supporters and as noted involved calls for forcible circumcision (KNCHR, 2006, p. 45; Warungu, 2008). The KNCHR has reported fully on the use of dehumanizing rhetoric and hate speech by politicians on both sides of the political divide during the referendum (KNHCR, 2006). In a later report, *Still Behaving Badly* (KNCHR, 2007), the organization said that the 2007 election campaign had been marked by continuing use by politicians of insults against opponents, threats of violence and effective incitement to violence. The commission said that 'covert hate speech, defamatory and unsavoury language continues unabated' and that 'unfortunately, Kenyans continue to condone and cheer hate speech and have themselves become active agents of proliferation of hate campaigns against politicians and fellow Kenyans' (KNHCR, 2007).

Some of the discourse – as happened in Rwanda with the use of the term cockroach or *inyenzi* for Tutsis and innocuous expressions like 'go to work' to mean killing Tutsis – was seemingly unrelated to politics but was clearly understood by protagonists. There were frequent references to the need for the 'people of the milk' to 'cut grass' and complaints that the 'mongoose' has come and 'stolen our chickens'. This, to Kenyans, is easily understandable with the pastoralist Kalenjin referring to themselves as people of the milk, the 'grass' refers to non-Kalenjin or non-Masaai in areas claimed as land originally belonging to them, and the mongoose is a reference to Kikuyus who have bought land in Rift Valley and are viewed by the Kalenjin and Masaai as interlopers and essentially thieves (AllAfrica.com, 2008). The calls by pro-ODM leaders for its supporters to 'cut the grass' was open incitement to attack what were viewed as foreigners in the Rift – cutting the grass meant killing them or driving them from land claimed as Kalenjin. This language was understood widely among the targets audiences (confirmed by Kenyan journalists and media specialists in interviews in Nairobi, February 2010).

Kikuyu and PNU politicians and public figures (often on radio or television as well as at public meetings) derided Odinga, his political allies and ODM supporters generally as 'baboons' or 'animals' or 'beasts from the West' (AllAfrica.com, 2008). Although the comments on occasion were accompanied by direct calls for violence, they drew on cultural differences and negative stereotypes and referred back to disputes about access to land, wealth and control of state power. The human rights commission concluded in its report on the 2005 referendum that even where there wasn't a direct call for violence, this political language and 'the resulting stigmatization, dehumanization and hatred is just as harmful' (KNHCR, 2005, p. 26).

The 2007 electoral campaign showed little change in the level or seriousness in violent and offensive political rhetoric – there was no perceived decline despite the reports and pleas for restraint that followed the 2005 referendum campaign. Once the dispute over the result turned to violence and that violence had developed an ethnic edge, the rhetoric of genocide and ethnic cleansing came into play – but not calls for genocide, rather accusations that their opponents were carrying out genocide against supporters of the targeted group. Hate rhetoric became an accusation and a polemical weapon to be wielded against your opponents, denigrating them not only in the eyes of Kenyans, but also internationally and, in particular, in the eyes of the foreign dignitaries (such as Ghanaian President Kofi Annan, African Union Mediator John Kufuor and US Assistant Secretary of State for African Affairs Jendayi Frazer) involved in negotiating an end to the violence.

By early January, both sides in the conflict were using the term 'genocide' to refer to the policies and actions of their opponents. On 2 January, President Mwai Kibaki's government accused rival Raila Odinga's party of unleashing 'genocide' in Kenya as the number killed in the violence passed 300 – 'It is becoming clear that these well-organized acts of genocide and ethnic cleansing were well planned, financed and rehearsed by Orange Democratic Movement leaders prior to the general elections,' according to a Kibaki government statement delivered by the lands minister, Kivutha Kibwana (Reuters, 2008). The ODM wasn't slow in replying and it accused the government of repressive policies 'bordering on genocide' by ordering police to shoot protesters demonstrating against Kibaki's victory (Reuters, ibid.). A website was set up by Kibaki and PNU supporters entitled 'Chronicles of the Kenyan Genocide', which sought to amass evidence from the PNU side that Kalenjin and other pro-ODM ethnic groups were carrying out systematic genocide against the Kikuyu. The site accused an ODM MP of inciting Kalenjin and Luo youths to drive Kikuyu and Kisii people from Molo district, to attack and kill them (Chronicles of the Kenyan Genocide, 2008).

Despite this, it is clear that despite the organized nature of many of the attacks, there was no obvious intention on the part of any group to annihilate another. The hate rhetoric was not part of a campaign to rid Kenya of all members of any one or a collection of identifiable ethnic/linguistic groups. The Kalenjin and their political allies showed no intention of wiping out the Kikuyu and the Kikuyu were not powerless victims – they were involved in tit-for-tat killings of Kalenjin, Luo and Masaai, as is becoming increasingly clear not just from the reports by Kenyan human rights bodies at the time, but also from the ICC indictments.

In Kenya, the killings and ethnic cleansing were clearly organized by political and community leaders and had definite goals – creating a situation of ungovernability that would force the Kibaki government to negotiate over the disputed election results; to create a new political landscape in areas like the Rift or in PNU-dominated regions, in which perceived opponents from other communities were driven out and given a clear message not to return; and also the clearing of land claimed by one community of what were seen as 'others' or interlopers. Some of the instigators have been remarkably candid about their intentions. In an interview with the BBC's Pascale Harter, Kalenjin community and political leader Jackson Kibor openly advocated the killing of Kikuyu and said, 'We will fight. This is war. We will start the war. We will divide Kenya' (BBC World Service, 31 January 2008 and HRW, 2008, p. 39). Human Rights Watch also details threats made by Kalenjin and ODM leader and former Moi lieutenant William Ruto against the Kikuyu and incitement to violence by him on the basis of Ruto's belief that Kibaki was governing 'this country on the basis of tribalism' (ibid.). The media was one way for those advocating violence or disseminating hate speech to get their messages across.

Vernacular radio and hate speech

'Radio is the premier means of reaching the public with news and information in countries where most of the population is illiterate and television sets are rare' (Chalk, 2000, p. 93). Kenya has a higher rate of literacy than many of its neighbours (above 70 per cent, but with an uneven spread across age ranges, urban/rural divides and gender). It also has an increasingly diverse network of newspapers, TV and online news providers. But as Frank Chalk identified in relation to Rwanda, with the limited access of populations in

Africa, particularly in rural areas, to TV let alone the internet, and greater levels of illiteracy or partial literacy in the countryside, radio remains a key source of news and other information. It is cheap, does not require reading skills, is immediate and, with the growth of FM stations across Kenya, available with strong local content and in vernacular languages (ibid.).

Kenya does not have a long history of vernacular radio. Independent Kenya inherited the colonial radio system – geared mainly towards the interests of administration, economic development and settler interests. The Kenyatta and Moi governments retained close control over radio and emphasis was put on national unity and to broadcasting in KiSwahili and English rather than vernacular languages.

It was the end of single-party rule and the gradual opening up of the media to greater freedom of expression that led to pressures for local, vernacular radio. Fearing its use for political purposes by the opposition and the loss of control of a key means of influencing opinion, Moi initially opposed granting FM licences to commercial stations – particularly as the first request for a licence to broadcast came from Royal Media Services owned by S.K. Marcharia, a prominent businessman with close links to leading opposition politicians. He wanted to set up a Kikuyu FM station, Kameme FM. Despite Moi's opposition, pressure on the government led to the licensing of commercial FM stations in 1996 (Wafula, 2008). But the government was not happy with the situation and, in 2000, banned Kameme on the grounds that it was being used to campaign for the opposition – exactly what Moi was using KBC for on behalf of KANU.

Realizing the power of vernacular broadcasting, the government launched its own Kikuyu station, Inooro FM, to compete with Kameme, which was eventually allowed to broadcast again. Both Joshua arap Sang, chief of operations and lead presenter for Kass FM, the Kalenjin station, and Macharia Wamugi, operations head for Kameme FM, the popular Kikuyu station, told the author in interviews in February 2010 that the governments of Moi and then Kibaki had been suspicious of vernacular radio because large parts of the population would not be part of the dialogue between local stations and the audience in their own languages and that they thought this would be both divisive and beyond their control. Both broadcasters insisted that while they spoke in their own languages to their own language communities and used colloquialisms and expressions that might seem odd to outsiders, they were doing so not to incite their audience, but because it was the language they knew and understood.

Following KANU's electoral defeat in 2002, there was a rapid expansion in FM stations – particularly those broadcasting in Kikuyu, Kalenjin, Luo and Luhya. Kass FM became the most influential Kalenjin station, while Lake Victoria FM and Ramogi FM were the leading Luo stations. They were criticized by human rights groups during the 2005 referendum campaign for inciting political violence – Inooro FM was pro-Kibaki and broadcast songs deriding 'beasts from the West', meaning Odinga and his supporters (KNCHR, 2007). The Kibaki government briefly suspended Kass FM in November 2005, accusing it of inciting violence during the referendum campaign (Wafula, 2008). Odinga supporters accused the government of attacking Kass because it was independent from the government and broadcast the views of Odinga supporters opposed to the planned new constitution. Kass was allowed to resume broadcasting when it produced transcripts of programmes and succeeded in proving that no hate messages had been broadcast. This gave the station greater credibility among Kalenjin listeners and increased suspicion of the Kibaki government. The government accusations and Kass's successful defence against them, convinced Kalenjin listeners that Kass was on their side and was willing to criticize the government where necessary (Sang, Nairobi, 2010). This gave it a level of credibility with its audience that increased its ability to influence opinion among the Kalenjin, something that presenter and operations chief at Kass was open about in interview with the author.

In a survey of Kenyan broadcasting, the BBC referred to reports of the broadcasting of hate speech by a number of vernacular radio stations in 2005 and to continuing fears that vernacular stations 'could influence ethnic tensions' (BBC World Service Trust, 2008). These fears appeared to be realized with the publication of a slew of reports in early 2008 that vernacular radio stations were playing a negative role in the violence following the elections. The journalist and media commentator Evans Wafula sounded an alarming and ominous note when he wrote that 'reminiscent of the notorious RTLM in Rwanda, the media in Kenya is partly to blame for the post-election bloodshed in Kenya. There are worrying echoes of a planned genocide being incited by local radio stations that urged people to "arm themselves" against their enemies' (Wafula, 2008). The BBC reported on 14 February that the government had ordered an investigation into claims that vernacular radio stations had engaged in hate broadcasting during and after the elections (BBC News, 2008).

Unfortunately, there are few transcripts available of the vernacular radio broadcasts. The stations involved are small and do not keep large archives, while major monitoring organizations (notably the BBC Monitoring Service, which has a monitoring station at Karen, on the outskirts of Nairobi) were not monitoring vernacular radio, only mainstream Kenyan broadcasters using English or KiSwahili (interviews with BBC Monitoring's Greenway, 2009; Muindi, 2010). There was some monitoring of press and broadcasting by the Steadman Group and Strategic Public Relations Research Ltd on behalf of human rights groups and the UNDP, but even they have relatively few transcripts.

The Kenyan Human Rights Commission (KHRC) believes that there is cause for concern over the language broadcast by some of the stations and there is evidence that in the past the vernacular stations (Kass FM, Lake

Victoria, Kameme and Inooro are named) have been responsible for 'spinning information to support candidates and parties who are of the same tribe as their audience while openly castigating those who are not of the same tribes' (KHRC, 2008) – evidence perhaps of bias, but hardly a convincing argument that stations were adopting practices similar to RTLM in Rwanda. The usually authoritative and widely read UN-linked IRIN news agency reported that 'inflammatory statements and songs broadcast on vernacular radio stations [...] all contributed to post-election violence' and warned that behaviour of vernacular stations was worrying given the role of RTLM in Rwanda (IRIN, 2008). The agency cited Caesar Handa of Strategic Public Relations Research Ltd, who carried out media monitoring for UNDP, as saying that 'there's been a lot of hate speech, sometimes thinly-veiled. The vernacular radio stations have perfected the art.'

The stations singled out in the IRIN report were Kass, Kameme, Inooro and Lake Victoria. Handa told the agency (and also supplied the author with further information in emails) that talk and phone-in shows were the worst and that callers or politicians/local leaders interviewed on the stations engaged in incitement against other communities, which the radio presenters seemed powerless to prevent or control. IRIN said that Kass FM repeated the hate speech used by Kalenjin politicians against the Kikuyu, notably the warnings that 'the mongoose has stolen our chickens' and that the 'people of the milk' had to 'cut the grass' and were 'getting rid of the weeds' (Handa, emails, 2009; IRIN, 2008). What is not detailed is whether Kass journalists themselves made these comments or whether they were from contributors via phone-ins, emails, SMS messages or in interviews with politicians.

Joshua arap Sang, who presented programmes on Kass FM during the elections and the violence, denied that his station broadcast hate speech; he said they were just broadcasting to their people (the Kalenjin) and explaining the situation to them in language they would understand. When presented with transcripts detailing incitement, for example, to beat opponents, he denied that they had been broadcast. In interviews with the author and the 'Radio for Development' website (Radio for Development, 2010), Sang said that there was no issue that the radio station wouldn't cover and they wanted to get across how the Kalenjin people were receiving government policies on the ground. He said that they were empowering the Kalenjin and enabling them to resist things like police harassment. Sang admits that Kass 'sensitizes' the audience about important issues and that it talks in the language they appreciate and understand, but denies that this means incitement. Sang admitted that Kalenjin public figures connected with Kass have been influential with the Kalenjin community both in Kenya and abroad, and that the station has a strong and trusted position.

Kass FM broadcasts in the Kalenjin language – and reaches an audience of about 4.5 million listeners across Kenya daily. Sang presents *Lene*

Emet, the station's popular breakfast show, which involves phone-ins, email contributions and both SMS and social networking links with the Kalenjin audience in Kenya and the Kalenjin diaspora (Radio for Development, 2010). Kass can also be heard by Kalenjin speakers globally through its website broadcasting. This makes it extremely influential within the community and explains the focus on Sang when it comes to accusations of incitement and hate broadcasting. He is the key presenter, as he told me himself, as well as operations manager and chief editor. Other journalists to whom I spoke in Nairobi about Kass, including some with past links with the station, said that Sang was the most popular broadcaster on the station and that the Kalenjin audience had great trust in him. Some added, on condition of anonymity, that during the violence his language was unrestrained, as was that of Kalenjin political leaders who appeared on *Kass*.

When they appeared before an initial hearing at the ICC in the Hague on 11 April 2011, Ruto and Sang faced charges of murder, forced eviction of people from the Rift Valley and persecution – the charges said that the offences were mainly committed around the Eldoret and Nandi areas – the focus of the Rift violence of 2008. They denied the charges. Ruto described the charges as 'the stuff of movies', which had been concocted in 'a devilish manner', claiming that it was not possible for murder and persecution to happen like that in Kenya. Sang described himself as an 'innocent journalist' who did not deserve to be 'hurled before the court' (AllAfrica.com, 2011). Despite the protestations of innocence, there is evidence, both in the few transcripts and in the recollections of media monitors and local journalists, of regular use of ethnically demeaning and threatening language by some presenters and contributors to Kass and to other vernacular stations. Because of the levels of violence in the Rift Valley and now because of the ICC indictment, attention has focused on Sang and Kass. The other stations such as Lake Victoria FM, Inooro and Kameme which, in the view of journalists to whom I spoke in confidence in Nairobi in February 2010, were just as unrestrained and freely attacked politicians and other communities in their broadcasts have not come under the same spotlight because of the concentration of violence in the Rift and the particular image and prominence of Sang – again, transcripts are lacking and most of the evidence is second-hand and anecdotal.

Western journalists covering the violence in 2008, also drew attention to the content of vernacular broadcasts. Mike Pflanz, reporting for the British *Daily Telegraph* and the Irish *Independent*, said 'there is growing evidence that hate-filled broadcasts have poured fuel on the fire of Kenya's post-election killings and contributed to "ethnic-cleansing" in certain areas'. He said that this was 'a chilly echo' of Rwanda and the role of hate radio in the genocide. He went on to say that programmes and songs broadcast on the vernacular stations 'had helped incite tribal killings' and he quoted Kamanda Mucheke of the KNCHR as saying, 'it has been thinly-veiled, but it is clearly hate speech and to a large extent the violence we're seeing can now be attributed to that' (Pflanz, 2008).

What is lacking from many of the reports about the role of hate radio is clear evidence, beyond the dozen or so transcripts available and plenty of anecdotal accounts, of the content that is said to have had such an effect in inciting violence. Pflanz does not cite the content of a single broadcast and transcripts are lacking for references in the human rights report. Of 13 transcripts supplied to the author by Caesar Handa, only one, from Kass FM on 3 October 2007, in the run up to the elections, has any incitement to violence and that could be as much symbolic as real incitement to cause harm. The offending broadcast had a presenter reading out the following SMS from a listener – 'Leaders who abuse ought to be shown, they should not be elected at all or they be beaten and their property be burnt' (Handa, emails, 2009). A broader survey sent to the author by Mr Handa indicates that strongly partisan content was broadcast by Kass, Kameme and Inooro, but little that could be compared with RTLM's output in 1993 and 1994, which set the agenda for the genocide against the Tutsi.

Greater credence is given to the accusations of hate broadcasting by East African media organisations and by Kenyan journalists themselves, including some working for FM stations. The Tanzanian-based IPS media organisation looked at the monitoring information available and at comments by Caesar Handa and concluded that the Kass, Kameme, Inooro and Lake Victoria FM stations had been the worst offenders in spreading hate messages, especially through talk shows with guests and phone-ins (IPS, 2008). Another local journalist, Dennis ole Itumbi, said that all the above stations had been broadcasting hate messages and that a journalist broadcasting for Kass had called on his Kalenjin audience to 'leave your houses, war has begun' and to 'arm themselves'. Itrumbi also said that a Reverend Kosgey, who broadcast on Kass, was active in organizing attacks on Kikuyu communities in the Rift Valley. He also said that the Kikuyu station Inooro 'was particularly blamed for organising revenge attacks in Kenya's Central Province' (Itumbi, 2008 – confirmed in conversation with the author in Nairobi, 10 February 2010).

Other evidence about Kass output and Sang's role in it has come from Nairobi-based journalist Robert Corey-Boulet. In an analysis of Sang's role, published in 2011 after the ICC indictment, he cites the case and testimony of Elizabeth Cherotich Karanja. In the last days of December 2007, Karanja's village, a pocket of ethnic Kikuyu families in the western part of Kenya's Rift Valley, was set upon by Kalenjin rioters angry about the election. Karanja is herself a Kalenjin, but she discovered, hiding from the mobs as she watched homes burn, that in marrying a Kikuyu man 20 years prior she had surrendered the benefits of belonging to the area's majority tribe. According to Corey-Boulet, one of Karanja's most vivid memories of the violence is of listening to Sang's show, *Lene Emet* (or *What the Nation is Saying*), on

Kass and hearing a message, delivered in 'code but clear to anyone paying attention', that seemed intended for people like her. She heard Sang say, 'Kalenjin girls who played football the wrong way will regret it, because they will have scored an own goal.' The journalist goes on to detail how the ICC Chief Prosecutor Luis Moreno-Ocampo believes that Sang accomplished his incitement of Kalenjin to violence against the Kikuyu and Kisii, 'not with subtle soccer metaphors but rather with overt calls to arms'. The article cites Ocampo as referring to broadcasts in which Sang asked his audience, 'What are you waiting for? [...] What are you doing at home?[...] The war has begun' (Corey-Boulet, 2011). According to this account of Ocampo's evidence, such statements were paired with specific instructions about what was to be done.

Corey-Boulet says in answer to these accusations, Sang claimed, 'Our job is to educate, entertain, and inform, not to incite.' And when it comes to specific allegations against him, he said, 'According to my own conscience, these are framed allegations. I don't remember in my conscience saying things like that.' Sang also hinted that this was about freedom of speech, arguing that the ICC was in danger of threatening protected speech, 'If they take me to The Hague and I know I was doing my job professionally, then what are they telling journalists?' (Corey-Boulet, 2011). Those on the receiving end of Kalenjin violence do not accept Sang's version of events. Corey-Boulet gives Elizabeth Karanja's reaction in which she says that Sang is plainly hoping to take advantage of the fact that his broadcasts are only fully understood by Kalenjin-speakers; 'You can lie to other people who don't understand, but you cannot lie to me because I understand,' she told the journalist (ibid.). The analysis goes on to quote Stella Ndirangu, legal officer for the International Commission of Jurists in Kenya, who believes that there are transcripts available to the prosecution (clearly not the ones seen by this author) that, though limited, will point to Sang's involvement in specific crimes – 'They [Kalenjin involved in planning the violence] gave updates using Sang's radio show on what they had conquered, what they had achieved, and [they were] giving plans for what they should be doing to advance their cause,' Ndirangu said. 'They would say, "Today we have attacked this village and we're heading to this village." The foot soldiers would know where they needed to go' (ibid.).

The viewpoint that hate broadcasting of this sort was being carried out is supported by journalists who attended an Inter-Press workshop in Nairobi in January 2008 to discuss the role of the media in Kenya's crisis. The reports of the meeting quote a number of Kenyan journalists lamenting the failures of journalists and, worse, the role of some journalists in perpetrating hate broadcasting. David Ochami of the Media Council of Kenya says that, from long before the elections, the vernacular radio stations had served to ignite 'ethnic consciousness' among their listeners, making them 'support leaders from their own tribe and harbour bad feelings about people from other communities'. Ochami cites an unnamed journalist working in vernacular radio as disclosing that 'the ethnic hate our radio station was propagating about those from outside the community was unbelievable. I can't repeat any of those expressions at this forum'. The journalist went on to say, though, that the expressions of hate came largely from calls to phone-ins, but 'the unfortunate thing is we let these callers speak vile and then laughed about [them]'.

The report of the workshop cites another anonymous journalist as admitting that 'we took sides in the issue and we became subjective, forgetting our professional tenet of objectivity and neutrality. In fact, this polarisation was so bad in the newsrooms that some broadcast journalists refused to cover or read news that wasn't favourable to the candidate or the party they supported.' Other participants said that broadcast and print media were too ready to accept money to carry campaign messages and they put money ahead of responsibility by 'accepting and conveying hate material'. Some also spoke of objectivity almost always giving way to partisanship in reporting and blamed media station owners who had 'vested interests in either camp of the political divide' (all quotes from IPP, 2008).

Because of the lack of substantial transcript, it is impossible to measure accurately the time period over which vernacular stations broadcast hate messages, the proportion of air time they took up, the role of journalists in directly inciting hatred and violence and the extent to which journalists through insufficient training, experience and editorial direction became caught up in partisan reporting and allowed, almost by default, hate speech to be broadcast.

Using the analytical tools from discourse analysis and from the study of hate radio in Rwanda is difficult with the dearth of verifiable broadcast material. However, from the little available and the reports of observers and journalists from the stations quoted above, there is at least an opportunity to look at the general agenda setting, framing and representation of subjects within vernacular broadcasts. Kass FM is most often accused of partisanship and broadcasting hate messages in 2005 and again in 2007–08. Along with Kameme and Inooro and, to a lesser extent, Lake Victoria FM, it seems to have followed a general editorial line of favouring candidates from its own community, broadcasting material that favoured local Kalenjin candidates supporting the 'No' campaign and the ODM, and denigrating those, generally Kikuyu or Kisii, who supported the 'Yes' campaign and then the PNU. Strongly derogatory terminology was used and periodic calls were broadcast to 'cut the grass' and get rid of 'weeds' – generally accepted as shorthand for clearing outsiders from what was considered Kalenjin land. But the frequency of such broadcasts, the proof of their origin (whether Kass journalists or interviewees/callers) and whether they were exceptions to the rule or part of a routine pattern of partisan broadcasting is impossible to assess accurately.

What we can conclude is that there is evidence of vernacular stations having a partisan agenda and of using language capable of inciting hatred and even violence. They clearly framed references according to this agenda – local candidates were supported and praised while the representation of opponents was couched in inflammatory and at times offensive and dehumanizing language. The approach of stations to politics was biased and the language extreme and, at times, violent. News about other parties or candidates was omitted and some journalists became very partial in their approach to reporting certain kinds of news. This suggests a discourse on these stations that was partial, open to the charge of inciting contempt or even hate for others and lacking any clear standards of impartiality, balance and responsible journalism. Joshua arap Sang of Kass FM admitted in an interview that his station was outspoken but claimed that this was just because it was in touch with what it knew its audience wanted to hear. He said that he and other presenters spoke in the language the audience would understand and appreciate. He confirmed that they had strong views about particular parties, politicians and issues and broadcast what they wanted to say in the way they wanted to say it (Sang interview, Nairobi, 12 February 2010).

Kenyan vernacular radio, as far as can be discerned from limited broadcast, printed and anecdotal evidence and material from the author's interviews in Kenya, periodically broadcast hate speech about perceived opponents from other communities, at times appeared to condone or even incite violence or the expulsion of people from particular areas and did demonstrate considerable partisanship. However, unlike RTLM in Rwanda, there is so far no compelling evidence of a coordinated campaign, of an organized, long-term setting of an agenda of ethnic attacks, let alone extermination; there is evidence of partisan and propagandistic agendas tinged with incitement at times of conflict.

Many journalists were partisan and prepared to seriously raise tensions through their broadcasting but others may have given in to pressure from owners and local/national political leaders and through this allowed hate messages to be broadcast during talk shows, interviews or phone-ins. In a lot of cases, it was sheer inexperience in hosting phone-ins or talk shows that meant that by default rather than design hate speech or incitement (some planned by politicians, but some the spontaneous contributions of ordinary citizens) was broadcast. Many of the vernacular stations had clear political agendas and these then could easily, by design by owners or politicians or in the heat of the moment, slip over from partisanship into incitement and it may be, though transcript evidence is not there to prove it, that presenters actively pursued the same agendas as politicians.

What there is evidence of, as identified by studies by Maina, the UNDP, BBC World Service Trust and others, is clear partisanship on the part of the FM stations mentioned in this paper, poor editorial standards and a willingness to become 'purveyors of the numerous rumours that circulated'.

They perpetuated divisions and images of 'those who were perceived to be the aggressors and those who were aggrieved' (UNDP, 2008). The stations allowed themselves at times to be used by powerful political and community groups with their own agendas. Kass, according to HRW, was not proved to be responsible for having a policy of hate speech, but it allowed guest speakers and callers to express hatred and engage in incitement against targeted groups without hindrance (HRW, 2008, p. 36). The station, as demonstrated during my visit there, clearly has a Kalenjin agenda relating to issues like land and this leads to strongly partisan output and a clear editorial agenda, but that alone is not proof of concerted hate broadcasting.

It may be that when the ICC trial commences, more evidence will be put before the public, beyond the current small number of transcripts and other supporting material, and this could prove whether or not there was a more concerted campaign of hate broadcasting by vernacular stations. But as the evidence currently stands, the most one can conclude is that hate broadcasting of a sporadic nature took place in 2007–08 (and most likely also in 2005) and that vernacular radio stations were the main culprits.

It should also be noted that, despite some improvements after the 2008 violence, the future of the media in Kenya and vernacular stations, in particular, is an uncertain one. The political and economic environment in which they operate is still marked by resort to the incitement of hatred, denigration of opponents and a willingness to use violence and the manipulation of community grievances as means to desired political ends. This was demonstrated during the 2010 referendum campaign. This did not see the levels of violence of 2005 or 2007–08, but six Kenyans died in a grenade explosion at a political rally, while three MPs, an assistant minister and William Ruto were questioned by the police over accusations that they used hate speech at political rallies. Three unnamed radio stations were investigated by the recently established Kenyan National Cohesion Committee Commission over reported hate broadcasting (Itumbi, 2010; Somerville, 2010a).

7
Conclusions: Propaganda, Hate and the Power of Radio

In the preface and opening chapter I set out to examine the development, nature, content and role of propaganda, highlighting examples of where propaganda evolves into forms of incitement to hatred. The objective was to try to delineate between different forms and uses of propaganda to be able to find a workable definition of hate propaganda. In the historical chapters and case studies, it has been demonstrated that popular perceptions of propaganda as a tool used only by those with evil intent or by the 'enemy' (however defined) but not by those with a more righteous cause is inaccurate and leads to a skewed picture of what propaganda is and how it works. It is a much wider phenomenon in communication than just the manipulative definition that took hold in the middle of the 20th century, notably following the First World War and then with the rise of fascism and communism in Europe. Propaganda is an integral part of political and social life and is inherent in many forms of human communication. Propaganda in its developed forms stresses 'the control of opinions and through them the actions of men' (Jowett and O'Donnell, 2006, p. 73). It is primarily concerned with the management of opinion and the use of significant symbols to achieve this (Lasswell, 1971, pp. 9 and 13). It operates on a spectrum from the well-intentioned (such as the British Broadcasting Corporation (BBC) World Service in the 1980s and 1990s seeking to provide its audience with the news and comment necessary for them to make informed decisions about the world around them), through the clearly manipulative forms of propaganda used within modern polities in the form of media owned by groups of individuals seeking to use that media for their own political or economic ends, to propaganda in societies with more (or even heavily) restricted media and public opinion networks where propaganda often takes the place of competing opinion or free dissemination of news and comment. At the extreme end of this spectrum is where propaganda is aimed at managing opinion, controlling that opinion and through it attempting to determine the actions of the target audience and seeking not just to attack the opinions of others, to establish the propagandist's ideology as the ruling set of ideas but to incite hatred and, through that incitement of hatred, elicit support for extreme programmes of action against the objects of the hatred and sanctify or elicit active involvement in violence against those objects. What has become clear is that no clear and simple line can be drawn on one side of which stands an acceptable form of propaganda, even one advocating violence, fear or forms of hatred of an enemy in times of war or in defeating aggression or invasion, and the other side of which stands propaganda where the intent and content is focused on the development and utilization of hatred to bring about the destruction, displacement or dehumanization of a perceived enemy or 'other'.

British, French and later American First World War propaganda sought to vilify the Germans, to seize on real, alleged, exaggerated and even invented atrocities to convince both the fighting forces and the public at home of the need to combat the barbarian Hun, the brutal Boche, or evil and heartless Prussian. They used fear and atrocity to develop contempt and even hatred for the enemy – yet this did not develop into a total, constant and repetitive dehumanization of the German nation or Germans as individuals. They were to be beaten in war but not destroyed as a nation, exterminated en masse or – despite the strictures, territorial changes and reparations demanded in the Treaty of Versailles – to be displaced from their homeland or subject to harsh and continuing repression purely because they were Germans. German propaganda prior to and during the Second World War was multifaceted and included what one might consider normal war propaganda aimed at boosting morale, trying to ensure support for the war effort and deriding opponents – as with propaganda aimed against the British and Americans. But there was the other side of propaganda – that which sought over time and with horrific consistency and repetition to build up a dehumanized image of the Jew (so dehumanized that this encompassed the entire nature of all Jews and brooked no individuality) or of the Russian, Pole, gypsy or Slav. This image was used to set an agenda for an entire population, an agenda that presented the image of a sub-human, consumed by evil intent towards Germans and the whole of European civilization and whose defeat and ultimate destruction was the only sure guarantee of German survival. The propaganda aimed at convincing Germans that total war against these peoples was the only option, a total war brought on Germany by the evil intent of the 'other'. Similarly, in Rwanda the image of the Tutsi was one of total evil and eternal threat to the Hutu, and an agenda of hatred was constantly drummed into Rwandans (see Kellow and Steeves, 1998).

For Hitler and the Nazis, the Second World War brought the opportunity to go beyond hate and the elimination of Jews from German public life and civil society and to start a concerted campaign of extermination – the propaganda broadcast during the war was consistent in its judgement that the Jews had caused the war and the Jews would therefore be exterminated. Because the German state had the machinery and manpower to implement a programme of extermination, there was no need to incite Germans as individuals and as a mass to carry out killings; in Rwanda, war brought the opportunity to exterminate the Tutsis and Hutu political opponents but the lack of a sufficiently large army or police force meant that incitement was not just of hatred but of the need for direct and immediate violence. In these cases, as in the historical examples of the preaching of the Crusades, the propaganda battles of the Thirty Years' War and the Serbs use of propaganda in the late 1980s and 1990s, propaganda was aimed at developing a level of hatred, a fear of the objects of that hatred and a progressive dehumanization of the objects and desensitization on the part of the audience for the propaganda. As a result, the most extreme and brutal methods of war and mass killing became accepted as the only solution. In Germany, the Nazi solution was the destruction of the entire Jewish population in Europe; in Rwanda it was the destruction of the Tutsi; in Yugoslavia the ethnic cleansing of Great Serbia and the use of mass killings to achieve this (though without perhaps the final aim of genocide); and in Kenya the objectives were both political and economic and involved the seizure of political power at all costs and the maximizing of control of land and other assets at the expense of the rival community, but lacking a long-term agenda for either genocide or lasting conflict.

In the 20th century, the development of broadcasting and particularly of radio as a form of cheap, mass communication revolutionized propaganda dissemination and particularly forms of propaganda, such as hate speech, that sought to get a strong, lasting emotional response from an audience. Print could disseminate ideas and engender strong feelings. Radio could convey not just the same ideas at print but bring to propaganda the power of the human voice, of the emotion contained within that voice to a mass audience at the same time. As explained in Chapter 1 with reference in particular to the works of Jowett and O'Donnell and Ellul, propaganda works on the individual but only as part of a greater mass. It is not aimed at individuals per se but as individuals as part of a greater societal unit. Radio works particularly effectively in making the individual part of that mass. A paper or journal can be read and reread and different interpretations developed with a second or third reading. Radio is immediate and heard once (though of course messages – whether of mobilization, hate or fear – will be repeated regularly in propaganda campaigns) – the power, intonation and emotion contained within the human voice appeals in an emotional way and can develop fervour in a way that print cannot. Even when a radio listener is on their own with their radio, they are still aware of being part of a wider, mass audience listening in that moment. The ability to convey ideas steeped in emotion, to appeal to man and the mass at one and the same time makes radio powerful. It can convey the atmosphere of a meeting or rally, bring into the home, the car, the workplace or wherever people listen the raw feeling of the voice as well as the power of the message.

In Africa, with lower rates of literacy, a slower development of access to TV and the internet, radio is the medium that can reach the widest audience and has a particular power – especially when speakers on the radio, as Luther found during the Reformation, can speak in simple, easily understood terms and in the language of the listener, conveying ideas in terms that he or she will understand. Radio has provided an effective tool for the dissemination of ideas, for political and social debate, for national development but also for the development of agendas of hate, discourses of dehumanization and has the ability to elicit strong responses.

Defining hate broadcasting

If there is a wide area of agreement about how propaganda works, that discourses of hate are a clear part of the spectrum of propaganda and that radio has been an effective means of propagating hatred, there remains a lack of clarity about how to define hate radio or hate discourses to make clear where they go beyond other forms of propaganda. The term 'hate radio' came into regular use in the contemporary study of journalism and the media through the role of the broadcast media in the break-up of Yugoslavia and of Radio Televison Libre des Mille Collines (RTLM) in Rwanda in 1993 and 1994. Journalists and academics seem to have an instinctive feel for what is meant by the term or by 'hate speech' but there is an absence of rigour in the way it is described and defined. This has been recognized by Article XIX, the non-governmental organization (NGO) campaigning for freedom of expression. The organization's executive director, Agnes Callamard, told a United Nations (UN) conference in 2008 that recent events related to freedom of expression had 'highlighted the substantive ambiguities as to the "demarcation line" between freedom of expression and hate speech' (Article XIX, 2008). This identified the issue but brought us no closer to identifying where the freedom to express ideas and to report the expression of those ideas and of the freedom to broadcast a range of opinions, no matter how propagandistic, ends and where incitement to hatred and violence begins?

The legal and political starting point for defining hate speech and material that is broadcast is set out in the UN's International Covenant on Civil and Political Rights (ICCPR) The basic description, in Article 20, is that 'Any advocacy of national, racial or religious hatred that constitutes incitement to discrimination, hostility or violence shall be prohibited by law.' This is balanced against Article 19, which is the dominant statement on freedom of speech and expression: 'Everyone shall have the right to freedom of expression; this right shall include freedom to seek, receive and impart information and ideas of all kinds, regardless of frontiers, either orally, in writing or in print, in the form of art, or through any other media of his choice.' The Covenant lays down that 'the exercise of the rights [of freedom of expression] [...] of this article carries with it special duties and respon-sibilities. It may therefore be subject to certain restrictions, but these shall only be such as are provided by law and are necessary.' The prohibition of incitement to hostility or violence is the only exception.

This single sentence description is hardly a clear or codified definition of what constitutes incitement to hostility or violence. Will definitions differ as to what constitutes incitement, hostility and violence? Does an exhortation to a people defend themselves, their sovereignty and land by a government whose territory has been unlawfully invaded constitute incitement to hos-tility and violence towards the invader? When Churchill made his rousing speeches after the fall of France in 1940, was he effectively mobilizing people for a just war of defence or was he actually engaging in a discourse of hate?

Surprisingly, practical, legal and academic work on the issue of hate speech has not progressed far in providing a comprehensive definition. Radio Netherlands, which has set up a programme to identify and combat hate broadcasting, still uses a very simple definition: 'hate media is defined as encouraging violent activity, tension or hatred between races, ethnic or social groups, or countries for political goals and/or to foster conflict by offering one-sided and biased views and opinions and resorting to decep-tion' (Radio Netherlands). But this definition doesn't, for example, mention religion and again could be interpreted to outlaw a call to arms in defence of an invaded land or people.

Jurists advocating legal, physical and even military action have not been much more explicit in defining hate broadcasting. One leading advocate of the jamming of hate radio, former UN human rights officer, Jamie Metzl, is adamant that hate radio does shape people's behaviour in times of con-flict and that 'many of the humanitarian disasters of the 20th century were spawned or exacerbated over the airwaves' (Metzl, 1997a, p. 1). But he is less precise about how to define hate radio or its characteristics. In his *For-eign Affairs* article arguing for the jamming hate radio and stations that incite violence, he doesn't address how you decide which stations are to be jammed. In a more substantial contribution to the *American Journal of Law*, Metzl again argues the case for intervention but fails to provide a clear taxonomy of hate speech or broadcasts. He points to the 'standard of causal-ity between targeted words and specific events' established as a benchmark at the Nuremburg trials for judging hate or genocide propaganda. Metzl highlights the case of Nazi radio head Hans Fritzsche, who was acquitted of crimes against humanity as the court was not prepared to accept that statements broadcast on radio 'were intended to incite the German peo-ple to commit atrocities on conquered people' (Metzl, 1997b, p. 6). The court decided that his aim was to generate popular support for Hitler and the German war effort. He was acquitted while the editor of Der Sturmer, Julius Streicher, was found guilty of actively inciting genocide and being part of the planning and implementation of a campaign of genocide – Streicher was hanged, Fritzsche was acquitted (though later jailed for a short period by a German de-Nazification court). The court decided that to be actionable 'incitement required specificity and a direct link to the action for which it called'. The 1948 Genocide Convention, adopted after Nuremburg, took a similar viewpoint regarding incitement to genocide (ibid.). In his analysis, Metzl notes that the ICCPR's Article 20 prohibits both propaganda for war and advocacy of hatred that constitute incitement to discrimination, hostility or violence, but does not expand on what he believes this to mean and how it can be applied when it comes to his desire for international action to prevent hate broadcasting (ibid. pp. 8–9). He does not provide a definition of hate broadcasting that would unambiguously identify hate content or broadcasters.

During the late 1930s and throughout the Second World War, there is little doubt that German radio under the Nazis consistently propagated hatred of the Jews and, when Nazi policy required it, of Roma, the Russians and Slavs as a whole. But even German radio at this time did not call for direct violence by its listeners against the objects of hatred – it was rather about support for long-term racist policies or war aims (see, for example, Gombrich, 1970; Herf, 2006; Welch, 1993). This was reflected in the Nuremburg trial acquittal of Hans Fritzsche.

The lack of precision in legal terms is exacerbated by the broad use of the term 'hate radio' to examples lacking clear and direct incitement to violence or hatred. As highlighted in the Kenyan case study, human rights bodies, journalists and politicians in Kenya all referred to the propagation of hatred, including by radio stations, in the election campaign and post-election violence 2007–08 but without many concrete examples and without a clear definition of what they mean by hate radio. Similarly, during the break-up of Yugoslavia in the first half of the 1990s, hate radio was a term used widely to describe the Serb and Croat broadcasts (see Thompson, 1999). The extended narrative provided of the Yugoslav conflict and propaganda discourses indicates how the Serbs (and to a lesser extent the Croats) used radio and TV to develop a climate of fear and hatred – how atrocity stories, historical examples of mass killing and the distortion of news and current events were used to develop discourses of hate. This discourse was used to mobilize support for and participation in the wars that accompanied the disintegration of the country – radio and TV stations in Serbia and Serb areas of Croatia and Bosnia built up images of the brutal, inhuman and essentially evil nature of their enemies and called for an all-out effort to defend against their alleged aggression but also to be willing to support a war of ethnic cleansing. An agenda of hate and fear was broadcast but not one of actual incitement to direct and immediate violence by individuals or groups. This does not, though, absolve the broadcasters and their political masters of the charge of broadcasting hatred – they, like the Nazis, broadcast a discourse intended to inculcate hatred and the acceptance or involvement in extreme state policies against enemies but did not directly incite individual or mass acts of spontaneous violence.

Hate radio broadcasting involves just as much the development of an agenda and a discourse of hatred as the direct incitement to acts of violence. What makes hate radio or other forms of broadcasting effective is the combination of the broadcasting of propaganda, of agendas of hate or of instructions to carry out acts of violence with the capacity to carry out policies of violence or even ethnic cleansing or genocide or to follow up broadcasts calling for violence with the direct pressure (peer pressure or threats of violence) to carry out personal acts of violence as part of the mobilized mass.

So can we come to a definition of hate radio/speech that encompasses both agenda setting and direct incitement to violence on the basis of hatred? I would argue that both forms are examples of hate broadcasting and would include within the definition of hate radio not just the broadcasting of content directly inciting violent activity or hatred between races, ethnic or social groups, or countries, but also the long-term setting of agendas of hatred between races or social groups or states. Using my original two measures of content and intent – does the content of a broadcast engender hatred, is it intended to develop within the listener hatred of a particular nation or group (however defined) and for the listener to act on this hatred, and by 'act' I include the acceptance of an agenda of hatred and the support (even passive) of policies that flow from that? Is it the intention of the broadcaster to use a discourse of hatred to enable the implementation of policies based on it – whether these involved the repression, permanent exclusion from power and effective denial of civil or political rights to a group, ethnic cleansing of target groups, physical elimination of target groups within a specific area or the genocidal extermination of whole groups?

In their study of the role of radio in the Rwandan genocide, Kellow and Steeves establish some basic prerequisites for examining the role of radio and identifying characteristics. They make the important point that, 'the role and influence of the media cannot be divorced from the historical, cultural and political-economic environments in which they function' (Kellow and Steeves, 1998, p. 108). In examining the role of RTLM in Rwanda, they emphasize the environment in which the radio operated and examine the way that over time the station (along with the Hutu journal *Kangura*) framed its reporting of the conflict and its representation of Tutsis but also at the consistent setting of an agenda of fear and hatred that was intended to engender 'collective reaction effects' from the audience (ibid.).

Framing is about selection and salience of content and in times of conflict or potential conflict might include depiction of risk or danger to the audience from others, dramatization of the conflict and inflation of the power or strength of opponents. Events and perceptions are framed and agendas are identified and in this way for those engaging in the broadcasting of hate messages; 'a media campaign is a conscious, structured attempt to use media to influence awareness, attitudes or behaviour' (Kellow and Steeves, 1998, p. 111). And in influencing awareness, attitudes and behaviour, the media use instruments such as emphasizing danger, the danger of general and specific threats to the lives, families or livelihoods of the audience and the dramatization of the threat of violence. The objective of such framing and the representation of individuals or groups as threats is, over time, to set an agenda that provides the prism through which the audience views political, social and economic developments, identifies friend and foe and assesses possible courses of actions – clearly this was a common characteristic in Nazi, Serb, Rwandan Hutu and, at times, Kenyan vernacular radio. One could also say that it was represented in the preaching of the Crusades and the propaganda of the Thirty Years' War.

Framing and representation can also be used to elicit more immediate and active responses. In Rwanda, an agenda was set for the Hutu audience of RTLM: emphasizing that all Tutsis were a threat to all Hutus on a long-term basis; that the Rwandan Patriotic Front invasion in 1990 was aimed at Tutsi supremacy; that Tutsi rule meant oppression and ultimately destruction of the Hutu; that Hutus had to act to prevent Tutsi dominance; that the only way to protect the Hutu was to destroy the Tutsi; that as the threat was deemed by Hutu leaders to be immediate and local, that you as a Hutu should join the collective effort in exterminating the Tutsi. It was a cascading series of actions deriving from the framing and representation of the Tutsi as the enemy. By establishing such an agenda and constant representation of Tutsis, Hutus were intended by the propagators of the message to automatically view Tutsis in a certain way and act towards them in particular ways. The Nazis did the same regarding the Jews, though they did not want to have spontaneous mass actions to exterminate the Jews, but a clandestine, controlled programme of state-run genocide that had the acceptance or support rather than active involvement of the mass of Germans, except where the duties of Germans in various spheres of military, police or other activity required their involvement.

The incitement of hate works on all the levels described above and can be put as follows:

- set an agenda of suspicion and ultimately hatred of a target groups or groups;
- attribute malign motivations to those groups;
- utilize fear through the propagation of a discourse of atrocity relating to the malign motivations of the target group;
- relate the long-term threat and/or grievances against a group to current developments;
- prepare people to 'defend' themselves and their community against this threat;

- place the blame for violence on the target group, thus justifying violence as a response to attack or threat;
- incite and justify action.

The ability to translate these points into actual policy and to implement that policy is dependent on the propagandist's ability to marshal and use force, coercion and violence to accompany the propaganda. Politicians, movements or governments may propagate ideas and even developed discourses of hatred, but they become a deadly weapon when allied with the capacity to carry out violence. Nazi propaganda, Slav radio and TV, RTLM and the Kenyan vernacular radio stations came to prominence and were labelled as propagandists of hate not merely through what was broadcast but because the intent and content of the broadcasts was then reflected in actual violence, killings, ethnic cleansing and, in the cases of Nazi Germany and Rwanda, attempted genocide. This does not mean that hate speech and the broadcasting of hate is mere harmless noise when not allied to military or other deadly force, but the propagation of hate becomes a deadly weapon when the two coincide.

Bibliography

African Union (no date) *Rwanda: The Preventable Genocide, International Panel of Eminent Personalities.*

AllAfrica.com (2008) *News Report from Kenya*, http://allafrica.com/stories/200801220692.html (accessed 23 September 2008).

AllAfrica.com (2011) *Ruto, Kosgey, Sang Come Face to Face with The Hague*, 8 April 2011, http://allafrica.com/stories/201104080150.htmlce (accessed 20 May 2011).

Allcock, John B. (1992) Rhetorics of Nationalism in Yugoslav Politics, in Allcock, John B., Horton, John J., and Milivojevic, Marko (eds.) *Yugoslavia in Transition: Choices and Constraints* (New York: Berg), pp. 276–296.

Anderson, Benedict (1991) *Imagined Communities: Reflection on the Origin and Spread of Nationalism* (London: Verson).

Anderson, David (2008a) Kenya on the Brink, *Prospect*, no. 142, January 2008.

Anderson, David (2008b) *Kenya's Agony*, Royal African Society website, http://www.royalafricansociety.org/ras-publications-and-reports/443.html (accessed 2 February 2009).

Article XIX and Thompson, Mark (1994) *Forging War: The Media in Serbia, Croatia and Bosnia-Hercegovina* (Avon: Bath Press).

Article XIX (2008) *Expert Meeting on the Links between Articles 19 and 20 of the ICCPR: Freedom of Expression and Advocacy of Religious Hatred that Constitutes Incitement to Discrimination, Hostility or Violence*, UNHCR 2–3 October 2008, Geneva, http://www.article19.org/pdfs/conferences/iccpr-links-between-articles-19-and-20.pdf (accessed 20 July 2010).

Article XIX (1996) *Broadcasting Genocide: Censorship, Propaganda and State-Sponsored Violence in Rwanda 1990–1994* (London: Article XIX).

Asch, Ronald G. (1997) *The Thirty Years War: The Holy Roman Empire and Europe, 1618–1648* (Basingstoke: Macmillan).

Asia Times (4 June 2009) http://www.atimes.com/atimes/South_Asia/KF04Df02.html (accessed 17 July 2011).

BBC (17 December 1942) *On this Day*, http://news.bbc.co.uk/onthisday/hi/dates/stories/december/17/newsid_3547000/3547151.stm (accessed 12 December 2011).

BBC Newsi (24 February 1999).

BBC Newsi (2008).

BBC World Service, news report by Pascale Harter, 31 January 2008.

BBC World Service Trust (2008) *The Kenyan 2007 Elections and their Aftermath: The Role of Media and Communications*, http://downloads.bbc.co.uk/worldservice/trust/pdf/kenya_policy_briefing_08.pdf (accessed 7 July 2009).

BBC World Service Trust, WST (April 2008) *Policy Recommendations* (London: BBC).

BBC, SWB, *Summary of World Broadcasts* (Caversham, Reading: BBC). This source available online via Nexis UK or in print at BBC Written Archives.

Badsey, Stephen (2011) Mass Politics and the Western Front, *BBC History*, http://www.bbc.co.uk/history/british/britain_wwzone/war_media_01.shtml (accessed 3 May 2011).

Barnouw, E. (1968) *The Golden Web: A History of Broadcasting in the United States, 1933–1953* (Oxford and New York: Oxford University Press).

Beck, Glenn (2009) *Father Coughlin and Glenn Beck,* http://wn.com/father_coughlin_ and_glenn_beck (accessed 10 February 2010).

Beller, Elmer A. (1940) *Propaganda in Germany During the Thirty Years' War* (Princeton, NJ: Princeton University Press).

Benesch, Susan (2008) Vile Crime or Inalienable Right: Defining Incitement to Genocide, *Virginia Journal of International Law,* 48, no. 3: 486–528.

Bergmeier, Horst J.P. and Lotz, Ranier E. (1997) *The Inside Story of Radio Broadcasts and Propaganda Swing* (New Haven, CT: Yale University Press).

Berkeley, Bill (2002) *The Graves Are Not Yet Full* (New York: Basic Books).

Berman, Bruce (1990) *Control and Crisis in Colonial Kenya* (London: James Currey).

Bernays, Edward (2005) *Propaganda* (New York: Brooklyn).

Berry, John A. and Berry, Carol Pott (2001) *Genocide in Rwanda: A Collective Memory* (Washington, DC: Howard University Press).

Boelcke, Willi A. (1967) *The Secret Conferences of Dr Gobbels, October 1939-March 1943* (London: Weidenfeld and Nicholson).

Bramsted, Ernest Kohn (1965) *Goebbels and National Socialist Propaganda* (East Lansing, MI: Michigan University Press).

Braeckman, Collette (January 2007) Accusations suspectes contre le régime rwandais, *Le Monde Diplomatique,* http://www.monde-diplomatique.fr/2007/01/BRAECKMAN/ 14367 (accessed 10 February 2010).

Branch, Daniel and Cheeseman, Nic (2009) Democratization, Sequencing and State Failure in Africa: Lessons from Kenya, *African Affairs,* 108, no. 430: 1–26.

Briggs, Asa (1970) *The History of Broadcasting in the United Kingdom: The War of Words 1939–1945 III* (Oxford: Oxford University Press).

Brinkley, A. (1982) *Voices of Protest: Huey Long, Father Coughlin and the Great Depression* (New York: Vintage).

Bullock, Alan (1962) *Hitler: A Study in Tyranny* (Harmondsworth: Pelican).

Bytwerk, Randall L. (2001) *Julius Streicher: Nazi Editor of the Notorious Anti-Semitics Newspaper Der Sturmer* (New York: Cooper Square Press).

CIA (27 August 1948) *Evidence of USSR Military Intentions in Soviet Propaganda Broadcasts* (ORE 64–48) (Langley, VA: CIA).

Caesar, J. (1976) *The Civil War* (Harmondsworth: Penguin).

Caesar, J. (2006) *The Gallic War* (New York: Dover Editions).

Cantril, Hadley (1940) *The Invasion from Mars: A Study in the Psychology of Panic* (New York: Transaction Books).

Chalk, Frank (2000) Hate Radio in Rwanda, in Adelman, Howard and Suhrke, Astri (eds.) *The Path of A Genocide: The Rwanda Crisis from Uganda to Zaire* (New Brunswick, NJ: Transaction Publishers), pp. 93–107.

Cheeseman, Nic (July 2008) The Kenyan Elections of 2007: An Introduction, *Journal of Eastern African Studies,* 2, no. 2: 166–184.

Chretien, Jean-Pierre *RTLM Propaganda: The Democratic Alibi,* The International Development Research Centre (IDRC), http://www.idrc.ca/rwandagenocide/ev-108180- 201-IDO_TOPIC.html (accessed 22 August 2011).

Chronicles of the Kenyan Genocide, http://kenyangenocide.blogspot.com/ (accessed 24 September 2008).

CIPEV (2008) Report of the Commission of Inquiry In to Post-Election Violence.

Coe, Lewis (1996) *Wireless Radio: A Brief History* (Jefferson, NC: McFarland and Co).

Collin, Matthew (2001) *This is Serbia Calling: Rock 'n' Roll Radio and Belgrade's Underground Resistance* (London: Serpent's Tail).

Corey-Boulet, Robbie (16 May 2011) Kenyan Trial Asks, Can Journalism Be a War Crime? *The Atlantic*, http://www.theatlantic.com/international/archive/2011/05/kenyan-trial-asks-can-journalism-be-a-war-crime/238692/2/ (accessed 19 May 2011).

Coughlin, Charles Recordings of speeches on You Tube, http://www.youtube.com/watch?v=uFDuGNCxyl0; http://www.youtube.com/watch?v=IS9_gqCytV4&NR=1; http://www.youtube.com/watch?v=RzLMRAz5G_4&feature=related

Cull, Nicholas J., Culbert, David and Welch, David (2003) *Propaganda and Mass Persuasion: A Historical Encyclopedia 1500 to the Present* (Santa Barbara, CA: ABC Clio).

Dallaire, Romeo (2004) *Shake Hands with the Devil* (London: Arrow Books).

Daniels, Gordon (1982) Japanese Domestic Radio and Cinema Propaganda, 1937–1945: An Overview, *Historical Journal of Film, Radio and Television*, 2, no. 2: 115–132.

Davidson, Basil (1992) *The Black Man's Burden: Africa and the Curse of the Nation-State* (London: James Currey).

Davies, Alan (1999) The First Radio War: Broadcasting in the Spanish Civil War, 1936–1939, *Historical Journal of Film, Radio and Television*, 19, no. 4: 473–513.

Dawn (7 July 2011).

Des Forges, Alison (1999) *Leave None to Tell the Story: Genocide in Rwanda* (New York: Human Rights Watch).

Des Forges, Alison (2002) Silencing the Voices of Hate in Rwanda, in Price, Monroe E. and Thompson, Mark (eds.) *Forging Peace: International Intervention, Media and Conflict (International Communications): Intervention, Human Rights and the Management of Media Space* (Edinburgh: Edinburgh University Press), pp. 236–258.

Des Forges, Alison (2007) Call to Genocide: Radio in Rwanda, 1994, in Thompson, Allan (ed.) *The Media and the Rwanda Genocide* (London: Pluto), pp. 41–54.

Doyle, Mark (2008) Kenya's Geographic and Political Rift, *BBC News*, 28 January 2008.

Ehrlich, Matthew C. (2011) *Radio Utopia: Postwar Audio Documentary in the Public Interest* (Urbana, Chicago and Springfield: University of Illinois Press).

Ellul, Jacques (1973) *Propaganda: The Formation of Men's Attitudes* (New York: Vintage).

Erni, John Nguyet (2009) War, 'Incendiary Media' and Human Rights Law, *Media Culture Society*, 31: 867–886.

European Union Election Observation Mission, EUEO (2008) *Kenya General Election, 27 December 2007, Preliminary Statement.*

Evans, Richard J. (2006) *The Third Reich in power: How the Nazis Won Over the Hearts and Minds of a Nation* (London: Penguin).

Fairclough, Norman (2003) *Analysing Discourse* (Oxford: Routledge).

Frere, Marie-Soleil (2007) *The Media and Conflicts in Central Africa* (Boulder, CO: Lynne Reiner).

Fukuyama, Francis (2006) *The End of History and the Last Man* (New York: Free Press).

Gellner, Ernest (1983) *Nations and Nationalism* (Oxford: Oxford University Press).

Gilchrist, J. and Murray, W.J. (1971) *The Press in the French Revolution: A Selection of Documents Taken from the Press of the Revolution for the Years 1789–1794* (Melbourne: Cheshire).

Glenny, Misha (1996) *The Fall of Yugoslavia* (London: Penguin).

Goebbels, Josef (1940) *My Part in Germany's Fight* (London: Hurst and Blackett).

Goebbels, Josef (1978) *Final Entries 1945: The Diaries of Josef Goebbels* (New York: Avon).

Goebbels, Josef (1982) *The Goebbels Diaries 1939–1941* (London: Sphere).

Goebbels, Josef (1984) *The Goebbels Diaries 1943–1943* (London: Hamish Hamilton).

Goebbels, Josef (1993a) The Tasks of the Ministry for Propaganda, Speech to Representatives of the Press, 15 March 1933. Reproduced in Welch, David (ed.) *The Third Reich: Politics and Propaganda* (London: Routledge), pp. 172–182.

Goebbels, Josef (1993b) Goebbels Address to Representatives of Radio. Reproduced in Welch, David (ed.) *The Third Reich: Politics and Propaganda* (London: Routledge), pp. 183–184.

Goebbels, Josef and Helmut, Heiber (1962) *The Early Goebbels Diaries: The Journal of Josef Goebbels from 1925–1926* (London: Weidenfeld and Nicholson).

Goldhagen, Daniel Jonah (1996) *Hitler's Willing Executioners: Ordinary Germans and the Holocaust* (London: Abacus).

Gombrich, E.H. (1970) *Myth and Reality in German War-Time Broadcasts* (London: University of London Athlone Press).

Gourevitch, Philip (1998) *We Wish to Inform You That Tomorrow We Will be Killed With Our Families* (New York: Acado).

Granville, Johanna (2005) "Caught with Jam on our Fingers": Radio Free Europe and the Hungarian Revolution of 1956, *Diplomatic History*, 29, no. 5: 811–839.

Griffith, William E. (1979) Communist Propaganda, in Lasswell, Harold D., Lerner, Daniel and Speier, Hans (eds.) *Propaganda and Communication in World History* (Honolulu: Published for the East-West Center by the University Press of Hawaii), pp. 239–258.

Gulseth, Hege Lovdal (May 2004) *The Use of Propaganda in the Rwandan Genocide: A study of Radio-Television Libre des Milles Collines (RTLM)*. A thesis for the Candidate Polit, Degree at the Department of Political Science, University of Oslo.

Hadamovsky, Eugen (1933) *Propaganda and National Power: The Organization of Public Opinion for National Politics*, http://www.calvin.edu/academic/cas/gpa/hadamovsky.htm (accessed 25 November 2011).

Hadamovsky, Eugen (1934) *The Living Bridge: On the Nature of Radio Warden Activity*, http://www.calvin.edu/academic/cas/gpa/hada3.htm (accessed 27 November 2011).

Hale, Julian (1975) *Radio Power: Propaganda and International Broadcasting* (Philadelphia, PA: Temple University Press).

Hand, Richard J. (2006) *Terror on the Air!: Horror Radio in America, 1931–1952* (Jefferson, NC: Macfarland & Company).

Handa, Caesar (2009) E-mail to the author, 01/07/2009.

Hanley, Wayne (2005) *The Genesis of Napoleonic Propaganda, 1796–1799* (New York: Columbia University Press).

Haugerud, Angelique (1997) *The Culture of Politics and Modern Kenya* (Cambridge: Cambridge University Press).

Heath, Carla W. (1997) Communications and Press Freedom in Kenya, in Eribo, Festus and Jong-Ebot, William (eds.) *Press Freedom and Communication in Africa* (Trenton, NJ: Africa World Press), pp. 29–50.

Herf, Jeffrey (2006) *The Jewish Enemy: Nazi Propaganda During World War II and the Holocaust* (Cambridge, MA: The Belknap Press).

Herman, Edward S. and Chomsky, Noam (2002) *Manufacturing Consent: The Political Economy of the Mass Media* (New York: Pantheon Books).

Herodotus (1998) *The Histories* (Oxford: Oxford University Press). Translated by Robin Waterfield with an Introduction and Notes by Carolyn Dewald.

Herzstein, Robert Edwin (1979) *The War That Hitler Won: The Most Infamous Propaganda Campaign in History* (London: Hamish Hamilton).

Higiro, Jean-Marie Vianney (2007) Rwandan Private Print Media on the Eve of Genocide, in Thompson, Allan (ed.) *The Media and the Rwanda Genocide* (London: Pluto), pp. 73–89.

Hill, Christopher (1991) *The World Turned Upside Down: Radical Ideas During the English Revolution* (Harmondsworth: Penguin).

Hitler, Adolf (1988) *Mein Kampf* (Ahmedabad: Jaico Publishing House).

Hobsbawm, E.J. (1990) *Nations and Nationalism Since 1780: Programme, Myth, Reality* (Cambridge: Camridge University Press).

Holtman, Robert (1950) *Napoleonic Propaganda* (Baton Rouge, LA: Louisiana State University Press).

Horten, Gerd (2003) *Radio Goes to War: The Cultural Politics of Propaganda During World War II* (Berkeley, CA: University of California Press).

Hough, Jerry F. and Fainsod, Merle (1979) *How the Soviet Union is Governed* (Cambridge, MA: Harvard University Press).

House of Commons Library (2011) *In Brief: Kenya – Six Politicians Fight Their Indictment by the International Criminal Court*, Standard Note International and Defence Affairs Section 17 March 2011, http://www.parliament.uk/briefingpapers/commons/lib/research/briefings/snia-05905.pdf (accessed 13 May 2011).

Human Rights Watch, HRW (2008) *Kenya: Ballots to Bullets*, www.hrw/en/reports/2008/03/16/ballots-bullets (accessed May 10, 2009).

ICTR (Nahimana) *The Prosecutor Against Ferdinand Nahimana, Amended Indictment*, http://www.unictr.org/tabid/128default.aspx?id=298mnid=4 (accessed 9 February 2011).

ICTR (Ruggiu) (1 June 2000) *The Prosecutor v. Georges Ruggiu (Judgement and Sentence)*, ICTR-97-32-I, International Criminal Tribunal for Rwanda (ICTR), http://www.unhcr.org/refworld/docid/415920394.html (accessed 30 September 2011).

International Criminal Tribunal for Rwanda, ICTR (2003a) The Verdict: Summary Judgement from the Media Trial. Reproduced in full in Thompson, Allan (ed.) (2007) *The Media and the Rwanda Genocide* (London: Pluto).

ICTR (2003b) *The Prosecutuor v Ferdinand Nahimana, Jean-Bosco Barayagwiza and Hassan Ngweze*, Case no ICTR-99-52-T, Arusha, Tanzania.

Institute for Propaganda Analysis, IPA (1939) *The Fine Art of Propaganda: A Study of Father Coughlin's Speeches* (New York: Harcourt Brace and Co).

Integrated Regional Information Networks, IRIN is part of the UN Office for the Coordination of Humanitarian Affairs, http://www.irinnews.org/Report.aspx?ReportId=76346 (accessed 23 February 2009).

International Criminal Court, ICC (15 December 2010) *SITUATION IN THE REPUBLIC OF KENYA Public Redacted Version of Document ICC-01/09-30-Conf-Exp Prosecutor's Application Pursuant to Article 58 as to William Samoei Ruto, Henry Kiprono Kosgey and Joshua Arap Sang* (Hague: ICC), http://www.icc-cpi.int/iccdocs/doc/doc1050835.pdf (accessed 13 May 2011).

International Criminal Court, ICC (8 April 2011) *Background information for the case The Prosecutor v. Francis Kirimi Muthaura, Uhuru Muigai Kenyatta and Mohammed Hussein Ali* Case No ICC-01/09-02/11, http://www.icc-cpi.int/iccdocs/PIDS/cis/MuthauraKenyattaAliEng.pdf (accessed 13 May 2011).

International Criminal Tribunal for the Former Yugoslavia, ICTY, de la Brosse, Renaud (2003) *Political Propaganda and the Plan to Create a "State for all Serbs": Consequences for using the Media for Ultra-Nationalist Ends*, Office of the Prosecutor for the International Criminal Tribunal for the Former Yugoslavia, http://hague.bard.edu/icty_info.html (accessed 8 February 2011).

International Military Tribunal, IMT (1949) XXVI, pp. 266–267, http://avalon.law.yale.edu/imt/count.asp (accessed 12 December 2011).

IPS News (2 February 2008) http://www.ipsnews.net/news.asp?idnews=41049 (accessed May 12 2009).

Itumbi, Dennis (2008) *Kenyan Radio Stations Criticised in Human Rights Report*, http://blogs.journalism.co.uk/editors/2008/08/20/journalism_in_Africa_Kenyan_ radiostations (accessed 21 March 2009).

Itumbi, Dennis (2010) *Kenyan Stations Slammed for Hate Speech*, http://www. journalism.co.za/index.php?option=com_content&task=view&id=3275& Itemid=37 (accessed 2 December 2010).

James, Eric (2008) Media, Genocide and International Response: Another Look at Rwanda, *Small Wars and Insurgencies*, 19, no. 1: 89–115.

Seaton, Jean (2003) Broadcasting History, in Curran, James and Seaton, Jean (eds.) *Power Without Responsibility: The Press, Broadcasting and New Media in Britain* (London: Routledge), pp. 107–234.

Jowett, Garth S., and O'Donnell, Victoria (2006) *Propaganda and Persuasion* (Thousand Oaks, CA: Sage).

Judah, Tim (2000) *The Serbs: History, Myth and the Destruction of Yugoslavia* (New Haven, CT: Yale University Press).

Kabanda, Marcel (2007) Kangura; The Triumph of Propaganda Refined, in Thompson, Allan (ed.) *The Media and the Rwanda Genocide* (London: Pluto), pp. 62–71.

Kallis, Aristotle A. (2008) *Nazi Propaganda and the Second World War* (London: Palgrave).

Kaye, Michael and Popperwell, Andrew (1992) *Making radio: A Guide to Basic Radio Techniques* (London: Broadside Books).

Kazan, Fayad E. (1993) *Mass Media, Modernity, and Development: Arab States of the Gulf* (New York: Praeger).

Keene, Judith (2009) *Treason on the Airwaves: Three Allied Broadcasters on Axis Radio During World War II* (Westport, CT: Praeger).

Kellow, Christine L. and Steeves, Leslie H. (1998) The Role of Radio in the Rwandan Genocide, *Journal of Communications*, 48, no. 3: 109–128.

Kenya Human Rights Commission, KHRC (2008) *General Elections 2007: A Preliminary Assessment*.

Kenya National Commission on Human Rights, KNCHR (2006) *Referendum Report*.

Kenya National Commission on Human Rights, KNCHR (December 2007) *Still Behaving Badly*, http://www.knchr.org/dmdocuments/Election_Report.pdf (accessed 23 March 2009).

Kershaw, Ian (1983) How Effective was Nazi Propaganda? in Welch, David (ed.) *Nazi Propaganda* (London: Croom Helm), pp. 180–205.

Kershaw, Ian (1987) *The 'Hitler Myth': Image and Reality in the Third Reich* (Oxford: Oxford University Press).

Kershaw, Ian (2001a) *Hitler1889–1936: Hubris* (London: Penguin).

Kershaw, Ian (2001b) *Hitler 1936–1945: Nemesis* (London: Penguin).

Kershaw, Ian (2008) *Hitler, The Germans, and the Final Solution* (New Haven and London: Yale University Press).

Kettenacker, Lothar (1983) Hitler's Impact on the Lower Middle Class, in Welch, David (ed.) *Nazi Propaganda* (London: Croom Helm), pp. 10–28.

Kimani, Mary (2007) RTLM: the medium that became a Tool for mass Murder in Thompson, Allan (ed.) *The Media and the Rwanda Genocide* (London: Pluto), pp. 110–124.

Klopp, Jacqueline M. (2001) Ethnic Clashes and Winning Elections: The Case of Kenya's Electoral Despotism, *Canadian Journal of African Studies*, 35, no. 3: 473–517.

Knightley, Phillip (1982) *The First Casualty: The War Correspondent as Hero, Propagandist and Myth Maker* (London: Quartet).

Kolsto, Pal (2009) *Media Discourse and the Yugoslav Conflicts: Representation of Self and Others* (Farnham, Surrey: Ashgate).

Kontler, Lazlo (1999) Superstition, Enthusiasm and Propagandism: Burke and Gentz on the Nature of the French Revolution, in Taithe, Bertrand and Thornton, Tim (eds.) *Propaganda: Political Rhetoric and Identity 1300–2000* (Stroud, Gloucestershire: Sutton Publishing), pp. 97–113.

Kriegler Commission (September 2008) *Report of the Independent Review Commission.*

Kris, Ernst and Leites, Nathan (1953) Trends in Twentieth Century Propaganda, in Berelson, Bernard and Janowitz, Morris (eds.) *Reader in Public Opinion and Communication* (Glencoes, IL: Free Press), pp. 267–277.

Kris, Ernst and Speier, Hans (1944) *German Radio Ropaganda: Report on Home Broadcasts During the War* (London: Oxford University Press).

Kwamboko, Oyara (2008) *KENYA* The Media is Not Innocent, *IPS News*, http://www.ipsnews.net/news.asp?idnews=41049 (accessed May 12 2009).

Lasswell, Harold D. (1995) Propaganda, in Jackall, Robert (ed.) *Propaganda* (New York: New York University Press), pp. 13–25.

Lasswell, Harold D. (1971) *Propaganda Technique in World War I* (Cambridge, MA: MIT Press).

Lee Thompson, J. (1999) *Politicians, the Press and Propaganda: Lord Northcliffe and the Great War, 1914–1919* (Kent, OH: Kent State University Press).

Lemarchand, Rene (1970) *Rwanda and Burundi* (New York: Praeger).

Lenin, V.I. (1971) *Where to Begin; Party Organization and Party Literature; The Working Class and Its Press* (Moscow: Progress Publishers).

Li, Darryl (2007) Echoes of Violence: Considerations on Radio and Genocide in Rwanda, in Thompson, Allan (ed.) *The Media and the Rwanda Genocide* (London: Pluto), pp. 90–109.

Linden, Ian (1977) *Church and Revolution in Rwanda* (Manchester: Manchester University Press).

Linkugel, Wil and Carpenter, Ronald H. (1998) *Father Charles E. Coughlin: Surrogate Spokesman for the Disaffected* (Santa Barbara, CA: Greenwood Press).

Lonsdale, John (July 2008) Soil, Work and Civilization, and Citizenship in Kenya, *Journal of Eastern African Studies*, 2, no. 2: 305–314.

Loughran, Gerard (2010) *The Birth of a Nation: The Story of a Newspaper in Kenya* (London and New York: I. B. Tauris).

Lynch, Gabrielle (2007) *Kenyan Politics and the Ethnic Factor: The case of the Kalenjin*, PhD dissertation, University of Oxford, 2007.

Lynch, Gabrielle (2008) Courting the Kalenjin: The Failure of Dynasticism and the Strength of the ODM Wave in Kenya's Rift Valley Province, *African Affairs*, 107, no. 429: 541–568.

MacArthur, Julie (July 2008) How the West Was Won, *Journal of Eastern African Studies*, 2, no. 2: 227–241.

MacDonald, David Bruce (2002) *Balkan Holocausts? Serbian and Croatian victim-centred propaganda and the war in Yugoslavia,* (Manchester: Manchester University Press).

Mafeje, A. (1971) The Ideology of Tribalism, *Journal of Modern African Studies*, 9, no. 2: 253–261.

Maina, Lucy W. (2006) *Kenya Research Findings and Conclusions* (London: BBC World Service Trust).

Malcolm, Noel (2002) *Bosnia: A Short History* (London: Pan).

Mamdani, Mahmood (2002) *When Victims Become Killers: Colonialism, Nativism, and the Genocide in Rwanda* (Princeton, NJ: Princeton University Press).

Marcus, Sheldon (1972) *Father Coughlin: The Tumultuous Life Of The Priest Of The Little Flower* (Boston: Little, Brown and Co).

Medieval Sourcebook (1966) *Urban II: Speech at Council of Clermont, 1095, According to Fulcher of Chartres*, http://www.fordham.edu/halsall/source/urban2-fulcher.html (accessed 26 April 2011).

Meller, Paul Jonathan (2010) *The Development of Modern Propaganda in Britain, 1854–1902*. Doctoral thesis, Durham University. Available at Durham E-Theses Online, http://etheses.dur.ac.uk/246/ (accessed 5 May 2011).

Meller, Paul (2011) E-mail correspondence with the author, 18 June 2011.

Melvern, Linda (2000) *A People Betrayed: The Role of the West in Rwanda's Genocide* (London: Zed).

Melvern, Linda (2004) *Conspiracy to Murder: The Rwandan Genocide* (London: Verso).

Metzl, James F. (November 1997a) Information Intervention: When Switching Channels Isn't Enough, *Foreign Affairs*, http://bss.sfsu.edu/fischer/IR%20305/Readings/intervention.htm (accessed 21 July 2010).

Metzl, James F. (1997b) Rwandan Genocide and the International Law of Radio Jamming, *American Journal of International Law*, 628: 1–28, http://lexisnexis.com?uk/legal/delivery=2821%A2159 (accessed 5 January 2010).

Mihelj, Sabina, Bajt, Veronika and Pankov, Milos (2009) Reorganizing the Identification Matrix: Televisual Construction of Collective Identities in the Early Phase of Yugoslav Disintegration, in Kolsto, Pal (ed.) *Media Discourse and the Yugoslav Conflicts: Representation of Self and Others* (Farnham, Surrey: Ashgate), pp. 39–60.

Misser, Francois and Jaumain, Yves (1994) Death by Radio, *Index on Censorship*, 4, no. 5: 72–74.

Monasebian, Simone (2007) The Pre-Genocide Case Against Radio-Television Libre des Milles Collines, in Thompson, Allan (ed.) *The Media and the Rwanda Genocide* (London: Pluto), pp. 308–329.

Mueller, Susanne D. (July 2008) The Political Economy of Kenya's Crisis, *Journal of Eastern African Studies*, 2, no. 2: 185–210.

Murrow, Edward R. (1968) *In Search of Light: The Broadcasts of Edward R. Murrow 1938–1961* (London: Macmillan).

Ndayambaje, Damascene and Mutabarika, Jean (2001) Colonialism and the Churches as Agents of Ethnic Division, in Berry, John A. and Berry, Carol Pott (eds.) *Genocide in Rwanda: A Collective Memory* (Washington, DC: Howard University Press), pp. 30–51.

New York Times, 27 April 1995.

New York Times, 11 January 2004.

Newbury, Catherine (1992) Rwanda: Recent Debates over Governance and Rural Development, in Hyden, Goran and Bratton, Michael (eds.) *Governance and Politics in Africa* (Boulder, CO: Pynne Reiner), pp. 193–219.

Nicholas, Sian (1995) 'Sly Demagogues' and Wartime Radio: J.B. Priestley and the BBC, *Twentieth Century British History*, 6, no. 3: 247–266.

Nicholas, Sian (1999) The People's Radio: The BBC and Its Audience 1939–1945, in Hayes, N. and Hill, J. (eds.) *'Millions Like Us' – British Culture in the Second World War* (Liverpool: Liverpool University Press), pp. 62–92.

Nove, Alec (1977) *The Soviet Economic System* (London: Allen and Unwin).

Oates, Sarah (December 2007) The Neo-Soviet Model of the Media, *Europe-Asia Studies*, 59, no. 8: 1279–1297.

O'Kane, Maggie (1996) *The Role of the Media in Bosnia*, Balkan Papers/Interview Series, http://ics.leeds.ac.uk/papers/pmt/exhibits/807/okane.pdf (accessed 25 October 2011).

O'Shaughnessy, Nicholas Jackson (2004) *Politics and Propaganda: Weapons of Mass Seduction* (Manchester: Manchester University Press).

Pakenham, Thomas (1979) *The Boer War* (London: Weidenfeld and Nicholson).

Pauley, Bruce F. (1981) *Hitler and the Forgotten Nazis: A History of Austrian National Socialism* (Chapel Hill, NC: University of North Carolina Press).

Paulu, Burton (1975) *Radio and Television Broadcasting in Eastern Europe* (Minneapolis, MN: University of Minnesota Press).

Pavkovic, Alesandr (2000) *The Fragmentation of Yugoslavia: Nationalism and War in the Balkans* (Basingstoke: Macmillan).

Phillips, Davison W. (1971) Some Trends in International Propaganda, *The ANNALS of the American Academy of Political and Social Science*, 398, no. 1: 1–13.

Podeh, Elie (2004) The Lie That Won't Die: Collusion, 1967, *Middle East Quarterly*, XI, no. 1, Winter 2004, http://www.mafhoum.com/press7/194P6.htm (accessed 18 July 2011).

Power, Samantha (2001) Bystanders to Genocide: Why the United States Let the Rwandan Genocide Happen, *The Atlantic Monthly*, 288, no. 2: 89.

Prunier, Gerard (2008) *The Rwandan Crisis: History of a Genocide* (London: Hurst).

Radio Cairo (6–8 June 1967) *British Broadcasting Corporation, Summary of World Broadcasts: The Middle East.*

Radio for Development (2010) *Kenya: Kass FM, Joshua arap Sang*, http://radiofor development.org.uk/?p=748 (accessed 18 May 2011); www.radionetherlands.nl/ features/media/dossiers/hateintro.html (accessed 12 December 2010).

Ramet, Sabrina P. (1992) The Role of the Press in Yugoslavia, in Allcock, John B., Horton, John J. and Milivojevic, Marko (eds.) *Yugoslavia in Transition: Choices and Constraints* (New York: Berg), pp. 414–442.

Rawnsley, Gary D. (1996) *Radio Diplomacy and Propaganda: The BBC and VoA in International Politics, 1956–64* (Basingstoke: Macmillan).

Reuters (2 January 2008) *Kenya Government Denounces "Genocide" as Toll Hits 300*, http://www.reuters.com/article/topNews/idUSL277107920080102?feedType=RSS& feedName=topNews (accessed 24 September 2008).

Reuth, Ralf Georg (1993) *Goebbels* (London: Constable).

Riegel, O.W. (January 1937) Press, Radio, and the Spanish Civil War, *The Public Opinion Quarterly*, 1, no. 1: 131–136.

Robbins, Jane (2001) *Tokyo Calling: Japanese Overseas Radio Broadcasting 1937–1945* (Firenze: European Press Academic Publishing).

Roberts, Jeremy (2000) *Joseph Goebbels: Nazi Propaganda Minister* (New York: Rosen Publishing Group).

Robertson, Geoffrey (2007) *Geoffrey Robertson Presents the Levellers, The Putney Debates* (London: Verso).

Rodrigues, Simon (2008) Corruption Trumps Tribalism, *International Herald Tribune*, 10 January 2008.

Runciman, Steven (1951) *A History of the Crusades, Volume 1 the First Crusade* (Harmondsworth: Penguin).

Schejter, Amit M. (2009) *Muting Israeli Democracy: How Media and Cultural Policy Undermine Free Expression* (Champaign, IL: University of Illinois Press).

Sebahara, Pamphile (1998) *The Creation of Ethnic Division in Rwanda*, http://www. un-ngls.org/orf/documents/publications.en/voices.africa/number8/7sebahara.htm (accessed 28 July 2011).

Seib, Philip (2006) *Broadcasts from the Blitz: How Edward R. Murrow Helped Lead America into War* (Washington, DC: Potomac Books).

Shirer, William (1960) *The Rise and Fall of the Third Reich* (London: Pan).

Shirer, William (1999) *'This is Berlin' Radio Broadcasts from Nazi Germany* (Woodstock, NY: The Overlook Press).

Short, K.R.M. (1983) *Film and Radio Propaganda in World War Two* (London: Croom Helm).

Silber, Laura and Little, Allan (1996) *The Death of Yugoslavia* (London: Penguin).

Smith, Carl O. and Sarasohn, Stephen B. (1946) Hate Propaganda in Detroit, *Public Opinion Quarterly*, 10, no. 1, Spring 1946.

Soley, Lawrence C. (1989) *Radio Warfare: OSS and CIA Subversive Propaganda* (New York: Praeger).

Somerville, Keith (1986) *Angola: Politics, Economics and Society* (London: Pinter).

Somerville, Keith (1990) *Foreign Military Intervention in Africa* (London: Pinter).

Somerville, Keith (2009) British Media Coverage of the Post-Election Violence in Kenya, 2007–8, *Journal of Eastern African Studies*, 3, no. 3: 526–542.

Somerville, Keith (2010a) The Language of Hate in Kenya: Balancing Freedom and Equal Rights, *New Africa Analysis*, 6–20 July 2010, p. 21.

Somerville, Keith (March 2010b) *Kenya: Violence, Hate Speech and Vernacular Radio*, Montreal Institute for Genocide and Human Rights Studies, Occasional Paper, http://migs.concordia.ca/papers.html (accessed 23 March 2010).

Somerville, Keith (2011) Violence, Hate Speech and Inflammatory Broadcasting in Kenya: The Problems of Definition and Identification, *Ecquid Novi: African Journalism Studies*, 32, no. 1: 82–101.

Sparks, Colin (1998) *Communism, Capitalism and the Mass Media* (London: Sage).

Stepakov, V.I. (1967) *Partiinoi propaganda – nachny osnovy* (Moscow: Progress).

Straus, Scott (2006) *The Order of Genocide: Race, Power and War in Rwanda* (Ithaca, NY: Cornell University Press).

Straus, Scott (2007) What is the Relationship between Hate Radio and Violence? Rethinking Rwanda's "Radio Machete", *Politics Society*, 35, no. 609: 609–637.

Swain, William N. (1999) Propaganda and Rush Limbaugh: Is the Label the Last Word? *Journal of Radio and Audio Media*, 6, no. 1: 27–40.

Taylor, Phillip M. (1981) Techniques of Persuasion: Basic Ground Rules of British Propaganda During the Second World War, *Historical Journal Film, Radio and Television*, 1, no. 1: 57–66.

Taylor, Philip M. (1983) Propaganda in International Politic, in Short, K.R.M. (ed.) *Film and Radio Propaganda in World War Two* (London: Croom Helm).

Taylor, Richard (1983) Goebbels and the Function of Propaganda, in Welch, David (ed.) *Nazi Propaganda* (London: Croom Helm), pp. 29–44.

Taylor, Philip M. (1997) *Global Communications, International Affairs and the Media Since 1945* (London: Routledge).

Taylor, Philip M. (2003) *Munitions of the Mind: A History of Propaganda from the Ancient World to the Present Day* (Manchester: Manchester University Press).

Thomas, Hugh (2003) *The Spanish Civil War* (London: Penguin).

Thompson, Mark (1999) *Forging War: The Media in Serbia, Croatia and Bosnia-Hercegovina* (London: Article XIX).

Thompson, Allan (ed.) (2007) *The Media and the Rwanda Genocide* (London: Pluto).

Thompson, Mark and De Luce, Dan (2002) Escalating to Success? The Media Intervention in Bosnia-Hercegovina, in Price, Monroe E. and Thompson, Mark (eds.) *Forging Peace: International Intervention, Media and Conflict (Internaftional Communications): Intervention, Human Rights and the Management of Media Space* (Edinburgh: Edinburgh University Press), pp. 201–235.

Time (12 November 1956) http://www.time.com/time/magazine/article/0,9171, 824576,00.html (accessed 18 July 2011).

Tusa, John (2009) Lecture to Brunel University Students on International Broadcasting, Brunel University, 18 February 2009, unpublished.

Tyerman, Christopher (2007) *God's War: A New History of the Crusades* (London: Penguin).

UN Trusteeship Commission (1961) *Report* (New York: UN), http://www.un.org/en/ mainbodies/trusteeship/ (accessed 28 July 2011).

UNESCO (1993) *Extrajudicial, Summary or Arbitrary Executions, Addendum – Report by Mr B W Ndiaye, Special Rapporteur on His Mission to Rwanda from 8 to 17 April 1993*, UN Doc. E/CN.4/1994/7/Add.1, 11 August 1993.

UNITA, Voice of the Resistance of the Black Cockerel *BBC Summary of World Broadcasts Part Four*, 1979, 1983–2002

United Nations Development Programme, UNDP (2008) *Media Monitoring: The Experience and Future* (Nairobi: Strategic Public Relations Research Ltd).

United Nations Trusteeship Council, http://www.un.org/en/mainbodies/trusteeship/ (accessed 26 July 2011).

United States Department of State (2010) *Country Report on Human Rights Practices 2010*, http://www.ecoi.net/local_link/158227/260661_en.html (publication date 8 April 2011) (accessed 14 July 2011).

United States Holocaust Memorial Museum, USHMM, *Incitement to Genocide in International Law*, http://www.ushmm.org/wlc/en/article.php?ModuleID=10007839

Urban, George (1997) *Radio Free Europe and the Pursuit of Democracy* (New Haven, CT: Yale University Press).

UWE, *Hitler's Speech to the Reichstag 30 January 1939*, http://www.ess.uwe.ac.uk/ genocide/statements.htm (accessed 20 December 2011).

Vaughan, James (2002) Propaganda by Proxy? Britain, America and Arab Radio Broadcasting 1953–1957, *Historical Journal of Film, Radio and Television*, 22, no. 2: 157–172.

Wafula, Evans (2008) *I Heard Them Cry for Help as the Media Watched*.

Walton, Douglas (October 1997) What is Propaganda, and What Exactly is Wrong With It, *Public Affairs Quarterly*, 11, no 4: 383–413.

War of the Worlds (2010) http://www.war-ofthe-worlds.co.uk/war_worlds_orson_ welles_mercury.htm (accessed 19 December 2010).

Warren, Donald (1996) *Radio Priest: Charles Coughlin, the Father of Hate Radio* (New York: The Free Press).

Warungu, Joseph (13 February 2008) Kenya in Crisis, *BBC College of Journalism Seminar* (London: Television Centre).

Washburn, Philo C. (1992) *Broadcasting Propaganda: International Radio Broadcasting and the Construction of Political Reality* (Westport, CT: Praeger).

Welch, David (ed.) (1983) *Nazi Propaganda* (London: Croom Helm).

Welch, David (1993) *The Third Reich: Politics and Propaganda* (London: Routledge).

WHA (AM) 970 – Madison (2011) http://www.wpr.org/schedule/displayschedule.cfm? istationid=2 (accessed 10 June 2011).

White, Thomas H. (no date) *United States Early Radio History: Radio During World War One (1914–1919)*, http://earlyradiohistory.US/sec013.htm (accessed 23 May 2011).

White, Stephen (July 1980) The Effectiveness of Political Propaganda in the USSR, *Soviet Studies*, 32, no. 3: 323–348.

Wilby, David (2011) *Suez Crisis 1956*, http://www.bbc.co.uk/historyofthebbc/resources/bbcandgov/pdf/suez.pdf (accessed 25 July 2011).

Windrich, Elaine (2000) The Laboratory of Hate: The Role of Clandestine Radio in the Angolan War, *International Journal of Cultural Studies*, 3, no. 206: 206–218.

Wood, James (1994) *History of International Broadcasting* (London: Peter Peregrinus).

Zeman, Z. (1964) *Nazi Propaganda* (Oxford: Oxford University Press).

Pflanz, Mike (2008) Hate Radio Spreads a New Wave of Violence in Kenya, *Irish Independent*, 28 January 2008, www.independent.ie/world-news/africa/ (accessed 13 August 2008).

Interviews

Sweeney, John, *Observer*, Correspondent in Croatia, *Telephone Interview from Vukovar*, 24 November 1991.

Younger, Sam, Former Head of BBC World Service, *Telephone Interview*, London, 20 April 2009.

Greenway, Chris, BBC Caversham, *Telephone Interview*, 27 April 2009.

Harmes, Neville, Former Head of Swahili and Great Lakes Broadcasting, *BBC World Service*, London, 27 April 2009.

Ammar, Benny, Former Head of Africa and Middle East Regions, *BBC World Service*, London, 6 June 2009.

Doyle, Mark, BBC Correspondent in Rwanda 1994, and BBC Africa Correspondent, London, 6 June 2009.

Mutua, Alfred, Chief Government Press Secretary, Office of Public Communications, Nairobi, 6 February 2010.

Gitau, Martin, Head of the Kenyan Journalists' Association, Nairobi, 10 February 2010.

Ole Itumbi, Dennis, Journalist and Editor of the *Fountain Post* Blog, Nairobi, 10 February 2010.

Muindi, Matthias, Chief Editor, *BBC Monitoring*, East African Unit, Karen, 11 February 2010.

Rono, Moses, *Former Kass FM Journalist*, Karen, 11 February 2010.

Joshua arap Sang, Head of Operations and Presenter, *Kass FM*, Nairob I, 12 February 2010.

Hardy, Claire, Former Chief Serbo-Croat Monitor and Editor, *BBC Monitoring*, East Africa Unit, Nairobi, 14 February 2010.

Wamugi, Macharia, Operations Editor, *Kameme FM*, Nairobi, 15 February 2010.

Jooste, Ida, *Internews Kenya Resident Advisor*, Nairobi, 17 February 2010.

Rambaud, Brice, *Internews Kenya Resident Journalist*, Nairobi, 17 February 2010.

Obera, Fred, *Kenyan Freelance Journalist*, Nairobi, 18 February 2010.

Bilic, Mladen, Serb media monitor and analyst, *BBC Monitoring*, Caversham, 9 June 2010.

Butcher, Tim, Former *Daily Telegraph* Defence and Africa Correspondent, *Telephone Interview*, Cape Town, 9 October 2010 (Covered conflicts in the Balkans and Africa).

Index

  wartime propaganda, role of, 41–5
  in Yugoslavia, 64–72
Radio Cairo, 62–3
Radio Commissioner, 111
Radio for Development, 231
radio documentaries, 223
Radio France International, 176
Radio Free Europe (RFE), 56, 58–61,
    59–61, 169–70
  in Hungary, 59–61
Radio Knin, 79–82
Radio Liberty, 56, 58
'radio machete,' 201
Radio Marti, 58
Radio Moscow, 56, 57
Radio Muhabura, 180
Radio Nacional de Espana, 43
Radio Netherlands, 242
Radio Rwanda, 165–6, 170–4, 176,
    178–80, 182–5, 189, 196, 202–3
Radio Swan, 58
radio telegraphy, 33
Radio Television Libre des Mille Collines
    (RTLM), 83, 152–3, 173, 177, 180,
    182, 200–4, 209–10, 230–1, 233,
    236, 241, 244–6
  in Rwanda, 183–9
Radio Union, 42
Rakosi, Matyas, 59
rallentando, 101
Ramet, Sabrina P., 72
Ramogi FM, 229
Rath, Ernst von, 123
Rawnsley, Gary D., 57
Raymond of Aguilers, 13
Red activities, 40
Red Army, 147
Red Cross, 30, 140
Reformation, 13–24
  Catholic Church's response to, 13, 15
  Protestantism, spread of, 13
  religious schism of, 14
Reich Chancellery, 141, 150
Reich Defence Law, 125
Reich government, 118
Reich Press Chamber, 110
Reich Press Office, 135
Reich Propaganda offices, 140

Reich Radio Company
    (*Reichsrundfunkgesellschaft* RRG),
    111–14
Reichstag, 100–1, 119–20, 122, 125, 127,
    130–1, 142, 145–6
Reichswehr Ministrerial Office, 104
Reifenstahl, Leni, 122
religious broadcasting, 37
religious propaganda, 10
republican propaganda, 9
'Return Home to the Reich' (*Heimkehr ins
    Reich*), 129
Reuth, Ralf Georg, 101, 103, 104, 105,
    106, 108, 115, 116, 121, 122, 124,
    128, 129, 131, 133, 141, 148
Revolutionary Movement for National
    Development (MRND), 167
Rheinland-Nord Gau, 100
Ribbentrop, 128, 130
Richelieu, Cardinal, 17
Riegel, O.W., 43
Robbins, Jane, 33, 49, 51
Robert the Monk, 12
Roberts, Jeremy, 87
Robertson, Geoffrey, 18
Rodrigues, Simon, 213
Rohm, Ernst, 92–5, 98, 105, 118–20
Roman people, 155
Rome-Berlin Axis, 126
Roosevelt, Franklin D., 38–9, 49, 132,
    145, 146, 150
Royal Media Services, 229
RPA, 169, 200
Rucogoza, Emmanuel, 207
Rucogoza, Faustin, 187, 190–1, 195
Ruggiu, Georges, 185, 199–200, 205–6
Runciman, Steven, 11, 12
Russell, William, 21–2
Russian Revolution, 142
Ruto, William, 208–9, 215, 220, 223, 228
Rwabukumba, Seraphim, 185
Rwanda
  genocide of, 165–83
  independence of, 159–65
  media law in, 184
  RTLM in, 183–9
Rwandan Armed Forces (FAR), 153, 170,
    175, 188
Rwandan Democratic Rally (Rader), 162
Rwandan Literacy Committee, 160